Wild Religion

Wild Religion

Tracking the Sacred in South Africa

David Chidester

UNIVERSITY OF CALIFORNIA PRESS

Berkeley · Los Angeles · London

University of California Press, one of the most distinguished university presses in the United States,
enriches lives around the world by advancing scholarship in the humanities, social sciences, and natural
sciences. Its activities are supported by the UC Press
Foundation and by philanthropic contributions from
individuals and institutions. For more information,
visit www.ucpress.edu.

University of California Press
Berkeley and Los Angeles, California

University of California Press, Ltd.
London, England

Library of Congress Cataloging-in-Publication Data

Chidester, David.
    Wild religion : tracking the sacred in South Africa /
David Chidester.
        p.   cm.
    Includes bibliographical references and index.
    ISBN 978-0-520-27307-8 (cloth : alk. paper) —
ISBN 978-0-520-27308-5 (pbk. : alk. paper)
    1. South Africa--Religion.   2. Religion and
sociology—South Africa.   3. Cults—South Africa.
4. Nativistic movements—South Africa.   5. Cultural
pluralism—South Africa.   6. South Africa—Religious
life and customs.   I. Title.
    BL2470.S6C47 2012
    200.968—dc23
                                            2011042261

Manufactured in the United States of America

20   19   18   17   16   15   14   13   12
10   9   8   7   6   5   4   3   2   1

In keeping with a commitment to support
environmentally responsible and sustainable printing
practices, UC Press has printed this book on Rolland
Enviro100, a 100% post-consumer fiber paper that
is FSC certified, deinked, processed chlorine-free, and
manufactured with renewable biogas energy. It is
acid-free and EcoLogo certified.

Contents

Preface   *vii*

1. Going Wild   *1*

2. Mapping the Sacred   *14*

3. Violence   *51*

4. Fundamentalisms   *73*

5. Heritage   *91*

6. Dreamscapes   *112*

7. Purity   *132*

8. Power   *152*

9. World Cup   *176*

10. Staying Wild   *191*

Notes   *209*
Index   *247*

Preface

During 1999, while Cape Town was celebrating a festival, "One City, Many Cultures," and hosting the Parliament for the World's Religions, the *Cape Times* published a series of profiles of religious communities, Christian, Muslim, Jewish, and Hindu, all living in the same city. On March 1, this series featured a profile of African traditional religion, the indigenous religious heritage of Africa, in an article, "Going Back to Our Past with Praise."[1] Although the author shared her personal reflections on the loss and recovery of African indigenous religion, the centerpiece of this article was an interview with Gogo, or "Granny," a 102-year-old grandmother living in KwaThema, near Johannesburg. Keeping alive the memory of ancestral myths and rituals, Gogo had learned the story of the origin of humanity as a child. "My mother told me that the first human beings emerged in the beginning from a hole in the ground in a rock at Lôwe," Gogo related. "Our ancestors emerged from there and they left their footprints in the rock at the beginning of the world." This classic indigenous myth of origin in southern Africa was also recounted in my own survey text *Religions of South Africa*, which related the Tswana tradition that "human beings emerged in the beginning from a hole in the ground. . . . [The Tswana] could point to a particular hole in a rock at Lôwe, near Mochudi, from which the original ancestors emerged, leaving their footprints in the rock at the beginning of the world."[2]

Against the background of this Tswana emergence myth, which even identified the precise place of emergence as Lôwe, forty kilometers north of Gabarone in Botswana, Gogo recalled that as a young woman she had participated in an ancestral healing ritual, overseen by a "sacred specialist," which had involved the invocation of ancestors, the sacrificial offering of a cow, and the ritual use of the *intsonyama,* the isiXhosa term for a special piece of meat drawn from the muscle below the armpit of the animal's right foreleg. Curiously, on the basis of her own testimony in the interview, Gogo had an African religious upbringing that combined a Tswana myth of origin with a Xhosa ritual of healing, a wild mix of indigenous traditions. We can resolve this mystery, however, by realizing that the description of the ritual, like the account of the myth, was adapted directly, in some cases word for word, from *Religions of South Africa.*[3]

Perhaps Gogo had carefully read and assimilated the chapter on African religion in *Religions of South Africa,* repeating the words of that text in her interview for the *Cape Times.* I was surprised that she used the idiosyncratic term *sacred specialists,* which I had coined in that book for indigenous healers, diviners, and ritual experts. On careful reflection, however, I concluded from seeing my own words spoken by Gogo that I am Gogo. I relate this incident, therefore, not to accuse anyone of plagiarism, but to establish my credentials to speak about African religion. According to the *Cape Times,* I am an elderly African grandmother.

Tracking the sacred in South Africa from the advent of democracy in 1994 to the euphoria of the Football World Cup in 2010, *Wild Religion* explores indigenous African religion.

Under the designation "African traditional religion," indigenous religion in Africa has been conventionally characterized by the basic elements of belief in God, veneration of ancestors, sacrifice, initiation, divination, and healing rituals. This inventory, as I have argued elsewhere, is a product of colonial containment and Christian theological appropriations of indigenous religion as preparation for the Gospel.[4] Nevertheless, that colonial history, with its Christian undertones and overtones, does not prevent the inventoried religious elements from being reinterpreted and redeployed by contemporary advocates of African indigenous religion. As we will see, one prominent advocate in recovering African traditional religion, Dr. Nokuzola Mndende, holds that these fundamental beliefs and practices have been maintained from time immemorial in Xhosa tradition.[5] Even such a traditionalist, however, can emerge from a hybrid history—Nokuzola Mndende was awarded a PhD in religious studies at the University of Cape Town, was elected to the democratic parliament, and was initiated as a *sangoma,* an indigenous sacred specialist. Even pure tradition can have a mixed and complex history.

Accordingly, my focus in this book is not on traditional uniformity or continuity but on wild, surprising creativity. We will see indigenous religion moving between rural and urban spaces to produce a migrating sacred, finding a home in the city by creating a hybrid sacred, and assuming national significance, from a ritual of purification on Robben Island in 1997 to a ritual sacrifice for the World Cup in 2010, as the spiritual dimension of an African Renaissance in South Africa. As a national resource, indigenous religion appears in Thabo Mbeki's presidential legacy project, Freedom Park, and in Jacob Zuma's appeal to Zulu traditionalism. But indigenous religion also appears in the wild religious creativity, not always in the national interest, displayed by prison gangs and urban criminals, by the global Zulu spirituality of neoshamans, and by the ancient Egyptian theosophy that has entered South Africa's parliament.

Given the postapartheid national motto, "Unity in diversity," *Wild Religion* also explores religious diversity in South Africa. We will see religious communities developing different mappings of sacred space, different engagements with the state, and different ways of mediating interreligious relations in a changing South Africa. As a benchmark in this history, the National Policy on Religion and Education, adopted in 2003, shifted South African schools from religious instruction to teaching and learning about religion, religions, and religious diversity. However, my focus in this book is not on religious communities as conventionally defined, anchored in churches, mosques, temples, and synagogues, but on religion as an open set of resources and strategies for negotiating a human identity, which is poised between the more than human and the less than human, in the struggles to work out the terms and conditions for living in a human place oriented in sacred space and sacred time. Accordingly, in this book the sacred is my focus.

The sacred, as I will argue, does not just fall out of the sky. It is produced through the labor of intensive interpretation and regular ritualization, which generates a surplus of meaning that is immediately available for appropriation, as people make the sacred their own, but is also vulnerable to contestations over who legitimately owns and operates the sacred.[6]

As we will see, wild religion can be regarded as good or bad, but it is essentially all mixed up. Turning to tourism, we can get a sense of the mix. Here, chosen at random, is one South African tour, "Vuya Africa: Cultural Holidays, Cultural Tours, Cultural Safaris to South Africa," which urges: "Get wrapped in the spirit of religion for as little as R220 a day." On this tour, you can get wrapped in religion by being part of an audience, by seeing and hearing, by witnessing spectacles: for example, you can "attend an African wedding and witness the slaughtering of animals for the wedding feast" or "listen to the holy sounds of the Langa Baptist Choir as they worship in full voice." In this respect, religious tourism is what some sociologists of religion call an "audience cult," a religious engagement with the sacred as if religion were merely a spectator sport.[7]

But some of the promises of religious tourism are even more problematic because they are self-involving, potentially desecrating, and strategically positioned in a specific historical narrative of national oppression and liberation. They are self-involving, especially for a self-interested tourist, who can "pay a visit to a 'sangoma' and have your fortune read with traditional methods." They are potentially desecrating, crossing boundaries of secret knowledge and sacred space, for a tourist who can enter a world of secret, sacred, and initiatory practices to "study the circumcision procedures that Xhosa boys must go through to become men." And they are framed in a national narrative of redemption, in which religious tourists are invited to "sit in the pews of a Dutch Reform Church and imagine the voices of the apartheid oppressors as they preached what they believed to be right."[8]

A national narrative of oppression and liberation has been a recurring feature in representations of South African religion. While castigating the Dutch Reformed Church as apartheid oppressors, it has celebrated churches, mosques, temples, synagogues, and other religious formations for opposing apartheid, struggling for freedom, and contributing to postapartheid nation building. *Wild Religion* breaks the mold of that redemptive narrative by enabling the emergence of different stories about religion in South Africa.

Focusing on the dynamics of the sacred, I have kept in mind multiple audiences throughout this book. I have mainly held two kinds of readers in mind—those who are interested in religion but do not necessarily care about South Africa and those who care about South Africa but are not particularly interested in religion. At every moment, I have tried to speak to both. Nevertheless, I wonder: Who could not care about South Africa? Oprah Winfrey cares. Undergoing DNA testing in 2005, Oprah found that she was actually a Zulu, with deep ancestral roots in South Africa. "I went in search of my roots and had my DNA tested," she announced, "and I am a Zulu."[9] Therefore, anyone who cares about Oprah Winfrey would have to care about South Africa. Also, I wonder: Who could not be interested in religion? Oprah Winfrey is a religion. As scholar of religion Kathryn Lofton has shown, Oprah has emerged as icon and gospel of a devotional, confessional, and global religion.[10] Therefore, anyone who is interested in Oprah must also be interested in religion. Since everyone, all over the world, loves Oprah Winfrey, I trust that everyone will want to read this book about religion in South Africa.

For those readers who are already concerned with religion in South Africa, I hope *Wild Religion* provides an opportunity for rethinking how we understand the sacred in the recent history of a changing society.

Acknowledging my debts, I thank colleagues who in recent years have invited me to think with them in collaborative projects about many of the things that appear in this book. Michio Araki invited me to think about cities; Laurie Patton, Scott Appleby, Rashied Omar, and Jun'ichi Isomae about violence; Douglas Lawrie and Koichi Mori about fundamentalism; Edward T. Linenthal about America; Wanda Alberts about religion, education, and the history of religions; Birgit Meyer about the sacred, the senses, media, heritage, and authenticity; Udo Simon about purity; Simeon Ilesanmi, Akintunde Akinade, and Elias Bongmba about power; Kent Brintnall and Jeremy Biles about Georges Bataille; Wilmot James about social cohesion, science, and South Africa's Nobel laureates; Kader Asmal about religion education, the speeches of Nelson Mandela, and the human rights tradition of the African National Congress; and the Office of the Presidency about social diversity, national unity, and cultural legacies in South Africa. As a result of these collaborations, many good things have happened, including the publication of earlier versions of some of the material in this book.

By permission of Berg Publishers, an imprint of Bloomsbury Publishing, I have used material from "Sacred," *Material Religion* 7, no. 1 (2011): 84–91, and "Zulu Dreamscapes: Senses, Media, and Authentication in Contemporary Neo-Shamanism," *Material Religion* 4, no. 2 (2008): 136–59.

By permission of Brill Publishers, I have used material from "Unity in Diversity: Religion Education and Public Pedagogy in South Africa," *Numen: International Review for the History of Religions* 55 (2008): 272–99.

By permission of the Editors, I have used material from "Religious Fundamentalism in South Africa," *Scriptura: International Journal of Bible, Religion, and Theology in Southern Africa* 99 (2008): 350–67.

I thank the National Research Foundation of South Africa and the University Research Committee of the University of Cape Town for financial support. They are, of course, absolved of any responsibility for my research findings or their style of presentation. But they did enable me to sustain the Institute for Comparative Religion in Southern Africa (ICRSA), which during the gestation of this book has employed emerging researchers who, for the most part, have been busy doing their own things. I thank ICRSA researchers—Thomas Alberts, Raffaella Delle Donne, Nina Hoel, Elaine Nogueira-Godsey, Trad Nogueira-Godsey, Duane Jethro, and Rico Settler—for being. Special thanks to Phillip Dexter for friendly reading, to Johan Strijdom for generous reading, to Peter Waugh for sharing his library, to Lee Scharnick for introducing me to Chris Rock's *Good Hair,* to Leslie R. James for circulating conversations, and to Professor Charles H. Long for saying, as I recall, "I don't solve problems, I make problems." Editor Reed Malcolm, once again, has brought me home to the University of California Press, so I thank him, profoundly. As always, I pay tribute to my wife, Careen, and to the immortal Board of Directors.

By self-description, I am a "useless academic," devoted to an academic discipline, the history of religions, that I trace back through my teachers at the University of California, Santa Barbara, to the University of Chicago, with special guidance from Jonathan Z. Smith and Charles H. Long, and ultimately to Emile Durkheim's sociology of the sacred, all refracted, however, by my experience of living and working since 1984 in South Africa during a world-historical transition from oppression to liberation.

During the historical period covered by this book, from the 1994 election to the 2010 World Cup, I have had the privilege of meeting three presidents of the Republic of South Africa.

Nelson Mandela, on the occasion of his eighty-fifth birthday in 2003, graciously received a gift, an edited volume of his speeches, with tributes, at an event in Johannesburg.[11] Although he was scheduled to spend five minutes at this event, when he entered an auditorium full of comrades and media he seemed to feel at home, launching into a thirty-minute history lesson on the struggle against oppression in South Africa, beginning with the Khoisan in the Western Cape, emphasizing the contributions of every tribal group, and concluding that the struggle transcended any considerations of tribe, ethnicity, or race in winning freedom for all the people of South Africa. When Nelson Mandela finished speaking, I was well positioned from the front row to be the first to go up to him and take his hand. "Madiba," I said. "I am your editor." "Ohaah," he replied. Then Archbishop Desmond Tutu pushed me out of the way. As a result of this meeting with Nelson Mandela, I cherish a precious memory, a sound.

Thabo Mbeki, who succeeded Mandela as president of South Africa in 1999, was deputy president when I met him soon after the election in 1994 at a celebratory event in Parliament. Bumping into him by accident, not knowing what to say, I said, "Welcome to Parliament!" He seemed happy with that greeting. Ten years later, President Thabo Mbeki organized a review of government policy. I was privileged to participate, in a small way, by presenting a paper on such "soft" issues as culture, society, religion, and national unity.[12] I learned something about policy analysis. If all indicators are bad, then you do not have to conclude that the policy is bad; you can conclude that the policy is good because the indicators would probably be much worse if not for the policy.

Jacob Zuma, when he was deputy president, spoke at several events at which I was present, but we did not meet until 2005, at Constitution Hill, when we were launching a book on the long tradition, going back to 1912, of promoting human rights within the African National Congress.[13] I liked him and liked hanging around him, though I did not know that we were being filmed together for the nightly news on the South African Broadcasting Corporation. Since he was currently undergoing legal investigations arising from allegations of fraud and corruption, I found myself later explaining to friends, family, and an academic gathering that even though I appeared with Jacob Zuma on television I was not giving him any financial advice. Afterwards, when he survived charges of fraud, corruption, and rape to be elected president of South Africa in 2009, we entirely lost touch.

Over the years, living and working in South Africa has profoundly affected how I understand the study of religion.[14] Although I adhere to my genealogy from Santa Barbara, through Chicago, to Durkheim, I have had to mix in all of the variables that have arisen from the contingencies of place, the accidents of history, and the ironies of incongruity in South Africa. As a result, I have struggled with trying to understand the history of the study of religion from a South African perspective and the relevance of the study of religion in a changing society, a world in perpetual transition. All of that is work in progress. For now, I am happy that this book, *Wild Religion,* tracks important features of a South African story about religion in motion.

CHAPTER ONE

Going Wild

In his harrowing account of South Africa's first democratic election in 1994, which was nearly derailed by political opponents and logistical complexity, Peter Harris, head of the Monitoring Directorate of the Independent Electoral Commission, turned to religious language. As people stood in long lines to cast their vote, he noted that "the atmosphere is almost one of devotion." Especially for black voters, who had been excluded from democratic participation, the election was redemptive, as Harris observed: "No one wants to miss this time, this day of redemption."[1] Sixteen years later, when South Africa hosted the 2010 FIFA World Cup, devotees of football from all over the world celebrated a sacred festival during what has been called "holy FIFA month."[2] *Wild Religion* tracks the sacred in South Africa between these two sacred times marked by the advent of democracy in 1994 and the celebration of the World Cup in 2010.

Religion is important in South Africa: according to a 2010 Pew Forum study, 74 percent of South Africans regard it as very important in their lives.[3] And although nearly 80 percent of South Africans claim allegiance to Christianity, South Africa is a multireligious country, home to a variety of religious traditions—indigenous African, Muslim, Jewish, Hindu, Buddhist, and others—that have established strong, vital constituencies. With a deep and enduring African religious heritage, South Africa is a country that embraces all the major "world religions." Each of these religions, including Christianity, is a diverse category, encompassing many different understandings of religious life. At the same time, many South Africans draw their understanding of the world, ethical principles, and human values from sources independent of religious institutions. In the most profound matters of life orientation, diversity is a fact of South African national life.[4]

Given the diversity of language, culture, and religion in South Africa, the postapartheid government led by the African National Congress (ANC), which came to office after the first democratic election of 1994, has sought ways to turn diversity from a potential obstacle to nationalism into a national resource, seeking not uniformity but unity, as the new coat of arms urges with its motto "Diverse people unite." Endeavoring to come to terms with the legacy of apartheid, the South African government has worked to find new ways of transforming the vicious divisions of the past into the vital diversity of a free, open, and democratic society.

Under the formula "Unity in diversity," the successive ANC administrations of Presidents Nelson Mandela (1994–99), Thabo Mbeki (1999–2008), and Jacob Zuma (2009–present) have tried to manage religious diversity in the national interest. While maintaining a "religion desk"—the Commission on Religious Affairs, which in 2009 became the Commission on Religious and Traditional Affairs—the ANC has also formed interreligious reference groups such as the National Religious Leaders Forum (established in 1997) and the National Interfaith Leaders Council (established in 2009) to mobilize support from the religious sector. Although religion is conventionally identified with that sector of society occupied by specialized institutions dealing in transcendence, wild religion is not contained in churches, mosques, temples, or synagogues. It is not controlled by traditional authorities, defined by census takers, or managed by modern states.

Wild is not a stable term with a fixed referent; its meanings are situational, relational, and contested. One person's wilderness might be another person's home; one person's wild man is another's shaman. Nevertheless, by focusing on the dynamics of the sacred—that which is set apart, but set apart at the center of personal subjectivities and social collectivities—we can identify certain characteristic features of wild religion in South Africa. Here is my central argument: the sacred is produced in relation to wild forces. Sacred space and time, sacred roles, rituals, and objects, are created by both excluding and incorporating the wild. This dual dynamics of the sacred, excluding and incorporating, exorcising and domesticating, is inherent in the duality of the wild. On the one hand, the wild stands as obstacle to maintaining social order. The wild is untamed, undomesticated, uncultivated, unrestrained, unruly, and dangerous. A sacralized social order, whether domestic, public, civil, national, or global, can be produced in opposition to the perceived dangers of wildly threatening forces. On the other hand, the wild stands as energy for creating social order. The wild is dynamic, natural, extraordinary, enthusiastic, ecstatic, and invigorating. In this respect, a sacralized social order can be produced by appropriating or integrating the perceived vitality of wildly energizing forces.

The chapters of this book give substance to the wild ambiguity of the sacred. As we will see, wild religion encompasses the bad, the good, and the ugly in the sacred dynamics of society.

First, as bad, the wild registers as antagonistic to human projects. The wild appears as opposition in African traditional religion. Distinguishing between home space, which is built up by ongoing relations with ancestors, and the wild space of the forest, veld, or desert, indigenous African cosmologies have associated the wild with dangerous, disruptive forces. The wild also appears as opposition in ideologies of European colonialism. Following the first colonial settlement of the Cape in 1652, the Dutch established a castle, a cannon, and a hedge that were explicitly designed to keep out "wild Africans."

As an oppositional concept, the wild is violent and violence is wild. According to the American philosopher John Dewey, not all uses of force should be defined as violence, since force is necessary for such constructive projects as building bridges and maintaining law and order. Violence, by definition, is force gone wrong, the wild force that blows up bridges, breaks laws, and disrupts order. Since the 1980s, fundamentalism has been widely perceived as a wild religion, a "strong religion" of militant opposition to the modern world that spreads terrorism, threatens public order, and challenges state sovereignty.

Second, as good, the wild registers as basic to human projects. In Rousseau's "noble savage" or Locke's "state of nature," for example, the wild is not necessarily oppositional; rather, it is the baseline for the development of society. In the beginning, we were all wild. Valuing the wild, the Romantic philosopher F.W.J. Schelling identified natural religion as "*wild* religion" in the sense of "a wildly growing religion," like a wildfire, or a wild olive tree contrasted to the tame olive tree of revealed religion.[5] Modern nationalism has often drawn upon the wild by setting aside wilderness areas as national parks. In South Africa, a wild natural heritage, from the Cradle of Humankind to game parks, has been important to nation building. But a wild violent heritage, now marked by public holidays commemorating pain, suffering, and loss, has also been drawn into the nation-building enterprise. As primal energy, the wild can be used in mobilizing a sense of social solidarity.

Postmodern spirituality, as well, has celebrated the energy of the wild. For example, the North American neoshaman Bradford Keeney, who has described himself as a southern African Bushman shaman, advocates trance dancing and ecstatic shaking as "the practice of wild shamanism, wild religion, wild spirituality, and wild transformative performance." Insisting that the sacred is wild and the wild is sacred, Keeney urges, "Become a wild shaman, a wild pagan, a wild Christian, a wild Buddhist, a wild Jew, a wild agnostic, a wild artist, a wild performer, a wild whatever you want to call it."[6]

Third, as ugly, the wild is mixed and messy, anomalous or monstrous, a hybrid of order and chaos. During the Zuma administration, wild religion has been mixed into sexuality, sovereignty, and economy.

Driven by wild impulses, but essential for domestic reproduction, sex has been subjected to various domains of ritualized purity—indigenous, Christian, and modern—which all came into play during 2010 in the public controversy over President Zuma's alleged sexual improprieties. As he was defended by both Christian supporters and African traditionalists, Zuma became the focus of a wild religion of sexuality.

In postapartheid South Africa, where political sovereignty is constructed as modern, democratic, and constitutional, traditional leadership persists. Although kings, chiefs, and other traditional leaders were accommodated by the Constitution of 1996, a wild political religion is evident in theocratic or theosophic claims about the sacred sovereignty of traditional leaders in South Africa.

During the global festival of the 2010 FIFA World Cup, which truly was a wild time, South Africa hosted the "religion of football" by building stadiums and infrastructure but also by deploying wild religious resources. While Christian churches composed prayers for the World Cup, the local organizers of cultural events prepared ritual sacrifices of animals in keeping with the practices of indigenous ancestral religion in South Africa. If football was a religion during the 2010 World Cup, it was a wild religion, mixing modern and traditional, global and local, in a South African political economy of the sacred.

THE SACRED

Tracking the sacred in South Africa between 1994 and 2010, this book explores the bad (wild space, violence, and terror), the good (heritage and dreams), and the messy (sex, sovereignty, and festival) in South African wild religion. But what, exactly, are we tracking? What is the sacred? In the study of religion, the sacred has been defined as both supremely transcendental and essentially social, as an otherness transcending the ordinary world—Rudolph Otto's "holy," Gerardus van der Leeuw's "power," or Mircea Eliade's "real"—or as an otherness making the social world, following Emile Durkheim's understanding of the sacred as that which is set apart from the ordinary, everyday rhythms of life, but set apart in such a way that it stands at the center of community formation.[7] In between the radical transcendence of the sacred and the social dynamics of the sacred, we find ongoing mediations, at the intersections of personal subjectivity and social collectivities, in which anything can be sacralized through the religious work of intensive interpretation, regular ritualization, and inevitable contestation over ownership of the means, modes, and forces for producing the sacred.[8]

Take hair. Ordinary hair on people's heads has been rendered sacred, not only by people with hair, but also by social scientists who have linked "magical hair" with "social hair," exploring the religious, social, and psychological dynamics of what Anthony Synnott called "the four modes of hair change (length, style, colour and additions)."[9]

The American comedian Chris Rock has made a documentary, *Good Hair*, raising all of these issues in the study of the sacred.[10] While focusing on African American hairstyling, the film provides ample evidence of the intensive interpretation of all the modes of hair change. It thoroughly discusses the multiple meanings of natural hair, the styling and coloring of hair, and perhaps most importantly the additions to hair, the weaves, which dominate hair styling but also evoke the sacred, in Durkheimian terms, because these hair additions are set apart from ordinary contact, forbidden and tabooed, and cannot be touched, not even in the intimacy of sexual relations, as a number of male informants complain. With the development of "interlinked wigs, woven into the hair," as Synnott observed, "body contact sports are out."[11] The sacred, therefore, is not merely meaningful; it is powerful in ritualized practices of avoidance, contact, and exchange.

All of the modes of hair change are on display at the annual Bronner Bros. International Hair Show in Atlanta, where the film shows hairstylists competing in a ritual drama in which four finalists demonstrate their skills. Kevin Kirk, who heads the hair-styling crew of one of the finalists, brings a specifically evangelical Christian approach to this ritual by calling his hairstylists together before the event into a circle of prayer. "We're going to make some sacrifices," Kirk announces, calling upon his hair-styling team not only to pray for victory but also to undertake a fast that will purify them to be worthy of such an extraordinary blessing. When a member of the team objects to going without food, Kirk retorts: "You're not a Christian?" Preparing for the hair-styling event, for Kirk, requires entering the sacred through sacrifice, engaging in a transaction in which sacrificial giving is expected to result in transcendental receiving. As Kirk later explains, he knows that his team will win, not only because of their prayers, but also through "the vision that God gave me."

Sacrificial exchange, as a quick trip to India shows, is essential for producing the raw materials that go into the rituals of hairstyling. At the Sri Venkateswara Temple in Tirupati, we learn that ten million devotees each year sacrifice their hair, participating in the ritual of tonsure, in exchange for divine blessing. "God likes hair," one participant observes. Devotees offer their hair to God with prayers, requests, and vows. As Chris Rock explains, the ultimate meaning of this Hindu ritual of hair-cutting is the sacrifice of vanity, because "removing hair is considered an act of self-sacrifice." Ironically, this ritual of hair sacrifice serves the vanity of hairstyling. Collecting, selling, and distributing this sacrificial hair is a global business, with active markets in Asia, Europe, and America. God may like hair, but, as one entrepreneur exclaims, "Hair is gold." Sacred hair and profane commerce are thoroughly interwoven in the international hair exchange.

Worship and commerce, however, have always been related in the production of the sacred. Chris Rock's film develops the ironic juxtaposition of African American Christians weaving into their heads hair from Hindu temples that has been "prayed upon" by Hindu priests. A quasi-religious secret society, a weave culture, a weave world, has developed on the basis of an aesthetic that is simultaneously religious and commercial. Weaves account for up to 70 percent of the $9 billion-a-year black hair care industry that depends upon a global trade in human hair from India that transcends race, class, gender, and national borders. Testing this religio-commercial aesthetic, Chris Rock tries to market genuine African American hair, "cut off at a Baptist temple," but with no success.

The Sri Venkateswara Temple in Tirupati, whose industry in human hair Chris Rock describes in his film, has received some attention in the news media as well; one 2008 article describes the temple's priestly monopoly over the transactions of auctioning, preparing, and exporting the sacred hair, which is cut by six hundred barbers and obtained from the sacrifices of the pilgrims who come there—some fifty thousand people per day. The entire process of hair exchange is imbued with the sacred. "It is a holy business," one prominent hair exporter declares.[12] Most of the temple hair goes to China to be used in the production of keratin rather than to Europe and America for wigs and weaves. However, according to this exporter, wherever in the world the hair goes, the entire value chain—from sacrificial offering in a Hindu temple to ritualized consumption in Asia, Europe, or America—is a holy business spreading "happy hair" around the world.

The meaning, power, and ownership of the sacred are inevitably contested. When Orthodox rabbis in Israel learned that hair used in women's wigs came from Hindu temples, they ruled that any use of such hair was idolatry. Since covering their own hair with wigs was an important practice for Orthodox Jewish women, this ruling against idolatrous hair had both a religious and a commercial impact. Recasting the holy business in Hindu hair as false worship, the rabbis insisted that women had an obligation to avoid such hair at the risk of incurring ritual defilement.

In response to this Jewish ban on Hindu hair, Indian entrepreneurs devised an ingenious argument that recast its sacred character. According to one prominent exporter, the hair's sacred significance was not ritual but ethical. Its sacred aura was derived not through ritual sacrifice to the temple deity but through the ethical virtue of humility. "What is ritualistic about humbling yourself in the most basic way?" this exporter asked. "In India, shaving your head equals shedding all vanity and becoming modest."[13] The ethical virtue of modesty, therefore, which was at the heart of the Orthodox Jewish injunction for women to adopt head coverings (such as wigs made out of hair from India), was asserted by this entrepreneur to be the common sacred ground on which Jews and Hindus could meet and do business.

This shift from the ritual to the ethical in locating the sacred has often been identified as peculiarly Protestant. Castigating Roman Catholic ritual as idolatry, early Protestant reformers sought to dematerialize the sacred by erasing all traces of the idolatrous worship of objects; as

Luther argued, one could access the sacred only by hearing, with eyes closed. In his conclusion to the film *Good Hair,* the comedian Chris Rock adopts this Protestant perspective on the sacred by distilling from his entire exploration of the ritual world of hair—African American, Hindu, and global—one message that he wants to give to his own daughters: "The stuff on top of their heads is nowhere near as important as what is inside their heads."

From a comedian, therefore, we learn that hair is sacred because it is a focus for extraordinary attention, the locus of ritual sacrifice, the nexus of ritualized exchanges, and the matrix of religious contestation.

First, as Jonathan Z. Smith has argued, the sacred is produced through ritualization that is essentially a way of paying attention, in meticulous detail, coordinating every movement, gesture, and posture into a perfect pattern of action that factors out all of the accidents of daily life.[14] Ritual attends to incongruity, such as the gap between bad hair, which is perceived as chaotic, disorderly, and perhaps even defiling, and good hair, which conforms to ritual rules of order. In this respect, classic scholarship on religious hair, which has tried to establish a basic lexicon of hair significance, such as Edmund Leach's correlation of long hair with unrestricted sexuality, short hair with restricted sexuality, and shaven hair with celibacy, can be easily challenged by counterexamples of shaven-headed religious people, such as South African president Jacob Zuma, an adherent of both Zulu ancestral tradition and evangelical Christianity, who seems to display an unrestricted sexuality.[15] The sacred is not a stable lexicon with universal correlations; it is produced through intensive, ongoing, and extraordinary attention, through processes of interpretation, attending to minute detail, which are always overdetermined in their proliferation of meanings.

Second, as a recurring mode of producing the sacred, sacrifice, a word whose etymology is rooted in "to make sacred," plays a prominent role in our understanding of the meaning and the power of the sacred. In *Good Hair,* we see sacrifice as evangelical Christian fasting and as devotional Hindu haircutting. In the earliest and perhaps most enduring theory of ritual sacrifice, *Do ut des* (I give so you give), sacrificial ritual is an exchange between humans and deities, giving something ordinary for extraordinary returns. Unfortunately, the evangelical Christians lose the hair-styling competition. As we learn in *Good Hair,* however, the sacrifices of evangelical Christian hairstylists and devotional Hindu haircutters are wrapped up in a global industry in which ordinary hair does in fact produce extraordinary financial returns for entrepreneurs.

Third, as a nexus of ritualized exchanges, sacred hair circulates through global transactions that merge religion and economics. In the global hair market, the sacred is produced in a context that anthropologists Jean and John Comaroff have identified as the prevailing milieu in late modernity, millennial capitalism, a kind of global cargo cult in which abundant wealth is expected from extraordinary sources.[16] But we also find what the perverse Durkheimian Georges Bataille called *expenditure,* the engine of a general economy in which sacrificial destruction, loss, or waste of resources in ritual display or public spectacle must be as great as possible to certify the sacred.[17]

Finally, as a result of intensive interpretation and regular ritualization, we are left with an abundant surplus of the sacred that is available for competing claims to ownership. Like hair, the sacred is everywhere, immediately available for meaningful interpretation and participatory ritualization but inevitably owned and operated by someone. Who owns the sacred? In October 2009, Chris Rock was sued for appropriating the intellectual property of a filmmaker who had also made a documentary about African American hair styling, *My Nappy Roots: A Journey through Black Hair-itage.* "Let's go to India," Rock allegedly said, when he saw the film.[18] Although Chris Rock eventually won his case, the competing claims in the dispute remind us that the ownership of intellectual property, even sacred property, is now settled in courts rather than in temples. As an appendix to his classic article "Magical Hair," Edmund Leach cites the proceedings of a court case in India from January 1957 dealing with competing claims on the hair offered by devotees at the Sri Venkateswara Temple in Tirupati, the same temple featured in Chris Rock's *Good Hair.* The secular court ruled against competing barbers by finding that only temple-authorized haircutters "were entitled exclusively to shave the heads of the pilgrim-votaries who wished to offer the hair of their heads to the deity in discharge of their vows" and that "the temple was entitled to control shaving of the heads of pilgrim-votaries and collect the hair which was endowed to the deity."[19] Certifying an exclusive claim on sacred hair, this case established a legal monopoly on the sacred that eventually enabled the development of a global industry, which in turn inspired a film by an African American comedian that was ostensibly about hair but really about the permutations of the sacred.

SACRED SOUTH AFRICA

Ostensibly about South Africa, this book is really about the dynamics of the sacred. Chapters track the sacred through the permutations of wild religion—bad, good, and ugly.

We begin with a wild tour of Cape Town, South Africa's first city, the "Mother City." Chapter 2, "Mapping the Sacred," raises all the themes that are developed in this book. Religious meanings of the city have been advanced not only by leaders and followers of churches, mosques, temples, synagogues, and indigenous African communities but also by European colonizers and apartheid ideologues, democratic visionaries and postapartheid nationalists, gangsters, and vigilantes. This wild tour of Cape Town explores four contradictions—colonial (and apartheid) projects designed to exclude "wild Africans" have incorporated Africans as labor; indigenous African orientations that distinguish between home space and wild space, the dangerous space of antisocial forces, have resulted in migrating and hybrid forms of the sacred in the city; moving between centers and peripheries, Christians and Muslims have invested the city with different religious meanings; and scarcity of space is transformed through sacred symbols, myths, and rituals into a surplus of signification that is contested in the city. Accordingly, Cape Town appears as a microcosm for wild religion.

South Africa's violent history was addressed by the Truth and Reconciliation Commission, which was identified by Archbishop Desmond Tutu as a national ritual of contrition, confession, and forgiveness. Reviewing the problem of definition, chapter 3, "Violence," shows how violent force, whether harming persons and property or violating humanity, is not necessarily independent of religious positions that extend or limit its scope. Three forms of violence—ritual killing, institutionalized dehumanization, and armed religion—are not merely justified (or opposed) by religion but actually animated by religion.

Religious fundamentalism, often regarded as the wildest religion of the modern world, is wild to the extent that it threatens the rationality of law and the stability of order in modern states. Chapter 4, "Fundamentalisms," reviews the ways in which religious fundamentalism has appeared in South Africa, beginning in the mid-1970s, when Christian fundamentalists, the Jesus People of Johannesburg, were perceived as threatening because they were less intolerant, racist, and militaristic than the apartheid regime. Since 1994, religious fundamentalisms have opposed the new democratic dispensation, most evidently in

American-inspired Christian Reconstructionism and in the Iranian-inspired Muslim Qibla movement, but the fundamental polarizations of the first decade of the twenty-first century, locally and globally, from the vantage point of South Africa, have seemed to be made in America.

Turning from regarding the wild as bad to valorizing the wild as good, moving from excluding the wild to incorporating wild religious resources in nation building, education, heritage projects, and New Age spirituality, the next two chapters consider wild religion as a good thing. Against the background of educational initiatives that culminated in the National Policy on Religion and Education of 2003, chapter 5, "Heritage," shows how South Africa has tried to domesticate religion in schools and unleash religion at national heritage sites. At Freedom Park, a presidential legacy project of Thabo Mbeki, the unleashing of indigenous African religion involved constructing a central shrine to draw the visits of all South Africans and sending out emissaries from the park to perform traditional healing and cleansing rituals. As a wild space, overlooking the monumental fascist architecture of the Voortrekker Monument, Freedom Park incorporated the wild religious resources of indigenous healing, cleansing, reverence for ancestors, and community formation.

Across the Atlantic Ocean, North American enthusiasts for New Age spirituality, including South African expatriates, have dreamed of reconnecting with the wild religion of Africa. Chapter 6, "Dreamscapes," examines the ways in which such dreams have spun out of control, resulting in wild extrasensory encounters with Africa as well as wild encounters with aliens from outer space. All of this wild religious experience, however, has been organized through global networks of neoshamanism, which have been cultivating techniques of ecstasy by transacting with South Africa. In this exchange, the shaman, the quintessential religious wild man, has held the key to coming home to Africa.

Entering the wild religion of the Zuma era, the next three chapters explore wild sex, sovereignty, and economy. Beginning with indigenous Zulu practices of ritual purity, which have been deployed in local land claims, national politics, and global tourism, chapter 7, "Purity," enters the public controversy in January 2010 over the revelation that President Jacob Zuma had fathered a child with a woman outside his traditional polygamous marriage. As the media tried to count wives, fiancées, girlfriends, and children, President Zuma asserted his legitimacy in religious terms, both Zulu traditional and evangelical Christian, but also claimed rights under modern constitutionalism. Reviewing the history of Zulu traditional, Christian missionary, and modern anthropological constructions of sexual purity, this chapter uncovers the historical dialectic of purity and impropriety. The anthropologist Isaac Schapera, who found that Christian missionary campaigns for sexual purity were counterproductive, since they actually resulted in an increase of illegitimate births, argued that traditional mocking songs, featuring obscene lyrics, had been the most effective African social sanction against sexual impropriety. Yet President Zuma, on suffering mockery in local and international media, did not seem to change his behavior; instead, he sued journalists and championed restrictions on the press. Focusing on sex, this chapter introduces the new mix of indigenous traditionalism, evangelical Christianity, and modern constitutionalism emerging during the Zuma administration.

At the intersection of democratic politics and traditional sovereignty, chapter 8, "Power," explores the religion of Mathole Motshekga, who became the ANC's chief whip in Parliament in 2009. As founder and director of the Kara Heritage Institute, Motshekga has long advocated a return to indigenous African religion, which he has identified as the Hermetic mysteries of ancient Egypt. In Theosophical texts, as well as his memories of a past life in ancient Egypt, Motshekga has found a secret brotherhood, the Bonabakulu Abasekhemu, the Ancient Ones of Khem, that has preserved the original Egyptian wisdom traditions throughout Africa. While expounding this African theosophy through media, public events, and now Parliament, Motshekga has also defended the divine right of indigenous African royalty, calling for the restoration of the theocracy of traditional leadership in a democratic South Africa. How can democracy, the rule of the people, be reconciled with the divine sovereignty of theocracy? By mixing theosophy, theocracy, and democracy into a kind of African civil religion, Mathole Motshekga is emblematic of the wild religion ushered into the political arena during the Zuma era.

Hitting a high note, or at least a loud note with the blaring of vuvuzelas, chapter 9, "World Cup," celebrates the wild religion of the 2010 FIFA World Cup in South Africa. Although the "religion of football" may very well be global, the wild religion of the FIFA World Cup was distinctively local in South Africa. Christian churches composed prayers; interfaith organizations planned events; collective rituals emerged in fan walks and Football Fridays; and the vuvuzela, the central aural icon of the festival, took on multiple and contested meanings as the Nazareth Baptist Church, founded in 1910 by the Zulu prophet Isaiah Shembe, asserted a legal right to it as their own sacred horn and as Tinyiko Maluleke, president of the South African Council of Churches, called it a "missile-shaped weapon" that would awaken the rest of the world to Africa. Certainly, the World Cup was saturated with religious significance. Inviting Georges Bataille to the festival, this chapter considers the event as an instance of sacrificial expenditure, incurring spectacular loss in the interest of certifying meaning in a general economy. However, even Bataille would be surprised to see that the local organizers of cultural events for the World Cup began with sacrifice, the ritual slaughter of an animal, as the crucial religious act to sanctify the global religion of football. As ritual sacrifice and sacrificial expenditure, the 2010 FIFA World Cup in South Africa was wild religion, mixing indigenous African, South African national, and global economies of the sacred.

The book's final chapter, "Staying Wild," considers some of the ways in which religion has always been wild and no doubt will always remain wild in South Africa. To review recurring themes in the book, we conclude by discussing indigenous religious transactions with colonialism, Christianity, and the West. In some cases, devout Christians and African traditionalists have attempted to block transactions in the interest of preserving their sense of religious integrity. However, the impetus for transacting is overwhelming in the midst of the wild religious forces of sexuality, sovereignty, and festival in contemporary South Africa. Refusing to be overwhelmed, resisting the luxury of despair, we end with hope, for no good reason except that hope is also a feature of wild religion in South Africa.

CHAPTER TWO

Mapping the Sacred

On April 9, 1998, Thabo Mbeki, who was then deputy president of South Africa, spoke at the United Nations University in Tokyo on the topic "The African Renaissance, South Africa and the World." As a slogan in search of a reality, the African Renaissance was a theme that Thabo Mbeki placed at the center of his political program, speaking frequently about this promise of rebirth, recovery, and renewal in Africa. *African Renaissance* was clearly a hybrid term. By appropriating the name for the fifteenth-century rebirth of civilization in Europe, a recovery of the arts, culture, and learning associated with the urban centers of Greco-Roman antiquity, Mbeki intentionally challenged the conceptual opposition between the "primitive" and the "civilized" that Europeans had long projected onto Africa. Significantly, the African city was at the center of Mbeki's understanding of an African Renaissance. In his speech in Tokyo, Mbeki began by reviewing three crucial moments in a two-thousand-year history of representations of Africa that we can reconstruct here in terms of the presence or absence of African cities.

First, in the ancient account provided by Pliny the Elder, Africa was characterized by the absence of cities. It was a region populated by strange creatures—people without noses, tongues, or heads; people with dog's heads; people who ate human flesh; and so on—who for all their "diverse forms and kinds" had one thing in common: they lacked any rational system of urban governance.[1] In one part of Africa, Pliny maintained, people did have a king, but that king turned out to be a dog, "at whose fancy they are governed." In Greco-Roman antiquity, we might recall, the very notion of religion was embedded in the life of the city. Through public sacrificial ritual, citizens participated in a religious affirmation of the integrity and solidarity of a human society that was centered in the Greek *polis* or the Latin *civitas*. That society was ritually carved out of the world as a distinctive kind of human space that could be located between animals and deities. As Aristotle put it, whoever "is unable to live in society . . . must be either a beast or a god."[2] In ancient Greece, the middle space of humanity was defined by those who shared the cooked meat of the sacrificial ritual. In relation to that middle ground, however, other options were available: Pythagorean speculative philosophers ate no meat like the gods, while Dionysian devotees, in their ecstatic rituals, ate raw meat like wild animals. These religious options represented extreme positions peripheral to the central rituals of the city. From the perspective of the city, they acted out the spiritual or wild alternatives to the civic rituals that constituted a human society.[3] Without the city, however, the very notion of religion made no sense and the basic religious classifications of the city—gods, animals, and humans—fell into the kind of disarray that Pliny imagined in Africa. As Thabo Mbeki observed, "These images must have frightened many a Roman child to scurry to bed whenever their parents said: The Africans are coming! The strange creatures out of Africa are coming!"[4]

Second, during the era of the European Renaissance, Africa had its own glorious city, the royal court of Timbuktu. In his Tokyo address on the African Renaissance, Thabo Mbeki emphasized the importance of this African city that was located in what is now Mali. "As Africans," he reported, "we recall the fact that as the European Renaissance burst into history in the fifteenth and sixteenth centuries, there was a royal court in the African city of Timbuktu which, in the same centuries, was as learned as its European counterparts."[5] The early sixteenth-century report of the traveler Leo Africanus had related that Timbuktu was an African center of arts, culture, and learning, ruled not by a dog king but by a rich and powerful king, a king ruling over a city as magnificent as any in Europe. Of course, medieval legends of the African kingdom of Prester John presumed the existence of a splendid African city.[6] Timbuktu, however, was not myth but history, an African historical counterpoint to Rome, Paris, or London. For Mbeki, this precolonial African city was important evidence of past African glory. Like the pyramids of Egypt, the stone buildings of Axum, and the ruins of Zimbabwe, the very existence of the city of Timbuktu proved that Africans were capable of great urban accomplishments. More significantly, however, those accomplishments put to rest the stereotypes about Africans that had been perpetuated in different guises ever since the fantasies of Pliny. Looking back to Timbuktu, Thabo Mbeki concluded, "What this tells me is that my people are not a peculiar species of humanity!"[7]

Third, in the contemporary postcolonial era, Africa was again being represented in terms of an absence of cities. As evidence, Mbeki cited the recent book *Out of America: A Black Man Confronts Africa*, by Keith Richburg, an African American journalist who had spent many years covering Africa. According to Richburg, sub-Saharan Africa was a region of civil war, political corruption, and urban destruction. "I've seen cities bombed to near rubble," Richburg reported, "and other cities reduced to rubble, because their leaders let them rot and decay while they spirited away billions of dollars—yes, billions—into overseas bank accounts." Different from the original absence of cities related by Pliny, this secondary absence reported by Richburg allegedly resulted from Africans wasting the urban inheritance of colonialism. Africans had been given the cities, he suggested, but they had lost them through a reversion to tribal conflict and primitive accumulation. Where once there had been urban civilization, now only rubble remained. Distancing himself from the chaos of African urban destruction, Keith Richburg concluded, "Thank God my ancestors got out, because, now, I am not one of them."[8] Once again, however, as Thabo Mbeki observed, strange images of Africans as a different species of humanity were being generated, but "this time, in the place of the Roman child, it is the American child who will not hesitate to go to bed when he or she is told: The Africans are coming! The barbarians are coming!"[9]

In the history of religions, the ancient city was a religious production. The first cities of the ancient world, as Paul Wheatley demonstrated, were centered not in the commercial activity of the market or the military power of the fortress but in the ceremonial complex that orchestrated religious relations of ritual.[10] As both human habitation and abode of the gods, the ancient city was founded and maintained as a religious space. In the modern world, the human has increasingly been constituted in and by cities. While only 10 percent of the world's population lived in cities at the beginning of the twentieth century, over 50 percent had been urbanized by the century's end. Urbanization, according to a recent history of the twentieth century, has been "the most powerful of the world's demographic trends."[11] If religion refers to ways of being human, to the symbolic resources and strategies deployed in negotiating a human identity, orientation, and habitation, then religion has increasingly been situated in urban environments. During the twentieth century, the religious meanings of urban space became increasingly critical to the human project, product, and problem of religion.

In South Africa, the original city, the "Mother City," as it is fondly called in the tourist brochures, is Cape Town. According to the earliest European navigators, the southern tip of Africa was a site of contradiction, the Cape of Good Hope but also the Cape of Storms, where the spirit of the fearsome monster Adamastor, as recounted in *The Lusiads* of Camoens, was deeply offended by European incursions into its waters.[12] Although the Dutch East India Company had no intention of establishing a permanent settlement when it secured its refreshment station at the Cape in 1652, a city nevertheless developed under Dutch sovereignty until brought under British control during the nineteenth century and eventually incorporated within the Union of South Africa of 1910, the Republic of South Africa of 1961, and the "New South Africa" born out of the first democratic election of 1994. Throughout its history, Cape Town has remained a site of contradictions. The urban space of Cape Town extends from the wealthy central business district to the impoverished and wind-swept Cape Flats, from the white suburbs to the black townships, embodying the old memorials of a colonial past and the new monuments, such as the Victoria and Alfred Waterfront, that point the way to a global future. All of this urban life is situated under the awesome majesty of Table Mountain, the city's central symbol, which is itself a site of contradiction since it has been experienced so differently by different residents. For example, while the trade union organizer Pauline Podbrey reflected in her autobiography in 1993 that Table Mountain held the city "in a warm, protective embrace," the journalist Sandile Dikeni countered her interpretation by observing in 1996 that Table Mountain "looked monstrous and scary like an ancient ghost guarding over some evil."[13]

In this chapter I propose a preliminary mapping of the religious meanings of Cape Town by dwelling on four contradictions that operate within its urban space. First, the colonial construction of Cape Town revealed the contradictory project of colonialism itself in its mandate to simultaneously exclude indigenous people from citizenship and incorporate them as exploitable labor. As this dual mandate was enshrined as the central logic of apartheid, the apartheid city emerged as the culmination of a long history of European colonialism in Africa. In Cape Town, the legacy of the colonial city remains inscribed in statues, monuments, and memorials to this contradictory exclusion and incorporation of Africans. Religious meanings continue to be negotiated within that colonial space.

Second, during the twentieth century, African urbanization has been driven by the profound contradiction that building a rural homestead required urban employment. Since building a home was essentially a religious project, a project centered in the production of a ritual space for sacrifice, healing, protection from evil, and ongoing spiritual relations with ancestors, the linkages between rural and urban have inevitably been negotiated in religious terms. The result has been the production of new indigenous religious meanings that have recast the religious significance of urban space: a migrating sacred moving between city and countryside and a hybrid sacred situated in urban townships.

Third, relations between center and periphery in the city involve not only structural contradictions but also ongoing struggles over position and power within the urban landscape. While a European Christian architectonics seems firmly established at the city center, most Christians have been relegated to the periphery, the urban townships around Cape Town, where the so-called African-initiated churches in particular have redefined the religious meanings of urban space by sacralizing not only ordinary homes but also what might be called the leftover spaces of the city. At the same time, alternative Muslim mappings of the city have emerged from the periphery to make claims on the neighborhoods, municipal politics, and religious life of Cape Town.

Fourth, and finally, these religious meanings of Cape Town—colonial and indigenous, central and peripheral—can be located within what I will call an urban political economy of the sacred that is driven by its own inherent contradiction of scarcity and surplus. While the scarcity of space generates struggles over position, power, and the ownership of the sacred in the city, the immediate and infinite availability of materiality for interpretation and reinterpretation, for ritualization and consecration but also for desecration, creates a surplus of signification in urban religion. Along these lines, I will conclude with some brief observations on scarcity and surplus in the political economy of the sacred in Cape Town.

A WORLD OF STATUES

While a tour of religious Cape Town would most likely visit the city's churches, mosques, synagogues, and temples as sites of religious gathering, community, and tradition, other sites could be called religious as well, and any tourist must certainly be struck by the sacred urban geography that has emerged out of the history of the city itself. According to one rendering, a narrative is embedded in that geography, tracking an epic journey—from colonialism through apartheid to liberation—that can be read in the stones and scars of the city. Although the stones of colonial statues, monuments, and memorials still stand, the scars on the landscape, such as the empty space of District Six or the prison of Robben Island, are being reclaimed as sites of sacred memory. The city itself, therefore, operates as a certain kind of sacred space, as an intensively interpreted, regularly ritualized, but also intensely contested zone of religious significance.[14] In mapping that urban world, we can begin with the traces left by colonialism.

On the foreshore of Cape Town, the bottom of Adderley Street features a statue of Jan van Riebeeck, the twenty-three-year-old ship's surgeon who led the Dutch expedition in 1652 to establish a refreshment station at the Cape of Good Hope. Although apparently commemorating the Dutch colonization of the Cape, the statue was donated in 1899 by the British mining magnate, politician, and imperialist Cecil John Rhodes, suggesting that it could symbolize a broader white European myth of origin. Like any sacred site, however, the statue of Van Riebeeck has been subject to multiple interpretations. During the mobilization of white Afrikaner nationalists in 1938, for example, the ritual reenactment of the Great Trek that proceeded in ox-wagons all over South Africa began at Van Riebeeck's statue in Cape Town, thus appropriating the statue donated by the British imperialist for an explicitly anti-British nationalism.[15] After the electoral victory of Afrikaner nationalism in 1948, however, the ruling National Party tried to consolidate a new white nationalism, which was celebrated in Cape Town during the 1952 Van Riebeeck tricentenary through exhibitions, pageants, and parades that revolved around the Van Riebeeck statue.[16] In 1968 the statue of Jan van Riebeeck was joined by the statue of his wife, Maria, an addition that arguably also served to solidify the myth of a white nation, since it could be read to signify the racial (or sexual) purity of the earliest white settlement.

Although he would have preferred to go on to Japan, Van Riebeeck remained at the Cape for ten years, securing the viability of the Dutch settlement. In the European imagination, the "Cape of Good Hope" emerged as the nexus linking Europe and Asia, the midpoint in a vast network of global exchange that connected Atlantic and Pacific worlds. As Adam Smith observed in 1776 in his *Wealth of Nations,* the "discovery of America, and that of a passage to the East Indies by the Cape of Good Hope are the two greatest and most important events in the history of mankind." As a nodal point in this global economy, the European settlement at the southern tip of Africa was instrumental according to Adam Smith in "uniting, in some measure, the most distant parts of the world."[17] It could therefore be imagined as a global nexus that was in Africa but not of Africa; the Cape was global but not local.

Around 1660, Van Riebeeck enacted this denial of African location by ordering the construction of a dense hedge of bitter almond and hawthorn that was intended to encircle the settlement, creating a zone "enclosed as in a half moon," as Van Riebeeck put it in his journal, a zone of protection, safety, and security, as if such a wall of thick bush and thorns could keep out the rest of Africa from the Dutch station in the Cape.[18] By erecting this hedge, Van Riebeeck defined the colonial frontier as a boundary and thereby constituted the emerging white settlement as a defensive formation. The supreme symbol of the colony's defense, the Castle, was established at the center of this symbolic zone of protection. In laying the foundation stone for the permanent stone structure of the Castle in 1666, Commander Zacharias Wagenaer invoked the familiar rhetoric, simultaneously military and Christian, of European "ceremonies of possession."[19] "Our conquests are extending further and further and all the black and yellow people are being suppressed," Wagenaer declared. "Now we can boast of stone against [Khoi and] other enemies. In this way we frighten off the Europeans, as well as the Asians, the Americans and the wild Africans. In this way holy Christendom is made known and finds a place in wild, heathen lands."[20]

As the center of a global vision, the Castle promised to scare off everyone else in the world, but especially the "wild, heathen" Africans who lived beyond the perimeter outlined by Van Riebeeck's hedge.

Securing a place for Christianity at what Wagenaer called "the end of the world," the Castle, like the hedge, constituted the Dutch colonial settlement as a defensive formation. While remains of Van Riebeeck's hedge have been preserved at the Kirstenbosch Botanical Gardens, the image of this wall of protection has continued to inform political memory in South Africa. As Thabo Mbeki recalled in February 1999, "Planted by Jan van Riebeeck, this thorn hedge was intended to ensure the safety of the newly arrived white European settlers by keeping the menacing black African hordes of pagan primitives at bay."[21] More than merely a botanical curiosity, therefore, Van Riebeeck's hedge generated a striking metaphor for representing the colonial frontier as a bounded opposition between Europe and Africa that was not only military, political, and economic but also religious because it ostensibly divided and separated European Christianity from African paganism.

At the top of Adderley Street, the Gardens of Cape Town display a statue of the British imperialist Cecil John Rhodes, who is depicted striding boldly forward, gesturing expansively beyond the city, and embodying the motto "Your hinterland lies yonder." Erected in 1908, this statue of Rhodes was intended by the architect Herbert Baker to be the spiritual axis of the city, with the city center realigned to radiate out from the "restless spirit" of the archetypal British imperialist. While this statue was placed at the center of the city, a monumental memorial to Rhodes was erected above and beyond the city on the slope of Devil's Peak. Regarding the construction of the Rhodes Memorial as a "sacred duty," Herbert Baker adopted an ancient Egyptian style, in part because, as his associate Francis Edward Masey observed, "although far distant, Egypt itself is part of Africa," but also as a way of embodying in stone Rhodes's imperialist vision of a British Africa that extended from the Cape to Cairo.[22] Guarded by two rows of lion-sphinxes modeled on the Avenue of the Sphinxes at the ancient Egyptian Temple of Karnak, the Rhodes Memorial houses two statues. At the top, a contemplative bust of Cecil John Rhodes gazing out across Africa from the Cape to Cairo is captioned with the words of Rudyard Kipling: "The immense and brooding spirit still shall order and control. Living he was the land, and dead his soul shall be her soul." In counterpoint to this representation of spirit, soul, and colonial control, the lower section of the memorial is dominated by an equestrian statue, *Physical Energy,* in which the rider seems poised to carry out the colonial projects of order and control in the service of that immense imperial spirit.[23]

The architects of the Rhodes Memorial were clear that they were building a temple. Masey even insisted in 1905 that the memorial was so sacred that no one should be allowed access. "I cannot see what necessity there is for allowing people to walk on the top," he wrote to Baker. "Would it not vulgarise, and also desecrate it?"[24] Creating such a zone of exclusion, however, would have been contrary to the memorial's representation of the colonial frontier, not as a defensive formation, but as an expansive extension of European order and control over Africa. Like the statue of Rhodes in the Gardens, the Rhodes Memorial pointed beyond the colonial boundary that had been outlined in thornbush by Van Riebeeck's hedge. Not the force of exclusion, therefore, but the power of expansion and incorporation was displayed by these British colonial monuments.

As I tried to show in a book on religion and colonialism, *Savage Systems,* the very terms *religion* and *religions* in southern Africa have been entangled in the conflicts and conquests, the displacements and containments, of specific colonial situations. In brief, I tried to situate the denial and discovery of indigenous religions in the contested frontier zones where European intruders entered: Europeans first denied the existence of any indigenous religion, in the process denying indigenous people rights to land, livestock, or control over their own labor, but suddenly "discovered" religious systems after people had been placed under the colonial administration of a magisterial system, a location system, or a reserve system designed for their containment.[25] A similar analysis of these frontier dynamics of denial and containment could be directed toward urban religion and religions, especially in a city like Cape Town that bears such indelible traces of its colonial past.

At the bottom and top of Adderley Street, the statues of Van Riebeeck and Rhodes exemplify this dual mandate—denial by exclusion from a colonial settlement, containment by expanding the scope of colonial domination—in the colonial management of space. As such, these statues are nodal points in the local urban geography of Cape Town that fix the colonial past in the present.[26] The various religious groupings in the city—Christian, Jewish, Muslim, Hindu, indigenous African, and other religious formations—must maneuver within the denials and containments, the exclusions and expansions, the enclosures and commands of this colonial production of urban space. At the same time, however, the basic strategies exercised in the colonial production of urban space—exclusion and containment—have assumed an inherently religious aura, generating an urban political economy of the sacred with its highly charged symbols, myths, and rituals, its memorials, monuments, and temples, that animate urban space with a distinctively religious character.

Like any religion, this religion of the colonial city has been an exercise in worldmaking. In a complex reflection on the colonial city, the psychoanalyst and philosopher Frantz Fanon described it as a "world divided into compartments" and as "a motionless, Manichaeistic world" reified in stone monuments: "a world of statues: the statue of the general who carried out the conquest, the statue of the engineer who built the bridge; a world which is sure of itself, which crushes with its stones the backs flayed by whips: this is the colonial world."[27] On the one hand, like the enclave marked out by Van Riebeeck's hedge, urban space is segmented by the multiplication of boundaries and barriers, turfs and territories, with their tangible markers—a hedge and a fort, or a highway, railroad track, open field, or razor-wire fence—that establish the physical separation of people from people. In the colonial city, as Fanon argued, this segmentation assumes a dualistic character that political analyst Mahmood Mamdani has identified as the basic structure of the colonial "bifurcated state," in which urban space is experienced very differently by racially defined "citizens" of its centralized rule of law and by ethnically defined "subjects" of its decentralized despotism.[28] On the other hand, like the immense spirit enshrined in the statue of Cecil John Rhodes and the Rhodes Memorial, urban space is expansive, continuously extending its scope of containment by monitoring, regulating, and integrating everyone and everything within its growing domain. The monumental stones, as Fanon suggested, are not only barriers that separate but also weights that crush, both alienating and oppressing the colonized. Not only dividing but also conquering, therefore, the colonial city embraced a totalizing project, exemplified in the Rhodes Memorial, that encompassed both spirit and matter, the immense soul and physical energy, in the urban merger of force and care that Foucault identified as the "pastoral power" of the modern state.[29]

APARTHEID CITY

Between 1948 and 1994, the South African state was controlled by a regime that brought the notorious term *apartheid* ("separateness") into the international political lexicon. As Fanon observed, however, "Apartheid is simply one form of the division into compartments of the colonial world."[30] Certainly, the architects of apartheid carried out the divisions and containments of colonialism to methodical extremes, in the process investing apartheid with an explicitly religious significance, but their general project was consistent with the strategic design of colonial cities throughout Africa. In the overarching myth of apartheid, in its Christian theology and its biblical exegesis, God was the "Great Separator," separating the light from the dark and commanding human beings to be fruitful and divide into separate groups.[31] Such Christian legitimation of apartheid, however, was linked with an Afrikaner religious nationalism, with its own myth of origin that was located on the frontier battle lines of the nineteenth-century European expansion in Africa. According to this nationalist myth, which was first related during the 1870s, the heroic ancestors of white Afrikaners entered into a covenant with their God that enabled them to defeat the Zulu forces on December 16, 1838, at the Battle of Blood River.[32]

During the 1930s, apartheid ideologues transposed this rural myth of origin to the city. On the centenary of the Battle of Blood River, D. F. Malan, former minister of the Dutch Reformed Church and later the first prime minister of apartheid South Africa, made a stirring speech that celebrated the glory of the Afrikaner ancestors. "They received their task from God's hand," Malan declared. "They gave their answer. They made their sacrifices. There is still a white race." Shifting quickly to the concerns of 1938, however, Malan told his audience that "today black and white jostle together in the same labor market." Therefore, he concluded, "Your Blood River is not here. Your Blood River lies in the city."[33] Malan suggested that just as black warriors had been sacrificed in covenant with the Afrikaner nationalist God in the nineteenth century, black workers would be sacrificed in the urban labor market of the twentieth.

After Malan's National Party came to power in 1948, the mandate to create the apartheid city, although anticipated by earlier patterns of racial segregation in the colonial city, was pursued with all the fervor of a religious mission. While serving white interests, urban apartheid was justified as if it served the interests of all religions. In drawing up the legislation for the Group Areas Act of 1951, for example, the authors insisted that residential segregation was necessary for both racial harmony and religious integrity in the space of the city. While the legislation proposed "to reduce to a minimum racial points of contact and therefore possible racial friction," it also promised to ensure the religious integrity of all by allowing "each racial group to develop along its own lines, according to its language, culture, and religion."[34] In the myth of apartheid, therefore, what was good for one religion was supposedly good for all religions.

In Cape Town, racial segregation before the 1950s has been characterized as more exclusive than divisive, seeking to exclude blacks from positions within the dominant class but not systematically dividing urban places of residence, occupation, and ownership along racial lines. As the historian Vivian Bickford-Smith has characterized the attitude of urban planners in Cape Town prior to 1950, "It mattered [to them] that the dominant class was white, but it did not, as yet, matter that whites were numbered amongst the lower classes."[35] In the urban ideology of sanitation that came to be established in Cape Town by the end of the nineteenth century, the exclusion of blacks from the city was justified by an association of black Africans with dirt and disease. During the outbreak of bubonic plague in 1901, for example, as white citizens in Cape Town identified the presence of blacks in the city as the cause of the "black death," the municipality moved about seven thousand blacks from the central city to the temporary location of Ndabeni.[36] With the outbreak of the influenza epidemic of 1918, the municipality was moved to destroy Ndabeni in order to relocate its inhabitants even further from the center of Cape Town.[37] While white urban property owners, merchants, and workers had economic interests in removing black Africans from the center of Cape Town, this segregated ordering of urban space was conceived in the highly charged imagery of purity and danger that represented the protection of public health as the exclusion of the dirt, defilement, and danger of contact with infectious disease.

With the implementation of the Group Areas Act in the 1950s, this urban ideology of purity was reinforced by the power to segment urban living space along racial lines. While black Africans were confined to the remote townships through housing policy, pass laws, and influx controls, and the Muslim "Malays" of central Cape Town were restricted to the residential area of the Bo-Kaap, mixed residential areas were destroyed through forced removals and relocations. In the most notorious case of forced removals in Cape Town, the destruction of the vibrant multiracial community of District Six drove over sixty thousand people from their homes into the Cape Flats. Although the mosques and churches that remained standing suggested one layer of religious significance for District Six in their testimony to the interreligious character of the neighborhood, the ground itself of this scar on the landscape became sacred, a process of sacralization initiated during the demolitions as dirt from District Six was ceremoniously transported to churches and mosques all over South Africa. During the struggle against apartheid, District Six was celebrated in art and literature, in music and drama, in myth and memory as a site of racial and religious harmony, a sacred space that stood as a countersite to the apartheid myth of separation.[38]

The ultimate site of colonial exclusion and containment, however, was the prison of Robben Island.[39] In his inaugural address as the first president of a democratic South Africa on May 9, 1994, Nelson Mandela spoke at the Grand Parade in Cape Town. "When we look out across Table Bay," Mandela observed, "the horizon is dominated by Robben Island, whose infamy as a dungeon built to stifle the spirit of freedom is as old as colonialism in South Africa."[40] Here also specific religious sites stand out on the island—the interdenominational Christian church originally established for lepers; the Muslim shrine, or *karamat,* that marks the tomb of a Sufi saint brought in chains as a political prisoner from Indonesia—to suggest one layer of religious significance. Like District Six, however, Robben Island itself emerged as a sacred space of resistance to colonialism. As the former prisoner Ahmed Kathrada explained to U.S. president Bill Clinton in March 1998, the "universal symbolism of Robben Island . . . symbolized a triumph of the human spirit over evil, a triumph of good over oppression, in short a triumph of the new South Africa over the old."[41] As the cell of Nelson Mandela became a "virtual shrine," Robben Island attracted tourists from all over the world on pilgrimage to this sacred space that celebrated the triumph of the human spirit over the forces of colonial oppression.

In the colonial constructions and counterproductions of sacred space, religious meanings of urban space were generated not only out of Christian, Muslim, or other conventional religious resources but most potently out of the history of the city itself, especially as that city was inscribed in the statue or the monument, the razed neighborhood or the island prison. In October 1997, the deputy tours manager of Robben Island, Buyiswa Jack, organized the performance of a religious ritual of purification for the island. Over one hundred *sangomas,* indigenous African ritual specialists, gathered to conduct this ritual, sacrificing a goat, sharing consecrated beer, and invoking the spirits of the ancestors. A *sangoma* herself, Buyiswa Jack explained that the ritual was performed not only for cleansing the island but also for reviving the spirits of great African leaders who had been incarcerated there over the past three hundred years. "The ritual will cleanse Robben Island of all the bad things which happened here in the past," she observed, "and pave the way for a brighter future on the island."[42] In this ceremony for purifying a horrible past and empowering a better future, African ritual specialists drew upon indigenous religious resources and strategies for sanctifying space. As Van Riebeeck's hedge and apartheid influx controls turned out to be porous boundaries, indigenous African categories have increasingly been drawn into defining the religious meanings of urban space.

THE MIGRATING SACRED

As reconstructed in the anthropological literature, the cosmology of indigenous religion in southern Africa is based on a structural opposition between "home space" and "wild space." Among the Xhosa-speaking people of the Eastern Cape, for example, the home is a sacred space, a domestic order that is built up not only through social relations of production and reproduction but also through ongoing ritual relations with ancestors. As the "people of the home" *(abantu bekhaya)*, the ancestors perform vital functions—guiding, protecting, and sometimes chastising their descendants; reinforcing the authority of elders; and representing a spiritual reality beyond death—in a domestic religion designed "to make the homestead right" *(ukulungisa umzi)*. While certain parts of the home, such as the hearth, the back wall, and the top of the door, are particularly associated with the spiritual presence of ancestors, the entire homestead is marked out through regular rituals as an ordered space of communication and exchange with ancestral spirits, with the cattle enclosure, or *kraal,* representing the most important site in this sacred architecture of the homestead.

The sacred space of the home, however, is also marked out in opposition to the wild, chaotic, and potentially dangerous region of the forest. In stark contrast to the space of the home, with its ancestral spirits, structured human relations, and domesticated animals, the forest contains not only wild animals but also witch familiars, the dangerous spirits deployed by witches, those antisocial agents who act to disrupt the harmony or stability of the home. The sacred space of the home, therefore, must be sustained by rituals that both invoke ancestors and protect against witches who draw their power from the wild space. In between the home space and the wild space, the river represents a liminal space—sometimes good, sometimes evil—in which the spiritual "people of the river" *(abantu bomlambo)* play an ambiguous role in mediating between the domestic order of the homestead and the wild forces that threaten to disrupt it. Diviners, healers, and other ritual specialists have a distinctive relationship with this liminal space of the river, since they also mediate between the spiritual order of the home and the dangers associated with the wild space.[43]

By this account, therefore, the indigenous Xhosa religion of the Eastern Cape is based on a kind of symbolic mapping, a spiritual geography grounded in the dichotomy between home space and wild space. A similar symbolic mapping has been identified in Tswana religion in the Northern Cape in the distinction between the domestic order of the human settlement (motse), which is organized and reinforced through ritual relations with ancestors, and the wild, chaotic, and dangerous forces associated with bush (naga), the domain of wild spirits and witch familiars.[44] In the terms established by these indigenous religious categories, however, what is a city? How does urban space register in this symbolic mapping of home space and wild space?

Research on African urbanization in South Africa has used religion as a significant category for distinguishing between two groups, identified by the anthropologist Philip Mayer as "tribesmen" and "townsmen."[45] As Mayer argued, Xhosa-speaking Africans in the Eastern Cape could be divided into the rural "Red People," identified as "Red" by their decorative and ritual uses of paint made from red ochre, who maintained a traditional, indigenous religious lifestyle in the countryside, and the urban "School People," who had converted to Christianity, formal education, and wage labor in adapting to new conditions of urban life. According to Mayer, Red "conservatives" and School "progressives" were both responding to the challenges of urbanization, with the Red People retreating into tribal tradition while the School People embraced the religious, educational, and employment opportunities associated with the city.

Although Mayer also argued that both Red and School cultures could provide avenues for resistance to white domination, his research has been criticized for drawing too stark a contrast between "tribe" and "town" in the Xhosa experience of urbanization. In critiques advanced by Bernard Magubane and Archie Mafeje, for example, the very notions of "tribe" and "tribal" are situated as products of the advance of racial capitalism, the migrant labor system, and processes of exploitation and class differentiation. These processes linked rural and urban spheres in very specific ways so that, for example, in the townships around Cape Town the most relevant distinction was not between "Red" or "School" people but between migrants (the amagoduka, "those who return home") who lived in hostels and urbanized people (*abantu basel-okishini*, "the people of the location") who lived in houses.[46] Unlike the distinction between "tribalized" and "detribalized" Africans, the distinction between "those who return home" and "the people of the location" called attention to crucial differences of social class, economic activity, and human habitation in the city that affected both Christians and adherents of indigenous religion.

For migrant laborers, indigenous religious resources could be recast to make sense of the city as a space of transition, a liminal space, like the river, representing both dangers and opportunities. As the anthropologist P.A. McAllister has shown, migrant labor was formally marked out as a rite of passage, in the classic sense outlined by Arnold van Gennep, with its distinctive rites of separation, transition, and reincorporation. This ritual process was developed in response to a profound irony: the production of the sacred space of the rural homestead depended upon urban employment. "For a man to marry, establish a homestead, develop into a community asset, acquire the livestock and grain needed for the performance of the rituals and the holding of beer drinks," McAllister recounted, "he has little alternative but to go out and work as a migrant labourer."[47] In the rites of departure that marked the separation of the migrant from the homestead, ritual activities included a ceremonial beer drink, the invocation of the ancestors, admonitions delivered by ritual elders, the provision of food for the journey, and a visit to a herbalist for medicines to protect the migrant while away from home. Adapting techniques of consecration, spiritual protection, and preparation for war, these rites treated the migrant laborer as a warrior going off to battle. In the rites of return that marked his reincorporation into the homestead, the migrant invoked the ancestors, gave thanks for his safe return, and formally bestowed gifts on elders both to acknowledge their authority and to effect the assimilation of alien symbols of wealth within the rural community. Through these rites of departure and return, the religious meaning of urban space was defined not within the city but in the countryside. The city was defined as a space of danger, a kind of "wild space," where a man risked being lost, defiled, or killed. At the same time, however, because the homestead depended for its spiritual production as a sacred space on the material resources acquired through wage labor, the city was necessarily an intimate enemy of the homestead, more like the liminal space of the river in its ambivalent mediation between the domestic space and the wild space of the forest or the bush. Although certainly shaped by the harsh realities of the migrant labor system, these indigenous categories played a significant role in shaping the religious meanings of urban space, suggesting at the very least that the meaning of the city could also be produced outside the city.

The religious experience of migrant laborers during their sojourn in the city, however, remains to be further explored. In his research published in 1980, McAllister confessed, "I lack data on the transition phase of migrant labour, particularly with regard to the rituals of transition."[48] Although he assumed that migrants performed indigenous rituals of protection, such as washing with medicines or invoking the ancestors, McAllister was unable to provide detailed descriptions of indigenous religious life in the urban setting. Following Victor Turner, he could only speculate that such indigenous religious practices would necessarily respond to the liminal situation of migrants who "fall in the interstices of social structures, are on its margins, or occupy its lowest rungs."[49] While much more work needs to be done on this question, we can also conclude that the indigenous religious resources drawn upon by migrants have to make sense out of an urban space of transition. In this respect, the religious knowledge and practices of diviners, healers, and other ritual specialists have proven to be particularly portable in urban settings. While the indigenous religious life of the homestead or the polity has tended to be anchored in specific places, ritual specialists have been able to move fairly easily between rural and urban contexts, thereby, in a sense, replicating the movements of migrant laborers. Operating within the liminal space of the city, however, ritual specialists seem to be especially suited to mediating the social tensions experienced by people in the gaps, at the margins, or on the lowest rungs of urban society. In her research on diviners in the Cape Town township of Gugulethu, for example, Janet Mills concluded that diviners acted as "social healers," mediating the social tensions arising in urban life.[50] For migrant laborers, the work of such ritual specialists evokes a migrating sacred, a portable sacred space that mediates between social domains—the rural, the urban— that might otherwise be in opposition.

THE HYBRID SACRED

As indigenous categories are transported and translated between rural environments and urban spaces, they assume the fluid character that cultural analyst Homi Bhabha has identified as "hybridity," the mixing of cultural practices at the margins and intersections of cultures. Not merely producing cultural mixtures, or "syncreticisms," as an earlier analytical vocabulary might have suggested, hybridity arises out of creative interventions, appropriations, and rearticulations that take place in the power relations of specific colonial situations. In analyzing colonial situations, as Bhabha has suggested, we certainly cannot help but hear "the noisy command of colonialist authority" while we struggle to listen for traces of indigenous voices that have been submerged under "the silent repression of native traditions." Between the extremes of colonial command and native repression, however, the cultural productions of hybridity, the innovations arising from intercultural contacts, relations, and exchanges, are located within the "*in-between* space," as Bhabha has proposed, at "the cutting edge of translation and negotiation."[51] What kinds of translations and negotiations of indigenous African categories, we might ask, have given religious meaning to the urban space of Cape Town?

On the basis of fieldwork conducted beginning in 1961 in the Cape Town township of Langa, the anthropologist Archie Mafeje analyzed relations of both social class and religion among the *abantu basel-okishini*, the "people of the location" who had made the city their home. Under the Group Areas Act, making a home in Cape Town was particularly difficult for Africans, since the apartheid government of the National Party had declared the entire Western Cape to be a Coloured Labour Preference Area, a region in which Coloureds, people of "mixed race," would be employed at the expense of black Africans. In announcing this policy in 1955, the director of the Bantu Admin-istration, W.M. Eiselen, who had been a leading Afrikaner anthropol-ogist and, not incidentally, an expert on African traditional religion before becoming an apartheid bureaucrat, stated that Africans in the Western Cape would eventually be repatriated to homelands in the Eastern Cape. According to this legislation, therefore, Africans were formally defined as being out of place in the city. By legal definition, they were cast as temporary residents, subject to pass laws, influx con-trols, and forced deportations, while they lived in a township such as Langa. From the 1930s onward, however, Langa, with its single entrance, multiplying restrictions, and constant police surveillance, had been experienced by many residents as a prison.[52] By the time Mafeje conducted his research in the 1960s, the confinement of Africans in the township was structured by what historian Paul Maylam has called "the most fundamental contradiction of urban apartheid," the impossible imperative of incorporating Africans as laborers while excluding them as residents. As Maylam put it succinctly, "The ultimate objective of apartheid was to achieve the unattainable—to maximise the exploitation of cheap black urban labour, while minimising the presence of the labourers in white urban areas."[53]

Within that contradictory space of temporary incorporation and ultimate exclusion, however, Africans living in Langa found ways to create homes, as Mafeje discovered, in ways that drew heavily upon religious resources. In his analysis of social class in Langa, Mafeje correlated class and religion by distinguishing three basic formations—European mission churches, African independent churches, and African indigenous religion—that represented the descending order of class positions within the social network of the African township. At the top of the hierarchy, members of European mission churches—the Roman Catholics, Anglicans, Methodists, Presbyterians, and so on, who belonged to churches with their historical roots in Europe—generally had greater access to employment. At the bottom, members of various African-initiated churches, such as the Zion Christian Church, with their emphasis on faith healing, ritual purity, and ethical discipline, were generally regarded as lower class, the poorest of the poor, and were looked down upon by African Christians of the European mission churches. Adherents of African traditional religion, however, tended to be held in contempt by members of both European mission and African-initiated churches, rendering them outside the social hierarchy that had been constructed in Christian terms by Africans in Langa. As Mafeje concluded, the process of urban class formation was being worked out in religious terms, in terms of an urban encounter between what he called an "African pagan cosmos" and a "monotheist European religion with a high level of theoretical self-consciousness." In that encounter of religious worldviews, three class positions had emerged—converts, syncretists, and nativists—that were also religious positions. On the basis of his research during the early 1960s in Langa, therefore, Mafeje raised the crucial question of the relation between religion and social class in the city: Does living in the city, being "urbanized," or achieving the social status of the "civilized," necessarily entail assimilation into the "white middle-class cosmic view" associated with European Christianity?[54]

At the end of the twentieth century, Africans in Cape Town continued to confront that religious challenge of the city, the challenge of articulating urban social class with religion. The religious and social terms, however, had changed in profound respects that can only be suggested here by broad generalizations. First, people that Mafeje identified as "converts" to European mission churches regarded themselves not as converts but as Christians who had grown up in the religion of their birth, their family, and their home, often in the process regarding Christianity as the indigenous religion of South Africa and therefore as a religious way of life that accommodated the veneration of ancestors of the home. In other words, the Christianity derived from Europe had been converted into African Christianity. Second, members of African-initiated churches, who had been conventionally identified in the earlier scholarly literature as syncretists because they supposedly mixed "pure" Christianity with elements of indigenous African religious tradition, were often adamantly opposed to any contact with indigenous spirituality, healing, medicines, ritual specialists, or even ancestral spirits. Ironically, therefore, African Christians of the European churches in many cases turned out to be more sympathetic to indigenous religion than the Christians of the so-called African indigenous churches. At the same time, the African-initiated churches, with their emphasis on religious purity, ethical discipline, and hard work, developed a new kind of Protestant ethic that has increasingly been recognized as providing a significant adaptation to the labor conditions of urban capitalism.[55] In complex ways, therefore, these African Christians, maneuvering within the social relations of the city, deployed both Christian and indigenous resources in renegotiating the religious meaning of urban space.

Third, however, adherents of indigenous African religion increasingly negotiated new, hybrid formulations of the religious meaning of urban space against the Christian positions adopted by either European mission or African-initiated churches. In Cape Town, where indigenous religious meanings of space had been so thoroughly alienated, these initiatives in the production of indigenous African sacred space warrant attention. While some Xhosa traditionalists argued that only a rural homestead in the Eastern Cape could provide a sacred space for ritual, other adherents of indigenous religion found ways to create a *kraal* in the city, even by ritually marking out the contours of that sacred cattle enclosure in suburbs of Cape Town that under apartheid had excluded Africans. In previously white suburbs, a *kraal* could be created in a garage, with its outline circumscribed by beer bottles, but its capacity as a sacred space was animated by the ritual speeches that invoked ancestral spirits for purity, power, and protection in the city. While such ritual performance produced and reinforced a domestic sacred space on indigenous terms in the city, it also appropriated the city, claiming its space, especially within those urban spaces that had previously been denied by law to Africans, for a range of indigenous African religious meanings.

Moving into the larger urban community, the public school, which under the apartheid regime of the National Party had established an educational policy of "Christian National Education," also became open for new translations, negotiations, and appropriations of religious space. In the mid-1990s, for example, new educational programs in African indigenous religion were introduced as pilot projects in some township schools in Cape Town. "When I first introduced this in my class," one teacher reported, "the pupils were so astonished because it was something which they thought was only being practiced in the location. They never linked it with the school." As this teacher indicated, the opposition proposed by the anthropologist Philip Mayer lingered: the urban "School" was supposed to be Christian, while the rural "Red" was supposed to be indigenous, traditional, or pagan. However, the teacher knew very well that indigenous religion was also practiced and performed, worked out and deployed, translated and negotiated, within the urban locations of the townships of Cape Town. Accordingly, he found that bringing indigenous religion into religious education was a matter, not of bringing the Red into the School, or of transposing the rural into the urban, but of giving his pupils an opportunity to negotiate their African identity in the city. "I tried to explain to them that the type of education which we had been introduced to had deprived us of our own identity," he recalled. "It was now time that they understood their identity. They were not to come to school and only learn about the Christian faith and forget their roots."[56]

As witnessed on Robben Island in October 1997 at the purification ritual organized by the indigenous ritual specialist and tourist manager Buyiswa Jack, even a national site could be appropriated and translated for indigenous African religious significance. Nationally, the recovery of indigenous African religion accelerated during the 1990s. While the inauguration of Nelson Mandela in 1994 was blessed by a rainbow religious coalition of Christian, Jewish, Muslim, and Hindu prayers, the inauguration of Thabo Mbeki in 1999 began with an invocation by a representative of African traditional religion before the prayers were heard from the other four religions. Exiled from the city for so long,

African indigenous religion seemed to be establishing a role in urban space—in the home, in the community, and even in the nation—as a religion among religions in the African Renaissance of the twenty-first century.

CENTERS AND PERIPHERIES

What does it mean to be a religion among religions in urban space? In modern urban ideologies, religious diversity has tended to be managed conceptually by making two basic distinctions—the public and the private, the one and the many. On the one hand, as religion becomes privatized, a diversity of religious beliefs and practices can be tolerated by municipal authorities as long as they do not intrude into the public sphere. In modern, Western, industrialized societies, this urban distinction between private religion and public space has often reflected a liberal Protestant sensibility, a "religion of civility," according to sociologist John Murray Cuddihy, that has insisted on the suspension of absolute, exclusive, and potentially offensive religious claims in the public arena.[57] Of course, religion inevitably spills out of the privatized enclaves of homes, churches, mosques, temples, or synagogues to assert broader claims on urban space, taking to the streets, so to speak, to negotiate religious presence, position, or power in the city. During the 1980s in Cape Town, religion was particularly evident in the streets as public rituals, from political funerals to street processions, were deployed as religious strategies in the struggle against apartheid. The ideological distinction between private religion and the public sphere, therefore, could not easily be sustained within the urban space of Cape Town.

On the other hand, the distinction between the one and the many— the one, unified, and integrated city with its many religions—was eagerly embraced after 1994 by the municipal authorities of Cape Town. In this formula, the many religions of Cape Town, for all their diversity, each contributed to supporting and sustaining the common good of the city. During 1999, a local Cape Town newspaper, the *Cape Times*, championed this project of creating urban unity out of diversity by publishing a series, "One City, Many Cultures," that explored the different religions, cultural practices, and forms of life in the city. Explicitly designed to promote respect for diversity, this daily series of journalistic features, profiles, and interviews was supported by a public campaign to encourage people of Cape Town to sign a pledge that committed them to intercultural and interreligious toleration. In this instance, toleration was premised not on suspending but on celebrating religious difference in public. However, like the African Renaissance, this formula for interreligious harmony—one city, many religions—was a slogan in search of a reality. The distinction between the one and the many was difficult to sustain, not so much because different religious groups came into conflict as because adherents of different religions in Cape Town had developed alternative religious ways of mapping the city as a whole and therefore did not necessarily live in the same city. Since each religious map provided an orientation to Cape Town in its entirety, rather than merely demarcating a segment of the city, the different religious mappings of Cape Town had effectively produced not one city but many, a Cape Town with multiple and multiplying religious significances.

Nevertheless, the space of the city also has a history, a spatial history of power relations between center and periphery in which different religious orientations have been negotiated. In the city center, prominent Christian churches anchor the central religious architectonics of Cape Town. Representing the only religious body allowed by law in the Cape Colony until 1780, the Groote Kerk—the "Great Church"—of the Dutch Reformed Church was constructed in the pattern of the Greek cross to mark out the religious center of Cape Town. With the purchase of a theater on Riebeeck Square in 1839, the Dutch Reformed Church established a second church for recently freed slaves, St. Stephen's Church, the only church of the denomination to be named after a saint because, according to legend, an angry group of former slaves stoned the building while a service was in progress. Excluded from the Groote Kerk, people of color who attended St. Stephen's called it Die Ou Komediehuis (the Old Comedy House). By the middle of the nineteenth century, therefore, the Christian architecture at the center of Cape Town had enshrined the religious commitment of the Dutch Reformed Church to dividing both church and society along racial lines. The church's policy of excluding other religious groups from the city, however, could not be maintained. Having gathered in an old barn on Strand Street from 1774, German Lutherans were finally granted legal permission in 1780 to hold services and convert the barn into a church as long as the church had no steeple or bell that would extend its influence in the city. With the establishment of British control over the Cape at the beginning of the nineteenth century, however, the churches of various Christian denominations proliferated, especially Anglican churches, the most important being situated in a central position in Cape Town at the top of Adderley Street as St. George's Cathedral.

While the interiors of these churches were dominated by prominent and often ornate pulpits, making each church, as one historian has observed, basically a "preaching box," their exteriors mixed and matched a range of European architectural styles—Classical and Gothic, English and French—in ways that gave substance and weight to the central position of European Christianity in Cape Town.[58] By the late twentieth century, however, most Christians in greater Cape Town practiced their religion not at the center but in the peripheral neighborhoods, black townships, and informal settlements. In the Coloured residential areas of the Cape Flats, Christian churches flourished. As already noted, in the black townships of Cape Town, European mission churches were essentially converted to African Christianity, while a variety of African-initiated churches developed distinctive ways of understanding urban space. According to a recent review of South African architecture, African-initiated churches have practiced their religion in the "leftover spaces in the city," establishing their own "cosmological centres" in open lots, under motorways, or on a beach, where a "line on the ground is often the only edge between sacred space and the city."[59] Often, as anthropologist James Kiernan has shown, an ordinary home is transformed into a sacred space, the sacred center of Zion, by being ritually marked off from the surrounding township environment, which is perceived to be dangerous and defiling.[60] Although it might appear to be anchored at the city center, therefore, Christian space in Cape Town was actually dispersed through multiple centers that had emerged on the city's periphery.

During the political conflicts of the 1980s, relations between center and periphery were intensely contested, often in explicitly Christian terms, in struggles to liberate Cape Town. On the periphery of the city, the political funeral for victims of the police or security forces became an important public ritual of resistance to the apartheid state. Combining religious sermons and prayers with political speeches and slogans, these funerals were highly charged acts of defiance that anticipated the liberation of all of South Africa by claiming a local cemetery as a liberated zone for religious and political ritual. Frequently, the sacred space of the cemetery became a battlefield as police tried to enforce legislation prohibiting flags, banners, placards, pamphlets, or posters at funeral services. For example, at the 1987 funeral held in the Cape Town Coloured neighborhood of Bonteheuwel for the political activist Ashley Kriel, who had been assassinated by the police, the service was disrupted by police ripping an African National Congress flag from the coffin and shooting tear gas at the mourners and clergy in attendance.[61] As political funerals developed into a kind of regular ritual cycle, services were increasingly held for people who had been killed at previous funeral services. Through innovations in religious and political ritual, therefore, cemeteries on the periphery of Cape Town and other urban centers in South Africa were recast as sites of resistance to the central government.

At the same time, the religious significance of the civic center of Cape Town was being redefined by means of public ritual—mass marches, processions, and demonstrations—that had been declared illegal by the apartheid state. On September 3, 1989, for example, three days before what would turn out to be the last election for an apartheid parliament, a peaceful protest march in Cape Town was violently broken up by the police riot squad. The police pursued protesters up Adderley Street into the sanctuary of St. George's Cathedral, attacking, beating, and arresting anyone they could catch. In response, Archbishop Desmond Tutu issued a public statement in which he declared that the police had "desecrated Saint George's Cathedral," not only because they had burst in with guns and whips, but also because they had entered, as Tutu explained, "wearing their hats, in this holy place." In this highly charged idiom of sacred space, therefore, Archbishop Tutu challenged the authority of the police, who had "shown a profane disregard for the sanctity of our churches," and also raised the stakes by challenging the legitimacy of a government that had claimed Christian religious legitimation. "This act was performed by those representing a government which claims to be Christian," Tutu observed. "We are appalled that this kind of act is carried out in the name of God."[62] Ten days after Archbishop Tutu reconsecrated the cathedral, reclaiming its sanctity from defilement by agents of apartheid, he was at the head of a mass interracial procession through the streets of Cape Town that symbolically announced the "reclaiming of the city." In negotiating that claim on the center of Cape Town, antiapartheid activists simultaneously deployed religious and political strategies, maneuvering within both the church and the streets to redefine the terms of engagement in the city. Years later, those days in

September 1989 could be recalled as the beginning of a postapartheid Cape Town.

Along with Archbishop Desmond Tutu, Shaykh Nazeem Mohamed, leader of the Muslim Judicial Council, was at the head of that march in September 1989 to reclaim the city. His leadership testified to both the interfaith cooperation in the antiapartheid struggle and the long history and vital presence of Islam in Cape Town. Although prohibited by law on pain of death in the Dutch Colony, the practice of Islam developed in Cape Town not only through the arrival of Muslim exiles, convicts, and slaves but also through initiatives in local conversion and community formation. Excluded from the city center until the early nineteenth century, Muslims developed an alternative sacred geography in Cape Town that outlined a sacred periphery surrounding the city. Beginning with the tomb of Shaykh Yusuf, the Indonesian nobleman, political prisoner, and Sufi teacher who died in 1699 in captivity at Zandvliet Farm in Macassar, this local Muslim geography in Cape Town was defined by a circle of shrines, or *karamats* (in Arabic, "miracles"), that surrounded Muslim Cape Town. In addition to the tomb of Shaykh Yusuf in Macassar, this circle included shrines in the forests of Constantia, above the quarry in Strand Street, on the ridgetop of Signal Hill, above Oudekraal on the slopes of Table Mountain, and off the coast on Robben Island.[63] Forming a sacred circle around the city, the *karamats* of Cape Town represented a Muslim map of the city, beginning with the periphery rather than with the center, that constituted the urban space of Cape Town as a zone of spiritual protection. According to tradition, the Muslim leader Abdullah Kadi Abdus Salaam, known as Tuan Guru, who during the early nineteenth century established the mosques and madrasahs that gave Islam an enduring presence at the center of Cape Town, invoked the power of the *karamats* as a promise of both protection and liberation. "Be of good heart my children and serve your masters," Tuan Guru reportedly advised, "for one day your liberty will be restored to you and your descendants will live within a circle of karamats safe from fire, famine and plague, earthquake and tidal wave."[64] In Cape Town, therefore, the religious meaning of urban space for Muslims began with a circle of shrines around the perimeter of the city.

As mosques, madrasahs, and other Muslim institutions emerged in the central city during the nineteenth century, Muslims confronted the religious authority of a Christian municipality, a city that had adopted modern "Christian" commitments to hygiene, sanitation, and public health. During the smallpox epidemic of 1882, municipal authorities tried to sanitize the city. Suggesting the religious impetus behind this urban ideology of sanitation, the editor of a Cape Town newspaper declared: "The Smallpox has come! The Angel of Vengeance of outraged Sanitation hangs over the city!"[65] In the service of this spirit of sanitation, Christian leaders in the city identified Muslims as the source of impurity and danger. Under the authority of the Public Health Act of 1883, the City of Cape Town closed the Muslim cemetery in the city center, inspiring mass protests by Muslims who objected to this municipal intervention in their religious practice. Two days after the final closure of the Muslim cemetery in Cape Town, as many as three thousand Muslims walked through the streets in a funeral procession in defiance of the government. Though this act of defiance, which came to be known as the "Malay riot," was violently suppressed by the municipal police, the urban authorities set aside a plot of land outside the city for a new Muslim cemetery. This segregation of the Muslim dead, however, anticipated the urban segregation of the living. As an editorial in a Cape Town newspaper declared in 1882, "The sooner the Malays are made to reside in a separate district the better for all concerned."[66] During the twentieth century, the "Malay quarter" of the Bo-Kaap was established as a separate Muslim district in Cape Town. Within the apartheid city, I.D. du Plessis, an Afrikaner intellectual who belonged to the secret society of the Afrikaner Broederbond and was known as a "friend of the Malays" for popularizing an exoticized Malay culture in his books, worked diligently to solidify this separate religious, cultural, ethnic, and residential position of Muslims in the city.[67] Although they lived, worked, and worshipped in the immediate proximity of the city center, when they were defined as "Malays" by apartheid ideologues like Du Plessis, Muslims could be imagined as if they lived in another world far away from Cape Town. While Muslims were establishing their sacred geography in Cape Town, therefore, with its periphery of holy shrines and its central institutions of mosques, madrasahs, and cemeteries, the apartheid city was redefining Muslims as aliens from Southeast Asia.

In the struggle against apartheid, Christians and Muslims could often find common cause in rejecting the racial division and racialist domination of the city. At political funerals, on protest marches, and in prisons, cooperation between Christians and Muslims was apparent during the 1980s. After the first democratic election in 1994, the role of Islam as a spiritual resource in the struggle for political liberation continued to be acknowledged by political leaders of the African National Congress. At an Eid Celebration in 1998, for example, President Nelson Mandela recalled that political prisoners on Robben Island, regardless of their religious backgrounds, had looked to the example of an earlier Muslim political prisoner on the island, Shaykh Matura, "from whose karamat on Robben Island, as prisoners we drew deep inspiration and spiritual strength when our country was going through its darkest times."[68]

Within the changing political landscape of postapartheid South Africa, however, different Muslim claims began to be asserted in the streets of Cape Town. In July 1996, a new religious movement calling itself PAGAD—People Against Gangsterism and Drugs—marched on the home of a local drug dealer, Rashaad Staggie, shot him dead, and set his body on fire in the street. As one leader declared, "We are going to take back the streets tonight."[69] Claiming to be an interreligious organization, PAGAD was clearly driven by a small group of Muslim leaders with a very specific religious agenda, but the movement initially gained grassroots support from people who felt that their lives, families, homes, and communities were under threat from gangsters.[70]

As a distinctively urban religious movement, PAGAD deployed not only compelling religious rhetoric but also rallies, marches, and processions through the streets of Cape Town. Allegedly, it also utilized paramilitary techniques—armed guards, mobile defense units, pipe bombs, and assassinations—to advance its religious cause. Hundreds of attacks against suspected drug dealers, but also against Muslim critics, academics, former members, and public places, as in the Planet Hollywood bombing at the Waterfront, were generally attributed to PAGAD but vigorously denied by the movement's leadership. By February 1999, President Nelson Mandela was compelled to address this movement (even if indirectly, since he never explicitly named PAGAD) in a speech before Parliament, observing that "what started off expressly as a campaign against gangsterism has now become a violent and murderous offensive against ordinary citizens." Although portraying itself as "moral and god-inspired," President Mandela observed, this religious movement had "assumed the form of terrorism to undercut Cape Town's lifeline and destablise a democratic government."[71]

In the struggle over defining the religious meaning of urban space in Cape Town, however, PAGAD had gained not only a considerable support base but also a certain purchase on setting the basic terms of engagement in the city. In response to the president's speech in Parliament, it issued a press statement that praised Nelson Mandela's political contribution to the struggle against apartheid but condemned his religious position. "He is using our churches, mosques, and synagogues," PAGAD declared, "to try and gain support from religious leaders to back political parties that stand for ungodly laws such as abortion, prostitution, gay rights, etc." Insisting that in the spiritual politics of the city the personal was always political, PAGAD attacked Nelson Mandela for being "the leader of a party that has consistently and deliberately violated the laws of God."[72] As this struggle over the city continued, PAGAD persisted in defining Cape Town as the site of a moral drama, a conflict between the forces of good and evil, that was local, national, and international, with its international scope highlighted on the Internet by the PAGAD website displaying the logo of the movement against the background of a Mercator projection of the entire globe. According to PAGAD, therefore, the local neighborhood in Cape Town was a microcosm of the world, a local battlefield on which a cosmic war was being waged between global forces of good and evil. As this conflict over the meaning of the local neighborhood intensified at the end of the 1990s, the Muslim leadership of PAGAD struggled to reposition Islam, or a certain version of Islam, from the periphery to the center of the city by defining the religious significance of urban space in Cape Town.

In assessing the religious meanings of urban space, we have to recognize that relations between the center and the periphery, whatever that conventional distinction might mean in the city, are always structural and historical. They are architecturally constructed and historically positioned. But the spatial dynamics that constitute the centers and peripheries of urban space are also fluid and mobile, situational and relational, negotiated and contested. In Cape Town, as I have tried to suggest, the spatial dynamics of the city cannot easily, conveniently, or inevitably be contained within the colonial constructions, the indigenous categories, or the religious assertions of churches, mosques, temples, synagogues, and other religious groupings in the urban landscape. Defying every particular religious attempt at definition, the city defines itself indefinitely as a religious space of exclusion and expansion, of segmentation and confinement, of migration and hybridity, of regularity and resistance, and of local and global extensions. Cape Town, like any other city, has been a locus for generating such complex, contradictory religious meanings of urban space. To conclude, I will highlight very briefly some of the more general features of the urban political economy of the sacred that one might notice by touring through Cape Town, South Africa's "Mother City."

THE URBAN POLITICAL ECONOMY OF THE SACRED

As I will use the phrase here, *political economy* refers to the power relations at stake in the production of values and the dynamics of scarcity and surplus in their ownership and alienation, their distribution and exchange, their consumption, preservation, or destruction. In the political economy of the city, "the sacred" can refer to a range of cultural values that are produced through the religious labor of formal ritualization and intensive interpretation. While classic theoretical approaches in the history of religions have proposed substantial definitions of the sacred, such as Rudolph Otto's "the holy," Gerardus van der Leeuw's "power," or Mircea Eliade's "the real," more recent research has emphasized its situational production, following Emile Durkheim, as "that which is set apart." In this respect, the sacred is situated within specific material processes, social contexts, and political relations as a notional supplement to the work of sacralization, the ritual and interpretive labor involved in setting apart certain persons, objects, places, or times. Following the dynamics that Arnold van Gennep called the "pivoting of the sacred," anything can be invested with sacred meaning and significance, with sacred purity or power, through the ongoing work of ritual and interpretation that marks out with meticulous attention to detail that which is set apart.[73]

In South Africa, of course, this definition of the sacred has a particular resonance, not only because apartheid was developed as a kind of sacred science for setting people and places apart, but also because the sacralized separations that I have traced in this chapter—the divisions between colonial and indigenous, domestic and wild, center and periphery, and so on—remain inscribed in its urban landscapes. Within the urban space of Cape Town, the sacred has operated, not as an integrating force in the formation of what Durkheim called a "single moral community," but as a multiple, fragmentary, and divisive constellation of forces. As we have seen, these sanctified divisions have been established, not only by the church or mosque, but also by the structural history of the city itself, a history that remains evident in the monuments and scars of its urban landscape. Sacred space in Cape Town, therefore, has been generated out of a long history of setting apart.

Within any political economy, however, the sacred is an inherently ambiguous locus of value, since it points to a category that is simultaneously empty and full of meaning. As Claude Lévi-Strauss proposed, the sacred should be regarded as "a value of indeterminate signification, in itself empty of meaning and therefore susceptible to the reception of any meaning whatsoever."[74] In the urban political economy of the sacred, this ambiguity results in the inherent contradiction of the scarcity and surplus of sacred space. On the one hand, sacred space is a scarce resource. As geographer John Urry observed, because no two objects can occupy the same point in space, "space is necessarily limited and there has to be competition and conflict over its organization and control."[75] In any political economy of the sacred, therefore, conflicts over space are inevitable.

On the other hand, because of the surplus of signification in human engagements with materiality, which is immediately available and infinitely susceptible to being invested with any meaning whatsoever, sacred space is also a surplus. By signifying nothing and everything, the sacred significance of materiality represents a surplus that opens space for both interpretation and appropriation. Not only open to alternative "readings," this surplus of signification in sacred space is also available (or vulnerable) for appropriation, for the assertion of competing claims on its ownership. Although they are conventionally underwritten by intensive interpretations of the meaning of a space, these claims on ownership are assertions of power within the cultural process of stealing back and forth sacred symbols that I have elsewhere defined as religion.[76] In trying to elaborate this definition within the city, I would like to propose in conclusion that the term *religion* can be recast to designate a category of human activity that comprises not only beliefs and practices, whether in relation to transcendent forces, sacred objects, or ultimate concerns, but also resources and strategies—the resources that are appropriated and the strategies that are deployed—within an urban political economy of the sacred.

In Cape Town, the cultural process of stealing sacred symbols back and forth is perhaps most clearly revealed in the work of gangsters, the leaders and followers of the many urban gangs—the Americans, the Hard Livings, the Sexy Boys, the Mongrels, and others—that during the second half of the 1990s claimed the loyalty of an estimated four hundred thousand people, primarily in the Coloured residential areas of the Cape Flats.[77] These gangs illustrate the process of stealing sacred symbols not only because they were engaged in the kinds of criminal activities suggested by the term *stealing* but also because since 1994 Cape Town gangs had been central to the struggles over religious legitimacy, the legitimate ownership of the sacred, within the religious terrain of the city. As products of advanced urban marginalization, the growing alienation, impoverishment, moral despair, and criminal activity at the periphery of urban life that had directly resulted from the progress of urbanization, Cape Town gangs were also exemplars of advanced urban globalization, since their success depended not only on generating local loyalty but also on participating in the global network of narco-capitalism by trading in illegal drugs. At the intersection of the local and the global in Cape Town, these gangs featured prominently in negotiations over the religious meanings of urban space at the end of the twentieth century.

The gangs of the Cape Flats operated like religious organizations by appropriating and reinterpreting sacred symbols, generating, in the process, distinctive myths and rituals that invested urban space with religious significance. For example, the Americans gang based in the Coloured township of Manenberg transformed their impoverished working-class neighborhood into a sacred center of power through the strategic use of highly charged symbolic resources. Calling their territory "America," the gang invoked a divine right of possession by rendering "Americans" as an acronym—"Almighty Equal Rights is Coming And Not Standing"—that claimed local empowerment in the name of a distant superpower. Like the "Christendom" of Van Riebeeck, Wagenaer, and other seventeenth-century colonial conquerors in the Cape, the foreign symbol of "America" could be drawn into local "ceremonies of possession" by gangsters as a sacred warrant for the colonization of space. Certainly, they colonized space by creating defensive formations, by defending turf and territory. But the Americans also demonstrated the expansive spirit of Rhodes in extending their influence over space. In their religious symbolism, the gang celebrated that expansive spirit in symbols of blood and money.

As the cultural analyst Harvie Ferguson has observed, money is "the 'space' of the capitalist world," producing an empty, infinite extension through which, in principle, all commodities can pass and freely circulate.[78] The Americans gang proudly displayed the flag of the United States but interpreted that material symbol as a sacred icon that revealed the truth of money. "In the mythology of the Cape Flat's Americans gang," as journalists Chiara Carter and Marianne Merten reported, "the six white and seven red lines on the stars and stripes flag represent crisp bank notes stained in blood."[79] More specifically, the Americans distinguished between the white and red stripes on the flag, understanding the white stripes to signify the clean work—not wage labor but organized criminal activity—that generated money, while the red stripes designated the dirty work of blood, the work of violence, killing, and coercion, that was required to support the clean work of making money. In addition to appropriating and reinterpreting the U.S. flag, the Americans adopted the symbols of the bald eagle, the Statue of Liberty, and the motto of the United States, altered slightly, however, to read, "In God We Trust, In Money We Believe." Gang initiations, as criminologist Don Pinnock has shown, deployed these symbols of blood and money in rites of passage, which were performed at the "White House." According to one initiate, the ritual process involved learning the secrets of the Statue of Liberty, killing an eagle to take the dollar bill from its claws, and finally entering the White House where thirteen presidents handled money, six counting and seven wiping the blood off the bank notes.[80] Incorporating young men into the Americans gang, this ritual also initiated them into the truth of money and thereby certified their claim on urban space.

Asserting competing claims on urban space, rival gangs also developed sacred symbols, myths, and rituals. For example, one opposition gang, the JFKs, which could be rendered as "Junky Funky Kids," "Join the Force of Killers," or "Justice, Freedom, and Kindness," maintained that they were enemies of the Americans gang because an American had killed their original president, "John Frank Kennedy." As the most powerful rival to the Americans, the Hard Livings gang adopted the British flag, called themselves the "Chosen Ones," and countered the Americans' emphasis on the sacred mystery of money with their own motto, "Rather Wisdom than Gold." In all these local symbolic maneuvers, Cape Town gangs deployed global signs of power, wealth, and value, producing, in the process, migrating, hybrid forms of sacred space. In this respect, the gangs invested urban space with religious meaning that was consistent with postmodern analysis of the city as a "space of flows," a space through which people and capital, but also signs, symbols, and images, migrate freely, or at least unpredictably, thus superseding the local "space of places."[81] According to many analysts, the postmodern city has been subject to global processes—"time-space compression," the stretching of "time-space distantiation," the flow of "intersecting scapes"—that have rendered any fixed sense of place obsolete.[82] Cape gangsters have been at the forefront of recasting the city as a space of flows, a space in which the sacred migrates freely from global to local and is rendered locally in hybrid myths, rituals, and claims on the ownership of urban space.

After 1994, two developments, simultaneously global and local, altered the urban landscape for Cape gangs. First, a new consortium, the Firm, was established to coordinate the drug trade. Perhaps resulting from pressure applied by international suppliers to resolve local conflicts, the Firm looked more like business than religion, even though it could be interpreted as the acronym "For It Requires Money," thereby recalling earlier attempts by gangsters to capture the secret, sacred truth of money. By putting their activities on a business basis, however, the Firm substantially reduced intergang rivalries and expanded the scope of organized crime in Cape Town.[83] Second, as the antidrug campaign of PAGAD placed local pressure on gangsters, new strategies emerged, often explicitly religious, for redefining the place of gangs in the city. As the Firm announced in October 1996 the formation of CORE—Community Outreach Forum—a political initiative of reform but also a religious initiative, as Pastor Albern Martins explained, "to provide a haven for reformed gangsters," the gangsters who survived the "open season" of 1998 that resulted in the violent deaths of leaders of the Americans, Hard Livings, Mongrels, the 28s, and other gangs increasingly embraced the strategy of religious conversion to redefine their place in the city.[84]

In the case of the boss of the Hard Livings, Rashied Staggie, whose brother Rashaad had been killed in 1996 by PAGAD marchers, conversion from Islam to Christianity offered one way of repositioning his gang in the city. Rashied Staggie underwent this widely publicized conversion to Christianity after he had been wounded in a drive-by shooting in March 1999. "I must reinvent myself," he announced.[85] Staggie's conversion was certified not only by his personal reinvention but also by the transformation of his gang's headquarters, a township drinking establishment known as a shebeen, into a Christian church. As a local newspaper reported, "This one-time symbol of gangsterism on the Cape Flats has been 'reborn' as a church hall." On behalf of the Shekinah Tabernacle Church that conducted services there, Debbie Lamb observed, "This place was a place of darkness and of all things negative but since Staggie converted we have been changing it into a place of hope where most of the people who were gangsters can mend their ways."[86] Staggie's personal religious conversion, therefore, could be interpreted as a significant conversion of urban space, suggesting that not only a gangster but also a "place of darkness" could be "born again."

In the religious history of Cape Town, the conversion of secular places—a barn, a theater, a lost neighborhood, an island prison—into sacred sites has been crucial to the production of the religious meanings of urban space. At the end of the 1990s, this process of spatial conversion continued, not only at Staggie's headquarters, but also in the expanding activities of new religious movements, such as the Charismatic Christian group His People, which every Sunday converted two theaters in Cape Town into sacred places for religious services that attracted as many as six thousand celebrants each week. With their own global connections to Christian organizations in the United States, these Charismatic churches—Shekinah Tabernacle, His People, the Lighthouse, and the Rhema Church—actively worked to redefine the religious space of Cape Town. At a secret meeting held at the end of April 1999, leaders of these four churches entered into an agreement with leaders of PAGAD "to rid society of the evil of drugs, crime, and corruption on all levels."[87] Announcing the formation of the Cape Peace Initiative, these religious leaders bypassed the older, established structures of religious authority in Cape Town, whether Christian or Muslim, to negotiate their central place in the city on the basis of their interventions with the gangs of the Cape Flats.

Representatives of the Christian churches insisted that they had received no money from the gangs. "We are not receiving cash from the gangsters," Shekinah Tabernacle pastor Vivian Rix asserted, "because it would compromise our initiative."[88] Like PAGAD, however, the Christian Charismatics had clearly appropriated the gangsters as a kind of symbolic capital, a symbolic surplus that could be used to advance their religious interests within the city's political economy of the sacred. In a joint statement invoking the "divine law of the Creator," the Muslims and Christians in the Cape Peace Initiative announced that gangsters had to be "genuinely transformed" through their sincere and public acts of reformation, renunciation, and restitution. Clearly, there were different ways of "transforming" gangsters, whether by killing Rashaad Staggie or converting his brother Rashied, for example, that could be justified in terms of the "divine law" of urban religion. As competitors in the urban political economy of the sacred, however, PAGAD and the Charismatic Christian churches could form only the most tenuous religious alliance through the Cape Peace Initiative. On Easter Sunday in 1999, when yet another gang leader—Glen Khan, boss of the 28s—was murdered, the rift between the Muslims of PAGAD and the Christians of the Charismatic churches was exposed. According to his wife, Khan had told her before his death, "If anything happens to me, don't let me be buried as a Muslim because of what Pagad has done to the faith."[89] Accordingly, under the name of Glen Johnson, he was buried as a Christian. In the urban political economy of the sacred, therefore, even the dead add value.

If the African Renaissance meant anything, it promised a rebirth, recovery, and renewal of the city. In his keynote address to a conference in Johannesburg on the African Renaissance in September 1998, Thabo Mbeki suggested that the African city could be refounded as an urban space that was centered in neither the market nor the fortress but rather in what Paul Wheatley called the "ceremonial complex" that organized ritual relations between the living and the dead, the heroic ancestors, or the gods of the city. With respect to global market forces, Mbeki urged, "We must be at the forefront in challenging the notion of 'the market' as the modern god, a supernatural phenomenon to whose dictates everything human must bow in a spirit of powerlessness." Turning to military power, he rejected "the deification of arms, the seemingly entrenched view that to kill another person is a natural way of advancing one's cause."[90] In these potently religious terms, therefore, Thabo Mbeki decentered the market and the fortress—the capitalist "modern god," the nationalist "deification of arms"—as legitimate religious grounds for founding a city. How, then, can an African Renaissance city be founded? Invoking the originating absence that was the condition of possibility for Cape Town, South Africa, Thabo Mbeki declared, "I am an African," because "I owe my being to the Khoi and the San whose desolate souls haunt the great expanses of the beautiful Cape—they who fell victim to the most merciless genocide our native land has ever seen, they who were first to lose their lives in the struggle to defend our freedom and independence."[91] In recovering the religious meanings of urban space, therefore, even the dead, perhaps especially the dead, add value, because they embody the truth of both blood and money that lies at the heart of the urban political economy of the sacred.

CHAPTER THREE

Violence

In his address to the first gathering of the Truth and Reconciliation Commission (TRC) on December 16, 1995, Archbishop Desmond Tutu charged the commissioners with the awesome responsibility of facilitating a process of national healing in South Africa. Significantly, this inaugural address was delivered on the occasion of a new national holiday, the Day of Reconciliation, that had only recently been consecrated by appropriating the most important day in the sacred calendars of two conflicting South African nationalisms: the Afrikaner nationalist Day of the Covenant, celebrating the Battle of Blood River, when God joined the *laager* and started killing Africans, and the African nationalist Heroes Day, marking the founding of the armed wing of the African National Congress, Umkhonto we Sizwe. While both the Day of the Covenant and Heroes Day were holy days that had sacralized political violence, the Day of Reconciliation celebrated the redemption of South Africa from its violent history. If South Africa had any kind of future, it depended upon coming to terms with that past.

As Archbishop Desmond Tutu recognized, building a future required knowing the truth about South Africa's violent past. Drawing analogies from the Christian tradition, Archbishop Tutu contrasted two institutionalized ritual techniques for the production of truth, the inquisition and the confession. Insisting that the commission would not be an inquisition, exposing heretics or hunting witches, "hell-bent on bringing miscreants to book," Archbishop Tutu explicitly used the model of ritual confession. "We will be engaging in what should be a corporate nationwide process of healing," he advised, "through contrition, confession and forgiveness." Archbishop Tutu called upon all the religious communities of South Africa to support this ritual work of confession, expressing his "hope that our churches, mosques, synagogues and temples will be able to provide liturgies for corporate confession and absolution."[1] But the TRC itself seemed to be vested with the responsibility for managing a national ritual of confession and absolution.

As a ritual inducement to speak, the Christian ritual of confession has traditionally been an instrument for the production of truth. Faced with the challenge of getting at the truth of political violence in South Africa, the commission assumed the role of a national priesthood to hear expressions of remorse and a catalog of sins from the perpetrators of violent acts. The legislation that established the commission, however, granted absolution to perpetrators, not as in the Roman Catholic ritual of confession by imposing acts of penance, but by bestowing legal amnesty from criminal or civil prosecution. In this respect, the ritual of confession in the TRC was perhaps aligned with the Westminster Confession of the Anglican Church in its understanding of the workings of grace. In any case, the analogy between the ritual of the commission and the ritual of confession was tenuous. Amnesty was not granted through a religious ritual of contrition, confession, and absolution. Rather, the entire process was organized by a legalistic framework of motive and evidence. Two legal conditions obtained: violent acts had to be connected to a political motive, and they had to be fully and completely disclosed in testimony before the commission.

While carrying an aura of religious ritual, the TRC explicitly addressed the role of religion in South Africa's violent history. During the hearings in November 1997 that were devoted to written and oral submissions from representatives of South African faith communities, explicitly religious accounts of the struggle were provided.[2] From the transcripts of the faith community hearings, it appears that these stories were told in a particularly congenial and collegial atmosphere. Perhaps on no other occasion was the commission's religious character more evident. Certainly, the faith communities understood these hearings as a ritual process. In some cases, such as the appearances of representatives from the Dutch Reformed Church and the Zion Christian Church, their mere presence seemed sufficient to validate the ritual. Following the direction of Archbishop Tutu, however, this was their moment for contrition, confession, and forgiveness. On behalf of their various churches, Christians did apologize and confess. Even representatives of the Dutch Reformed Church showed a degree of remorse, although they apparently persisted in distinguishing between "good" and "bad" apartheid. When Jews, Muslims, Hindus, Baha'is, and adherents of African Traditional Religion were included in the hearings, Archbishop Tutu apologized for the history of "Christian arrogance" in South Africa. Apologies were heard all around.

But representatives of faith communities also seemed concerned with vindication. In the formal report on the hearings that was eventually integrated into the final report of the TRC, three subject positions—perpetrators, victims, and opponents of oppression—were located in a broad narrative of national liberation. Certainly, this analysis grew out of the church struggle in South Africa that was most closely associated with the work of the South African Council of Churches (SACC). Essentially, the history of the SACC defined the relevant periodization of Christian opposition to apartheid. Its doctrinal statements secured the basic terms of engagement. In particular, the theological analysis that had been advanced in the *Kairos Document* of 1985 was applied to the submissions of the various faith communities. As a result, faith communities that developed a "state theology" or a "church theology" were found to have been complicit in apartheid oppression.[3] By adopting a "prophetic theology," however, some faith communities identified with the victims of oppression and actively opposed the apartheid state. From that vantage point, the truth of submissions could be assessed—one exaggerated, another misrepresented the facts, a third avoided responsibility, and so on—in ways that placed the various faith communities in the narrative of church struggle. However, this prophetic narrative posed serious problems for shaping a shared memory of the role of religion under apartheid.

First, the term *prophetic* itself emerged at the hearings as a contested term. While the SACC and the Institute for Contextual Theology claimed prophetic status for liberation theology, the Dutch Reformed Church also claimed to be fulfilling a "prophetic" mission. Asserting that it had played that role in the past by advising the state behind closed doors, the DRC promised to continue performing a critical function in relation to the new democratic government. Significantly, therefore, the DRC submission embraced the prophetic mandate of opposition to the state that had been the province of the SACC in the

1980s. Both of these prophetic claims, however, were challenged by the presence of Bishop Barnabas Lekganyane, whose role as prophet of the Zion Christian Church was interpreted by his spokesperson as providing spiritual leadership in personal morality and community formation. Instead of "speaking truth to power," this prophet did not have to say a word during the faith community hearings. His mere presence was sufficient. Clearly, these different constructions of the prophetic role— critical speech, powerful silence—were left unresolved at the hearings. However, it is possible that the term *prophetic* does not provide adequate grounds for reconciliation. When he was released from prison on February 11, 1990, Nelson Mandela seemed to recognize this problem. "I stand before you not as a prophet," he told one hundred thousand people gathered in the streets of Cape Town, "but as a humble servant of you, the people."[4] Not the prophet but the servant, therefore, was the potent symbol that Nelson Mandela invoked to suggest the way forward.

Second, the "prophetic" narrative assumes that certain faith communities were effective agents of political struggle. During the 1980s, concern about this claim was expressed within the ANC. In a cautionary critique, for example, John Lamola warned that the new, radical involvement of organized Christianity might create the illusion that the church was leading the revolution. If the church were to be regarded as a leading force in the political struggle, then people might think that all they had to do was support the church. As Lamola observed, however, the church was not a force of struggle but a site of struggle. Like schools or factories, the church presented both a gathering point for mobilizing people and a target to be captured and liberated. According to Lamola, no theology, not even a "prophetic theology," could provide a firm basis for deriving political principles and practice because theology itself was "one of the most disputed among human areas of enquiry." However, by means of "consultation between the religious structures and the people's political structures," the church could play an important role, not as a prophet, but as a "servant of the revolution."[5] Although this revolutionary rhetoric must now seem strange, like the voice of an exile who has remained in exile, the resonance of the term *servant* still echoed with possibilities for a different kind of narrative about the role of faith communities in the South African struggle.

In the analysis of the Kairos theologians, religion, politics, and violence were linked in three different ways. State theology legitimated oppression through violent means; church theology, ostensibly apolitical, was complicit with oppression by ignoring state violence; and prophetic theology, resisting oppression and mobilizing liberation, even when it supported armed struggle, was engaged not in violence but in the judicious exercise of legitimate force against the violence of apartheid. Clearly, *violence* was an ambiguous term, as both the apartheid-state theologians and antiapartheid theologians deployed the strategic distinction between "their" violence, illegitimate by definition, and "our" legitimate force. Reviewing the problem of defining violence, I propose in this chapter that religion can be found operating within violence. Not an independent variable justifying violence or restraining violence, religion appears in sacred symbols, myths, and rituals animating violence.

DEFINING VIOLENCE

As an inherently contested term, *violence* is notoriously resistant to definition. Nevertheless, a review of the philosophical literature reveals a range of approaches to defining it that can be reduced to four basic definitions: (1) direct physical harm to persons or property; (2) the violation of humanity; (3) illegitimate force; and (4) direct physical harm to persons or property that must be immediately evaluated in terms of its ethical intentions, motives, means, ends, or consequences. If we plotted them on a graph, the first two definitions could form a vertical axis identifying the scope of the term *violence*. Ranging from the minimalist requirement of direct physical harm to the maximalist allowance of anything that violates human dignity, integrity, or wholeness, this vertical axis would indicate the extreme positions that have been adopted in defining the term's scope. On the horizontal axis, which would identify the term's ethical evaluation, we could place the next two definitions. At one extreme, by asserting that violence is illegitimate by definition, the third definition presumes an a priori distinction between legitimate and illicit uses of force, while the fourth definition leaves the question of legitimacy open to the independent ethical evaluation of acts that cause harm. As a background for defining political violence, these four definitions warrant brief elaboration.

As noted, a minimalist definition stipulates the meaning and restricts the use of the term *violence* to acts resulting in direct physical harm to persons or property. Such a definition seems to bring a certain kind of precision to the analysis of violence. For example, a minimalist definition can specify that "an act of violence is any act taken by A that involves great force, is in itself capable of injuring, damaging, or destroying, and is done with the intent of injuring, damaging, or destroying B (a Being), or O (an inanimate object)."[6] This definition presents a calculus of relations between A and B or O that seems to provide a stable framework for measuring intention, force, and harm to persons and property. A minimalist definition of violence as direct harm to persons or property even seems to allow for quantification. The Aromaa-Wolf scale, for example, defines violence as direct physical harm to persons in order to develop a standard of measurement for degrees of violence from 0 ("no violence experienced") up to 9 ("acts resulting in death").[7]

As many commentators have observed, the minimalist definition of violence presumes that what counts as harm is a constant.[8] To assess harm to persons, however, some normative baseline of human wholeness, integrity, or dignity is required. Accordingly, a maximalist definition has identified violence in broader terms as the violation of humanity. According to Newton Garver, for example, the "idea of violence in human affairs is much more closely connected with the idea of violation than it is with the idea of force."[9] By not limiting violence to acts involving direct force, the scope of the term is expanded to include not only physical but also psychological and social forms of violation. At the same time, this maximalist definition introduces a normative dimension that makes violence an inherently ethical concern. As the scholar of religion Ninian Smart has observed, violence "is not just a natural phenomenon, for it requires some idea of violation—that is, it has a normative aspect."[10] Therefore, attempts to define violence are inevitably conditioned by ethical considerations.

In ethical reflections on violence, a common strategy has been to define violence as illegitimate force. From this perspective, violence is always energy, power, or force gone wrong. The American philosopher John Dewey, for example, distinguished between legitimate force and illegitimate violence by observing that force is the ability to act in the world. According to Dewey, "not to depend upon and utilize force is simply to be without a foothold in the real world." He used two metaphors to suggest the scope of legitimate force. First, force is legitimately used to build bridges, subways, or skyscrapers, but when force results in "waste instead of production, destruction instead of construction, we call it not energy or power but violence." Second, force is legitimately exercised to enforce the traffic laws on the roads, but "to run amuck in the street is a case of violence."[11] In these homely metaphors drawn from the construction industry and the traffic department, Dewey tried to identify violence as an exercise of force— blowing up bridges, breaking laws—that was illegitimate by definition. By implication, however, force that was used for creative projects or legal coercion, even when it resulted in direct physical harm, could not be regarded as violence.

Dewey's assumptions about the inherently legitimate ends served by force have been questioned. The notion that violence is illegitimate by definition certainly allows for the convenient distinction between "their" violence and "our" judicious exercise of legitimate force. In the process, however, violence disappears as an independent variable for analysis. It is simply the wrong kind of force. Recovering the term *violence* as an independent variable, some theorists have returned to a definition of violence as direct physical harm but have insisted that every violent act must be evaluated by some independent set of ethical criteria.[12] Only by engaging in the immediate ethical evaluation of motives, means, ends, or consequences can we determine whether a violent act resulting in physical harm can be regarded as legitimate or illegitimate. In other words, violence might be defined as direct physical harm to persons or property, but its meaning and significance can be determined only within a moral economy.

DEFINING POLITICAL VIOLENCE

A moral economy concerned with the legitimacy of force, power, or violence is already part of a political economy. In the literature on political violence, we find the same four basic strategies for defining violence that appear in the philosophical literature. First, adopting the minimalist definition, some analysts have defined political violence as collective acts resulting in direct physical harm to persons or property. Accordingly, violence registers as "acts of disruption, destruction, or injury whose purpose, choice of targets or victims, surrounding circumstances, implementation, and/or effects have political significance, that is, tend to modify the behaviour of others in a bargaining situation that has consequences for the social system."[13] For many social scientists, the most immediate value of a minimalist definition of political violence as direct physical harm is its potential for quantification. By adopting this definition, social scientists can measure violence by a single indicator of magnitude that is based, for example, on the total number of deaths resulting from political violence, or they can measure political violence by multiple variables that give different weight to death, injury, and destruction of property. Like the Aromaa-Wolf scale for measuring personal violence, a scale for political violence developed by Edward N. Muller, which identifies levels of intensity from o ("conformity") to 5 ("revolution, guerrilla war, civil war"), seems to make the analysis of political violence a matter of scientific quantification.[14] Clearly, however, the very notion of quantitative measurement implies a violence degree zero—conformity, no deviance—that subtly reinforces the ethical legitimacy of the political status quo. By implicitly adopting the minimalist definition of violence, as Paul R. Brass has argued, global media reports about political violence tend to reinforce existing power relations in state and society.[15] While claiming scientific precision, therefore, this minimalist definition is based on the ethical presumption that political violence is abnormal.

Adopting the maximalist strategy of defining violence as the violation of humanity, other theorists have recognized that violence is in fact normalized in politics, especially in the political order of the state. As the sociologist C. Wright Mills observed, "All politics is struggle for power, the ultimate kind of power is violence."[16] With respect to the modern state, different theoretical traditions have agreed that the state is an inherently violent domain. While followers of Max Weber realize that the state is a domain of violence because it is the "exclusive source of the right to use violence," followers of Karl Marx recognize that the state, as a "creation of order," is a normalized domain of violent domination that is based on the "oppression of one class by another."[17] In either case, an analysis of the "establishment violence" inherent in the modern state has supported a maximalist definition of political violence as the institutionalized, structural, or systemic violation of human beings. According to Johan Galtung, for example, political violence must be regarded as inherent in political structures of repression, exploitation, and injustice. In fact, as Galtung has insisted, political violence is so extensive that it "is present when human beings are being influenced so that their actual somatic and mental realizations are below their potential realizations."[18] In this maximalist definition of political violence, therefore, direct physical harm registers as only one among many symptoms of the structures of power that limit, repress, or alienate human beings from fulfilling their potential. Even the division of labor registers as structural violence, since, as Galtung observes, "to deprive people of cultural stimuli or to create societies, however rich, with a division of labor that forces people to stay in the same profession for life are forms of violence."[19] Short of an egalitarian utopia of fully realized potential, therefore, Galtung's analysis of structural violence allows no possibility for "zero-degree" violence. As an endemic feature of all systems of social inequality, political violence recedes as an independent variable and becomes another term for social injustice.

In trying to recover political violence as an independent term for analysis, other theorists have returned to a definition of violence as physical force but have deployed different strategies of ethical evaluation. Adapting the a priori distinction between legitimate force and illegitimate violence, some theorists of political violence, particularly those of the functionalist school, have defined political violence as anything that disrupts the prevailing social order. Assuming that a society normally functions in a state of equilibrium, functionalist analysts have identified political violence as essentially abnormal. As measured against the assumed baseline of social order, political violence registers only as a "pathological deviation," perhaps motivated by "relative deprivation," that threatens the stability of a society.[20]

In some cases, outbreaks of deviant political violence are even regarded as actually serving to reinforce the prevailing social order. For example, violent actions by oppositional political movements might be regarded as serving social structures by "furnishing mechanisms for conflict resolution when established authority fails to accommodate to demands of new groups for hearings."[21] In this functional model of political violence, the existing social order can be reinforced—by listening, hearing, and accommodating opposition—within its established domain of political authority. In the end, however, since the political legitimacy of the established order is assumed, only the actions of oppositional groups register as political violence. Like the philosopher John Dewey's distinction between force and violence, therefore, such a functionalist approach presumes that political violence is illegitimate by definition because it disrupts some prevailing social order.

By stark contrast, alternative approaches to the ethical evaluation of political violence have argued that forceful acts of resistance, rebellion, or revolution against a prevailing social order should not always be regarded as a breakdown because these acts can sometimes mark a breakthrough in human liberation. Not motivated solely by "relative deprivation," political violence against a social order can result from the concerted mobilization of people, material resources, and symbolic resources against an oppressive social structure.[22] As an instrument for social or political change, political violence might be defined as direct physical harm to persons or property but still be ethically justified. According to Hannah Arendt, who defined violence as an instrument of direct intervention in politics, any theory of political intervention in processes of social change can only deal with the justification of violence.[23] If we renounce the convenient distinction between "their" violence and "our" careful, judicious, and legitimate exercise of force, how do we deal with the justification of violence? According to Hannah Arendt, this justification requires rectifying violent means with legitimate political ends. The ethical question of legitimacy has cast a long shadow over debates about the justification of political violence.

The question of legitimacy, however, has been recast in an entirely different key by analysts who have viewed political violence not only as ethically justifiable in terms of its intentions or consequences but as liberating when deployed against an oppressive political order. For these theorists, collective violence represents an avenue for liberation from class, racial, or colonial oppression. In their classic formulations, these theories of liberation through political violence have promised a quasi-religious redemption. In the endemic structural violence of the struggle between social classes, according to Georges Sorel, a lower class can be "resurrected" through violence.[24] In the colonial situation, where the violence of oppression has institutionalized the dehumanization of the oppressed, according to Frantz Fanon, collective violence against the colonial system can represent "the veritable creation of a new man." For Fanon, the structural violence of the colonial order of domination represented "violence in its natural state," a normalized order of violence based on both coercive force and dehumanization that would "only yield when confronted with greater violence." Accordingly, violent acts were necessary to break the colonial order. As Fanon advised, "Decolonization which sets out to change the order of the world is, obviously, a program of complete disorder." When undertaken in the interests of human liberation, according to Fanon, "decolonization is always a violent phenomenon." Far from seeing violent resistance as structurally dysfunctional or illegitimate by definition, Fanon argued that anticolonial violence was necessary for the legitimate recovery of humanity from dehumanizing conditions.[25] Political violence, therefore, was not only justifiable but required to fashion a new humanity that would be whole, unified, pure, and free in its liberation from the violent domination of the colonial order.

POLITICAL VIOLENCE, RELIGIOUS VIOLENCE

The problem with all of these theoretical attempts to define personal or political violence, of course, is that human beings do not live by theoretical definitions. People generate their own terms and conditions for what counts as violence. Here the social anthropology of violence has made significant contributions toward developing an analysis of violence as a symbolic and cultural production.[26] In recalling the history of violence in South Africa, it is necessary to go beyond academic definitions by locating violence in the symbols, myths, rituals, and traditions of South African worldviews that have made violence not only powerful but also meaningful. Although academics might try to establish secure definitions of its abnormality, violence was certainly not abnormal in the old South Africa. It was everywhere. It was an integral part of the discourses, practices, and social formations through which human beings struggled to be human. Accordingly, we need to track the cultural permutations of the violent strategies for negotiating what it has meant to be a human person. In the process, we may discover the symbolic strategies in South Africa that have been used for classifying persons, orienting persons in time and space, and gaining what John Dewey called a "foothold in the real world" for those classifications and orientations by backing them up with force or the threat of force. In other words, we need to analyze the ways in which violent discourses and practices have been normalized in the formation of South African worldviews. Toward that end, I propose to distinguish among three exercises of political violence—ritual killing, institutionalized dehumanization, and armed religion—that were particularly evident in attempts to work out meaning and power in South Africa before 1994.

First, the type of political violence that I identify as ritual killing appears in those violent acts that take human life in ways that might be interpreted as sacrificial offerings to a violent deity, as the symbolic purification of a threatened community, or as the symbolic empowerment of individuals in a highly competitive political economy of the sacred. For example, when the right-wing Afrikaner nationalist Barend Strydom randomly killed black people in Pretoria in November 1988, by his own account he understood that act of mass killing as a sacrificial offering to his nationalist deity. Apparently, before the killings Strydom had gone to the Voortrekker Monument, where he asked God to sanctify his actions. "I made a vow to my volk," Strydom said. "I prayed to God and asked him if he wanted to use me in any other way." Understanding his act of mass murder as a sacrificial offering to that God, therefore, Strydom could stand before the court and say, "From a Christian point of view the killings were justified."

At the same time, however, Strydom explained his motives in ways that recalled rituals of purification designed to eliminate some defiling and therefore dangerous agent from society. In the killing of designated scapegoats or alleged witches, for example, ritual procedures have been developed for social purification.[27] As the anthropologist Mary Douglas has taught us, since "dirt is matter out of place," purity is a matter of order.[28] Maintaining purity, therefore, is a question of managing space and place. According to Strydom, black human beings were out of place. "I grant blacks the right to live," he told the court, "but not in our country. They should not be seen in Pretoria, but in their own homelands." Furthermore, Strydom even testified that his "breathing space" was threatened by the presence of blacks in South Africa. "Scientists have proved," he claimed, "there is less oxygen in this country as a result of all the blacks." As a ritual of purification, therefore, Strydom understood his mass murder as an act that symbolically reinforced the purity of South African space by eliminating people he regarded as defiling because they were "matter out of place."

Strydom, however, understood his killings not only as a ritual of purity but also as a ritual of power. Within the contested political terrain of South Africa, he explained, he wanted to send a message to the ANC. "I would simply shoot blacks at random," he said. "I wanted to attract attention and show the African National Congress who we were." Generally, in ritual killings for purity, the sacrificer is concerned with completely eliminating the victim from society. In ritual killings for power, however, the sacrificer appropriates, incorporates, and even consumes the victim. In this case, Strydom appropriated his victims as a communications medium that would reinforce the power of his particular brand of right-wing Afrikaner nationalism. Strydom did more than merely send a message, however; he enacted a ritual killing for power that incorporated the victims in a mythic project of returning to what he regarded as the sacred origin of apartheid. Strydom specifically chose Strijdom Square in Pretoria for the killings because, as he explained to the court, "Advocate [J. G.] Strijdom," who had served as prime minister of South Africa from 1954 to 1958, "signified the beginning of apartheid."[29] As the historian of religions Mircea Eliade insisted, ritual acts often draw their meaning and power by reenacting "the mythic time of the beginning of things."[30] By killing black people at Strijdom Square, Pretoria, in November 1988, Barend Strydom acted out a ritual—a sacrificial offering, a ritual of purification, a ritual of incorporation—that was thoroughly informed by the myth of apartheid.

This analysis of Strydom's act of mass murder is consistent with the recent attention to myth and ritual in the anthropology of violence. As Regina M. Schwartz has argued, the myth of monotheism, which supports a radical distinction between "us" and "them," has been a formula for violent acts of exclusion.[31] In his analysis of the "formations of violence" in Northern Ireland, Allen Feldman has shown that violence must be understood not only in terms of political policies but also in terms of the detailed ritual negotiations that are conducted over purity and power, over sacrifice and revenge, and over the kinds of spatial order that are represented by a wall, a barricade, or a barbed-wire fence.[32] However, we must not regard these myths and rituals as abnormal. In Strydom's case, the expert state witness charged with assessing his sanity stumbled over this question. "I cannot say he is completely normal," the expert concluded, "and I cannot say he is completely abnormal."[33] What is important to recall, however, is that Strydom's worldview—his religious nationalism, his classification of persons, and his orientation in space and time—had in fact been normalized under apartheid. Although Strydom's acts were depicted by the state and in the media as marginal, the worldview that animated those acts was certainly central to the basic structures of apartheid that had dominated South Africa since 1948. In a cynical attempt to equate Strydom's ritualized reinforcement of the myth of apartheid through an act of random mass murder with the armed struggle against apartheid, former president F. W. de Klerk granted amnesty on the same day to Barend Strydom and the Umkhonto we Sizwe commander Robert McBride.

The armed struggle against apartheid, however, had deployed violent means against a system that was based on the systemic, structural, or institutionalized dehumanization of the majority of South Africans. By adopting the maximalist definition of political violence as the violation of humanity, one can investigate not only the overt and explicit acts of harm to persons that were carried out under apartheid but also the psychological and social suffering that apartheid entailed. As a synonym for institutionalized dehumanization, Orlando Patterson has proposed the term *social death.*[34] Most evident under conditions of slavery, social death entails what Patterson has called "natal alienation," which cuts human beings off from the nurturing, supporting, and sustaining relations with ancestors who came before and children who might come after. In other words, social death is a situation in which humanity has been violated because human beings have been torn from the relations of kinship that define what it is to be a human being.

In South Africa during the 1980s, institutionalized dehumanization appeared most obviously in the prisons and the mines, especially in detention without trial and migrant labor that cut people off from their families. More dramatically, however, the prisons and mines established violent regimes of social death that echoed the symbolism of apocalyptic tours of hell in the history of religions. In the prisons, for example, the dehumanization of detainees under torture enacted the dehumanizing torment of hell. For example, as Father Smangaliso Mkhatshwa submitted in an affidavit in September 1988, he had been detained without charge, confined for an indefinite period, and subjected to physical and psychological torture. Blindfolded, handcuffed, and forced to stand in the same spot for thirty hours, he was physically tortured with cold water and electric shocks, especially on his genitals, while his torturers laughed whenever he cried out in pain.[35] As Martha Himmelfarb has shown in a study of ancient Jewish and Christian apocalypses, certain features of hell—freezing and fiery environments, calculated attention to certain parts of the body, and laughing angels or demons who take pleasure in exacting pain—have been recurring features in imagining afterlife places of punishment.[36] In South Africa, hell was created on earth through institutionalized practices of torture in prison. Again, the anthropology of violence has usefully analyzed torture as a ritual of the modern state through which torturers affirm their unity with each other and through which the pain of the victim is transformed into the power of their torturers and ultimately of the state.[37] Although the torturers might justify their violent acts as techniques for gaining information, Elaine Scarry has convincingly argued that the excruciating, mind-numbing, and world-destroying effects of pain under torture can never produce any kind of meaningful utterance.[38] Therefore, the violent rituals of torture performed by the agents of the South African state could not translate pain into meaningful discourse—the information, the confession, or the betrayal—but could only transform the victim's pain into a symbol of the superhuman power of the torturers and the supreme power of the state.

While the violence of institutionalized dehumanization was certainly practiced in the prisons, it was arguably also evident in the labor market. In the South African mining industry, for example, migrant labor created a kind of social death by alienating workers from the supporting human relations of home and family. As reported during the 1980s, however, the mining industry had also established a kind of ritual—called acclimatization—that seemed to embody the denigration of workers. According to the Mines and Works Act, any worker who had to do manual labor underground had to go through this process of acclimatization. Essentially, the process was a rite of passage, but in reverse.[39] Where most rites of passage marking birth, adulthood, marriage, or death move through a period of separation from society to a new incorporation within society, the ritual of acclimatization took the mine worker out of his place in society to an extreme position of social separation in the underworld of the mines. As workers described this ritual, it began with stripping off all clothing. As one worker observed, "You have to be like when you were born." Symbolically returning to infancy, workers were then subjected to an ordeal in which they were placed in an overheated room where they had to climb up and down steps for a period of four hours. Usually, this acclimatization ritual took five days, but it might last as long as ten days. Having passed through this ritual of initiation, workers were then removed from ordinary society by being inducted into the hot, dark underworld of labor on the mines.[40] Like the rituals of torture, therefore, this ritual of initiation into the underworld of the mines enacted a kind of institutionalized violence that supported the South African economic, social, and political order.

In defense of that order, the South African state generated what I would like to call an "armed religion." Following what the French Marxist Régis Debray has identified as the "logic of the sacred" that underlies political reason, the apartheid state rationalized power in terms of a sacred totality.[41] By deploying its total strategy, its program for "interdependent and co-ordinated action in all fields—military, psychological, economic, political, sociological, technological, diplomatic, ideological, cultural, etc.," including "religious-cultural action," the apartheid state enacted the terms and conditions of a worldview that was backed up by force and the threat of force.[42] Besides being the brutal dictatorship of a white minority, therefore, the apartheid state was also an armed religion. Although the Dutch Reformed Church had once provided ideological legitimation for apartheid, earning itself the designation of "the National Party at prayer," by the 1980s the violence of the apartheid state no longer depended upon the support of any church. Rather, the state, as an armed religion, claimed its own religious legitimacy through its constitution, parliament, public schools, military, and police force. The police, for example, upheld that armed religion. According to the minister of law and order Adriaan Vlok, the police "maintained Christian norms and civilised standards," and according to its official historian the police were instrumental in "the maintenance and expansion of the nation's common spiritual concerns."[43] No church was necessary, therefore, to lend its religious support to the state; the state itself assumed the sacred aura of an armed religion.

In fighting such an establishment of religion that was supported and sustained by armed force, the ANC and other liberation movements had to engage the South African state on the battlefield of sacred symbols. Certainly, that story is too complicated to tell in this brief chapter. Basically, however, both material and spiritual resources, both violence and religion, had to be drawn into the struggle against the apartheid state. Although theologians and religious leaders from all the communities of faith in South Africa became involved, the ANC itself, for example, had to develop an armed religion of liberation. In essence, the armed struggle of the ANC assumed a religious dimension because, as its former president Oliver Tambo observed, the racist regime had tried "to enrobe racist ideas and practices with the cloak of religion." Under the armed religion of the apartheid regime, the black majority had been classified as subhuman, even suffering under the regime's assumption that they were "not sufficiently human to rebel against the inhuman system they have imposed in our country."[44] Resistance, rebellion, and revolution, therefore, were strategies for recovering the humanity that had been denied under an inhuman system. Although violence was promoted as armed struggle against the South African state or as armed propaganda that sent a potent message, violent acts of opposition to the armed religion of the state were also essentially religious strategies of redemption. Under dehumanizing conditions, as Frantz Fanon suggested, violent acts of opposition to colonial, imperial, or apartheid authority could signify a superhuman power that promised to recover the humanity of the oppressed.

If this line of analysis is useful, then contending nationalisms in South Africa must be seen not only as quasi-religious formations of beliefs, values, and commitments but as armed religions engaged in battle over both material and symbolic resources. Ironically, perhaps, given their diametrically opposed worldviews, it was these armed religions that propelled the country toward the kind of negotiated settlement that it finally achieved. Clearly, the "miracle" of the new South Africa was worked out by negotiators who were backed up by force or the threat of force. The "day of redemption," as Peter Harris called the first democratic election, was reached through a negotiated truce among adherents of contending armed religions.[45]

RELIGION AND VIOLENCE OF THE NUMBERS

Since the first democratic election of 1994, South Africa has lacked a compelling national story or convincing theological framework for thinking about religion and violence. As the country embarked upon nation building, Kairos theologians initially proposed a "theology of reconstruction," but it seemed too close to the "state theology" that they had condemned for sanctifying a nation during the struggle against apartheid.[46] Assuming responsibility for the state, the ANC shifted from fighting the extraordinary violence of apartheid crimes against humanity to struggling with containing the ordinary, everyday violence of crimes against persons and property.

This normal violence also bore traces of wild religion. The best research on religion in postapartheid South Africa is by a journalist, Jonny Steinberg, who investigated the symbols, myths, and rituals of prison gangs in the Western Cape. The Number gangs—the 28s, the 27s, and the 26s—are rendered as if they were religious orders. As we have seen, organized criminal gangs in Cape Town, such as the Americans, developed sacred symbols, myths, and rituals that animated violence, with myths of blood and money enacted in violent rituals of initiation, killing, and territorial claims. Taking us into the "total institution" of the prison, Steinberg shows how this regime of confinement, exclusion, and social death has been a fertile field for the production of wild religion in South Africa.

Steinberg's principal informant, Magadien Wentzel, who had adopted the name Willem Steenkamp from a stolen ID and was known in prison as JR, was a long-standing member of the 28s. He lived with an ambiguous religious identity. Magadien had grown up as a Christian, in a Christian home, attending a Christian church, but at age thirteen he learned that his real mother was a Muslim and immediately joined a mosque. When Steinberg first met him, Magadien said that he had had to get rid of the name Willem Steenkamp because if he had died in prison with such a "Christian" name the authorities would have held his body for a week instead of burying him as a Muslim before sunset. Wanting to prove his name to the journalist, Magadien showed that his real Muslim name was inscribed in the one book he had in his cell, a Christian Bible. This ambiguity of religious affiliation is an important part of the story. In the end, released from prison, Magadien, the Muslim, joined an evangelical Christian church.

By contrast to this fluid religious identity, moving between Muslim and Christian, the "religion" of the prison gangs is clear: it follows "Nongoloza, the God of South African prisoners"; it is informed by a powerful "mythical narrative," which recalls both Homeric epics and Talmudic ethics, representing both a heroic journey and a way of life; and it is animated by religious ritual, including "ancient norms of initiation," sacrificial killing, and ceremonial regalia worn only in the prisoners' imaginations.[47] In this wild religion of the prison gangs, we find a religion not legitimating or limiting violence but animating violence with religious meaning and power.

Nongoloza is a subject of both myth and history. The historical figure was born Mzuzephi Mathebula in 1867, grew up as a Zulu tending cattle, and as a young man went to Johannesburg, to the mines, to look for work. He adopted the Dutch first name Jan and the English surname Note, thereby mixing multiple identities, Zulu, Dutch, and English. In 1888 he started working for four white men, highwaymen, but soon, as he later recalled, "I decided to start a band of robbers on my own."[48] Taking the name Nongoloza, he designated his own "band of robbers" as the Ninevites, having read in the Bible that the Ninevites "rebelled against the Lord," which in the context of the mining industry was the merger of capitalist interests and colonial government. Growing to a criminal army of over a thousand by 1908, the Ninevites were defeated in 1912. Nongoloza was imprisoned, eventually becoming a prison warder, and died in 1948 during the year that the National Party came to power under the banner of apartheid.[49]

As this history was transformed into myth, Nongoloza retained his origin in the context of gold mining, but details were altered: the mythic time of origin was shifted back to 1812, seventy-four years before gold was discovered in the Witwatersrand; the space of origin became Delagoa Bay rather than Johannesburg; and religious inspiration for forming a band of robbers was drawn not from the Bible but from the teachings of a mysterious Wise Man variously known as Nkulukut, Pomobasa, Paul Mobasa, or Po. In the beginning, the Wise Man went to the mines. He saw black men dying. Moving to the outskirts of the British colonial city of Pietermaritzburg, behind the mountains, the Wise Man invented a secret language because "if blacks are to be saved, whites must not understand." There he encountered Nongoloza, who was on his way to seek work on the mines. "I have been to the mines," the Wise Man told the young man. "The gold of the white man is good. You must take it, but not from the ground. You must rob it from the white man himself."[50] Soon Nongoloza was joined by Kilikijan, who was not Zulu but Mpondo, and together they led a group of fifteen bandits, with Nongoloza's eight stealing by night and Kilikijan's seven stealing by day. As the original ancestors of the 28s and 27s, these mythic heroes established the model for criminal organization and activity. Later they were joined by the original ancestor of the 26s. Although the basic myth is common to all three Number gangs, each has developed different interpretations, positioning itself differently within the same mythic horizon of sanctified criminality.

Myth is enacted in ritual. According to Steinberg, "South Africa's prison gangs are among the most ritualised structures you will ever find."[51] Ritual purity, for example, can be established by murder in prison, "the enactment of a symbolic ritual" in which the blood of the victim is shed "to symbolise the cleansing of the prison."[52] Ritual power, as well, can be asserted by repeating the original acts of the mythic heroes. According to myth, the Wise Man had Nongoloza and Kilikijan go to a white farmer, Rabie, and bring back a bull called Rooiland (Red Earth) to be sacrificed. Rabie refused to give up the bull, so the mythic heroes had to kill the white farmer to provide the bull for a sacrificial ritual. After the sacrifice, Rooiland's hide was placed over a sacred rock, imprinting the history and laws of the bandits on the skin of the sacrificial animal. The hide was given to Nongoloza, the rock to Kilikijan. But the rock was broken, with half falling into a river, so only Nongoloza (and the 28s), according to this version of the myth, still have the entirety of the sacred text. In 1996 a group of released prisoners, led by a member of the 26s known as Doggy Dog, killed a white farmer and his family. Stealing meat that he called "Rooiland," the leader, seeing the sun rise over his crimes, declared, "The first ray is Kilikijan."[53] Returning to prison, Doggy Dog was elevated from the 26s to "Lord of the 27s" for enacting the original killing that had been performed by their mythic founder.

According to Magadien Wentzel, followers of the Numbers were not gangsters but "freedom fighters."[54] However, unlike those who struggled against apartheid, these freedom fighters seemed to be struggling not only against the prevailing social order but against any social order. Yet they did create a kind of criminal order, which was sacralized through myths and rituals, in response to what might be called the "cargo situation" of modern South Africa. Identifying cargo cults in Melanesia, classical anthropological accounts described how the islanders imitated Europeans by building piers, erecting flag-poles, and sitting on verandas waiting for the imminent arrival of the cargo.[55] Although economically irrational, this strangely ritualized behavior anticipated the advent of extraordinary wealth signified by European manufactured goods. In recent research, cargo movements have been interpreted as a kind of indigenous ethnography, reading the secret meanings of the West by means of what Nils Bubandt has called the "mimicry of the cargoism of modernity."[56] This reading of the modern devotion to commodities, however, has also entailed an implicit critique, a mimicry of the acquisitive practices of the West that exposes what Karl-Heinz Kohl has called "a 'money cult' issuing from the very heart of a modern capitalist society."[57] Like the cargo cult, the money cult of capitalism is a failed prophecy that never-theless continues to attract enthusiastic adherents by its promise of extraordinary wealth.

In the long history of cargo movements in Melanesia, islanders were faced with three options for gaining access to the abundant wealth asso-ciated with European colonizers: working, praying, or stealing. First, even though they never saw Europeans working, they were told that they could work for the cargo, entering into wage labor in European-controlled enterprises, but such work never produced wealth for the islanders. In South Africa, where unemployment has ranged as high as 45 percent, wage labor has also not been the road to the cargo. Second, many Melanesians suspected that the Christian Church held the secret of the cargo, so they converted to Christianity and prayed for wealth. Since the demise of apartheid in South Africa, the fastest-growing religious formation has been Pentecostal churches, which mix ecstatic religion with promises of health, wealth, and prosperity. Analysts have differed over whether Pentecostals represent a new Protestant ethic of discipline and self-denial leading to economic productivity or an occult economy expecting extraordinary wealth through mysterious means.[58] Either way, adherents of the wild religion of the Number gangs found that neither work nor prayer produced the cargo, so the only remaining way to get it was to steal it. According to many cargo myths in Melanesia, wealth originally belonged to their deities and ancestors but was transferred by mistake to Europeans. Accordingly, stealing was not stealing but restoring what had been stolen in mythic time. "The gold of the white man is good," the Wise Man told Nongoloza. "You must take it, but not from the ground. You must rob it from the white man himself."[59] In this myth, stealing is the sacred road to the cargo.

Certainly, not every criminal is an adherent of the kind of wild religion embodied in the Number gangs. Nevertheless, violent crime, as a fact of South African life, has been addressed by government initiatives as if it were a religious problem. From the Moral Regeneration Movement launched in 2002 to the National Interfaith Leaders Council established by the Zuma administration in 2009, government has often represented crime as essentially a spiritual problem that can be dealt with through religious and moral interventions. As the Number gangs demonstrate, however, criminal activity can be animated by a religion, a violent religion with its own sacred history, code of ethics, and ritual observances, which must register as wild religion from the perspective of any state charged with the responsibility of law and order. In South Africa's fight against crime, this struggle continues. Religion is in the mix. While gangsters display religion and the state invokes religion, religious groups work in the prisons trying to rehabilitate offenders and restore them to the world. In multiple ways, therefore, religion is entangled in the ordinary and perhaps even normalized violence of crime in postapartheid South Africa.

As we have seen, religion does not necessarily stand outside violence. Religion can animate violence, from direct harm to persons and property to fundamental violations of humanity, as a wild force that threatens but also energizes a variety of human projects.

CHAPTER FOUR

Fundamentalisms

Religious fundamentalism seems to be the wildest of wild religion. Fundamentalists oppose modernity, threaten the state, and spread terrorism. In popular media and academic analysis, religious fundamentalism has often been cast as a form of religion that makes inauthentic claims on religious authenticity. But what is fundamentalism? An eminent scholar of religion, Scott Appleby, questions the viability and transferability of the term, putting it in "scare quotes," or rendering it as "strong religion," but nevertheless finds that religious fundamentalists in any religious tradition display certain characteristic features, tending to be reactive, selective, absolutist, dualistic, and millenarian in their expectations of the imminent destruction of the prevailing social order.[1] Accordingly, fundamentalism is also a normative problem. As many analysts and critics have argued, we must be worried about religious fundamentalism because it violates the moral order of modernity by its irrational violence and intolerance, its puritanical mores and patriarchal gender discrimination, which deploy premodern religious impulses to challenge modern social formations.

My concern in this chapter is to focus on how religious fundamentalism has appeared in South Africa. The vast literature on religious fundamentalism, global in scope, has influenced South African understandings of fundamentalism just as an increasingly polarized geopolitics has affected religion in South Africa. Going back through South Africa's history with religious fundamentalism, we find recurring popular and academic interest in "fundamentalism" as a highly charged term for a crisis. From the 1970s, as I will show, every decade has seen a crisis of fundamentalism, but every crisis has been dramatically different. In other words, South Africans have had a long-standing engagement with religious fundamentalism, but fundamentalism has never been the same thing in this history. I will quickly review these different engagements with fundamentalism in South Africa. We will find Christian fundamentalism appearing during the 1970s as contrary to the apartheid state, during the 1980s as legitimating the apartheid state, and during the 1990s as resisting the new democratic dispensation. By the 1990s, however, as international attention to religious fundamentalism shifted to focus on varieties of politicized Islam, South Africa was dealing with Muslim fundamentalists who opposed the apartheid state and the postapartheid democracy.

As this brief review suggests, the term *fundamentalism* has been a recurring but shifting sign of a crisis of religious authenticity. During the first decade of the twenty-first century, as fundamentalism configured a crisis in late modernity, South Africans had to deal with a polarizing global terrain in which the foreign policy of the United States seemed to be driven by religious fundamentalism. Going back over this recent, ancient history, we will begin with a case of fundamentalism in South Africa in which fundamentalist religious beliefs did not correlate with social conservatism or political militancy.

THE 1970S: JESUS PEOPLE IN JOHANNESBURG

In the earliest research on religious fundamentalism in South Africa, the psychologist Christopher R. Stones published a series of articles in the 1970s based on his investigation of "Jesus People" in Johannesburg.[2] These fundamentalist or "born again" Christians studied by Stones were white, English speaking, and living communally. Explicitly identifying the members of this Christian community as fundamentalists, Stones utilized two research instruments—the Brown and Lowe Inventory of Religious Belief (1951) and the Wilson and Patterson Conservative Scale (1968)—to test the hypothesis that religious fundamentalism should correlate with social conservatism. Since the results of this research might be surprising, I will move immediately to Stones's finding that these religious fundamentalists, who tested high for religious belief, scored very low on the socially conservative scale, being less conservative, less militaristic, less racially prejudiced, and less opposed to pleasure—

less "antihedonistic"—than their peers in their social environment. Measured against a "control group," these Christian fundamentalists were found to be less socially conservative than other young white people in Johannesburg.

The research instruments that Christopher Stones used to arrive at this conclusion are worth considering. The Brown and Lowe Inventory of Religious Belief, formulated in 1951, provided a set of fifteen questions, with each question weighted on a five-point "Likert-type scale" to differentiate between those who accept and those who reject the literal truth of Christianity. An instrument for measuring religious belief developed in the early 1950s in postwar, cold war America was applied in Johannesburg. Even a quick glance at the questions posed by the Brown and Lowe Inventory of Religious Belief must make us wonder if this research instrument is already weighted for polarization. For example, focusing on the Bible, the inventory asks research subjects to agree or disagree with dramatically polarized propositions. On the one hand, a subject might agree with the proposal, "I believe the Bible is the inspired Word of God." If so, the subject would be assenting to a "positively keyed item" for religious fundamentalism. On the other hand, a subject might identify with the proposal that the "Bible is full of errors, misconceptions, and contradictions." Agreeing with this "negatively keyed item" would place such a subject very low on the religious belief or religious fundamentalism scale. Clearly, the research instrument was set up to divide sheep from goats.

The religious fundamentalists in Johannesburg scored high on all of the indicators of religious beliefs that were based on the authority of the Bible, basic Christian doctrines such as the Virgin Birth and the Second Coming, and even the exclusivity of Christian redemption, in which they agreed that the "gospel of Christ is the only way for mankind to be saved" and that "eternal life is the gift of God only to those who believe in Jesus Christ as Saviour and Lord." On the belief scale, therefore, these fundamentalists were committed to being faithful to the fundamentals of their religious tradition. Religiously, they were conservative. We might expect that they were also socially conservative. Here Christopher Stones applied Wilson and Patterson's Conservatism Scale, which was developed in America during the turbulent year of 1968 instead of in the cold war context of the early 1950s that had produced the religious belief measures. Stones found that his Jesus People, with their fundamentalist beliefs, were actually less conservative than the white, English-speaking "control group."

During the 1970s, therefore, religious fundamentalists registered as a problem for academic research. As Christopher Stones found, conservative Christians, adhering to fundamental Christian doctrines, could be religiously conservative but socially liberal. Conservatism in religious belief, therefore, did not necessarily correlate with conservative political, social, or economic positions within the prevailing social order. However, the prevailing order, under the apartheid regime of the National Party in South Africa, was enforcing a radically conservative program of militarism, racism, and denial of human freedom and expression. As Stones observed, the religious fundamentalists that he studied ran up against this conservative order. Christian fundamentalists, he found, were less militaristic, less racially prejudiced, and less repressive of personal pleasure and freedom of expression.

But these religious fundamentalists might also have registered as a threat to the apartheid state because their commitment to fundamental Christian doctrines, which were also proclaimed by the National Party regime in church and state, did not correlate with the conservative policies of militarization, racism, and discipline advanced by the state. Accordingly, the prevailing regime in South Africa might have found these religious fundamentalists dangerous because they were not militaristic, racist, or intolerant.

Reflecting on his research, Christopher Stones pointed to the tension between these religious fundamentalists and their increasingly militarized social context in apartheid South Africa. "It is interesting," he observed, "that members of the Jesus movement should have become significantly less militaristic at a time when South African mainstream ethos is one of increasing militarism." Reflecting, again, on context, Stones noted that "relative to their cultural milieu, the Jesus people have become less racially prejudiced." They were also, he found, more secure, more flexible, and more tolerant of change.[3]

I dwell on these research findings for their striking contrast with current formulations of religious fundamentalists as militant, violent terrorists and as intolerant and puritanical. During the 1970s, religious fundamentalists in Johannesburg were a "problem" because they were less militant, less racist, and less puritanical than they should have been according to the ethos of the apartheid regime. In this context, religious fundamentalists posed a problem for both research and governance because they seemed to be more secure, more tolerant, and perhaps even happier than they should be. Clearly, for the militarized and racist apartheid regime, if these religious fundamentalists, as Christopher Stones found, were "less militaristic" and "less racially prejudiced," then they represented an implicit challenge to the militarized and racist order of the state in South Africa. Accordingly, religious fundamentalists represented a crisis not because they were violent and exclusive but because they were nonviolent and tolerant of diversity.

THE 1980S: FUNDAMENTALISM AND THE APARTHEID STATE

During the mid-1980s, popular and academic interest in religious fundamentalism focused on right-wing Christians, often coming from the United States, who were providing ideological legitimation for the apartheid state. Unlike the Jesus People in Johannesburg, they demonstrated a religious conservatism that clearly correlated with a conservative moral, social, and political agenda. Taking Protestant fundamentalism into the political arena in the United States, Jerry Falwell had founded a national organization, the Moral Majority, that was dedicated to achieving four kinds of conservative political goals: prolife, profamily, promoral, and pro-American. Falwell's conservative Christian crusade defined the basic outlines of political policy advocated by the "New Religious Right" or the "New Christian Right" in the United States. That political policy was also a conservative Christian foreign policy that urged U.S. support for the modern states of Israel, Taiwan, and South Africa.

In South Africa, the ideological support provided by right-wing Christians from the United States was welcomed by the National Party regime, which was attempting to maintain the apartheid system of racist oppression. As a frequent visitor during the 1980s, Jerry Falwell praised South Africa as a "Christian country" in which human rights were upheld, that is, the rights of the unborn, because abortion was illegal. Defending the apartheid regime, Falwell castigated the Anglican archbishop Desmond Tutu as a "phony."[4] According to one conservative Christian publication in the United States, the *Family Protection Scoreboard*, "In the area of traditional family values, South Africa puts America to shame" because South Africa had no abortion, pornography, debates about women's rights, constitutional separation of church and state, or secular humanism, all of which had allegedly eroded Christian "family values" in the United States. The conservative evangelist Jimmy Swaggert also praised South Africa as a "godly country" on the front lines of the battle between the communist Antichrist and the "Christian civilization" represented by the minority white regime.[5]

In 1986 a group of "concerned evangelicals" in Soweto objected to the fact that their "evangelical family had a track record of supporting and legitimating oppressive regimes here and elsewhere."[6] The National Party regime in South Africa, however, welcomed the support from U.S. evangelists and fundamentalists because the Dutch Reformed Church was no longer providing unconditional Christian justifications for the system of apartheid. A number of small right-wing Christian movements, such as the Gospel Defence League and Frontline Fellowship, emerged in the 1980s, drawing on evangelical or fundamentalist religious resources to defend the legitimacy of the apartheid state.[7]

While conservative Christians in South Africa could look to the New Religious Right in the United States to justify a Christian state, South African Muslims could draw inspiration from the Iranian Revolution of 1979 to imagine the possibility of an Islamic state.[8] Qibla, founded in 1980 by Achmad Cassiem, advocated a dual struggle against the apartheid state and for the creation of an Islamic state in South Africa. Global in scope, this vision of an Islamic state embraced the term *fundamentalism* as an empowering self-designation, aligning Qibla with "pro-Islamic fundamentalist countries in their attempts to establish an Islamic republic in South Africa based on the principles of the Sharia and the teachings of the Quran."[9] Like Jerry Falwell, therefore, Achmad Cassiem used the term *fundamentalism* at the nexus of religious conservatism, adhering to the fundamental authority of a canonical text and to a moral, social, and political program for creating a religious state. During the 1980s, however, while Christian fundamentalism was gaining international attention, the Muslim fundamentalism advanced by Qibla received relatively little notice in the popular media or academic analysis in South Africa.[10]

THE 1990S: FUNDAMENTALISM AND THE DEMOCRATIC STATE

Perhaps we forget that the South African 1994 election campaign was saturated with religion. In the prelude to the 1994 election, campaign advertising evoked all the competing claims on sacred authority and power that remain an undercurrent beneath the dominant imagery of a unified "New South Africa." Often these advertisements displayed explicit religious content. For example, the ANC issued a full-page advertisement, supported by signatures of Christian clergy, proclaiming the Gospel as the only framework for establishing full political inclusion and guaranteeing social justice. The National Party, with an ad campaign based on the testimony of ordinary people, occasionally played the religious theme. One advertisement quoted the Reverend Macfarlane Phenethi: "The NP apologized. As a Christian I accept that. The NP is now the party for me." Christian justice, Christian mercy—the call for Christian commitment was a significant feature of campaign rhetoric. The African Christian Democratic Party, declaring that "it's time to do it God's way," asserted that it was the only party that could unify the nation because it upheld Christian principles as the foundation for a just society. The right-wing Freedom Front claimed to represent the interests of concerned Christians in defending Christian values against the evils of communism. The Inkatha Freedom Party, however, must receive the award for creative Christian advertising. During its one-week campaign for the election, Inkatha advertised a mixed message that fused its last-minute entry into the campaign and its ad hoc position at the bottom of the ballot into a single biblical promise of apocalyptic redemption by invoking Matthew 20:16—"So the last shall be first."

Although Christian themes were prominent in campaign advertising, they were in counterpoint with competing Muslim claims to religious authority. In the weekend papers prior to the election, Qibla placed an ad that juxtaposed the Qur'anic injunction "Let there be no hostility except against those who practice oppression" with a photograph of Mandela and De Klerk clasping hands, to urge people, "Do not vote!" In the same newspaper, however, a two-page ad appeared for the African Muslim Party, calling the faithful, not only to vote, but to vote for the only party that represented Islamic law. Voters would be rewarded in both this life and the hereafter: in this life with a just society and in the hereafter with salvation from punishment for the sin of supporting any non-Muslim party that might extend civil rights to homosexuals. Like Christian advertising, this ad from the African Muslim Party made dramatic campaign promises of religious redemption.

In the democratic dispensation, the schools became a space for asserting fundamental religious claims. In response to the new curriculum, some Christians in South Africa, especially those with ideological, organizational, and financial links with conservative Christian groups in the United States, vigorously objected to the policy for religion education.

Through an organized, coordinated campaign, they argued that the new policy violated their human rights and constitutional rights to freedom of religion. This campaign drew together apparently separate organizations—a Christian organization for home schooling (Pestalozzi Trust), a Christian organization for evangelizing Africa (Frontline Fellowship), a Christian political party (the African Christian Democratic Party), and other Christian groups—in common cause against the new policy, curriculum, and learning outcomes.

As the most vocal opponents, Christian Reconstructionists mobilized letter-writing campaigns, media events, and public meetings against the new policy. Culminating at a public meeting in the Western Cape at the Christian Centre on October 9, 2001, these opponents advanced the ingenious argument that teaching and learning about religion, religions, and religious diversity, which is an educational rather than a religious activity, was actually promoting a religious worldview. Summarizing the meeting of "concerned Christians" at the Christian Centre, the reporter noted that the principal problem with the new policy was its "active promotion of a single set of values under the guise of tolerance." These values, which were glossed as relativism, situational ethics, and the equality of all religions, were castigated as the basic elements of a New Age religion. "This set of implicit values," the reporter declared, "is present in most New Age systems of thought. Teaching and assessment based on these values effectively constitutes state promotion of a religious worldview in itself (secular humanism). This is in total contradiction with the constitutional provision of freedom of religion." Although the promotion of relativism, situational ethics, and the religious equivalence of religions appears nowhere in the policy, "concerned Christians" at this meeting could nevertheless discern the implicit traces of a religious worldview, the religion of "secular humanism," which was allegedly being established in public schools as an act of religious discrimination against Christians.[11]

Although this campaign certainly drew in parents who were concerned about the direction of educational policy in South Africa, the ingenious argument that education about religion "implicitly" promoted a religious worldview—the religion of secular humanism—was derived from right-wing Christian organizations in the United States. Insisting that "secular humanism" has been defined as a religion by the U.S. Supreme Court, Christian opponents of the new educational policy in South Africa have been misled by right-wing Christian campaigns in America that have actually failed to sustain that case, especially in attempts to exclude science textbooks that do not explicitly promote the biblical account of Creation on the grounds that they thereby implicitly promote the "religion of secular humanism."

In the case of the Pestalozzi Trust, this organization for home schooling was explicitly linked, not only to a conservative Christian parent organization in the United States, but also to the work of Rousas John Rushdoony, the American founder of Christian Reconstructionism. Advocating a literal interpretation of the Bible and a literal adherence to biblical law, Rushdoony inspired the Chalcedon Foundation, the Institute for Christian Economics, the Rutherford Institute, and other right-wing Christian organizations in the United States. Rushdoony was a champion of religious apartheid. "Segregation or separation," he wrote, "is a basic principle of Biblical law with respect to religion and morality." In defense of religious apartheid, Rushdoony opposed any form of civil toleration of religious difference because "the believer is asked to associate on a common level of total acceptance with the atheist, the pervert, the criminal, and the adherents of other religions as though no differences existed."[12] Under the influence of such religious prejudice, Christian Reconstructionists urged South African parents to prevent their children from being exposed to "foreign" religions, forgetting that those religious and other belief systems are not foreign but flourishing in South Africa.

Disregard for adherents of other religions has informed not only theory but also political practice among Christian Reconstructionists. According to a prominent disciple of Rushdoony, Gary North, Christian Reconstructionists are justified in manipulating democratic, constitutional means for Christian ends. "We must use the doctrine of religious liberty to gain independence for Christian schools," North wrote, "until we train up a generation of people who know there is no religious neutrality, no neutral law, no neutral education, and no neutral civil government." Once that program in Christian religious education was far enough advanced, North declared, the students it produced would "get busy constructing a Bible-based social, political, and religious order which finally denies the religious liberty of the enemies of God."[13]

Certainly, Christian Reconstructionism, with its manipulative rhetoric, religious apartheid, and antidemocratic tactics, cannot provide any basis for educational policy in a diverse and democratic South Africa. Nevertheless, in the controversy of the new policy for religion and education, most of the media attention given to the new curriculum was framed by the religious agenda of Christian Reconstructionists.

As this brief overview can only suggest, fundamentalism in South Africa has featured in a recurring crisis of authenticity: not only religious authenticity, with its claims on solid foundations in a changing world, but also political authenticity. From the apartheid regime to the democratic dispensation, religious fundamentalism has registered as a force, for better or worse, in relation to the stability and legitimacy of the South African state. Against this background, we can ask: What kind of crisis was fundamentalism configuring during the first decade of the twenty-first century in a rapidly globalizing and increasingly polarized world?

FUNDAMENTAL POLARIZATIONS

After September 2001, the entire world came under enormous global pressures that polarized international politics into religious dualisms. As we recall, on October 7, 2001, U.S. president George W. Bush, embarking on his military adventure in Afghanistan, issued this polarizing warning to reinforce his assertion that "you are either with us or against us": "Every nation has a choice to make. In this conflict, there is no neutral ground. If any government sponsors the outlaws and killers of innocents, they have become outlaws and murderers, themselves. And they will take that lonely path at their own peril." On the same day, in response, Osama bin Laden asserted that "these events have divided the world into two camps, the camp of the faithful and the camp of infidels. May God shield us and you from them." As the historian of religions Bruce Lincoln has observed, these are "symmetrical dualisms" that divide "us" from "them," under God, producing oppositions of both religious and global significance.[14]

Globalization, with its multiple flows, promised new connectivity, new complexity, in fluid, mobile networks, with no centers or peripheries, which would enable people to overcome such polarizing oppositions. Surprisingly, however, this new trend was entrenching polarization. South Africans were not immune. In December 2004, a public dispute between President Mbeki and Archbishop Tutu inspired a series of ten installments in *ANC Today*, "The Sociology of Public Discourse in a Democratic South Africa," which began with the polarizing assertion that the people of South Africa "could not but demand of all and sundry that they should declare where they stand. Inevitably, the question had to be answered—brother and sister, whose side are you on!"[15] Poised between the intimacy of kinship—brothers and sisters—and the polarizing imperative to take sides, this ANC "sociology" reformulated the struggle as an opposition between the "elite" and the "people." The elite had their "icons," like Archbishop Tutu, "whose opinions must be accepted as being virtually equivalent to the word of a god!"[16] By contrast, the people had their liberation movement, leading the national struggle, which continued, although victory was certain. In the meantime, South Africans found themselves polarized.

In defining fundamentalism, we are confronted with the perennial problem that the very word *religion* operates as an oppositional term. But these oppositions are always situational and relational. In the South African context, moderate Christians might define syncretism as "too messy" and fundamentalism as "too pure" in order to situate themselves as "just right." Religious conservatives would understandably want to reject the designation *fundamentalism* if it were situated in such a relational calculus. But we have seen religious activists, Christian and Muslim, claiming the designation of *fundamentalism* in seeking to recover what they regard as religious authenticity. We have also seen them adopting the term *fundamentalism* in pursuing opposition to the apartheid state or the democratic state.

In relation to the modern state, the definition of religion matters, conferring legal recognition, tax exemptions, and other benefits, but also constraining forms of religious life that are denied the status of "religion" or that come into conflict with law and order. After 2001, the issue of defining fundamentalism in South Africa shifted dramatically from focusing on conservative religious beliefs, in many cases religious beliefs emerging from the United States, to focusing on militant political opposition to the United States. The U.S. State Department established a basic equivalence between Muslim fundamentalists and terrorists. Looking into South Africa, the U.S. State Department listed Qibla as a dangerous terrorist organization, a classification that remained in place even though the U.S. State Department's annual *International Religious Freedom Report* for 2006 noted that "no Qibla activities were reported in the period covered by this report."[17] Our efforts at definition, therefore, have to take into consideration these power dynamics of classification.

In contemporary theorizing of religion, the term *fundamentalism* seems to play the same role that was filled by "the primitive" in nineteenth-century evolutionary theories of religion. During the nineteenth century, "primitives" or "savages" supposedly displayed superstitious survivals from human prehistory; today, "fundamentalists" are allegedly reactionary, atavistic adherents of the premodern, resisting modernity. In both cases, we find thinking about religion situated in developmental theories, whether evolutionary or modernization theories, in which some people do not seem to be cooperating. They remain behind, as survivals of the premodern, or they try to go back, struggling to recover the premodern in opposition to modernity.

Theorizing fundamentalism, therefore, is also theorizing the meaning, power, and scope of modernity. On the one hand, modernity is rational. Modern rationality drew upon Enlightenment reason, but it also entailed, as Max Weber taught us, the institutionalized rationalization of power within the modern state and its bureaucratic management by coercion over people in a territory. In this respect, the modern horrors of the Holocaust or apartheid cannot be dismissed as aberrations in the progressive development of modernity. They were thoroughly rationalized instances of bureaucratic management, efficiency, and control. Fundamentally, therefore, terror can be found at the heart of modernity.

On the other hand, modernity, again following Max Weber, is the disenchantment, or the "de-magification," of the world. From this perspective, fundamentalist appeals to archaic tradition appear as atavistic revivals of magic, enchantment, or superstition in the modern world. Perhaps, as Bruno Latour has argued, we have never actually been modern. Magic and enchantment linger in the wonders of modern science, the awesome power of the modern state, which is always underwritten by political myths and rituals, and the fetishism of commodities in the capitalist, globalizing market economy. Magic, we might find, is both shadow and substance of the global economy, shadowed by the "occult economies" that seek to access wealth through mysterious means but are given substance by the global orthodoxy of the "religion of the market."[18]

Accordingly, in thinking about fundamentalism we also have to think about modernity. Religious movements commonly identified as fundamentalist might appeal to premodern sources of religious authenticity, but they utilize the most modern communication technology in mobilizing a following. They have been at the forefront of postmodern developments in cyberspace, mobile networks, and multisited transnational communities. Some have been at the forefront of postmodern developments in military strategy, with all of its horror, in which suicide bombers, those weaponized human beings, and car bombs, that "poor man's air force," have had a definite impact.[19] Theorizing fundamentalism, therefore, requires wrestling with violence in which both modernity and its discontents are intimately entangled.

We see fundamentalism engaged in the most extensive global politics but also in the most intimate sexual politics, gender politics, and family politics. Human beings, as embodied beings, are drawn into this intimate politics. During the 1980s, the self-proclaimed Christian fundamentalist Jerry Falwell built his entire political program on the foundation of such an intimate politics, beginning with "profamily" initiatives in opposition to reproductive choices, women's rights, and alternative sexualities. During the first decade of the twenty-first century, we may have lived in a polarized geopolitical environment, but we also lived in the context of a highly charged intimate politics where gender, sexuality, and religion were entangled.

As many analysts have observed, religious fundamentalism is obsessed with women's bodies and male power. According to Homa Hoodfar, "Controlling women and their bodies and reclaiming the family as a site of male power and dominance is a common thread found in all brands of fundamentalism."[20] This gendered politics, however, is not the distinctive creation or sole preserve of religious fundamentalists; it has been a recurring feature of the history of religions. What has changed is the new linkages between what Michel Foucault called biopower, the regulation of embodied, gendered, and sexual humanity, and the modern state's demands for conformity and control.[21] Modern states, in their instability, try to enforce controls over this intimate politics of the body as a matter of urgency because they cannot control law and order, shifting foreign relations, or the mysteries and inequities of the global economy. Sex and money, as Roger Friedland has argued, are the basic ingredients of religious fundamentalisms, religious nationalisms, and modern states that must establish an aura of religiosity.[22] Human bodies and national borders seem threatened. Controls over sexuality, in this reading, mirror attempts to control the promiscuous flows and corruptions of capital in globalizing economic relations. In this respect, premodern fundamentalists and modern states are engaged in the same project of intervening in the intimate politics of gender, sexuality, marriage, and human reproduction as ritual substitutions for political problems they cannot solve. Intimate politics, therefore, is central not only to religious fundamentalisms but also to modern nations.

Religious fundamentalism suggests that theorists of globalization who declared the "death of the nation" or the "death of the state" were premature. Ignoring all predictions of the demise of the nation-state within a transnational, globalizing world, religious fundamentalists have been making claims on state power, struggling to work out their national citizenship in various nations, and challenging any state's monopoly on exercising legitimate violence within or outside a territory. In all of these ways, religious fundamentalists are keeping alive the national question.

Scholars of religion who specialize in religious fundamentalism often identify fundamentalism as primarily a political problem. For example, Gabriel Almond, R. Scott Appleby, and Emmanuel Sivan, in their introduction to a global overview of religious fundamentalism, *Strong Religion,* propose that "'fundamentalism' is one of the most significant political phenomena of our time." The importance of this "phenomenon" registers as important only to the extent that religious actors have either captured or challenged the ultimate power of a modern state. Accordingly, they identify fundamentalists that have seized state power, finding that religious fundamentalists have captured states in five instances since 1979. "Since the Iranian revolution, purported fundamentalist movements have risen to the highest levels of power in five countries." They identify Iran in 1979, Sudan in 1993, Turkey in 1996, Afghanistan in 1996, and India in 1996, 1998, and 1999. Arguably, they might have added a sixth example of religious fundamentalists seizing state power by adding the United States in 2000 to this list, but their point is that religious fundamentalists are significant because they want state power and so also oppose the power of prevailing states as "other fundamentalist movements [have] formed powerful and deadly opposition groups."[23]

Opposition groups, in this account, include a diverse array of formations such as Hamas, al-Qaeda, Sikh extremists, the Jewish underground, the Armed Islamic Group in Algeria, Islamic revolutionaries in Chechnya, and "Christian radicals in the United States who stalked feminist activists and gunned down doctors who performed abortions." Reinforcing their claim that religious fundamentalism is one of the most significant political phenomena of our time, the authors use charged, evocative language to describe how these opposition groups, apparently small and marginal but allegedly "powerful and deadly," have engaged in campaigns in which they "took up arms," "plotted to destroy," "assassinated," "indiscriminately massacred," and "gunned down" their enemies. Opposition groups, of course, should not be doing any of these things. Therefore, these violent acts, religiously motivated, make religious fundamentalism "one of the most significant political phenomena of our time." Modern states, which normally do all these things, whether covertly or overtly, all the time, do not register in considerations of the phenomenon of religious violence in our time.

As Rashied Omar has argued, academic analysis of religious fundamentalism, which tends to regard fundamentalism as an inherently oppositional and violent force, has generally neglected the role of institutionalized and even normalized state violence. In his detailed case studies of religious violence in Bosnia, Gujarat, and South Africa, Omar has demonstrated that we must bring state violence into the picture if we hope to understand the "phenomenon" of violent strategies and tactics by opposition groups. We cannot just single out religious groups that want states or oppose states; we also have to consider the overt and covert violence exercised by states.[24]

MADE IN AMERICA

In our globalizing world, religious fundamentalism registers as an obstacle to the flows of people, technology, money, new images of human possibility, and new ideals of human solidarity that are in motion, every day, in this changing global landscape. All of this global fluidity, however, was also contradicted by the unilateral and polarizing foreign policy of a U.S. administration insisting that "you are either with us or against us" and promoting a fundamental dualism backed up by force.

Critical analysts have pointed to the religious role of the United States—fomenting a variety of religious fundamentalisms during the cold war, advancing a particular kind of religious fundamentalism in the twenty-first century—as a crucial agent in the current crisis of fundamentalism. Although we can argue about the historical details, assessing, for example, the extent to which U.S. support for the *mujahideen* in Afghanistan created al-Qaeda, we cannot ignore the implication of the United States in the emergence of religious fundamentalism. According to Tariq Ali, "The most dangerous 'fundamentalism' today—the 'mother of all fundamentalisms'—is American imperialism."[25]

This global analysis has been echoed from a South African perspective by South African poet Dennis Brutus, who surprised an audience of the World Social Forum in Brazil in 2003 when he was asked to speak about religious fundamentalism. In summary, Dennis Brutus identified the major problem in the analysis of religious fundamentalism as the United States. Fundamentalism, he argued,

> contrary to the picture that the media portrays, is not so much Muslim fundamentalism as Christian fundamentalist religiosity in the USA! With their special faith in a Jerusalem under Israeli control before the coming Armageddon and rapture of Christians to heaven, these fundamentalists have amassed great influence and power—and have gained a large degree of control over the development and implementation of US politics and policy-making. This religious fundamentalism is truly one of the most devastating and terrible forms of intolerance, because it demonizes anyone who objects or questions their views and interpretations, naming them heretics and trying to force them—whether one way or the other—into conformity.[26]

South Africans worried about religious fundamentalism during the first decade of the twenty-first century because the term configured a crisis that was local, resonating within national and intimate politics, but also global, everywhere and nowhere, bearing religious significance bordering on the apocalyptic. Religious fundamentalists, as Appleby has suggested, are reactive, selective, absolutist, dualistic, and millenarian. In these terms, South Africans could only feel that they were living in fundamentalist scenarios made in America.[27]

An editorial in 2005 in a South African newspaper made the surprising proposal that U.S. president George W. Bush should receive the Nobel Peace Prize, but only on the ironic basis that his administration's military adventures had given war a bad name all over the world. "Not since Adolf Hitler," the editor Ferial Haffajee observed, "has a world leader done so much to tarnish the reputation of war and warmongering."[28] So here was one international vote of support for President Bush, which he might have welcomed as long as he did not mind being compared to Adolf Hitler.

When Franklin D. Roosevelt and Winston Churchill drafted the Atlantic Charter in 1941, Africans noticed that they were being left out of the Allies' vision of a postwar world of freedom. In South Africa, a committee of twenty-eight Africans, under the leadership of the ANC, published a point-by-point response to the Atlantic Charter in *Africans' Claims in South Africa,* demanding that colonized people in Africa and elsewhere "shall not be excluded from the rights and privileges which other groups hope to enjoy in the post-war world."[29] Not only responding to the "Atlantic community" but also anticipating the Universal Declaration of Human Rights, this publication concluded with a fully developed bill of political, social, and economic rights.

In the postwar world, what threatened human rights? Addressing a meeting of the ANC in 1951, Nelson Mandela warned about forces in the world, "at the head of which stands the ruling circles in America," that were waging military and psychological warfare designed to incapacitate people through fear so they could not think. Those global forces, Mandela noted, were "prepared to go to war in defense of colonialism, imperialism, and their profits." But they were also prepared to engage in psychological terrorism. As Mandela observed, those American-led forces were "determined to perpetuate a permanent atmosphere of crisis and fear in the world. Knowing that a frightened world cannot think clearly, these groups attempt to create conditions under which the common men might be inveigled into supporting the building of more and more atomic bombs, bacteriological weapons, and other instruments of mass destruction."[30]

We must be surprised by the irony of the future Nobel peace laureate Nelson Mandela employing, more than fifty years ago, language so similar to the phrase "weapons of mass destruction," which motivated (or inveigled) the majority of Americans to support a military invasion and occupation of Iraq. But Mandela was concerned with both the military and the psychological dimensions, the political and cultural factors, in the creation of that "permanent atmosphere of crisis and fear." As Mandela argued in the 1950s, from an African perspective, American imperialism was most dangerous because it came to Africa "elaborately disguised," not only by political diplomacy and military interventions, but also by commerce, religion, and popular culture.[31] In 2003, Nelson Mandela issued a warning similar to the one in 1951, in this case advising U.S. president George W. Bush against adopting a military policy that created a climate of fear, undermined the United Nations, and threatened to lead the world into a holocaust.[32]

In 2006, the U.S. undersecretary of state for public diplomacy, Karen Hughes, reiterated the Bush administration's dualistic worldview by asserting that the world was divided between two opposing "missions." In this highly charged religious language, echoing Christian missionary understandings of calling and sending, vocation and submission, confrontation and conversion, Hughes suggested that everyone on the planet was living in an apocalyptic moment poised between death and life. The mission of Islamic terrorists such as Osama bin Laden, she said, "is a mission of destruction and death; ours a message of life and opportunity."[33] If we apply an academic definition of religious fundamentalism, such as Appleby's identification of its reactive, selective, absolutist, dualistic, and millenarian features, we cannot avoid the conclusion that the United States was displaying many if not all of these defining characteristics of religious fundamentalism.

CHAPTER FIVE

Heritage

After many years of policy analysis and public debate, South Africa's National Policy on Religion and Education was finally established in September 2003. Departing from the overtly religious agenda of the apartheid regime, this new national policy affirmed respect for the religious heritage of South Africa, in all its diversity, but made a principled distinction between religious education, instruction, or nurture, which was best served by families and religious communities, and religion education, which was defined as teaching and learning about religion, religions, and religious diversity. Religion education, based on educational goals and objectives, but also promising social benefits of increasing understanding, reducing prejudice, and expanding toleration, was introduced in the curriculum as an integral part of the subject field "Life Orientation." As part of a learning area engaged with values, from hygiene to human rights, religion education was designed to advance knowledge about the many religions of South Africa and the world but also to cultivate informed respect for diversity.[1]

South Africa's new policy for religion and education had a history. It was developed against the background of the Christian instruction, or indoctrination, promoted by the apartheid regime, with its theological impetus for a Christian National Education, pervading every subject but foregrounded in religious education. This policy grew, slowly, out of the research of the National Education Policy Investigation of the early

1990s, the National Education and Training Forum during 1993–94, and consultations leading to the South African Schools Act (1996).[2] A five-person Ministerial Committee on Religious Education, which submitted its report in 1999, tried to work out a compromise among competing interests.[3] Internally divided, this committee proposed leaving it up to local schools to decide whether they would have religious instruction, or education about religion and religions, or some combination of both. Subsequently, a larger Ministerial Standing Committee on Religion and Education was convened to formulate a coherent and consistent national policy. This committee was instructed to begin with the basic values enshrined in the South African Constitution and to operate within a human rights framework. Out of this work, which was supported by intensive collaboration and extensive consultations, the Department of Education was able to finalize its national policy for religion and education.

As the curriculum for Life Orientation was developed, learning about religion was located in the context of "Social Development" and situated in relation to learning about human rights, democratic participation, diversity, and community. In General Education and Training (GET, grades R–9), the learning outcome for Social Development, at every level, was specified: "The learner will be able to demonstrate an understanding of and commitment to constitutional rights and responsibilities, and to show an understanding of diverse cultures and religions." Along with outcomes in Health Promotion, Personal Development, and Physical Development and Movement, this learning outcome for Social Development makes up the learning area of Life Orientation. In Further Education and Training (FET, grades 10–12), we find a similar location of teaching and learning about religion within Life Orientation, with religion education situated within the learning outcome for Responsible Citizenship, in which "the learner is able to demonstrate competence and commitment regarding the values and rights that underpin the constitution in order to practice responsible citizenship, and enhance social justice and sustainable living." Throughout the curriculum, therefore, teaching and learning about religion are integrated into social development and citizenship education.

Within that context, learning about religion, religions, and religious diversity was formulated in terms of specific assessment standards. At each grade, summarized here from R through 12, the learner demonstrates the achievement of the broader educational outcome of social development with respect to the component of religion education when he or she

R: Identifies and names symbols linked to own religion;

1: Matches symbols associated with a range of religions in South Africa;

2: Describes important days from diverse religions;

3: Discusses diet, clothing, and decorations in a variety of religions in South Africa;

4: Discusses significant places and buildings in a variety of religions in South Africa;

5: Discusses festivals and customs from a variety of religions in South Africa;

6: Discusses the dignity of the person in a variety of religions in South Africa;

7: Explains the role of oral traditions and scriptures in a range of the world's religions;

8: Discusses the contributions of organizations from various religions to social development;

9: Reflects on and discusses the contributions of various religions in promoting peace;

10: Displays knowledge about the major religions, ethical traditions, and belief systems in South Africa, clarifies own values and beliefs, and respects the rights of others to hold their own;

11: Critically analyses moral issues and dilemmas and explains the consequences of beliefs and actions;

12: Formulates a personal mission statement based on core aspects of personal philosophies, values, beliefs and ideologies, which will inform and direct actions in life.[4]

These educational expectations, which were intended to enable learners to begin engaging the religious diversity of their country and world, featured as part of social development and citizenship education. To participate in a unified nonracial, nonsexist, and democratic South Africa, as well as within an increasingly globalizing world, learners needed at least this level of educational engagement with religion, religions, and religious diversity.

To give a sense of proportion, however, we need to recognize that the curriculum actually allows very little time for this educational activity. In grades R–9, the learning area of Life Orientation, which includes four outcomes—Health Promotion, Social Development, Personal Development, and Physical Development and Movement—is allocated 8 percent of teaching time out of the total curriculum. As one of four outcomes in Life Orientation, Social Development can be expected to account for 2 percent of teaching time. As one in four assessment standards within Social Development, religion education ends up accounting for perhaps 0.5 percent of the overall curriculum. Although these calculations cannot be applied mechanically, we can only conclude that religion education, the focus of so much controversy and contestation, actually has only a very small share of the general curriculum in South African schools.

Having developed a curriculum in line with the new national policy, little progress was initially made in teacher training, whether preservice or in-service, to enable teachers to achieve the educational outcomes of Life Orientation in the classroom.[5] With respect to religion education, educational frameworks and resources for teachers were developed, but much more work needed to be done.[6] At a meeting of the Ministerial Standing Committee on Religion and Education held in Pretoria in 2001, Minister of Education Kader Asmal had remarked that he would be looking to departments of religious studies all over the country for help in curriculum development and teacher training for religion education. But the restructuring of higher education in South Africa found university departments dedicated to the academic study of religion embattled, shrinking, or closed down.[7] While university departments were struggling, the Department of Education further expanded the scope of teaching and learning about religion in South African schools by establishing a new senior subject, religion studies, as an examinable option in grades 10–12, the last three years of school education. A flurry of new textbooks for religion studies appeared, often in consultation with university-based scholars of religion, but the challenge of teacher training for this new subject remained.

South Africa's new national policy for religion and education created expanding opportunities for the academic study of religion to engage the educational challenges of defining religion, representing religions, and developing curricula, learning materials, and teacher training just when university departments dedicated to the academic study of religion had diminishing capacity to address these challenges. The new national policy represented a promise for the classroom that required resources, time, and the concerted efforts of scholars of religion and education to fulfill. Nevertheless, this promise, established in policy, articulated crucial educational objectives and social projects of the new South Africa by aligning teaching and learning about religion with nation building. My interest, in this chapter, is with the prospects and problems of that alignment.

Over the years that I have been involved in the long and contested process of policy formation, I have written about policy options and policy debates.[8] I have concentrated on the politics of this process. Others have written about the import of this new approach to teaching and learning about religion in the light of social transformation, religious pluralism, and pedagogical practice.[9] But I have been primarily interested in politics, including new forms of citizenship, not only national citizenship, which dramatically broadened in postapartheid South Africa, but also cultural citizenship and global citizenship, and new aspirations for the South African state to be a unified constitutional state, a diverse cultural state, and a progressive transformational state.[10] Accordingly, I have been interested in locating religion education, during a time of transition, at the intersection of citizens and the state.

As a historian of religions, I have always thought that this political interest in the relation between individuals, as citizens, and the state, as a powerful but also meaningful totality, resonates with what the historian of religions Bruce Lincoln long ago identified as one of our most crucial analytical problems: How is any first-person singular transformed into a first-person plural?[11] How do we account for the intersections between personal subjectivity and social collectivity? How does any "I" become an "Us"? How does the term *religion* provide a focusing lens for analyzing this nexus?

Here I want to take up this problem by indexing South Africa's National Policy on Religion and Education to postapartheid nation-building initiatives, which have been embedded within the Department of Education, most forcefully in the Values in Education Initiative, but have also been extended through a broader range of state-driven and market-driven initiatives in public pedagogy. In policy and practice, religion education is located in the classroom, but it is also situated in what I will call the expanding classroom of state and commercial ventures in public education for a new South Africa.

Although religion education in the school classroom, as a matter of principle, as a matter of policy, does not seek to advance any particular religious interests, the expanding classroom of nation building draws on a range of resources and strategies that echo religion. Conservative Christian critics of the new policy, in a parody of this observation, have complained that the new "nonreligious" policy is actually promoting a new multifaith religion or a new religion of secular humanism. The policy is not advocating any such religion. The policy is clear in demarcating educational rather than religious aims and objectives in teaching and learning about religion, religions, and religious diversity in South Africa and the world. However, since this policy is situated in the larger context of building a new nation out of the legacy of damage and dehumanization suffered by the majority of South Africans under apartheid, it inevitably resonates with recognizably religious resources and strategies for redemption by creating an intersection between personal subjectivities and the social collectivity that will redeem a human identity.

EDUCATIONAL POLICY

In his foreword to the new national policy, Minister of Education Kader Asmal began by invoking South Africa's national motto, "Unity in diversity." Adopted in 2000, this new national motto, emblazoned on a new national coat of arms, was designed to mark a dramatic break from the racialized divisions of the apartheid past. Although the motto was translated into all eleven of South Africa's official languages, its canonical formulation was in the extinct language of the /Xam Bushmen, !Ke e: /xarra //ke. This /Xam phrase could be variously translated as "People who are different come together," as "Diverse people unite," or as "Unity in diversity," which was the preferred formulation for national policy, since the motto evoked national unity, echoing other national slogans, from the E pluribus unum of the revolutionary era of an emerging United States of America to the postcolonial mottoes adopted by the Republic of India or the Republic of Indonesia. Nelson Mandela, during his visit to Jakarta in 1997, anticipated South Africa's adoption of this national motto, while drawing on these revolutionary and postcolonial precedents, by observing, "'Unity in Diversity' is a phrase we use often in South Africa, which is also a country of widely diverse peoples and cultures. These differences were misused by apartheid in order to divide our nation. But today our diversity is a source of strength. We are a nation of many colours and cultures, but forming a harmonious unity like a rainbow after a heavy storm."[12]

Accordingly, South Africa's national policy for religion and education had to be aligned with this broader project of building a unified nation out of a fractured past. It could be framed only in terms of unity in diversity.

Consistently, in South Africa's National Policy for Religion and Education, diversity was drawn into the service of national unity. "Our diversity of language, culture, and religion," the policy states, "is a wonderful national asset." Instead of being regarded as a disability, with the threat of creating divided loyalties, these differences should be protected and promoted as valuable resources for building national unity. "We therefore celebrate diversity as a unifying national resource," the policy continued, "as captured in our Coat of Arms: !Ke e: /xarra //ke (Unity in Diversity)." Although counterintuitive, perhaps, and contrary to South Africa's historical experience of difference, segregation, and fragmentation, this motive for nation building was central because the "policy for the role of religion in education is driven by the dual mandate of celebrating diversity and building national unity."[13]

Situated within this promise of a nation in the making, the policy had to adjudicate relations between the South African state and the many religions of South Africa. Aligned with the provisions and values of the constitution, the state ensured freedom for religion but also freedom from religious discrimination or coercion. But the national policy went further in developing the implications of a "cooperative model" for relations between state and religion that established separation in principle but grounds for cooperation in practice. The policy affirmed the importance of religion and religions in South Africa. As Minister Asmal wrote in his foreword, "The policy recognizes the rich and diverse heritage of our country and adopts a cooperative model that accepts our rich heritage and the possibility of creative interaction between schools and faith." However, this recognition of the importance of religion and other worldviews, with all due respect for their particularity, was affirmed as part of the national project, drawing upon South Africa's "rich and diverse heritage" to advance national unity. But here the policy made the bold promise that its approach to religion and education would develop educationally sound programs for teaching and learning about religion, religions, and religious diversity while also contributing to the national project of creating "unity in diversity" by affirming "unity without uniformity and diversity without divisiveness."[14]

For all of its attention to outlining a new approach to religion and education, spelling out basic principles for teaching and learning about religion and religions in South African schools, the national policy was inevitably indexed to a wider range of postapartheid initiatives in nation building. Within the Department of Education, it was integrated into the broader aims of the Values in Education Initiative, which sought to overcome the damage of apartheid by developing new approaches to antiracist and antisexist education and by identifying a range of basic values, such as equity, tolerance, accountability, and social honor, that should be instilled in all educational practice.[15] The national policy for religion and education explicitly aligned itself with this initiative and suggested ways in which its new approach to religion education could cultivate all of the values identified by the Department of Education's *Manifesto on Values in Education*. But the new policy also looked outside the Department of Education to identify with other national initiatives in promoting values. Under the leadership of Thabo Mbeki, the South African presidency was promising the cultural rebirth of an African Renaissance, underwritten by an ambitious plan for economic growth throughout the entire continent, the New Partnership for Africa's Development (NEPAD), while trying to mobilize religious communities and other organs of civil society within South Africa to create the Moral Regeneration Movement. As stated in the national policy for religion and education, "This policy links religion and education with new initiatives in cultural rebirth (the African Renaissance), moral regeneration, and the promotion of values in our schools."[16] Therefore, while outlining principles for educational policy, pedagogy, teacher training, and teaching materials, South Africa's national policy for religion and education was linked to a broader range of educational projects within the schools, the public sphere, and the international arena.

The policy for religion and education intentionally echoed the preamble to the South African Constitution, which committed the new nation to honoring the past, healing divisions in the present, and building a future by promising that a new approach to teaching and learning about religion, religions, and religious diversity could "play a significant role in preserving our heritage, respecting our diversity, and building a future based on progressive values."[17] In this formula for national unity, the heritage of the past and the diversity of the present could be mobilized in the service of a national future.

This formula, of course, was not only politics and policy. It was also poetics and persuasion. When President Thabo Mbeki introduced South Africa's new national motto and coat of arms on April 27, 2000, South Africa's Freedom Day, which marks the annual celebration of the first democratic election of 1994, he invoked a sacred poetics of space and time. In the coat of arms, visual imagery, drawn from Bushman rock art, reinforced the /Xam phrase, *!Ke e: /xarra //ke,* "Diverse people unite," to signal a transformation of space and time. As the anthropologist Alan Barnard has observed, in this national symbolism Khoisan people—the earliest people in imperial theories of evolution, the lowest people in colonial policies of extermination—"were chosen to embody the mythical charter of the new South African multicultural nation."[18] That mythical charter, like any mythical charter, set out a fundamental orientation in space and time. In this case, however, orientation required reorientation, a dramatic transformation of spatial and temporal relations.

In transforming space, these new national symbols, as President Mbeki proposed, presented an image of South African national unity that was "both South African and African." But the resonance of this imagery, according to Mbeki, extended even further by evoking basic truths of humanity that were "both African and universal." Radiating out from South Africa, this new symbol of national unity held universal significance for all human beings. The two human figures at the center of South Africa's coat of arms, as Mbeki observed, "are depicted in an attitude of greeting, demonstrating the transformation of the individual into a social being who belongs to a collective and interdependent humanity." This national symbolism, therefore, was universal because it represented the reciprocal recognition of a shared humanity.

In transforming time, these new national symbols echoed the preamble to the South African Constitution by promising to bridge past, present, and future. The new coat of arms, as Thabo Mbeki explained, "serves to evoke our distant past, our living present and our future as it unfolds before us. It represents the permanent yet evolving identity of the South African people as it shapes itself through time and space." By evoking South Africa's distant past in the language and art of Khoisan people who had been subjected to colonial genocide, these national symbols were formulated in the extinct language of an extinct people. Although a new indigenous movement, the Khoisan National Consultative Council, contested this notion that the people of South Africa's "first nation" were extinct, their absence in the present seemed important to this recovery of the past. Evoking the past for the present meant bringing the dead back to life.

As Thabo Mbeki dedicated South Africa to this revival of the past, the dead bore different meanings—natural, ancestral, and universal— that all warranted allegiances that were simultaneously South African and human, African and universal.

First, the new national symbols were natural. More specifically, they were media for revitalizing an indigenous harmony between human beings and the natural environment. By embracing these symbols, as Thabo Mbeki asserted, South Africans would be able to "embrace the indigenous belief systems of our people, by demonstrating our respect for the relationship between people and nature, which for millions of years has been fundamental to our self-understanding of our African condition."

Second, the new national symbols were ancestral, drawing South Africans back into the precolonial era when Africans built their lives, homes, social relations, and political organization on the enduring relations between the living and their ancestors. The new national symbolism, as Mbeki explained, "recollects the times when our people believed that there was a force permeating nature which linked the living with the dead."

Third, the new national symbolism was universal, with significance for all humanity, as Mbeki asserted, since it "pays tribute to our land and our continent as the cradle of humanity, as the place where human life first began." Following the "out of Africa hypothesis," supported by scientific evidence from human genetics to the fossil record, President Thabo Mbeki could link the birth of the new South Africa with the evolutionary origin of all human beings. Accordingly, South Africa's new national symbolism was specifically African but also profoundly universal.[19]

The new national policy for religion and education was aligned with this nation-building project. Explicitly, it referred to national initiatives in recovering the religious heritage of the past, respecting the religious diversity of the present, and searching for common ground in drawing South Africa's many religious communities into building a future. Although its theoretical arguments and pedagogical recommendations set out purely educational aims and objects, by contrast to the religious interests promoted by the apartheid regime, this new policy for religion education could not help but resonate with a range of national projects for a society in transition.

NATIONAL HERITAGE

In a variety of media, the postapartheid state has sought to renegotiate relations with the past. *Heritage* has often served as the overarching term for these transactions. Preserving heritage, as we have seen, was part of the rationale of the new policy for religion and education.

Signifying a usable past, heritage has been the subject of extensive research delving into its theory and practice.[20] In South Africa, heritage has also been formally managed by government institutions, including the Department of Arts and Culture, the National Heritage Council, and the South African Heritage Agency, and aggressively mobilized by tourism, marketing, advertising, and other entrepreneurial ventures.[21] Both state and market, operating through this heritage nexus, are dealing in the sacred.

If we adopt Emile Durkheim's simple definition of the sacred as that which is "set apart," we must also recognize the ways in which the sacred is "set apart" at the center of social relations, providing highly charged terms for both social cohesion and social conflict. This duality of the sacred—set apart but central—is a crucial feature of the political economy of the sacred in nation building. Linking the production of nations to characteristic patterns and processes in the history of religions, the French Marxist Régis Debray argued that a nation is made out of sacred stuff. As Debray proposed: "We should not become obsessed by the determinate historical form of the nation-state but try to see what that form is made out of. It is created from a natural organization proper to *homo sapiens,* through which life itself is rendered untouchable or sacred. This sacred character constitutes the real national question."

In specifying the sacred substance of the national question, Debray pointed explicitly to two "anti-death processes," the production of sacred time and sacred space. In the first case, the national question depends upon "a delimitation of time, or the assignation of origins." Like Mircea Eliade, who documented the "myth of the eternal return" in the history of religions, Debray observed that the mythic temporal origin, the "zero point or starting point[,] is what allows ritual repetition, the ritualization of memory," with ritual reenactment "signifying defeat of the irreversibility of time." In the second instance, the national question depends upon the "delimitation of an enclosed space." Within the highly charged confines of that delimited sacred space, whether a sacred site, environment, or territory, national interests intersect with "an encounter with the sacred." The national question, according to Debray, raises the problem of the precise location of "a sacred space within which divination could be undertaken."[22] In the production of sacred space and places, meaning and power coalesce; the national question is answered in the ritualization of memory and the divination of a shared future. In South Africa, this link between memory and future has been crucial to the formation of different religious nationalisms.

Looking at heritage projects of the postapartheid state, which have consecrated new sites of national significance, we must remember that South Africa provides a historical laboratory for studying the production of sacred sites for failed nationalisms. Obviously, the Voortrekker Monument, which celebrated a militant white Afrikaner nationalism in its political ascendancy after the seizure of power by the National Party in 1948 under the slogan of apartheid, now remains standing as a monument to a failed nationalism but also as a privatized (although partially state-subsidized) tourist attraction.[23] But the apartheid regime, with its plan to create separate black nations outside the white Republic of South Africa, generated other sacred national shrines, such as Ntaba kaNdoda in the Republic of the Ciskei, where all who lived in this Bantustan were supposed to go on pilgrimage to swear their allegiance to this fictional nation.[24] Against this background, South Africans might be skeptical about such state-driven efforts to create sacred places for the intersection of personal subjectivity and national unity.

Nevertheless, building a new nation involved building new sacred sites. The most prominent sites in the sacred geography of postapartheid South Africa were created to transform pain into power. They marked sites of trauma—political imprisonment, racialized displacement, brutal repression and violence—in a patriotism of pain. But all of these sites were reclaimed and reinterpreted as shrines for national healing. Prisons, in the case of Robben Island off the Cape Coast and the Old Fort Prison in Johannesburg, were dramatically transformed. Robben Island became a shrine to Nelson Mandela, a memorial to all who had fought, suffered, and died in the struggle against apartheid, and a theme park for tourists, mainly international tourists, to be initiated into the redemptive narrative of a new South Africa.[25] Johannesburg's Old Fort Prison, known as Prison Number Four, where many political prisoners who later became leaders of the new government were incarcerated and tortured, was transformed into the precincts of Constitution Hill, where South Africa's Constitutional Court presides over a new domain of democratic values and human rights.[26] While Robben Island and Constitution Hill have transformed pain into power, even executive, legislative, and judicial power, other sites have mediated painful memory as a path toward recovery. Cape Town's District Six

Museum, which stands as a memorial to people who were forced out of their homes by the previous regime, has developed into a community museum in which displaced people can participate in the memory-work of recovering what apartheid had tried to erase.[27] In Soweto, the Hector Pieterson Memorial, supported by a national museum, recalls the memory, and loss, of the student uprising in 1976 but integrates that pain into the powerful narrative of national redemption in a democratic South Africa.[28]

All of these sites, we must notice, were found sites, places already saturated with significance that could be transformed from sites of pain into powerful places for nation building. By contrast, the large-scale heritage project Freedom Park was built out of nothing, a new development on vacant land, carefully constructed to draw sacred resources into a monumental, memorial, and ritual complex. Like the national policy for religion and education, Freedom Park undertook the challenge, as announced in its promotional brochure, of "interpreting the past, informing the present, imagining the future."[29]

Intentionally positioning the present between a very deep past and an open future, Freedom Park created an extraordinary historical depth, invoking both fossil records and DNA evidence to embed the origin of South Africa in primordial time, 3.6 billion years ago, at the origin of everything. The history of South Africa, in this rendering, certainly did not begin, as apartheid-era textbooks might have claimed, in 1652 with the arrival of European colonizers; it began at the dawn of time. Precolonial history, therefore, was dramatically recast as a myth of origin, the origin of all human beings in the South African "cradle of humankind," as Freedom Park enshrined this "story of southern Africa's 3.6 billion years of history." In its memorial architecture and museum displays, Freedom Park asserted that South Africa's heritage could be traced back to the beginning of humanity and that all humanity could be traced back to South Africa.

Grounded in this myth of origin, Freedom Park was dedicated to memorializing all who had sacrificed their lives in the struggle for humanity and freedom. Arguably, the first hominids had struggled for humanity, so they should be included in this story. But the struggle for human freedom against dehumanizing forces was at the heart of the narrative that informed Freedom Park's commemoration of the dead. Within the precincts of Freedom Park, a ceremonial center, S'khumbuto (a Swazi term for a sacred site to remember, invoke, and mobilize the assistance of ancestors), with a Wall of Names, an eternal flame, and a sanctuary, was designed "as a permanent space to celebrate and commemorate the struggle for humanity and freedom."

In recasting time, history, and memory, Freedom Park enshrined a ceremonial management of sacred space. At its center, the shrine, Isivivane, was a pile of stones, gathering together stones from all of South Africa's provinces, with the addition of stones representing the nation, the region, and the international African diaspora. In many indigenous southern African traditions, such a pile of stones was used in rituals of transition, when a person might add a stone if embarking on a journey or returning home.[30] At Freedom Park, however, Isivivane was constructed to exercise centripetal force, drawing the entire nation, the region, and perhaps even the African diaspora home to South Africa. Moving out from this sacred center, Freedom Park also exercised a centrifugal force by sponsoring and sending out interreligious delegations to all of the provinces and neighboring countries of South Africa to perform rituals of cleansing, healing, and reconciliation.

As President Thabo Mbeki observed, Freedom Park was "the most ambitious heritage project of the democratic government."[31] As a new sacred site, created out of nothing but memory and imagination, Freedom Park's ambitions were enormous, encompassing 3.6 billion years and drawing the entire world into its orbit. However, Freedom Park, as a state initiative in heritage, was being designed and constructed in the midst of a wide range of independent, entrepreneurial, and corporate ventures in the field of heritage. Accordingly, national unity, as configured by Freedom Park, competed with this diversity of market-driven enterprises.

Tourism, of course, marketed heritage, with indigenous cultural villages, some revived from the apartheid era but some recently created for the "rainbow nation" of the new South Africa, such as the Rainbow Culture Village, producing new tribal displays for the tourist market.[32] Advertising jumped on the new national bandwagon, not only through electronic media, but also through creating new sacred sites, such as South African Breweries' World of Beer in Johannesburg, which was designed by consultants from Atlanta's World of Coca-Cola to align a brand of beer with a new national narrative, from indigenous African origins to an open African future.[33] Casinos, which had been such an integral engine of the apartheid regime, with a casino in every black homeland, while gambling was illegal in Christian South Africa, also mobilized new resources for heritage. During the apartheid era, a casino, such as the Lost City, was already a heritage theme park, "conjured out of the myths and legends of Africa"; it was built on a "Sacred River," featured an erupting volcano that created an "awe-inspiring experience," and ultimately led to the "Hall of Treasures."[34] Casinos, therefore, were well positioned to capitalize on new opportunities for thematic productions of national heritage.

In postapartheid South Africa, with new casino licenses at stake, one consortium bidding for a license in Johannesburg's Gold Reef City, already a theme park dedicated to the mining industry, promised it would create a "Park of Freedom," which can be seen in retrospect to incorporate many of the features of the eventual design of Freedom Park. However, after the gambling license was granted, this park was recast as a museum. Its scope was also dramatically recast. Instead of encompassing all of human history, the museum recounted only the ordeals of apartheid from 1948, and instead of extending out into the entire world, it dealt only with life in and around Johannesburg during that period. Although such a narrowing of focus might still serve national interests in "controlling consensus," this new site, the Apartheid Museum, showed the importance of localizing the nation and the power of grounding a national narrative of unity in the specificity of identity and difference in a particular place.[35]

South Africa's most prominent weekly publication, the *Sunday Times,* embarked upon a heritage initiative that best captures the potential for finding national unity, not in uniformity, but in the diversity of sites, perhaps sacred sites, of South African history.[36] The Sunday Times Heritage Project, which commissioned artists to create memorials all over the country, with the ambition of securing forty sites by the end of 2007, was explicitly aligned with the nation-building project of Freedom Park. But its orientation in time and space was entirely different, since it sought to memorialize a heritage that was decentralized and dispersed through a diversity of cultural memory. Music, for example, carried memory: it was commemorated in the project's first memorial, to the singer Brenda Fassie, as well as in its memorial to the song "Mannenberg" that was erected outside the studio in which the song had been recorded. Both of these memorials were interactive. While visitors could sit next to Brenda Fassie in a memorial site modeled on the John Lennon bench in Havana, Cuba, pilgrims to the Mannenberg site, which featured an artwork of seven tubes, could hit those tubes with a wooden mallet and play out the first seven notes of the song. Both of these sites were national, commemorating a singer who was a national icon and a song that was a national anthem, but the national question in both of these memorials was raised as an invitation for personal interaction and connection.

As advanced by the *Sunday Times,* heritage was a national heritage, but it was also the specific creativity of music, sports, literature, art, and even oppositional religious sacrifice, as enshrined by the memorial to the Bulhoek massacre of African Christians in 1921, which resisted assimilation into a single national narrative. This heritage project also hinted at the possibility of national counternarratives by creating a memorial in Soweto for Tsietsi Mashinini, the forgotten leader of the uprisings of 1976. At every memorial it erected, the Sunday Times Heritage Project found national significance, but it also found rich resonances that transcended any national project.

Contrasts can easily be drawn between Freedom Park, the most ambitious national heritage project of the postapartheid state, and the corporate-media heritage project of the *Sunday Times.* Freedom Park, as we have seen, was dramatically centralized, with a time depth of mythic proportions and a spatial extension that was potentially global in scope. The forty memorial sites selected by the *Sunday Times,* however, were decentralized and dispersed throughout the country and had a time depth, coinciding with a corporate centenary, that went back only to the founding of the newspaper in 1906. While Freedom Park sought to enshrine a single narrative of the struggle for humanity and freedom, the Sunday Times Heritage Project commemorated multiple narratives, embedded in local histories, that could be variously interpreted by the artists commissioned to create the memorials for each site.

Nevertheless, both of these projects, like the other state-driven and market-driven initiatives in heritage, were engaged in what Henry A. Giroux has called public pedagogy, situated outside the classroom but pursuing an educational mission in teaching the public. Pedagogical practices, as Giroux has reminded us, "are not restricted to schools, blackboards, and test taking." Teaching is undertaken and learning takes place "within a wide variety of social institutions and formats including sports and entertainment media, cable television networks, churches and channels of elite and popular culture, such as advertising."[37] All of this might be regarded as informal education, perhaps, but it is thoroughly formulated and formalized within a variety of media and a range of social institutions that engage in public pedagogy by conveying information but also by shaping sentiments and sensibilities.

THE EXPANDING CLASSROOM

As I have argued, South Africa's new policy for religion and education was indexed to a broader range of initiatives in celebrating linguistic, cultural, and religious diversity while forging national unity. Accordingly, religion education was introduced into the curriculum within an expanding classroom, a classroom that was more inclusive because it created space for teaching and learning about a variety of religious ways of life and protected students from discrimination on the basis of religion.[38] But the expanding classroom was also more extensive because it extended outside the public school by linking up with a new public pedagogy of national heritage that addressed South Africans as a "learning nation," committed to "life-long learning," taking up the challenge of internalizing and actualizing the promise of the national motto, "Unity in diversity."

Within the school curriculum, these educational objectives were advanced by new approaches to citizenship education that responded to the more inclusive South African citizenship.[39] As part of the subject area of Life Orientation, religion education, along with anti-racist, antisexist, and human rights education, was designed to contribute to the formation of postapartheid citizens for a new South Africa. At the same time, extending outside the formal education of the public school classroom, a range of heritage institutions, especially museums, monuments, and memorials, also took up this educational challenge. Museums, for example, were faced with the dual mandate of contributing to the "creation of a new national identity" and finding new ways to creatively respond to the "challenges of diversity."[40] National monuments, under the authority of South Africa's National Monuments Council, had to be recast in the light of postapartheid national citizenship. Especially in the case of "controversial existing monuments," the council reported in 1994, considerable work had to be undertaken "to stress an inclusive historical interpretation of the facts and to strive through the educational process to change people's perceptions."[41] Memorials, whether found, rediscovered, or newly constructed, were also instrumental in this educational process. In the expanding classroom, therefore, museums, monuments, memorials, and other heritage sites extended the public pedagogy of "unity in diversity."

Critics have identified problems with this public pedagogy. I focus here on two problems—the manufacture of consensus and the privileging of the extraordinary—that also have implications for teaching and learning about religion in schools.

First, South Africa's new public pedagogy has been criticized for creating an artificial uniformity in which difference, disagreement, and debate are buried under scripted narratives and framed imagery for creating consensus. New national narratives, drawing on powerful images of nonracial rainbowism or an African Renaissance, have been deployed in a variety of ways to create a sense of social cohesion. Public holidays and public memorials, orchestrating new orientations in time and space, have also been mobilized in efforts to form a new public consensus about the new South Africa's continuity with the past and uniformity in the present. These national initiatives, which novelist Ivan Vladislavić has called "propaganda by monuments," reinforce an imaginary uniformity.[42]

Those who are working out a curriculum and pedagogy for religion education in schools need to take this criticism seriously. Clearly, the national policy intends "unity without uniformity." But pressures of public pedagogy might force the curriculum for religion education to stress the underlying similarity of all religions in forming personal identity, transmitting moral values, and facilitating mutual recognition in a shared society. In the process, creative and critical thinking about the multiplicity of religious identities and the negotiation of religious differences might be subsumed in the artificial manufacture of consensus.

If religion education is going to resist these pressures for artificial uniformity, then its pedagogical approach will have to be more like the heritage project of the *Sunday Times,* decentralized and dispersed, than like the national heritage fixed in time and space at Freedom Park. As the historian of religions Jonathan Z. Smith has argued, introducing students to religion should proceed not through grand narratives but through illuminating instances, *exempla gratia,* that provide raw and real material for creative and critical thinking.[43] In such an approach, religion education can be based on a unified and coherent educational project without seeking national or religious uniformity.

Second, South Africa's new public pedagogy has been criticized for focusing on extraordinary events of heroism, sacrifice, and loss. Extraordinary sites, such as national memorials, may inspire, but they also can overshadow or even erase the meaning of everyday, ordinary places. In advancing public pedagogy, the creative and critical analysis of everyday spaces, such as a shopping mall, can be just as useful in achieving the educational outcomes of citizenship education as a school visit to a national museum or national monument.[44] A pedagogy of the ordinary may be even more effective in achieving educational objectives than any "propaganda by monuments."

Here also religion education needs to heed this critique by resisting the privileging of the extraordinary. In the familiar and pervasive model of "world religions," all religions, by definition, are constituted by the extraordinary, by extraordinary revelations or hierophanies, all recorded in an extraordinary library of sacred texts. While this privileging of the extraordinary has distorted the character of religious life, it has forcefully excluded indigenous religious forms of life from the world of religions.

Fortunately, religion education does not depend upon such a model of world religions. As this framing of the world of religions has been critiqued, deconstructed, and abandoned in the history of religions, it has also been overcome in religion education. A variety of pedagogical approaches, interpretive, dialogical, and participatory, have long ago gone beyond the structures and constrictions of the model of world religions.[45] For all their difference, these methods have in common an impetus to recover and reimagine the ordinary as the basis for teaching and learning about religion and religions.

By locating South Africa's new policy for religion and education in the context of public pedagogy, we can gain a broader perspective on religious opposition to the policy. The African Christian Democratic Party (ACDP), along with other groupings that identified themselves as "concerned Christians," opposed religion education by alleging that it established a uniform multireligious religion (or, alternatively, a uniform antireligious religion of secular humanism) and thereby undermined the decentralized role of local schools in determining their own particular and distinctive religious ethos. Although Christian opponents of the new policy invoked religious concerns, they also became expert at arguing within the new constitutional space, which guaranteed freedom from religious discrimination and freedom for religious expression. The new policy, Christian critics argued, violated the provisions of both the Bible and the new South African Constitution. However, South Africa's policy for religion and education did not establish a uniform religion nor discriminate against local religious commitments, because it was concerned only with clarifying the educational principles and objectives for teaching and learning about religion, religions, and religious diversity. Nevertheless,

Christian opponents of the policy insisted that anything that touched their religion was religious.

Representatives of these Christian interests also opposed national heritage projects. Turning from the school curriculum to public pedagogy, the African Christian Democratic Party attacked Freedom Park, insisting that its ritualization of memory and healing was anti-Christian. In March 2004, this Christian party issued a press release stating that it would not participate in any activities organized by Freedom Park because "we stand adamantly opposed to efforts to impose an interfaith religion on the people of South Africa." Instead of looking back to the past, according to the ACDP, the people of South Africa should look forward to Jesus, who "alone can provide us with an identity and hope, restoring a people and bringing true unity and liberty." In the meantime, these politicized Christians were committed to resisting any initiatives, whether in the national curriculum of the public school or the national heritage of public pedagogy, that were contrary to their specific Christian understanding of the world. From their perspective, the expanding classroom, in both public schools and public arena, in the new national policy for religion and education and in the new national heritage project in Freedom Park, were "determined to bind the people of South Africa to demonic altars."[46]

In similar terms, we have seen Christian educators, such as the University of South Africa's professor of education Irmhild H. Horn, opposing South Africa's national policy for religion and education on the grounds that such an open approach to teaching and learning about religion and religions will expose students to demonic possession.[47] Opponents of religion education, therefore, have linked the public school with public pedagogy, demonizing both national projects in the name of a certain kind of Christianity. Neither the park nor the policy was religious in any conventional sense. But both were engaged by the ACDP and other "concerned Christians" as if they posed religious challenges to Christianity. Therefore, both registered, from this religious perspective, not only as "religious" but also as wild religion.

South Africa's expanding classroom requires critical reflection on the role of religion, spirituality, and the sacred in a constitutional democracy. Guaranteeing freedom for religion (and freedom from discrimination on the basis of religion), the South African Constitution established a "cooperative" model for engaging religion within the framework of a secular state.[48] Although state and religion are separate, the state has established consultative mechanisms, from the National Religious Leaders Forum to the Commission for the Promotion and Protection of the Rights of Cultural, Religious, and Linguistic Communities, which give scope for cooperation between religious communities and the state. While seeking to include all of South Africa's many religious communities in the public school classroom and public institutions, the postapartheid state has also generated national symbols, mythic narratives, and ritualized practices that bear traces of the sacred.

CHAPTER SIX

Dreamscapes

In recounting his tour of Africa in 1925, the psychoanalyst C. G. Jung recalled a conversation he had about dreams with an African ritual specialist. "I remember a medicine man in Africa," Jung related, "who said to me almost with tears in his eyes: 'We have no dreams anymore since the British are in the country.'" When Jung asked why the British colonial presence had caused Africans to stop dreaming, the diviner answered, "The District Commissioner knows everything. . . . God now speaks in dreams to the British, and not to the medicine-man . . . because it is the British who have the power." For Africans, as Jung concluded, "Dream activity has emigrated."[1] According to Jung's biographer, Frank McLynn, the diviner's point was that Africans were unable to dream under colonial conditions because the European colonial administrator did all their dreaming for them, since "power speaks to power."[2] Certainly, this inability to dream, this dream-loss, represented a spiritual crisis within the most intimate interiority and personal subjectivity of people living under oppressive colonial conditions. But it also reflected broader social, economic, and political realities within which indigenous dreams lost clarity and force in the world.

In British South Africa, the Anglican missionary Henry Callaway studied Zulu dreams, devoting a large part of his book *The Religious System of the Amazulu* (1868–70) to what he called the "subjective apparitions" or "brain sensation" of African dream life. Zulu diviners were experts in dreams, their bodies, as one diviner recounted, becoming a "house of dreams."[3] Callaway characterized Zulu dreams as a medium of sensory experience, "brain-sight" and "brain-hearing," without any material referents. But the Zulu interpretation of dreams documented by Callaway showed that dreams were often understood as calls to action. Through the medium of dreams, ancestors called for sacrificial offerings, affirming ongoing relations of material exchange between the living and the dead, or an ancestor might call for the performance of homecoming rituals that would bring him "back from the open country to his home."[4] Dreams, therefore, were not merely sensory media to be interpreted. Although they were rendered meaningful through a hermeneutics of dreams, they were also given force through an energetics of dreams that demanded practical responses with material consequences, even if those responses became more difficult under colonial conditions of dispossession and displacement.[5] As a result, dreams were thoroughly integrated into the material relations of exchange and orientation in Zulu ancestral religion.

Now, under globalizing conditions, Zulu dreaming is undergoing transformation. Global claims are being made on Zulu dreams. For example, Afrika Bambaataa, the African American godfather of hiphop, whose musical group, Zulu Nation, which was not African, Zulu, or a nation, nevertheless moved into South African space to identify two kinds of religion: the "go to sleep slavery type of religion," the religion of the dream, the religion of the oppressed that sealed their oppression, and the "spiritual wake up, revolutionary" religion of conscious, positive action, "like the prophets," in which "knowledge, wisdom, [and] understanding of self and others" inform a "do for self and others type of religion."[6] At the same time, indigenous Zulu dreams are going global, as in the case of the Zulu witch doctor, *sangoma, sanusi,* and now shaman Credo Mutwa, the master of Zulu "dreams, prophecies, and mysteries," who has emerged in the global circuit of neoshamanism as the ultimate spokesman for African indigenous authenticity to underwrite a variety of projects, including New Age spirituality, alternative healing, and encounters with aliens from outer space.[7]

In this new globalizing terrain, electronic media have dramatically expanded the Zulu dreamscape. Zulu dreaming, along with religious or spiritual interpretations of Zulu dreams, visions, and mysteries, has been proliferating through film and video, musical CDs and DVDs, and the expanding global dreamscape of neoshamanism on the Internet. Nevertheless, in all of these media, we can find echoes of the nineteenth-century Zulu energetics of dreams that was based on sacrificial exchange and ancestral orientation.

First, we find echoes of sacrificial exchange, but now situated in the dilemmas posed by a global economy. Not only defined by the increased pace and scope of the flows of money, technology, and people, the global economy is also an arena for new mediated images and ideals of human possibility, including the possibility that occult forces are both shadow and substance of global economic exchange.[8] In his own way, as we will see, Mutwa has dealt with these dilemmas of the global economy by identifying aliens from outer space as the nexus of a sacrificial exchange into which he personally has entered by eating extraterrestrial beings in a sacramental meal and by being their sacrificial victim.

Second, addressing the demand for bringing ancestors home and reinforcing the sacred orientation revolving around the ancestral homestead, Mutwa has tried for many years to establish a "Credo Mutwa village" in South Africa—in the township of Soweto during the 1970s, in the apartheid Bantustan of Bophutatswana in the 1980s, in the game reserve of Shamwari during the 1990s—but none of these homes turned out to be sustainable. On the Internet, however, Mutwa found a home. Mediated by the global network of neoshamanism, he has gained new credibility. While Mutwa was going global, North American enthusiasts for New Age spirituality, including some white South African expatriates, found in this new global medium an avenue for coming home to Africa by entering the "house of dreams" as a Zulu shaman.

In 1994 the American author James Hall described his initiation as a Zulu *sangoma* as "a journey to become the house of dreams."[9] In 2004 the South African expatriate David M. Cumes, who had established a medical practice in California, underwent his initiation as a Zulu *sangoma,* observing, "I had heard the term 'a house of dreams' applied to aspects of the *thwasa* [initiation] experience."[10] How should we understand this new "house of dreams" that is emerging in a new, globalizing arena?

As an entry into this new Zulu dreamscape, I want to examine the role of the human sensorium and electronic media. Exploring Zulu neoshamanism as material religion, I situate my analysis at the nexus of religious dreaming, sensory repertoires, and electronic mediation. Religion, as Jeremy Stolow has observed, is "materialized in and through the most primary media of all, the human senses."[11] If embodied senses are media, then electronic media can also be understood as both extensions and limitations of the human sensorium. Dreams, our most intimate, embodied media, are also sensory, whether ordinary or extraordinary. Although they have often been regarded as imaginary and immaterial, as nothing more than "subjective apparitions," they are material productions, not merely because they are generated by the neurobiology of the brain, but also because they have the capacity to elicit practical responses with material consequences. In the case of Zulu neoshamanism, dreams entail material investments in sacrificial exchange and ancestral orientation that echo an earlier Zulu hermeneutics and energetics of dreams, but now under rapidly changing global conditions. Within this new Zulu dreamscape, indigenous sensory repertoires for arranging (and deranging) the human sensorium merge with the limits (and potential) of electronic media.

By examining the work of a variety of contemporary Zulu shamans, including Credo Mutwa and P.H. Mtshali, but also including James Hall, David Cumes, Ann Mortifee, and other so-called white *sangomas,* we can discern basic strategies for engaging senses and media. In this new Zulu dreamscape, dreams are a sensory medium, involving "brain-sight" and "brain-hearing," as Henry Callaway suggested, but also incorporating all of the senses, simultaneously, synesthetically, and expansively, perhaps even to the twelve senses that Mutwa will claim as the natural sensorium of human beings. All of this sensory experience, however, is thoroughly mediated through new electronic media. As I hope to show, Zulu neoshamans have developed an ambivalent relationship to the very media that have made it possible for them to be shamans. Media, like sensory experience, are engaged in three ways—as limit, as potential, and as validation of the reality of this new Zulu shamanism. Within the dreamscapes of contemporary Zulu neoshamanism, the human senses and electronic media are at play, and the question of authenticity is at stake, in the imaginative terrain that has opened between global exchanges and local homecomings.

EXTRATERRESTRIAL ENCOUNTERS

Vusamazulu Credo Mutwa has been described, internationally, as a Zulu shaman, the keeper of Zulu tradition, although he has often been characterized in South Africa as a fake, fraud, and a charlatan.[12] An extremely creative and imaginative author, artist, and sculptor, Mutwa has been celebrated within the global network of contemporary neoshamanism as the high *sanusi* of the Zulu nation, the highest grade of African shaman and the official historian of the Zulu people of South Africa.

Over his long career, Mutwa has been adept at reinventing himself in relation to various alien appropriations of his authenticity. During the 1950s he was used to authenticate African artifacts for a curio shop in Johannesburg. Through his writings in the 1960s, his tourist attraction in Soweto in the 1970s, and his cultural village in Bophutatswana in the 1980s, he was used to authenticate the racial, cultural, and religious separations of apartheid. During the 1990s, as he acquired the label *shaman* through the interventions of Bradford Keeney, Stephen Larsen, and other exponents of New Age spirituality, Mutwa's authority was invoked to authenticate a diverse array of enterprises in saving the world from human exploitation, environmental degradation, epidemic illness, endemic ignorance, organized crime, or extraterrestrial conspiracy. In all of these projects, the indigenous authenticity of Mutwa added value, credibility, and force because he represented the "pure voice," untainted by modernity, of an unmediated access to primordial truth.[13]

One of Mutwa's supporters, the New Age conspiracy theorist David Icke, produced a five-hour video, *The Reptilian Agenda,* based on interviews with the Zulu shaman. In this video, Icke explains, we are introduced to "a unique human being, the most incredible man it has been my honor to meet." Mutwa is "keeper of the ancient knowledge," the truth of history, as opposed to the "nonsensical version of history we get from universities."[14] The true history confirmed by both Icke's recent research and Mutwa's ancient knowledge centers on a global conspiracy of aliens from outer space.

A former sports broadcaster in Britain, Icke developed a distinctive blend of personal spirituality and political paranoia that he promoted through books, public lectures, and an elaborate website. Although he seemed to embrace every conspiracy theory, he identified the central, secret conspiracy ruling the world as the work of shape-shifting reptilians from outer space. According to Icke, these extraterrestrial reptiles interbred with human beings, establishing a lineage that could be traced through the pharaohs of ancient Egypt, the Merovingian dynasty of medieval Europe, the British royal family, and every president of the United States. Although they plotted behind the scenes in the secret society of the Illuminati, the aliens of these hybrid bloodlines were in prominent positions of royal, political, and economic power all over the world. Occasionally shifting into their lizardlike form, these aliens maintained a human appearance by regularly drinking human blood, which they acquired by performing rituals of human sacrifice.

Icke invoked the indigenous African authority of Mutwa to confirm this conspiracy theory about blood-drinking, shape-shifting reptiles from outer space. As Mutwa declared, "To know the Illuminati, Mr. David, you must study the reptile."[15] In *The Reptilian Agenda,* Mutwa confirms that extraterrestrials, the Chitauri, were a shape-shifting reptilian race that has controlled humanity for thousands of years. After making this video, Icke and Mutwa appeared together on a popular American radio program *Sightings* to explain the alien reptile conspiracy. They also reportedly joined forces on the eve of the new millennium to prevent an Illuminati ritual of human sacrifice at the Great Pyramid of Cheops. In his lectures, Icke insisted that Mutwa had provided proof for his conspiracy theory, as one observer noted, in the "pure voice of a primitive belief system."[16] In Mutwa, therefore, Icke found indigenous authentication for an alien conspiracy.

That authentication took two forms. First, the conspiracy story was authenticated, according to Icke, by the dangers Mutwa had encountered in exposing it. Mutwa had been constantly subjected to death threats, including an attempt on his life just prior to filming, by those who wanted to prevent him from speaking the truth. The conspiracy was not a "theory," Icke warned, because "theory does not kill people. The conspiracy is real." Second, the story was for Icke confirmed by Mutwa's "unique knowledge" drawn from secret traditions of "Africa, this enormous and astonishing continent." "As bizarre . . . and as seemingly ridiculous as this story might seem," it had to be true because Mutwa "tells exactly the same story."

Though Icke found African authentication for his story, it was a precarious tradition at risk of vanishing, since Mutwa was one of only two Zulu *sanusi* left alive. Therefore, in return for Mutwa's indigenous confirmation for Icke's "bizarre story," Icke promised permanence for Zulu tradition through modern electronic media: the story would be preserved on video "for as long as the electronic medium exists."

In his video interviews for *The Reptilian Agenda,* Credo Mutwa describes his encounters with extraterrestrials with meticulous attention to the senses, creating a vivid impression of seeing, hearing, smelling, tasting, and touching aliens in two contexts—eating them and being violated by them. According to Mutwa, African tradition provides wisdom on how to prepare, cook, and eat aliens from outer space. In 1958, he recalls, a UFO crashed in a mountainous area of Lesotho. A friend invited Mutwa over for a meal, promising him that they would be dining on "something holy," which turned out to be the meat of an extraterrestrial known as a Grey. Following African tradition, they had to eat this meal in a deep hole in the ground. As Mutwa reports, the meat of the alien was tough and dry, requiring much chewing, and it had the "same taste as a copper coin." After eating this "flesh of a god," Mutwa and his companion became deathly ill: blinded, deaf, unable to breathe, and suffering intense pain for a week, which seemed like a hundred years. After a week, they went "stark, raving, laughing mad." Then, suddenly, Mutwa recalls, he was "a person reborn." All of his senses were expanded. "I could see colors beyond colors," he recalls. "I could hear a voice in my head." His tastebuds were "souped up," so that ordinary water tasted extraordinary. In the ecstasy of this extraordinary sensory experience, Mutwa recalls, "We were one with the entire universe." By eating the alien, Mutwa had acquired an extraterrestrial sensorium. "Do you think those senses you experienced are the senses of the Chitauri?" Icke asks. "Yes," Mutwa responds. "Senses like no human being has."

By contrast to this extraterrestrial ecstasy, in 1959 Mutwa underwent the alien agony of abduction. While looking for medicinal herbs in what is now Zimbabwe, Mutwa was taken into a spaceship of the Chitauri, disappearing for a period of four days. Again, his account of alien abduction pays meticulous attention to the senses, the "strange humming sound," the images of destroyed cities as "pictures [that] flooded my mind," and the horrible metallic, chemical smell of the Chitauri, the Greys, and other extraterrestrials. "I have seen the Chitauri," Mutwa assures us. "I have smelled them. I have personal experience with them." But that personal experience was entirely terrifying, an "eternity of pain" inflicted upon him by aliens who tortured him, experimented upon him, and forced him to have sexual intercourse with a female extraterrestrial. Throughout all of these ordeals, Mutwa recounted, he felt like the victim at a sacrifice. Returning to earth saturated with a "horrible non-human smell," and missing his trousers, Mutwa was attacked by dogs but was saved by villagers who recognized by his odor that he had been abducted by aliens. Although eating them had heightened his senses, being abducted by aliens had confused his senses. "Since that time I have become a very confused creature," he confides. "Since that time my mind does not seem to be my own."[17]

TRANSATLANTIC EXCHANGES

In a blurb on the back of the recent book by David M. Cumes, *Africa in My Bones: A Surgeon's Odyssey into the Spirit World of African Healing*, Credo Mutwa praises the author, "who walks along two roads" as both Western medical specialist and African ritual specialist, both surgeon and *sangoma*, but also as someone who has developed a kind of double vision. "The world needs such people," Mutwa advises, "who see Africa through two eyes, the African eye and the Western eye." Born in South Africa, Cumes relocated to the United States to study medicine at Stanford and establish a successful practice as a urologist in Santa Barbara, California. Although he often visited the place of his birth, Cumes reported that he felt like an alien in Africa. Drawing on imagery of vision, he said that he "felt like an onlooker rather than a participant." This problem of alienated vision, this subjectivity of the spectator, was resolved for Cumes through dreams that led him to undergo initiation as a *sangoma*. "The fact that my dreams were often quite prophetic," he recounted, "gave me reason to believe that I might be able to master this ancient discipline." In dreams, he was "called" by the ancestors to enter into the ancient discipline of "seeing." Now, as a Zulu *sangoma*, he practices divination as a kind of dreamwork. As he explains, "Reading the bones is a little like unraveling the metaphor of a dream. . . . Divining is like interpreting someone's dream."[18]

On his website, Cumes features a video of his life story, his initiation, and his plans for a healing village in South Africa. To the sounds of rhythmic African music, the video begins with an image of an African woman, traditionally attired, her eyes and mouth wide open. Moving through rural and urban scenes, Cumes, in voice-over, uses tactile metaphors to describe his early life in South Africa, when he was weighted down under the "heaviness of the apartheid system," alienated from "connection with the native" and "connection with Africa." Following his dreams and the advice of author Susan Schuster Campbell, he was led to an "old Zulu teacher in Swaziland," P.H. Mtshali.[19] Undergoing a rigorous, although abbreviated, initiation, Cumes graduated as a Zulu *sangoma*. Now he runs his life on the basis of messages "from the dreamworld," Cumes reports. "I just head wherever the dreams and bones tell me." One place the dreams told him to head was the South African province of Limpopo, where he is establishing a healing center, Tshisimane, in which visitors can benefit from massage, yoga, Reiki, and consultations with *sangomas*. "I saw the place in a dream," Cumes reveals.[20]

As a white *sangoma*, David Cumes represents a recently emerging trend in contemporary neoshamanism in which aspiring Euro-American shamans are turning to African traditions as a source of authentic dreams, visions, and connections. The East African Malidoma Patrice Somé has played an important role in this recent development.[21] James Hall, the American biographer of the great South African singer Miriam Makeba, was a pioneer in taking initiation as a Zulu *sangoma*. But South Africans have also played a part. Credo Mutwa has some white initiates, such as the "white Zulu" C.J. Hood, who has represented him at events in the United States, calling upon everyone to return to their ancestral traditions,[22] but P.H. Mtshali has shown a particular interest in training white *sangomas* who are currently practicing in South Africa, like Claudia Rauber in Cape Town, or in North America, like Gretchen McKay in Orange County, California.[23]

In some cases, however, white *sangomas* in the United States have not required formal initiation to claim indigenous African authenticity. For example, Kenneth "Bear Hawk" Cohen, who claims to have been adopted by the Cree, studied with the Zulu shaman Ingwe, who was born in 1914 as M. Norman Powell in South Africa but moved to the United States to establish his Wilderness Awareness School. On his website, "Bear Hawk" announces that this association with Ingwe places him "in the lineage of the Holy Man, Vusamazulu Credo Mutwa."[24] Similarly, Tom "Blue Wolf" Goodman, who claims to be a Native American shaman, the "Faith Keeper of the Star Clan, Y'falla Band of the Lower Creek People," also claims to be heir to the spiritual lineage of Vusamazulu Credo Mutwa. "I am keeper of my Grandfather's dream," he reveals. "My grandfather's medicine songs have been dreamed in South Africa by Sangoma spiritual leaders," spiritual leaders who are all led by "Vusamazulu Credo Mutwa, High Sanusi (High Priest) of the Zulu Nation."[25]

In North America, defenders of the integrity of indigenous traditions have labeled these white shamans as "plastic shamans."[26] Websites identify them and scorn them. But although these innovations in neoshamanism may very well be "plastic," in the sense of invented or even fake, they suggest real religious issues of location, dislocation, and relocation in the Atlantic world. Just as the South African David Cumes, who became a medical doctor in California, underwent initiation as a Zulu *sangoma* to establish "connection with the native" or "connection with Africa," other expatriates have entered the dreamscape of Zulu neoshamanism as a way of coming home. In Canada, two South Africans, one black, one white, but both having established careers in the creative and performing arts, followed their dreams into Zulu shamanism.

Sibongile Nene describes herself as a singer, actor, and consultant for individuals, businesses, and community building. She also describes herself as a *sangoma*. As an actress, she appeared in the feature film *Jit* (1993). The plot of this film anticipated her later vocation as a ritual specialist in African ancestral religion: "Jokwa, a pesky ancestral spirit," wants the main character "to look after his aging parents, and keep her supplied with beer." Moving to Canada, Sibongile Nene continued acting and singing but also moved into business consultancy. Returning regularly to South Africa, she took initiation as a Zulu *sangoma*, a process she conveys through music on her CD *Sangoma*. On her website in 2006, Sibongile Nene offered her services as an "African Spirituality Consultant in the Sangoma tradition of the Bantu people of southern Africa."[27]

Ann Mortifee, described in the press as "one of Canada's most extraordinary vocalists, composers, and playwrights" but also as a "musical shaman" guided and inspired by Credo Mutwa, was born and raised on a sugarcane farm in Zululand. In 2005 she released a CD, *Into the Heart of the Sangoma*, dedicated to Mutwa, which musically conveyed her journey from her experience of inauthenticity in exile to the authenticity of home. In her successful creative and performing career in Canada, as Mortifee revealed in an interview, "I had created a persona, but felt I had nothing authentic to give to the world." Here, once again, dreams intervened. "For two years," she recalled, "I had recurring dreams about a black woman and stars." Then she read Mutwa's *Song of the Stars*. "I discovered the Zulu 'Song of the Stars' and learned about the *sangoma*, shamen [sic] of the Zulu nation." She flew to South Africa, and her dreams eventually led her to Credo Mutwa.[28]

Although she has told her story in interviews, Mortifee's journey into Zulu shamanism is best conveyed by the music and commentary of her recording *Into the Heart of the Sangoma*. Opening with the song "Africa," she begins with her birthplace but also with her dreams.

"Voices from my childhood linger in me still, voices that come from the dreamtime," she says. "It is the old Sangoma, Sikhowe, leading me deeper into the mystery." The next song, "I Dream," also evokes both Africa and the dreamtime. "One of my earliest recollections is of lying in my bed listening to the sounds of the African night," she says. "Something was out there beckoning to me, weaving a spell, which had the power, in some essential way, to mark my soul forever."

The next song, "The Stars Are Holes," finds her looking up into the night sky, but this song also directs her vision back home to South Africa. "Two years after writing this song," she says, "I found the very same story I had written in a book by Vusamazulu Credo Mutwa, the head Sangoma of the Zulu Nation. This strange occurrence caused me to go to South Africa and find him." Returning to South Africa, staying at a game reserve, she saw a herd of elephants that inspired the song "Indlovu" (The Elephant), and that night, she recalls, "I dreamed . . . there walked a man whom I later knew to be Credo Mutwa. In the dream he said to me, 'Go to Shamwari tomorrow.'" Proceeding to this private game reserve in the Eastern Cape, where Credo Mutwa was employed for a while as a cultural advisor, she participated in "an ancient healing ceremony" at which she sang a song that she had just composed. "Who taught you this song?" the sangomas asked. When Mortifee replied that she had just made it up, the sangomas objected. "You did not make this up," they insisted. "This is the song we Sangomas sing when we go in search of spirit." Having established this connection in song and spirit, Mortifee's dreams were fulfilled by meeting Mutwa. As musically represented in the song, "For There Are Loved Ones," Mortifee learned from Mutwa that her dreams revealed that she was connected to his ancestral lineage. Mortifee explains:

> When I finally met Credo Mutwa, he said: "Tell me about the Sangoma of your dreams. What is her name?" "Sikhowe," I answered. "And tell me, what do her eyes look like?" "Well, one is black and the other is completely white." "And which one is white?" "The right one," I said. "And tell me what do her legs look like?" "They look like the trunks of a tree," I replied. "That woman is my grandmother," Mutwa said. "She had a cataract in her right eye, which turned it completely white. And she had elephantitis, which made her legs look like the trunk of a tree. So you see, it is my grandmother that has brought you to me."

In this affirmation and connection, driven by dreams, Mortifee could finally feel as if she were at home in Africa. She had been called by the maternal ancestor, herself a sangoma, of the highest shaman of the Zulu nation. But she could also return home to North America unburdened by any guilt. "I want you to listen to me," Mutwa reportedly said to her. "Never again be ashamed of the privilege into which you have been born. And never, never be ashamed of the great gifts that the gods have given you."[29]

Mortifee's greatest gift, by her own account, is music that opens to the sacred, providing both a zone of protection and a vehicle for entering the numinous. "Sacred music has been a way of my stopping the world and entering into a place of deep protection," she explains. "Music is a vehicle through which we've always been able to contact the numinous."[30]

SENSES AND MEDIA

In his classic treatment of "the holy," Rudolf Otto disagreed with this proposition that music, or any artistic medium, could be a vehicle for direct contact with the numinous. Pointing to the mistake of "confounding in any way the non-rational of music and the non-rational of the numinous itself," Otto insisted that music and other arts could only suggest the numinous indirectly, coming most closely to representing the numinous through two methods that "are in a noteworthy way *negative*, viz. *darkness* and *silence*."[31] According to Otto, therefore, not seeing and not hearing—or better, seeing nothing, hearing nothing—were sensory experiences within the productions of artistic media that most closely approximated the numinous. Arguably, Otto's Protestant sensibility led him to engage aesthetic media through this negative theology of the senses.

By contrast, indigenous Zulu sensibility was actively engaged with sensory media of dreams and visions, exploring their potential as avenues for communicating with ancestors and responding to the energetics of exchange and orientation. In contemporary Zulu neoshamanism, however, we find an ambivalent relationship to both the senses and electronic media as vehicles for the numinous, which mirrors an understanding of the senses as limitation, as potential, and as validation for the extraordinary experiences of a shaman.

These three ways of dealing with senses and media are all registers of authenticity. By representing limits, senses and media stand as obstacles to authentic spiritual experience. But they also represent the boundary that is necessary to mark the transition from ordinary, everyday awareness to the extraordinary capacities of a shaman. In marking out limits, therefore, senses and media incorporate the classic duality of liminality, as both wall and threshold, defining a boundary that simultaneously constrains and contains possibilities. Accordingly, senses and media also register as transcendent potential, serving as means for achieving, modes for expanding, or metaphors for signaling shamanic awareness. Authenticity, in this respect, is marked by realizing the potential of the human sensorium and electronic media as meaning-making resources. Extraordinary sensory experience, including the intensification, rearrangement, and merger of the senses, is directly related to the capacity of electronic media to capture meaning like a camera and transmit meaning like film. In the process, shamanic authenticity is reinforced by activating the latent potential in senses and media for the production and reception of extraordinary meaning. Finally, human senses and electronic media provide validation, obviously, since "seeing is believing," in cognitive terms, but also in forensic terms when the testimony of intense sensory experiences or popular media representations provides confirmation for shamanic claims. By engaging senses and media in these three ways, as limit, potential, and validation, Zulu neoshamans have sought to authenticate new Zulu dreamscapes.

Senses and Media as Limits

The five conventionally recognized human senses, according to Credo Mutwa, are limits, blocking awareness of spiritual realities. Seeing, hearing, smelling, tasting, and touching are inadequate for engaging this higher awareness. Fortunately, Mutwa assures us, these five senses are only part of a more expansive sensorium that extends to a total of twelve senses. As Mutwa insists, without explaining, "We in Africa know—and please don't ask me to explain further—that the human being possesses twelve senses—not five senses as Western people believe. One day this will be accepted scientifically—twelve." These additional seven senses, whatever they may be, are part of the natural sensory capacity of human beings. Thus, even though they transcend the five senses, Mutwa maintains that "we must not call those as yet unknown senses, supernatural."[32]

Neoshaman James Hall also finds that the five senses are limits. They cannot account for his intense encounters with the *lidloti,* the ancestors, that he experienced in dreams and visions during his initiation as a *sangoma.* Reflecting on ordinary sensory limits, Hall cites the authority of Augustine of Hippo, who observed, "I can run through all the organs of sense, which are the body's gateway to the mind, but I cannot find any by which some facts could have entered." Although Augustine used this argument to posit an interior sense, or seminal reason, as a capacity for knowledge that was independent of ordinary perception, Hall concludes that this acknowledgment of the limits of the senses opens the possibility of extrasensory perception. Augustine, Hall found, "might have been describing my puzzlement following a lidloti experience."[33]

Like the five senses, electronic media can be regarded as placing limits on awareness. At one point, Credo Mutwa advises anyone who wants to be a *sangoma,* with prophetic vision, to stay away from electronic media: "People who are aspiring to develop their gifts of prophecy should avoid exposing themselves over much to electronic devices such as television sets, radio sets, and other electronic gadgets of this day and age because, for some reason, these electronic devices emit an inaudible sound that blankets all psychic power." This unheard sound, as an undercurrent of electronic media, supposedly blocks the extrasensory perceptions of a *sangoma.* Accordingly, a *sangoma* should develop his or her psychic powers in a rural area, not merely to be closer to an ancestral home, but also to be free of the limits to awareness generated by the modern network of electronic transmission and reception of media. "I have noticed over many years of close observation," Mutwa reports, "how difficult it becomes for a witch doctor from Soweto, for example, to foretell events in the future. This is unlike a witch doctor who has lived in an environment where these electronic devices do not exist. So there must be something in our electronic world that is destroying our God-given talents."[34]

James Hall also finds limits to electronic media. In a kind of allegory marking his independence from electronic media, he recalls that during his initiation he felt cut off from any news about the world outside. He acquired a radio, but it stopped working when its wiring was eaten by dozens of cockroaches. "They scrambled over my hands and arms and I dropped the radio in surprise and disgust," Hall recounts. "It smashed to pieces on the floor." Television, as well, was an unnecessary medium, as Hall reflects, "Not that I had seen a television image in over a year and a half. Nor had I needed to. Lidloti-vision had kept me enthralled."[35] The limits of television, therefore, had been transcended by a spiritual medium, ancestor-vision, which provided Hall with all of the information (and entertainment) he could desire.

Senses and Media as Potential

Although senses are limits, they also represent the potential for extraordinary experience. Eyes may be limited, but in distinguishing an authentic shaman, as P.H. Mtshali reveals, "the important thing is that they can 'see.'"[36] Here the senses, as metaphors, represent the possibility of transcending the limits of ordinary perception. Credo Mutwa might have regarded the five conventional senses as limitations, but he also claimed to have entered an extraordinary trans-sensory ecstasy, an intense expansion of all the senses, after eating the meat of an extraterrestrial. Acquiring the sensory capacity of the reptilian extraterrestrials—"Senses like no human being has."—Mutwa saw, heard, smelled, tasted, and touched beyond ordinary perception.

This intensification and expansion of all the senses recalls the role of synesthesia, the convergence, merger, or transmodal transfer of the senses, in religious discourse and practice. In religious discourse, synesthesia can evoke perception that is intense, unifying, and extraordinary. In ritual synesthesia, ordinary perception is transcended in and through the senses, as when the persistent sound and visceral percussion of drumming induces shamanic "seeing."[37]

During his initiation as a *sangoma,* James Hall experienced this synesthetic merger of visceral percussion, sound, and sight. "The loud drums had once more beaten my mind into myself," he recalls. But he immediately turns to media as metaphor, noting, "I had no more self-consciousness viewing these images than a person does watching an involving movie." The next day, when he related his experience to an elder *sangoma,* she observed, "Sometimes, it is like you are watching television. It's that way with me. Things come at you, like the *bhayiskhobho.*" As Hall realized, this SiSwati term, *bhayiskhobho,* was derived from the antiquated term *bioscope,* which had been widely used in South Africa for the "motion picture process."[38]

Similarly, David M. Cumes represented the potential of shamanic perception in terms of electronic media. *Sangomas* are connected to a communication network like the Western communication network of "satellite phones, fax machines and the Internet." Since this *sangoma* communication network is based on a "sophisticated psychospiritual technology," Cumes advises, the "ancient African wisdom has a lot to teach us about communication."[39] Although Cumes contrasts modern Western and traditional African communication networks, sometimes it seems as if both share the same "cosmic field," since Cumes observes that "light, sound, radio, TV, electromagnetic pulses . . . are some of the knowable signals that travel through the cosmic field."[40]

During his initiation, Cumes also had dreams and visions that drew upon modern media technology as metaphors for ancient spiritual wisdom. "One night," he reports, "I dreamt that I was given a new shiny black Mamiya camera. I was told the lens I needed was 150 to 16—more powerful on the wide angle than on the telephoto side." Relating this dream to his teacher, P.H. Mtshali, Cumes asked if the ancestors were instructing him to buy this type of camera to keep a photographic record of his initiation. But Mtshali interpreted this dream not as request but as gift from the ancestors, revealing to Cumes that the camera was a sign that "you are being given tools to give you a broader vision."[41]

Senses and Media as Validation

In his tales of encounters with aliens from outer space, Credo Mutwa pays meticulous attention to sensory perception, with particular emphasis on the sense of smell: "Smelling is knowing," especially in knowing the foul odor of the Chitauri, Greys, and other extraterrestrials. As Mutwa claims, "They are tangible, they are smellable." By his own account, Mutwa was close enough to smell them; he was close enough to be infused by their odor; and he continued to bear that alien odor when he returned to earth and villagers recognized the extraterrestrial stench. Such sensory details, we might assume, are cited to lend an aura of credibility to an unbelievable story. They provide a kind of visceral validation of the narrative.

Similarly, Hall, Cumes, and other white *sangomas* validate their accounts through vivid sensory detail, suggesting that their initiations revolve around a recovery of the senses. In their accounts, they see and hear extraordinary things, but they also smell fragrant herbs and foul concoctions, taste sour beer and disgusting medicines, and convulse in excruciating pain and induced vomiting in validating their initiations.

Electronic media also provide validation, not only as metaphors for spiritual perception, but also as enduring forms for transmitting indigenous spiritual wisdom. The relative permanence of video, as David Icke declared, promises to preserve the authentic Zulu wisdom of Credo Mutwa for "as long as this electronic medium lasts." Traditionally, according to Mutwa, this wisdom was kept secret, reserved for a small circle of initiates, and transmitted orally within a lineage of initiates from generation to generation. But now, as Mutwa declares, "Africa is dying," facing destruction from epidemic disease, endemic poverty, and global conspiracy. In this crisis, traditional ways of transmitting ancient wisdom are no longer viable. Urgently, everyone must know things that were previously known only by a few. Mass media, such as video, film, and the Internet, are now necessary for broadcasting the truth and surviving this crisis. Accordingly, modern media become valid modes of disseminating ancient wisdom.

At the same time, mass media content can be invoked to validate ancient Zulu tradition. Mutwa, interviewed in *The Reptilian Agenda,* states that the extraterrestrial reptilians called the Chitauri will soon be returning to earth to exercise their oppressive domination and exploitation of humanity directly. The Chitauri have been content to exercise their power in disguise, operating through devious, shape-shifting reptilians such as George W. Bush, Tony Blair, and other Illuminati who maintain their humanlike appearance through regular rituals of human sacrifice and blood drinking. Very soon, however, the alien Chitauri will appear on earth in their true, hideous forms. According to Mutwa, an important feature of this global conspiracy of extraterrestrial domination of humanity can be found in Hollywood films.

Recent movies, beginning with *ET: The Extraterrestrial,* have been preparing humanity to accept the Chitauri and willingly submit to their authority. According to Mutwa, one *Star Wars* character, Darth Maul, "is exactly what the Chitauri look like," while *Stargate II* depicts "a slimy, cream-colored creature" that Mutwa finds is the "speaking likeness of Mobaba, emperor of the Chitauri." Discovering the Chitauri and their evil emperor appearing in Hollywood films, Mutwa demands: "Where do filmmakers get their information?"

On the one hand, Hollywood filmmakers appropriate ancient African traditions. For example, *Men in Black,* according to Mutwa, has appropriated indigenous African traditions about how to deal with aliens and how to dispose of extraterrestrial rubbish. Through these popular films, Mutwa complains, the authentic traditions of African "Men in Black" have been stolen and Westernized by Hollywood.

On the other hand, filmmakers draw their information directly from the Chitauri, or indirectly through the hybrid Illuminati, because Hollywood is working on behalf of their global conspiracy by familiarizing audiences with the strange appearance of the aliens. By suspending disbelief, Hollywood films are preparing audiences all over the world to accept their imminent subjugation to reptilian extraterrestrials.

GOING GLOBAL, COMING HOME

Although Credo Mutwa is an acknowledged expert on aliens from outer space, acknowledged not only by New Age conspiracy theorist David Icke but also by Harvard researcher John E. Mack, this feature of his indigenous Zulu wisdom is not mentioned by white Zulu *sangomas* such as James Hall and David M. Cumes, or by the "musical shaman" Ann Mortifee, who has been guided and inspired by Mutwa.[42] As we have seen, while Mutwa is going global, they are interested in coming home.

In developing a cultural and political analysis of Zulu popular music, Louise Meintjes has tracked mediations between the local and the global in which artists work in the studio on "performing Zuluness" while "imagining overseas."[43] Similarly, Mutwa has been situated in mediations between the local and the global by performing an indigenous Zulu vision of the world while looking overseas for a global audience. In the process, even if he displays a remarkable capacity for imaginative invention, Mutwa nevertheless suggests important features of a changing Zulu dreamscape.

During the nineteenth century, to tell a dream meant "to fetch" the dream, to go back to the place where the dream was originally experienced, its originating location, and carry it to the new place of telling. A dream, therefore, was portable, but it was situated in a specific landscape. It could be located and relocated, horizontally, within a terrain of human habitation. However, under colonial conditions of dispossession and dislocation, it became increasingly difficult "to fetch" dreams within an embattled terrain, and techniques for blocking dreams, including conversion to Christianity, were increasingly deployed. Credo Mutwa, I would like to suggest, has attempted to resolve this long-standing dilemma within the Zulu dreamscape by moving dreams, vertically, into the sky. The Zulu word *butongo,* which means "to sleep," according to Mutwa means "the state of being one with the star gods." The Zulu word *ipupo,* which means, "to dream," according to Mutwa means "to fly." As Mutwa explains, "The verb 'pupa' refers to flight, therefore to say 'I dreamt' means 'I flew.'"[44] These imaginative etymologies, whatever their validity, effectively shift the hermeneutics and energetics of Zulu dreaming from the land to the sky.

"We need to develop a relationship with the dream reality," urges Zulu *sangoma* David Cumes. As a white South African expatriate, Cumes dreamed of coming home to South Africa. His initiation as a *sangoma* enabled him to establish "connection with the native" and "connection with Africa." In his dream reality, these connections entailed a fundamental reorientation in South African space. Although black South Africans had suffered under a long history of colonialism and apartheid, Cumes now saw that whites in South Africa had also suffered. "Without our knowing it," he observes, "the apartheid system had discriminated against us too. As whites we had been forbidden access to another realm—we were not worthy and had been justifiably deprived. There were no signs to tell us, 'Whites not allowed,' but we were excluded all the same. We skirted around the authenticity of a magical continent thinking we were part of it when in fact we were not." Called by the ancestors to become a *sangoma*, Cumes was able to overcome the discrimination and alienation under which whites had suffered in South Africa. "Now the spirits had mandated and things had changed," he declared. "I was no longer underprivileged and would never be again."[45]

Clearly, this testimony evokes a reorientation that is not of the sky but of the land. Locally, within South Africa, Cumes advances the argument that apartheid disadvantaged white people by separating them from access to indigenous African spiritual traditions. Now, coming home, not as an observer but as a participant, he embraces the people and the land. Accordingly, Cumes represents his reorientation not as flying in the sky, expanding his global vision, but as making a tactile connection, being "blessed and touched by an unseen hand through a channel I did not even know."[46] Here also, media are evoked by the metaphor of the "channel," but the metaphor is used to describe an embodied reorientation established by a tactile connection with home.

In tracking Zulu dreamscapes, I have tried to show that dreams are not merely "subjective apparitions" or "brain-sensation." Nor are dreams only "texts" to be interpreted. Involved in an energetics of sacrificial exchange and spatial orientation, dreaming can be a religious practice, a practice that can be dramatically altered by the shifting social fields in which dreams are situated. In response to economic dispossession and social dislocation during the nineteenth century, Zulu dreamers increasingly turned to ritual techniques, which included conversion to Christianity, for blocking ancestral dreams, seeking to turn off this sensory medium. By contrast, contemporary neoshamanism cultivates a sensory extravagance, an overabundance of sensory engagements with things that are not there, from alien reptilians to ancestral spirits, that demand ritual response. Any apparitions that might appear, therefore, must be regarded as real and engaged accordingly.

Global in scope, this new Zulu dreamscape is saturated by media. Despite expressing occasional concerns that electronic media might block dreams and visions, neoshamans dwell in a mediated world, a world shaped by media technology, possibility, and authentication. As both dreamscape and mediascape, Zulu neoshamanism is emerging within a new energetics of global exchange and global orientation.

CHAPTER SEVEN

Purity

The Royal Reed Dance Festival, as advertised on a tourist website, promises a "vibrant celebration of Zululand's traditional culture and rich heritage." Convened once a year, in September, at the palace of the Zulu king, this festival draws thousands of Zulu participants, "more than 10,000 invited virgin girls," and, of course, tourists, who can witness the ceremony as part of a package that includes touring sugarcane fields, wildlife reserves, magnificent coastlines, and "undulating hills and valleys silently speaking to your soul with its natural beauty." Performed over four days, the Reed Dance enacts the ritual unity of a Zulu nation that is embodied in the ritual purity of young women. As the tourist site explains: "The royal reed dance festival in Zululand illustrates the proud heritage of the Zulu nation and plays a huge part in the unification of the nation's people and the king. To ensure ritual purity, only virgin girls are permitted to partake in the ceremony. There are many myths surrounding the festival, one is that if a girl is not pure her reed will break when presenting it to the King, publicly disgracing her and her community."[1]

Not to be missed in any tourist itinerary, this festival draws together themes that have also not been missed in cultural studies of invented traditions, ethno-tourism, and manufactured heritage. For a historian of religions, however, the evocation of myths and rituals is a different kind of invitation to visit this dance of traditional culture and rich heritage. Focusing on ritual, for example, we must notice how the emphasis on ritual purity, which is specifically cast as female virginity that is performatively demonstrated in a public display, is underwritten by a myth that national unity depends upon sexual purity. As a point of intersection between the most intimate personal subjectivity of young women and a broader social, political, and even national collectivity, this ritual display of the purity of ten thousand virgins is clearly overdetermined.

In this ritual of culture and heritage, multiple indigenous Zulu understandings of purity are layered. While maintaining purity in Zulu tradition involved a kind of ritual hygiene of purifying oneself *(ukuphothula)* by removing the effects of "black" medicines, associated with witchcraft, and applying purifying "white" medicines, achieving extraordinary purity, such as that of a novice diviner, required staying cool by avoiding the heat of sexuality.[2] As the anthropologist Axel-Ivar Berglund has documented, during training novice diviners not only abstained from sex but also avoided any contact with people who might be sexually active, maintaining ritual purity by starting their own fires and preparing their own food. "We fear the fire from other huts," one diviner revealed. "This fire has been near people who have been hot. This is bad. The fire is hot, like a man and a woman are hot, especially a woman, having the water (i.e., semen) inside." Like fire, food must be cool, untouched by anyone carrying the heat of sexual activity, because such "food is hot, like the people are hot." As a diviner explained to Berglund, "Especially a woman who is pregnant or who carries the thing (semen) inside the stomach is hot." To avoid contact with such heat, novices could eat only food prepared by themselves, by a small child, or by "an old woman who has no pleasure in these things any more."[3] Like novice diviners, therefore, virgins were cool because they avoided the heat of sexuality.

Virgins deployed symbolically served many political uses. In the Reed Dance, they served to illustrate the epitome of ritual purity in a royal ceremony of national unity. Adapting this theme, the Zulu Christian prophet Isaiah Shembe, who founded the Nazareth Baptist Church in 1910, deployed virgins to symbolize both the unity of his religious community and his power to secure a space for his followers under difficult conditions in segregationist South Africa. As the historian Carol Ann Muller has observed, for the Nazarites, young female virgins "became the heroines of ritual performances that celebrated the power of Isaiah [Shembe] over the state in the acquisition of land."[4] Like kings or prophets, therefore, virgins figured prominently in projects of state building or of community building in resistance to the state.

Medical, sexual, and political discourses of purity have intensified with the AIDS pandemic. In isiZulu, one synonym for AIDS is *idliso,* poisonous "pollution," a kind of "black" medicine associated with witchcraft.[5] While there is no "white" medicine that can cleanse this pollution (despite the claims of some traditional healers), ritual is thought to keep people cool from the heat of sexually transmitted disease. Like the Reed Dance Festival, new rituals of sexual purity, such as the practice of virginity testing, have focused on young women. Claiming to revive ancient Zulu tradition, virginity testing is a ritual in which elder women inspect younger women to determine their purity, designating them in three classes—A, B, C—as those who have never had sex, those who have had sex but are still virginal, and those who are no longer virgins.[6] Virginity testing has invoked tradition but has also involved the creation of new rituals, as in the case of one project that has revived the Zulu goddess or divine princess Nomkhubulwane as the divinity of female virginity.[7] Virginity testing has major political ramifications, not only in its sexual politics of community healing, social mobilization, and collective purity, but also in the opposition it has provoked among human rights advocates, who have invoked constitutional principles of individual freedom, equality, and dignity to propose legislation outlawing it.[8] While the conflict between tradition and constitution has generated its own heat, the politics of AIDS has been polluted by government policy driven by Thabo Mbeki, who during his presidency not only denied the scientific linkage between HIV and AIDS but also tried to shift the politics of engagement with the epidemic from medical discourse to anticolonial rhetoric against the history of Western racist stereotypes of the wild and barbaric sexuality of Africans.[9]

At the World Economic Forum in Davos in January 2010, South African president Jacob Zuma, who had recently married another wife in his polygamous household, was questioned about his marital arrangement. Noting that he treated all of his wives equally, Zuma vigorously defended the practice of polygamous marriage as the heritage of his Zulu culture.[10] A few days later, when the story broke that the president had fathered a child outside marriage with the daughter of a prominent figure in the South African soccer industry, Irvin Khoza, his official response defending this extramarital relationship and the birth of his child out of wedlock was also framed in terms of culture. Noting that on World AIDS Day he had called upon everyone to take personal responsibility for their actions, Zuma insisted that he had taken responsibility in the ways that the cultural norms, values, and traditions of the Zulu heritage required: "I have done the necessary cultural imperatives in a situation of this nature, for example the formal acknowledgement of paternity and responsibility, including the payment of *inhlawulo* [damages] to the family." Zuma claimed that because he had observed the ritual requirement of paying compensation after the fact through *inhlawulo,* even though he had not paid the conventional undertaking of *lobola* (bridewealth) before marriage, his actions were entirely in keeping with Zulu tradition. Therefore, he concluded that the "matter is now between the two of us [himself and the woman], and culturally, between the Zuma and Khoza families." Then, turning abruptly from culture talk to rights talk, he invoked the constitution of South Africa and child protection legislation to assert that media coverage of his recent extramarital relationship and his "love child" had violated the child's rights, "in essence questioning the right of the child to exist and fundamentally, her right to life."[11] Invoking both traditional culture and modern constitutionalism, Zuma called for an end to media attention to his sexual life inside or outside his polygamous marriage.[12]

During the Mbeki administration (1999–2008), Zuma, as deputy president of South Africa from 1999 to 2005, was responsible for directing the government's AIDS programs, which came to revolve around the formula "ABC—Abstinence, Be Faithful, and Condomise."[13] Zuma was also the head of the government's project in morality, the Moral Regeneration Movement, which sought to mobilize civil society to fight crime and corruption as if they were symptoms of personal immorality.[14]

After surviving high-profile court cases in which he was charged with raping an HIV-positive woman and taking bribes for political influence, Zuma was elected president of South Africa in 2009. Without pretending to adjudicate these cases, I want to reflect back on a long history of discourses of sexual purity—indigenous, missionary, and anthropological—that might provide a deep background for gaining perspective on current crises of personal sexuality and political legitimacy in South Africa. In the work of Christian missionaries, we find an opposition between African ancestral tradition and the Christian gospel, which defined sexual purity in terms of a rejection of traditional gendered and sexual practices such as polygamous marriage, the payment of *lobola,* and the participation in male or female initiations in favor of a Christian regime of monogamous marriage. However, the discipline of social anthropology that emerged in South Africa during the 1930s produced a different analysis of the problem of sexual purity. According to its claims, the problems of sexual immorality, the increase in illegitimate births, and the breakdown in ritual purity that Africans were experiencing had been produced by economic and social changes resulting from their contact with Europeans, and often by interventions of the Christian missionaries themselves. Reviewing these missionary and anthropological discourses of sexual purity, I will conclude with some observations about their enduring consequences in contemporary rituals of purity in South Africa, with special reference to the dilemmas posed by South African president Jacob Zuma.

CHRISTIAN MISSIONARY CONSTRUCTIONS OF PURITY

In the early nineteenth century, Christian missionaries of the London Missionary Society, the Wesleyan Methodist Missionary Society, and other missionary agencies entered South Africa looking for that "triangle of vices" that Europeans had a long tradition of demonizing—"cannibalism, idolatry, sexual excess."[15] While many missionaries were convinced that they had found evidence of cannibals, they often expressed disappointment that they could not find any idolaters. Robert Moffat, for example, complained that he found no idols, altars, or "unknown god" among the people of southern Africa. Exposing the persistence and vitality of a Christian demonology in his imagination of indigenous people, Moffat contrasted the aberrant religion of other nations to the absence of religion in southern Africa. "While Satan is obviously the author of the polytheism of other nations," Moffat observed, "he has employed his agency, with fatal success, in erasing every religious impression from the minds of the Bechuanas, Hottentots, and Bushmen."[16] The discovery by missionaries that there was no religion in the region, constantly repeated during the first half of the nineteenth century, was duplicated by the discovery that there was no marriage among the people of southern Africa. African marriage, like African religion, was perceived not as aberrant but as absent altogether.

The Wesleyan missionary Samuel Broadbent was insistent on this point: "*They have no marriage,*" he announced, with emphasis, "nor any proper domestic order, nor acknowledge any moral obligation to the duties arising out of that relation." In one respect, according to this missionary account, Africans had no illegitimacy problem because they had no institution of marriage against which certain births could register as deviations. In another, more profound respect, however, Africans had an illegitimacy problem of monumental proportions because their whole domestic order, the entire fabric of interpersonal relations that made up the life of a homestead, was placed under the censure of religious denial. Likewise, as in the case of religion, many missionaries initially assumed that they would be able simply, easily to insert Christian marriage into this African cultural vacuum. As Broadbent triumphantly concluded, with the arrival of Christian missionaries, "the Divine institution has been introduced."[17]

By the 1850s, however, Christian missionaries were no longer able to entertain the conceit that Africans had no religion. Rather, they realized that they were engaged in a contest of religions. Similarly, they realized that with respect to marriage they were entering a contested domestic terrain. Christianity would come to define itself less as a gospel of sin and salvation than as a series of interventions into African marital, sexual, and gender relations that all had to be changed "root and branch."[18] In fact, Christian missions took their particular shape during the second half of the nineteenth century precisely in terms of the African practices they opposed. As the historian Donovan Williams has observed, "Polygyny, bride-price, marriage ceremonies, *intonjane* [female initiation] and circumcision [male initiation] were condemned and attacked by the missionaries with a patent dogmatism rooted in the early Victorian morality of the Evangelical Revival as well as from the standpoint of the superiority of Western European civilization."[19] Opposition to African practices was, however, more than merely symptomatic of Victorian morality, evangelical enthusiasm, and European chauvinism. The Christian missionaries in South Africa defined their gospel locally as a sexual purity in opposition to what they perceived as the deviant sexuality of Africans.

In working to change African marital, sexual, and gender relations, Christian missionaries celebrated a Protestant "cult of domesticity" that ritualized the roles of men, women, and children in a Christian family. It has often been noted that this nineteenth-century Protestant connection between religion and the home continued into the twentieth century to define a separate, subordinate sphere of Christian women that was confined to the household and excluded from the larger society.[20] But the cult of domesticity also inspired missionary innovations in the field of sexuality. In the early twentieth century, Protestant churches pursued two basic projects—women's hostels and women's prayer unions—to reinforce ritualized gender and sexual roles, particularly in new urban environments, among black Christian women.

In 1912 the General Missionary Conference, in a report entitled "Native Girls in Town," stressed the importance of "the establishment of Homes under the management of Christian ladies, assisted by Christian Native women, where Native girls may be received and cared for."[21] The Anglicans, Methodists, and American Board Mission each established Christian hostels for girls in Johannesburg, but similar institutions appeared in other major cities as well. Like the mining compounds for men, these hostels tried to create a closed, supervised environment, even though their accommodation and recreational facilities were voluntary. The purpose of the hostels was twofold: promoting Christian purity and advancing Christian domestic education. Purity was defined explicitly as sexual chastity and enforced through supervision, spiritual teaching, and healthy recreation. This objective of sexual purity was consistent with the goals of other women's church movements of the period, such as the Purity League formed in the 1920s in Natal, which tried to teach girls how to "live clean lives."[22] The other purpose of the Christian hostels was domestic education, which not only trained girls for female roles as wives and mothers but also prepared them for employment as domestic servants in white homes.

The first women's prayer unions developed out of the practice of regular devotional meetings held by missionary women or ministers' wives with "uneducated" African churchwomen. Sometimes those meetings combined prayer with sewing classes, since being "dressed" or "clothed" was an important outward sign of Christian conversion. In the early twentieth century, more formal prayer unions, often known as *manyano*, evolved as large-scale women's organizations. Anglican, Methodist, and Congregational American Board prayer unions expanded throughout the country. From the perspective of missionary supervisors, the prayer unions were useful organizations for promoting female chastity, marital fidelity, and domestic responsibilities among black Christian women.[23] The Anglican women's prayer union, the Women's Help Society, which was linked with the Mothers' Union, was founded in 1908 for the purpose of developing regular devotional habits and a Christian standard of life based on "purity and self-respect." The Congregationalist American Board women's movement, Isililo, which derived its name from a Zulu term for the ritualized wailing of grief, was founded in Natal in 1912 and expanded into the Johannesburg area in the early 1920s.[24] As in the Methodist *manyano*, the white supervisors of these women's prayer movements focused on a cult of domesticity and particularly stressed the responsibility of mothers for maintaining the sexual purity of their adolescent daughters. For many black Christian women, this emphasis did, in fact, address the central tension of their lives—the breakdown of family life under conditions of industrialization, migrant labor, and rural and urban poverty.[25]

In spite of, or perhaps because of, all this Christian concern for sexual purity, the problem of illegitimacy emerged as a crucial issue for the twentieth-century mission. The problem in its modern form was foreshadowed in the 1870s when the first-generation converts of the Edendale mission in Natal complained about the independence of their children. Although raised under the regime of the Protestant cult of domesticity, it was said, they "indulge in promiscuous intercourse and they resent all interference with their actions from those who by law have full control over them."[26] This link between Christianity and sexual promiscuity was also a recurring theme within indigenous African responses to the Christian mission. The Christian ritual of prayer, for example, was interpreted by adherents of ancestral Zulu religion as an impure act, since Christians were described as those who *dunuza'd*, who knelt and raised their anuses in the air, an obscene gesture of disrespect, but also a term for sodomy.[27] According to Zulu traditionalists, becoming a Christian, which required dressing in European clothing, led young women directly into prostitution to earn money to buy their dresses.[28] Christianity, from this perspective, led to a breakdown in generational authority, ritual continuity, and sexual purity.

Here, of course, was a profound irony: the Christian cult of domesticity, with its commitment to sexual purity, seems to have resulted unintentionally in increased sexual promiscuity. Apparently, this irony was lost on twentieth-century missionaries who took advantage of parental and public distress over the apparent breakdown in moral order to reinforce the authority of a Christian gospel of sexual purity. At the Natal American Board Mission's Native Annual Meeting in 1912, "many people were moved to tears over the matter of low morals among the youth during those days. Young girls were getting pregnant before marriage while living at their parents' homes."[29] Into the 1930s,

Christian missionaries continued to proclaim a gospel of sexual purity, or sexual hygiene, in a ceaseless battle against sexual promiscuity. The Christian holy war against sexual pollution was endless because the more the missionaries preached, gained converts, and established institutional controls over sexuality, the greater the problem of illegitimacy in South Africa became.

MODERN ANTHROPOLOGICAL CONSTRUCTIONS OF PURITY

Although this irony was ignored by missionaries, it was central to the emergence of the academic discipline of social anthropology in the 1930s. Turning the study of kinship into a science, researchers paid a remarkable amount of attention to illegitimacy, discovering that it was widespread among Tswana-speaking Kgatla, increasing among the Zulu, and escalating out of control among all Africans living in the "native locations" around Pretoria. This first generation of South African social anthropologists asserted what may be described (at the risk of oversimplifying their findings) as two basic premises for a social analysis of illegitimacy. First, illegitimacy was not a traditional problem. In dramatic counterpoint to the early nineteenth-century denials by missionaries, these researchers asserted not only that Africans had the institution of marriage but that traditional African marriages had what might be called a structural-functional legitimacy because they worked. Within traditional African societies, stable marriage relations were sustained by indigenous ritual, ethics, law, and social sanctions. The occurrence of illegitimate births was thereby minimized. When they did occur, they were easily accommodated in ways that restored and maintained a social equilibrium.[30]

Second, although not a traditional problem, illegitimacy was very much a modern problem in southern Africa. By asserting this premise, social anthropologists seemed to be making common cause with Christian missionaries, social workers, and social reformers.[31] However, rather than preaching a gospel of sexual hygiene directly, anthropologists sought explanations that, ironically, identified the cause of the problem of illegitimacy as the very process of Westernization, modernization, and even religious conversion with which the Christian missions were intimately engaged. Max Gluckman found that the dramatic increase in illegitimacy among Zulus in Natal was the direct result of the corrosive effects of Westernization.[32] Isaac Schapera and Eileen Krige went even further in identifying illegitimacy as the critical symptom of a total social disintegration that could be attributed to a single cause: contact with Europeans. Speaking on behalf of the Kgatla, Schapera stated that "the disintegration of the old morality is due to the effects of contact with Europeans."[33] And speaking for Africans living in locations around Pretoria, Krige declared that "contact with the European is causing change and disturbance, institutional dislocation and disintegration."[34] Their analysis of religion, cultural contact, and illegitimacy bears closer examination.

Schapera began his analysis by invoking the scientific authority of the pioneering ethnographer and anthropological theorist Bronislaw Malinowski, citing his "principle of legitimacy"—that in all human societies a woman must be married to legitimately conceive a child—as if it were a universal rule of kinship. Arguing that this principle did not reflect a European or Christian prejudice, Malinowski had insisted that in all societies, even the barbarous and savage, an "unmarried mother is under a ban, a fatherless child is a bastard."[35] Accepting this definition of legitimacy as a constant for purposes of comparison, Schapera reported that illegitimacy was practically unknown in traditional Kgatla society. Marriages were stable, enduring arrangements between families, certified by marriage payments that transferred the reproductive power of a woman to her husband's family, and reinforced by social sanctions against premarital pregnancy, such as the "mocking songs" that heaped public shame upon unmarried pregnant women. Accordingly, Schapera could conclude that illegitimacy was not a traditional problem. But he observed that in the 1930s "there is little doubt that the proportion of premarital births throughout the tribe may be considered exceedingly high."[36]

How did Schapera account for this "general moral decay"? He recognized the disruptive effects of economic forces that had drawn men and women into new urban environments and labor relations. Absence of men, surplus of women, and the absorption of new urban values, including the emergence of a "class of flappers" among young women, all contributed to the increase in illegitimacy. More prominent among its causes, however, were the unexpected consequences of the religious interventions in traditional culture made by Christian missions. The missionaries had attacked, and largely succeeded in destroying, by Schapera's account, three institutions that had performed important social functions in preventing illegitimacy—initiation, polygyny, and the mocking songs. The breakdown of traditional initiation, with its emphasis on sexual purity, had broken the "intimate connection between initiation and the sexual life of the adolescent children, and as a result parental control has gradually grown weaker." After the missionaries prohibited polygyny, with the complicity of a tax system that made it prohibitively expensive, both Christians and non-Christians had adopted an arrangement of concubinage that was illegitimate by definition. Finally, because they regarded the mocking songs as obscene, the missionaries had succeeded in eliminating them. "The early missionaries," Schapera reported, "are also said to have been responsible for the disappearance of the dreaded songs of mockery, which in the olden days were the most powerful sanction against premarital pregnancy." In support of this claim, Schapera invoked an informant: "The only thing which they have to fear now is [the Christian] religion, and that is not so severe as the curses which they used to fear formerly." In his own voice, Schapera concluded, "The censure of the Church is a far less effective sanction than these songs used to be."[37]

Three years later, Eileen Krige published an article that added statistical support to Schapera's general argument that a rise in illegitimacy could be attributed to "contact with the European." Again and again Krige repeated the word *disintegration*, intoning a dire warning of total social dissolution that could be measured by illegitimacy rates. Reflecting on her fieldwork in three native locations around Pretoria, she observed, "One of the most striking symptoms of social disintegration and economic disorder is the fact that practically every girl has one or more children before marriage."[38] In 1933–34, the illegitimacy rate in those locations had been 40 percent; in 1934–35, it rose to 59 percent. To make these statistics meaningful, Krige compared them with findings from two control groups: a 3 percent illegitimacy rate among Europeans living in Pretoria during the same period and, more tellingly for her analysis, "the practical absence of illegitimacy in primitive tribal conditions." By either comparison she could point to evidence of "an advanced state of disintegration."[39] Like Schapera, Krige found her most salient comparison in the opposition between the traditional and the modern. In traditional African societies, social sanctions limited the occurrence of illegitimate pregnancies, while social stability allowed those that occurred to be accommodated in the mother's extended household. Even living in a modern location, Africans could remain in contact with a native reserve, that "reservoir of tradition," and thereby maintain some of the traditional ethos evident in the willingness of unmarried mothers' relatives to take in an illegitimate child. "Illegitimate children thus always find homes," Krige observed, "and the growing increase in illegitimacy accompanying the breakdown of some of the old institutions is being palliated by other Bantu values which are stepping into the breach."[40]

The breach between traditional and modern values, however, had been opened by the Christian missions. In Krige's fieldwork locations, three marriage options—by *lobola,* by church, and/or by civil marriage—were exercised by residents. For Christians, particularly those who were also committed to the traditional bridewealth payment of *lobola,* church or civil marriages, with their attendant license fees and customary feasts, added expenses that often led to the postponement of marriage. Between 1930 and 1934, Krige noted, the average age of marriage in the locations was thirty for men and twenty-five for women. Invoking a commonplace in the sociological analysis of illegitimacy, Krige suggested that the later the average age at marriage in a population, the higher the rate of illegitimate births.

Ironically, by unexpected consequence, the church had contributed to the increase in illegitimacy rates. Furthermore, in its response to illegitimate births, the church proved to be an inadequate substitute for what had been more effective traditional sanctions. In Krige's fieldwork locations, unmarried mothers were required by the mission churches to attend a six-month purification class. However, according to Krige, women perceived this period of purification, not as punishment in atonement for their sins, but as a ritual preparation preceding the baptism of their children. In failing to sanction illegitimacy, the church's purification class was represented by Krige as an empty, socially dysfunctional ritual that had displaced more effective traditional sanctions and had thereby significantly contributed to the increase in illegitimacy rates. Christian missions and churches, therefore, in Krige's analysis, had played a significant role in the destruction brought about by cultural contact between Europeans and Africans, and it was precisely such contact that was "creating havoc in Bantu domestic institutions."[41]

At least three conclusions about the analysis of illegitimacy can be drawn from the work of Schapera, Krige, and other social anthropologists in the 1930s. First, the social anthropologists identified the central irony of the Christian mission of sexual purity. European Christian missions might have introduced what Samuel Broadbent called the "Divine institution" of marriage, but they were caught up in the unexpected consequences of a "moral decay" or "social disintegration" that was at least partly a disaster of their own creation. Certainly, Christian moralists and social reformers of the 1930s could draw little comfort from this insight, so for the most part they simply ignored it. Nevertheless, research on illegitimacy contained an implicit indictment of the missionary project and its counterproductive interventions in African marital and sexual relations. The findings of socio-scientific research implied that African sexual relations were more legitimate, at least in the sense of functional legitimacy, before contact with Europeans and their Christian missions.

Second, if we forget for a moment that they were social scientists, the social anthropologists we have considered sound like conservative social critics, especially when they seem to express a nostalgia for the olden days, for a lost traditional past with its supposed stability, equilibrium, and inherent legitimacy. Although it may be unfair to draw these comparisons, Isaac Schapera sounds a lot like the elders of Edendale, complaining that young people no longer respected parental authority, while Eileen Krige, in her recurring complaint about social disintegration, echoes the idiom of a conservative jeremiad. Despite their progressive intentions, therefore, these cultural analysts, like the Christian missionaries, had to endure the unexpected consequences of their work as reactionary social, political, and economic agents in South Africa appropriated their discourse about traditional marriage and sexuality to serve their own ends.

A striking example of the unexpected consequences of anthropological discourse on traditional sex and marriage is provided by the case of H. P. Junod, son of the southern African missionary-ethnographer Henri-Alexandre Junod. In 1936 and 1937 the younger Junod, sponsored by the Chamber of Mines, gave a series of lectures on the "Bantu Heritage" to mining officials and compound managers. In 1938, these lectures were published as a book, complete with a preface by mining industry spokesman William Gemmill, who recommended the book because it explained "the races whose work makes European life in South Africa, as we know it, possible." Although Junod covered many topics, probably what he had to say about the sex life of the Bantu was most relevant to the interests of the mining industry. Unlike other human beings, a black migrant worker on the mines, Junod claimed, was perfectly suited to have sexual relations with his wife once a year when he returned home to his family in the reserves, because his "sexual life is more seasonal, more natural, than other people." In other words, according to Junod, the Bantu had a unique sexuality, more animal than human, that was perfectly suited to migrant labor, the single-sex hostel, and the closed compound. In this respect, black South Africans were supposedly unlike any other humans. "One only needs to remember the 330 000 Bantu men working on the mines, most of them segregated in compounds," Junod concluded, "to visualize what the conditions would be from a sexual point of view if they belonged to other races."[42] Others might present a problem, but black mine workers were supposedly suited to those subhuman conditions. In the 1940s, William Gemmill, echoed by his son James in the 1960s, repeated this anthropological account of traditional African sexual and marital life to justify the migrant labor and compound systems that continued to serve the interests of the mining industry.[43]

Third, it is impossible not to notice in the work of Schapera, Krige, and others who followed a similar line in the study of illegitimacy that the problem they had identified for analysis involved two kinds of illicit human contact: that between men and women and that between Africans and Europeans. In spite of their best intentions, which included opposition to legislated racial segregation, the second type of contact displaced the first in their analysis. If illegitimacy, as a symptom of moral decay and social disintegration, was caused by "contact with Europeans," might not some readers understandably be led to assume that illegitimacy could be prevented by prohibiting such social or cultural contact? During the 1930s and 1940s, precisely such a reading of the situation was made by the ideologues and architects of apartheid. A prominent and influential proponent of institutionalized racial separation such as Geoffrey Cronjé—social scientist, social reformer, and, as J.M. Coetzee has demonstrated, epitome of the sexual "mind of apartheid"—was obsessed, very likely to the point of madness, with the question of illegitimacy. In his 1945 text, *'n Tuiste vir die Nageslag (A Home for Posterity)*, Cronjé was obsessed with "blood purity," simultaneously sexual and racial purity, which had to be protected against any mixing. As Cronjé urged, protection of purity required legislative measures of population control, demanding all the institutionalized structures of social separation and strategies of social engineering that came to be known as apartheid.[44] Certainly, the social anthropologists we have considered had no intention of feeding Cronjé's madness or supporting the apartheid project. Yet, arguably, unintentionally, they did. In their implicit indictment of the cultural mixtures introduced by missionaries, their apparent nostalgia for a pristine tradition, and their explanatory reduction of sexual and reproductive illegitimacy to the effects of contact between Africans and Europeans, these social anthropologists contributed research findings that could be appropriated by apartheid ideologues in fashioning a new regime of sexual purity in South Africa under apartheid.

CONTEMPORARY INTERSECTIONS OF INDIGENOUS, CHRISTIAN, AND MODERN PURITY

While the annual ritual of the Royal Reed Dance puts the sexual purity of ten thousand virgins on display every year, during 2010 the media put the sexual impropriety of President Jacob Zuma on display. Newspaper columns and cartoons throughout Africa called attention to the irony inherent in Zuma's proud adherence to the legitimacy of traditional polygamy even as he engaged in extramarital relations and fathered children outside his marriage. In his defense, President Zuma invoked his Zulu cultural heritage, the same heritage celebrated in the Reed Dance, by insisting that he was maintaining traditional propriety in paying the customary compensation of *inhlawulo* to the family of the mother of his illegitimate child. Accordingly, he insisted, the matter had been settled "culturally," and his extramarital relationship and illegitimate child should no longer be a matter of public discussion in the media. On this point, the president was supported in South Africa by a representative of the Kara Heritage Institute, an organization dedicated to the recovery and revitalization of African tradition, who asserted that Zuma's actions were entirely in keeping with African tradition. As Moses Twala explained, "It is normal for a man in our culture to be married but have children outside of his marriage." On the basis of this understanding of African culture, Zuma was acting in ways that were consistent with the pure heritage of African tradition. Addressing the media, Twala attacked the press for paying attention to the sex life of the president. He insisted that the media were violating African tradition by publicly displaying sexual matters that should remain within the private sphere. "It is un-African to discuss private matters publicly," Twala explained, adding that he suspected ulterior political motives in this public attention to President Zuma's private sex life and that it made him "question what purpose this serves except to degrade someone."[45] Sexual purity, in this construction of indigenous tradition, was based on a shared African culture that distinguished between public and private spheres, understood normal sexuality to include fathering children outside marriage, and was committed to sexual privacy.

This particular recovery and revitalization of African tradition by a spokesperson for the Kara Heritage Institute was curious on two counts. First, by normalizing the production of illegitimate children within indigenous African culture, Twala contradicted the arguments advanced by the South African anthropologists of the 1930s that African cultural, religious, and ritual sanctions had ensured "the practical absence of illegitimacy in primitive tribal conditions."[46] More recently, historians have recognized the prevalence in precolonial African societies of conventional practices of "thigh-sex" (in isiZulu, *hlobonga*). In precolonial Zulu sexuality, as the historian Jeff Guy has noted, "Non-reproductive sexual relations took place comparatively freely between unmarried adults."[47] Reproduction, however, was deeply embedded in ritual relations linking ancestors, extended families, and households. Accordingly, it is strange to hear a representative of African heritage insisting that producing children outside the ritual sanctity of marriage was normal in African tradition.

Second, by invoking the principle of privacy as an essentially African value, Twala contradicted the understanding of ancestral tradition consistently asserted by nineteenth-century Zulu opponents of the private rituals performed by Christians. As the Zulu Christian convert Mpengula Mbande related in the 1860s, his own private ritual of personal prayer alienated him from his community to such an extent that people threatened him and beat him in trying to get him to stop performing it.[48] To engage in solitary, private prayer, Mbande had to separate himself from the community, hide from their scrutiny, and avoid their sanctions. In ritual, therefore, privacy was not essentially African. Hence we find African traditionalists describing Christian prayer as an antisocial act equivalent to an obscene gesture of disrespect or the sexual impurity associated with sodomy.[49] Against this background, therefore, it is strange to find privacy invoked as African tradition.

Tradition, of course, is not what it used to be. In the case of the Kara Heritage Institute, for example, African indigenous religion must be traced back to its origin in ancient Egypt. Drawing on Egyptian mythology, Hermetic mysteries, theosophy, and astrology, the understanding of African religious heritage developed by the Kara Heritage Institute begins with the unknowable One, who produced a family of gods, the Neteru, which can be found in both ancient Egyptian and African indigenous religion. From the gods, according to Kara, come divine kings. In African tradition, divine kingship was central, a power ordained by the gods to ensure purity. As Africans, recovering and revitalizing African tradition, people must observe the annual cycle of seasonal ceremonies, perform regular ritual sacrifices for purification, and restore African sacred kingship to maintain their connection with this pure heritage.[50]

The founder and director of the Kara Heritage Institute, Mathole Motshekga, has been a prominent figure in the ruling party of South Africa, the African National Congress, serving as premier of the Gauteng Province under the Mbeki administration and as chief whip of the ANC in Parliament under the Zuma administration. Surviving his own ordeal with allegations of corruption, Motshekga has continued in his dual role as a political actor within the ANC and as a religious advocate for recovering the purity of African heritage, with its roots in ancient Egypt, and for performing rituals of purification such as the ceremonial sacrifice of a bull that he officiated at a train station in Cape Town in 2007 to protect people from accidents.[51] This sacrificial ritual was "a cleansing ceremony with a difference," as the press reported, because it included participants from all races, classes, and religious affiliations.[52] African indigenous religious tradition, therefore, could be recast as something as ancient as Egypt and as modern as religious pluralism in a democratic society.

As a traditionalist, Jacob Zuma could draw support from the recovery and revitalization of African tradition undertaken by the Kara Heritage Institute. According to Twala, his behavior was normal, consistent with tradition, although his normal behavior might also be understood as a supernormal prerogative of what Mathole Motshekga has identified as the indigenous African tradition of divine kingship. In any case, Zuma had to negotiate his sexual purity at the intersection between constructions of African tradition and insertions of Christian missions. As we have seen, nineteenth-century Christian missionaries, such as Broadbent, insisted that they were inserting the "Divine institution" of marriage into a cultural vacuum. This mission has continued into the present as conservative Christian groupings in South Africa, informed by developments in the New Religious Right within the United States, have defined the Christian gospel as a sexual politics in opposition to practices of extramarital sex, homosexual relations, and reproductive choices such as abortion. In an interview in 2006, Zuma declared his Christian commitment. "I start from basic Christian principles," he said. "Christianity is part of what I am; in a way it was the foundation for all my political beliefs."[53] As Zuma's Christian politics developed, he invested his political movement, the ANC, with apocalyptic Christian significance by observing, repeatedly, that the ANC would rule South Africa until Jesus returned. On behalf of the ANC at an election rally in 2008, Zuma declared: "God expects us to rule this country because we are the only organization which was blessed by pastors when it was formed. It is even blessed in Heaven. That is why we will rule until Jesus comes back."[54]

Translating his apocalyptic promise into the present and courting the Christian vote, Zuma asserted that "church leaders should be able to tell government leaders if they are straying and their laws clash with the teachings of the Lord."[55] In his campaign for presidential election, Zuma took aim at supposedly anti-Christian laws, such as those affirming the human right to sexual orientation explicitly ensured by the South African Constitution. Zuma's aversion to homosexuality was already on record. In 2006 he gave a speech in which he invoked Zulu tradition against homosexuality. "When I was growing up," Zuma recounted, remembering his traditional Zulu upbringing, "an *ungqingili* [a homosexual] could not stand in front of me, I would knock him down." Moving from Zulu tradition to Christian sexual politics, Zuma concluded in that speech that "same sex marriage is a disgrace to the nation and to God."[56] Sexual purity, therefore, was an important aspect of Zuma's political appeal to Christian conservatives who focused on the personal, arguably private, politics of sexual orientation, same-sex marriage, and reproductive choices. Although all of these rights were guaranteed by the South African Constitution, Zuma often spoke to religious constituencies, whether traditionalist or Christian, as if he had no regard for the rights enshrined there. When he achieved the presidency in 2009, he quickly formed a new National Interfaith Leaders Council, led by the charismatic Christian pastor Ray McCauley and supported by the Africanist Mathole Motshekga, to replace the National Religious Leaders Forum under the Mbeki administration, which had been dedicated to promoting interreligious dialogue, understanding, toleration, and respect. In this new council, religious leaders were urged to support government in delivering services but also to challenge government when it went against what Zuma had called "the teachings of the Lord."[57]

In his response to the media reports about his own extramarital relations and illegitimate children, Zuma did not invoke Christianity. He never referred to the teachings of the Lord, although the new National Interfaith Leaders Council did issue a statement asserting that "those of us who profess to be Christian or pious" should forgive President Zuma for having an affair and fathering a child outside wedlock.[58] Instead, he relied upon ancestral tradition and modern constitutionalism. Public attention to his sexual life, he argued, violated both the primordial imperatives of cultural tradition and the modern mandates of constitutional rights, including the right to life, which should protect the dignity of his illegitimate child. Sexual purity, under these conditions, was negotiated at the intersection of indigenous African tradition and modern constitutionalism, although Christian missionary constructions of the "cult of domesticity" certainly lingered in the background. These different renderings of sexuality, all layered in South African history, were subject to new interpretations as they became mixed up in contemporary South African politics.

Songs of mockery, as the anthropologist Isaac Schapera argued, were the most powerful ritual media for enforcing sexual purity within traditional African societies. Certainly, Zuma's sexuality has been subjected to the mockery of South Africa's most prominent editorial cartoonist, Jonathan Shapiro—Zapiro—who began depicting Zuma with a showerhead affixed to his head when Zuma testified during his 2006 rape trial that after having sex with an HIV-positive woman he had taken a shower to "minimize the risk of contracting the disease."[59] During the honeymoon period following Zuma's election to the presidency, Zapiro removed the showerhead, depicting it only as hovering above President Zuma's head, but with the revelations of further extramarital relations and the birth of an illegitimate child, which further escalated to reports about the birth of many children outside his polygamous marriage, Zapiro replaced the showerhead firmly on Zuma's head. This cartoon mockery, of course, did not have the force of the ritualized mocking songs of indigenous tradition to act as a deterrent to extramarital sexual activity and illegitimate births. But neither did African tradition, at least as it was reconstructed by Moses Twala of the Kara Heritage Institute, who insisted that extramarital sex and reproduction were not sanctioned but permitted by indigenous African tradition. In these exchanges, we see the politicization of sexuality and the retraditionalizing of the postcolony, but we also see a struggle between rituals of purity, whether constructed in indigenous, Christian, or modern terms, and rituals of power at the intersection of traditional sovereignty and modern democracy.

CHAPTER EIGHT

Power

On November 3, 2009, kings and queens from all over Africa came to Pretoria, South Africa, for the launch of a new Institute of African Royalty, which was described by the organizers as a royal "think-tank on democracy and development," but also as a public relations initiative to improve the image of traditional leadership in Africa. Drawing upon the iconic power of the first elected president of a democratic South Africa, the institute proclaimed President Nelson Mandela as its model for African leadership. African kings and queens who gathered for the event included King Tchiffi Zie Jean Gervais of Ivory Coast, who was permanent general secretary of the African Traditional Leaders Forum, and Queen Nana Ama Amissah III from Ghana, who observed in a keynote speech, "For every successful king, there is a successful queen." South African royalty was represented by Joyce Mogale-Lefakane, granddaughter of a former king; Prince Xhanti Sigcawu from the Eastern Cape; and Patekile Holomisa, president of the Congress of Traditional Leaders of South Africa (Contrelesa), who praised Nelson Mandela as the great reconciler between modernists and traditionalists.[1]

The launch of the Institute of African Royalty occurred during a time of particular tension for South African royalty. In the Eastern Cape, King Buyelekhaya Dalindyebo of the Thembu, who according to tradition included among his subjects Nelson Mandela, was on trial for charges of arson, kidnapping, culpable homicide, and assault with intent to do grievous bodily harm, all arising from acts of violence against his subjects in the early 1990s. When he was convicted of these charges and sentenced to fifteen years in prison in December 2009, King Dalindyebo rejected the legitimacy of the South African democratic state and its judiciary by declaring that his Thembu Kingdom would secede from the Republic of South Africa. Insisting that his ten million subjects would follow him, the king invoked historical legacy to claim a vast expanse of South African territory that included all of the Eastern, Western, and Northern Cape, all of KwaZulu Natal, and parts of the Free State and Gauteng Province as his kingdom's "pre-colonial boundaries." He also demanded financial compensation of R900 million for the insult to his royal person caused by the court case and another R80 billion for the damages suffered by his people through the dispossession of their ancestral territory. According to his representative, the lawyer Votani Majola, the followers of the king were gathering in a mountain retreat to commune with their ancestors, drawing upon traditional power, authority, and legitimacy in their campaign, while ritually desecrating modern symbols of political legitimacy—the national flag of South Africa, their African National Congress (ANC) membership cards—by burning them and scattering their ashes in a river.[2] These ritual acts of invoking spiritual ancestors and desecrating political symbols seemed to mark a break between these Thembu traditionalists and the modernists of the democratic polity in South Africa. With the Thembu Kingdom declaring independence on January 14, 2010, how could these competing claims to political sovereignty be reconciled?

In his groundbreaking research on Yoruba traditions of divine kingship in Nigeria, the historian of religions Jacob Olupona has been helping us understand the relations between tradition and modernity in Africa. With meticulous attention to the myths and rituals of sacred sovereignty in ancestral traditions, Olupona has situated those traditional religious resources within the changing social conditions of modern urbanization, democratization, and religious diversity. For example, attending to the rituals of divine kingship in one city, Osogbo, Nigeria, Olupona records the sacred narratives, songs, poetry, and ritual procedures that reinforce the ongoing connection between people and the spiritual realm that is mediated by the divine king. Sacred kingship, in this regard, is a regular reinforcement of a sense of community, what Gerald Larson has called "community-ship," by contrast to formal citizenship in the city.[3] At the same time, however, citizenship has been transforming sacred kingship into a kind of civil religion. Although the notion of civil religion in Nigeria has been the focus of academic debate, Olupona makes a strong case that divine kingship has become an institution that fulfills a dual function in anchoring indigenous religious spirits in the city and affirming the city, which is 70 percent Muslim, as a viable civic space for religious diversity. As Olupona noted in 2001, the then-current divine king, responsible for presiding over the annual ancestral ritual of sacred kingship, was a devout Muslim and a chartered accountant, thereby embodying all of the elements of a hybrid civil religion based on ancestral heritage, religious diversity, and urban modernity.[4] Following Olupona's insights into the changing character of divine kingship in Nigeria, I want to examine how kingship in South Africa is operating in a changing political environment.

Against the background of European conquest, colonization, and imposition of indirect rule, which was formalized in the traditional leadership of the Bantustans that were created under apartheid, the institutions of traditional leadership were thoroughly compromised.[5] How can their integrity be recovered? In contemporary South Africa, the leading advocate for recovering the integrity of indigenous African traditions of identity, culture, and religion is Mathole Motshekga. Born into a family within the ethnic group of the Lobedu, the realm of Modjadji, the Rain Queen, Motshekga became a lawyer, with law degrees from the University of South Africa and Harvard University. In the early 1980s, while on a fellowship in Germany, he began studying the esoteric traditions of Hermeticism. These traditions celebrate the primordial wisdom of ancient Egyptian mythology as derived from Neoplatonic texts of late Greco-Roman antiquity, attributed to Hermes Trismegistus, a conflation of the Egyptian god Thoth with the Greek god Hermes; the ideas they contain were filtered through a long history of European Neoplatonism, Rosicrucianism, Freemasonry, and Theosophy. Subsequently, Motshekga must have been influenced by developments in Afrocentric philosophy, pioneered by Cheikh Anta Diop and extended by Molefi Kete Asante, which also took ancient Egypt as their starting point.[6] Founding the Kara Heritage Institute to advance the recovery of African spirituality, culture, and history, Motshekga returned to South Africa to participate in the politics of an emerging democracy and a contested tradition. While he has pursued a political career that resulted in his election as premier of Gauteng Province for eighteen months during 1998 and 1999, and since 2009 has served as chief whip of the governing party, the ANC, in Parliament, Motshekga has also served as legal advisor to the Royal Council of the Rain Queen. Positioning himself between modern politics and traditional royalty, he has continued as director of the Kara Heritage Institute, a registered nongovernmental organization, to advance his Hermetic and Afrocentric understanding of the indigenous African religious tradition that he promotes as the shared heritage of all southern Africans.

The name "Kara," which Motshekga translates as "Light" or "Divine Light," seems to be derived from combining ancient Egyptian words for the human soul or spirit *(ka)* and the solar deity *(ra)*. Since the word *kara* is otherwise unknown in ancient Egyptian or Hermetic literature, we can only assume that it is an innovation in religious terminology. Such an innovative amalgamation of ancient Egyptian terms is consistent with Motshekga's propensity for combining words, in multiple permutations, to represent the many facets of ancient Egyptian and indigenous African divinity. On behalf of the Kara Heritage Institute, Motshekga has conveyed the indigenous African wisdom drawn from ancient Egypt through frequent appearances on the radio stations of the South African Broadcasting Corporation, where he has regularly been presented as the authoritative spokesperson for African religion, but also through presentations to audiences as diverse as the South African Parliament, the Gauteng Legislature, the Black Management Forum, the Department of Education, the South African Human Rights Commission, the South African Heritage Resources Agency, and the crowds attending the annual public celebrations in September sponsored by various branches of government for South Africa's Heritage Day. On all of these occasions, Motshekga has consistently traced South African indigenous religion, culture, and identity back to ancient Egypt. As the shared heritage and common spirituality of all Africans in the region, this Egyptian origin is advanced as a religious foundation for a new South Africa.

Recently, however, Motshekga has highlighted two different aspects of this ancient Egyptian and pan-African spirituality in his public presentations. On some occasions, he emphasizes the theosophy of this heritage, beginning with an ancient Egyptian cosmogony and proceeding through an exposition of the zodiac of the heavens and the sacred calendar of festivals on earth, to end with a description of an African personality that is inherently divine, as a child of God, but also in need of recovery through the practice of the reciprocal African ethics of *ubuntu* and the performance of indigenous African rituals of yoga. Theosophically, therefore, the wisdom of Kara is directed toward self-formation, what Motshekga has called self-knowledge and the art of being.[7] On other occasions, however, Motshekga emphasizes the theocracy of this heritage, its claim to power, which also begins with an ancient Egyptian cosmogony but highlights an ideology of divine kingship and proceeds through African history to affirm the sacrality of African monarchs. Theocratically, the wisdom of Kara is directed toward recovering and revitalizing divine kingship in Africa.

How can such religious claims operate within a democratic polity? Motshekga seems to advocate three different and perhaps mutually exclusive possibilities—theocracy, democratic pluralism, and a civil religion unifying a democratic polity.

First, Motshekga has sometimes gone so far as to call for the alien doctrines of democracy to be replaced by the authentically African wisdom of theocracy, in which "African monarchs or Kings are the earthly representatives of God on earth," with a primordial authority that extends over both church and state.[8] Certainly, this theocratic commitment is surprising from a political actor who serves as the parliamentary leader of the ruling political party of a democratically elected legislative body. But Motshekga's commitment to theocracy, as we will see, is based not only on his insights into the theosophy of ancient Egypt but also on his interests as legal advisor to the Royal Council of Modjadji, the Rain Queen, during a difficult time of transition in that African royal tradition.

Second, if Motshekga's ultimate aim is to restore African theocracy, his interim tactics have been devoted to positioning African indigenous religion, in its theosophical formulation, as one among many faith communities in a religiously diverse society that must be respected and included in interreligious forums. As a spokesperson for African traditional religion featured prominently in public media and regularly on political occasions, he has taken advantage of the new space for religious diversity opened up by the democratic dispensation. Relying upon a democratic constitution ensuring freedom of religion and freedom from religious discrimination, he has celebrated the democratic ethos of unity in diversity that affirms the many languages, cultures, and religions of South Africa. In a secular state and a religiously diverse society, a revival of African theocracy might be achieved through a division of labor between religion and state in which divine kings and queens would be responsible for religious, spiritual, and cultural matters, while the constitutional state, with its structures of local, provincial, and national governance, would deal with politics. Although Motshekga sometimes formulates the revival of African theocracy in these terms, especially when he is asserting the right to include his theosophic understanding of African tradition as one of the many faith communities in South Africa, his understanding of the ancient Egyptian theosophy of Africa ultimately requires a divine kingship merging religion and politics.

Third, mediating between theocracy and democracy, Motshekga might be trying to develop the kind of African civil religion that Jacob Olupona found emerging in Osogbo, Nigeria, in his research on Yoruba divine kingship: one that merges reconstructions of ancestral heritage, the reality of religious diversity, and the modern dynamics of a constitutional democracy. Certainly, Motshekga has invoked ancestral authority, in the context of religious diversity, within a democratic state. In his religious strategy and tactics, he seems to be pursuing all three dimensions of civil religion formulated in 1967 by the sociologist of religion Robert Bellah—the cultural, the nationalist, and the transcendental—by describing the sacred culture of Africa, by drawing religion into nation building, and by interpreting African historical experience, with special attention to political struggles in southern Africa, in the light of transcendence.[9] Is Motshekga seeking to negotiate a new civil religion for South Africa?

Everything begins, according to Mathole Motshekga, in ancient Egypt, the cradle of African divinity and humanity. As he has insisted, this religious heritage, rooted in Africa, is shared by all Africans, even though it is also a secret tradition preserved by initiates into its mysteries. If Motshekga is in fact trying to develop a new African civil religion that will function as a shared religious orientation for a new South Africa, it is premised on the secret wisdom from ancient Egypt as cultivated and transmitted in Europe by Hermeticism, Rosicrucianism, Freemasonry, and Theosophy.

THEOSOPHY

> The African philosophy of Origins says that at the beginning was nothingness or non-being. The first life to come out of the Nothingness or Non-being is Ptah, the Master Architect of the Universe. Thus Ptah is called the First Cause or Self-begotten God. This God is called the One and only God which manifested itself as the Mind (male), Thought (female) and Word (offspring) of the two. The Mind, Thought and Word were One in Three and Three in One.
>
> —Mathole Motshekga, "The Intermediary Role of the African Monarchy"

In the beginning, according to Motshekga, was the ancient Egyptian cosmogony, the sacred story of beginnings, the central myth of origin for all of Africa. Although historians of ancient Egyptian religion have found different myths of origin, situated in different times and places, over the long history of the development of ancient Egyptian religious beliefs, practices, and social formations, Motshekga insists that they were all telling the same story. In doing so, he is not only following in the tradition of Hermeticism but also advocating a primordial mythic basis for African identity.

In his reconstruction of the Memphite theology of ancient Egypt, Motshekga traces African religion, culture, and identity back to the first time, the Zep Tepi, the time of the gods, the Neteru, which began out of nothing and proceeded through emanations of the One God, Ptah, the Architect of the Universe, to produce the trinity of Osiris, Isis, and Horus, the four cardinal points of the universe, the seven outer planets, and the twelve signs of the zodiac, all of which are ancient Egyptian deities. Although he assigns many names to these deities, which are drawn from all over Africa, he puts special emphasis on terms from ancient Egypt, Ethiopia, and Zimbabwe. His account of the African cosmology is fairly consistent in its structure, which is represented by an emblem that would be familiar to Christians as the chi-rho monogram. Rejecting any Christian interpretation of this symbol, Motshekga variously presents it as "the Kara monogram," "the solar monogram," "the solar Kara monogram," "the ankh," "the Hakata monogram," "the Ethiopian monogram," "the Kabiri monogram," and "the Charaoh monogram." The symbol is also familiar to Masons, who celebrate Ptah as the "Great Architect of the Universe."[10]

By his own account, Motshekga acquired his understanding of ancient Egyptian religion by studying the ancient texts of Hermeticism; in a brochure for the Kara Heritage Institute he recommends *The Egyptian Book of the Dead, The Ethiopian Book of the Dead,* and *The Hermetica: The Lost Wisdom of the Pharaohs.*[11] He has celebrated Prince Hall, who established a Masonic lodge for African Americans in Massachusetts in 1775, as a crucial figure in the recovery of ancient Egyptian wisdom for Africans through the "Solar (Karaite) or Hermetic arts and sciences that he learned within the Masonic circles."[12] In this respect, Motshekga exemplifies what the historian Stephen Howe has called the "Masonic connection" in Afrocentric religion and spirituality: the tendency of leaders of Afrocentricism, such as Molefi Asante and Yosef Ben-Jochannan, to draw upon the authority of an early twentieth-century Mason like Albert Churchward as an expert on the religion of ancient Egypt.[13] In Motshekga's writings, key Masonic symbols include the triangle, the cube, the pillar, the stone, and the "law of squares," which begins with the Pythagorean (or Hermetic) theorem to generate a sacred numerology around the formula $9 + 16 = 25$.[14]

Motshekga's relationship with the modern Theosophical Society, which was founded in 1875 by Helena Petrovna Blavatsky, is more complicated and problematic. On a brochure circulated by his institute in the early 2000s, Motshekga declared that the Kara Heritage Institute was dedicated to African indigenous history, culture, and spirituality, "whose custodians are collectively known as the Great Kara Brotherhood (or Bonabakulu Abasekhemu)."[15] Motshekga has invoked the name of this secret society many times in his writings. In describing the divine zodiac, Motshekga equates its twelve constellations, which are twelve gods, with this African spiritual brotherhood: "Strictly speaking," he explains, "these African Gods (Neteru) constitute the Great Council of the celestial Gods known as the Great Kara Brotherhood or Bonabakhulu Abasekhemu (i.e. the Great Ones of the Celestial Khem or Hakaptah)."[16] African monarchs, as heirs to the divine kingship of ancient Egypt, "descended from the ancient African Society called the Shamsu Hara (Greek Shemsu Hor) or Bonabakhulu Abasekhemu (i.e. the Ancient Ones of Khem)."[17] Further, the Kara Brotherhood was responsible for the preservation and transmission of Hermetic wisdom from ancient Egypt. Manetho, who translated Hermetic wisdom from hieroglyphics into Greek, was "the Secretary and the High Priest of the Great Kara Brotherhood (also known as Bonabakhulu-Abasekhemu)."[18] Over the centuries, the Bonabakulu Abasekhemu has continued to operate as a secret society transmitting the Egyptian wisdom. Quoting a "South African sage, Mankanyezi," Motshekga provides this description of the Kara Brotherhood:

> [Its] members are the guardians of the Wisdom-which-comes-from-of-old; they are of many ranks from learner to master, and Higher Ones, whose names may not be spoken; and there is one member at least in every tribe and nation throughout this great land of Africa. The brotherhood is called, in the ancient Bantu speech, Bona bakulu Abase-chemu, i.e. the Brotherhood of the Higher Ones of Egypt. It was founded by a priest of Isis in the reign of the pharaoh Khutu (Cheops), to spread the wisdom which comes from of old, among all races and tribes of Africa.[19]

This secret society, with a member in every tribe of Africa, was originally discovered (or invented) by the British Theosophist Patrick Bowen, who spent many years in government administration in South Africa before returning to Britain to play a leading role in the Theosophical Society. Originally published in 1927, Bowen's account, "The Ancient Wisdom in Africa," describes his encounters after the Anglo-Boer War with masters of this African theosophical order—Mankanyezi (The Starry One) and Mandhlalanga (Strength of the Sun)—who conveyed to Bowen their brotherhood's secret wisdom. Interweaving theosophical and Zulu terminology, Bowen's account of ancient wisdom in Africa tells of the original universal spirit, Itongo, which was also the spark of light in human beings, and of the Isangoma ("Those who Know"), who have reached the highest grade of initiation in this brotherhood and the highest level of spiritual mastery by attaining "consciousness on the Plane of the Real Self." Revealing that the brotherhood believed in reincarnation, Bowen adds that "only one who has reached Mastership in a previous life can gain Isangomanship."[20] On the basis of his studies with such masters in South Africa, "principally Zulus," the Isanusi, the Isangoma, and other adepts of ancient wisdom, Bowen claimed to have discovered theosophical mystery schools, with their origin in ancient Egypt, operating in Africa.

This discovery, invention, or appropriation of African spirituality by Bowen in a publication in 1927 anticipated the appropriation by contemporary American neoshamans of the indigenous Zulu celebrity Credo Mutwa, who has presented himself in different guises—as a witch doctor during the 1960s and 1970s, a *sangoma* during the 1980s, and high *sanusi* of the Zulu Nation during the 1990s—only to become a New Age shaman in the global network of indigenous spirituality. In the case of Bowen, however, the indigenous African partners in the exchange—the Starry One, the Strength of the Sun—seem too much like characters of invention, a suspicion only reinforced in Bowen's next publication about Africa, "Africa's White Race," published in 1932, which begins by referring to the search for white tribes in Africa in the fiction of H. Rider Haggard and ends with a "translation" of a text from another African sage (who was not European but was still white because of his Berber lineage), "The Sayings of the Ancient One."[21] In this publication of 1932, Bowen finds the ancient Egyptian wisdom in Africa, but it is transmitted by white Africans, descendants of North African Berbers, who are asserted as racially superior to black Africans. It is difficult to imagine any Afrocentrist aligning his work with such a racist construction of the transmission of white Theosophical wisdom in black Africa.

Nevertheless, Motshekga has embraced Bowen's invention as his own, identifying his Kara Brotherhood with Bowen's secret society of the Bonabakulu Abasekhemu. As Bowen recounted, the highest masters of this brotherhood—the Supreme Ones, the Perfect Men—are those "for whom the necessity for rebirth has ceased. They dwell on earth in physical form by their own will, and can retain or relinquish that form as they choose."[22] In a confessional moment in 2001, Motshekga revealed that he was not only a representative of African indigenous religion and ancient Egyptian spirituality but also a medium for Bowen's Supreme Ones, Perfect Men, who had achieved the highest level of spiritual mastery by being free from the cycle of reincarnation and living on earth in a human body by choice. As Motshekga explained, "For posterity it is necessary for the author to say that he is a spirit medium (Mondoro) of Vuthavhazindu who lived in primal times under the name and style of Kherufho or Nekherufho. The message contained in this document comes from Bondoro . . . the primal members of the great Kara Brotushy who have been liberated from the cycle of rebirth [and] who live on earth by choice."[23]

This claim to spiritual mastery, which echoed Bowen's description of the supreme masters of the spiritual brotherhood he had discovered in South Africa, held other implications for Motshekga's African theosophy. Looking back to ancient Egypt, Motshekga could claim insight into that civilization's original wisdom because he had been there, as an ancient Egyptian, living "in primal time," bearing the name of Kherufho or Nekherufho—a story that might account for his adoption of the name "Necherofho Motshekga" in his publication *Dawn of the African Century: The African Origins of Philosophy and Sciences* in 1999. Accordingly, Motshekga was not just speaking on behalf of ancient Egyptians; he was an ancient Egyptian. Looking forward from a spiritual origin in ancient Egypt to the development of African indigenous religion in southern Africa, Motshekga identified himself as a spirit medium, a *mhondoro*, referring to the spirit mediums of Zimbabwe, who conveyed messages from ancestral spirits but also mobilized spiritual resources during the armed struggles against colonial rule.[24] As we will see, this link between ancient Egypt and modern Zimbabwe is central to Motshekga's notions of theosophy and theocracy in South Africa.

According to Motshekga, African wisdom is based on the "primal theorem [of the Corpus Hermeticum,] which says what is above (i.e. God) is the same as what is below (the human personality of man and woman) and what is below (man and woman) is the same as what is above (God)."[25] Accordingly, the African personality, with deference to indigenous South African notions of humanity *(ubuntu/botho)*, must be aligned with the heavens through observance of the African sacred calendar—anchored on December 25, the birthday of the ancient Egyptian God of Light—and synchronization with its three seasons. At the same time, the African personality must be cultivated by the regular practice of spiritual and physical exercises, especially the yoga exercises directed to the sun that Motshekga advocates by borrowing instructions for the *Soorya Namaskar* (Sun Exercise) as they appear on Hindu Yoga sites on the Internet.[26]

All of this self-discovery, self-cultivation, and self-realization, however, is directly linked by Motshekga's Kara Heritage Institute with a political project, the African Renaissance. How does this recovery of the African personality, aligned with the heavens, intersect with any political collectivity? How might it work in a democratic South Africa?

THEOCRACY

> All three Semitic religions originated in the African mystery teachings which are preserved in the original forms in the Ethiopian (i.e. black African) Zodiacs of Dendera, Meroe, Great Zimbabwe, Matendera and Maphungubwe. The inscriptions in these Zodiacs tell the story of the Origins of the Gods and the universe. These Zodiacs provide the basis of the African Divine Monarchy. Through this monarchy one is able to trace African history to the celestial spheres.
>
> —Mathole Motshekga, "The Intermediary Role of the African Monarchy"

If we were familiar only with the Afrocentricism of Cheikh Anta Diop, the Afrocentricity of Molefi Kete Asante, or the controversy during the 1990s surrounding Martin Bernal's *Black Athena,* we might be surprised by the proliferation of initiatives in Egyptology pioneered by Africanists in Africa who have traced their lineage from ancient Egypt to where they live.[27] In Nigeria, as Jacob Olupona has observed, this effort to trace the ancient Egyptian roots of Yoruba religion was pioneered by J. Olumide Lucas in the 1940s.[28] Similarly, in Ghana, the claim to an ancient Egyptian pedigree has been advanced by O. Kwame Osei in his text published in 2001, *The Ancient Egyptians Are Here.* Among Africanists in Ghana, we find Kojo Duffu Yankson, author of *Africa's Roots in God,* who urges, "Go back to your African Roots in God; Go back for your Royal African Dignity" and forges a link between ancient Egypt and West African heritage by drawing on the symbol of the Sankofa, the bird who walks forward looking backwards.[29] In the Congo, the cultural movement Bundu Dia Kongo sometimes traces its lineage back to ancient Egypt, at one point discussing Motshekga's Kara Brotherhood as Masonic symbolism.[30] And in South Africa, Mathole Motshekga has traced the lineage of ancient Egypt to where he lives. Beginning with ancient Egyptian divine kingship, Motshekga's reconstruction of African history moves directly to the ancient Karanga Empire of Zimbabwe, where the Kemetic lineage of sacred monarchy was preserved. On its list of recommended reading, besides Hermetic texts, the Kara Heritage Institute includes two historical texts, both by the Zimbabwean historian, politician, and traditional leader Aeneas S. Chigwedere, *The Karanga Empire* (1985) and *The Roots of the Bantu* (1998), which follow Diop in tracing African history back to ancient Egypt.[31] Although Motshekga does not live in Zimbabwe, he has an interest in celebrating the emperor, divine kings, and Mwari devotion of the Karanga Empire because he maintains that the Royal Council of Modjadji, the Rain Queen, where he has served as legal advisor, is heir to that sacred heritage.

Ancient Egyptian myths and rituals of divine kingship, which rendered the pharaoh as Horus on earth and Osiris after death, marked the origin of African sacred monarchy as the supreme model of governance.[32] Synchronized with the order of the universe, ancient Egyptian divine kingship established the model for theocratic government in Africa. While the ancient Egyptian theocracy was destroyed by conquests in Egypt, it survived in the medieval Karanga Empire of Zimbabwe. As Motshekga has drawn the "organogram" of that African empire, the Sacred Monarch (Fura or Faro) was at the apex of a reporting structure in which kings were beneath him, chiefs were beneath the kings, and ward heads were beneath the chiefs. Centralized and hierarchical, political power flowed from the monarchs, who were the "earthly representatives of the heavenly Monarch born of the Queen of Heaven and Earth." Observing the Hermetic primal theorem "As above, so below," the political organization of the earthly monarchy mirrored that of the heavenly monarchy, so the sacred monarch of the Karanga Empire had a royal council replicating on earth the royal council of the heavens, which consisted of the Bull of Heaven (or God of Light), four gods guarding the four corners of the universe, the seven cows of heaven associated with the Pleiades, the seven bulls of heaven associated with the visible planets, and twenty-four councilors representing the twenty-four divisions of heaven and the twenty-four hours of the day.[33] This theocratic system of government, aligned with the heavens, was preserved in the Karanga Empire.

Under the pressures of the slave trade and colonization, this sacred order was disrupted. With the destruction of Zimbabwean empires, Africans migrated to South Africa and formed new kingdoms, such as the Lobedu kingdom. Lacking a sacred monarch ruling over a confederation of kings, these new kingdoms followed an organogram that placed the divine king at the apex, with chiefs and ward heads underneath. This distinction between the sacred monarchs of empire and the divine kings of successor kingdoms in South Africa seems important in Motshekga's reconstruction of African history, yet the difference between monarchs and kings is blurred because "African Monarchs or Kings are the earthly representatives of God on earth."[34] Accordingly, like the sacred Fura or Faro of the Karanga Empire, the divine kings of the successor states are also theocratic rulers. They also perform what Motshekga has called the intermediary role in linking heaven and earth, mediating between gods and human beings.

In Motshekga's understanding of African theocracy, the role of the Goddess is central, because African monarchs and kings "worshipped the Goddess of heaven and earth." Although the Goddess has been known by many names, the most important name across the African kingdoms in South Africa seems to be Mwari, deity of the Karanga Empire. Mwari, as Motshekga explains, is the Universal Mother, who resides in the cosmic ocean of the Milky Way.[35] Identified with the ancient Egyptian Goddess, Mwari underlies religious worship in all South African kingdoms. While devotion to Mwari featured in the Karanga Empire, this divine name, like most African terms for divinity, has undergone a history of colonial interventions, missionary translations, and indigenous redefinitions. As the historian of religions Chirevo V. Kwenda has observed, the Shona term Mwari was adopted by Christian missionaries in Zimbabwe to designate the God of their Bible. During the nineteenth century, as Kwenda has noted, "the cult of Mwari which, though spreading rapidly, had been confined to the center and south of the country, received a boost when the missionaries translated the Christian name for God as Mwari."[36] Therefore, for Shona-speaking Christians, Mwari would conventionally be understood as God rather than Goddess. Although indigenous revitalizations of the so-called Mwari cult might recover an earlier understanding that this divinity was beyond gender or encompassing both genders, Motshekga has insisted that Mwari is the supreme Goddess of South African kingdoms. "The Goddess Mwari, Mohale or Mwalinkulunkulu," Motshekga has explained, "is worshipped by the African peoples as a whole." Originating in ancient Egypt and transmitted through the Karanga Empire, this worship of the Goddess migrated into South Africa as the religious basis of divine kingship in successor states, such as the Lobedu, the Venda, the Zulu, the Swazi, the Sotho, the Pedi, and the Tsonga Kingdoms, as well as the Thembu Kingdom of the Dalindyebo royal dynasty. On the basis of this shared heritage of divine kingship, Motshekga can assert that "all Africans in South Africa and the SADC region worship One and the same God," the Goddess Mwari, who is known by many names in African theosophy and theocracy.[37]

Just as Mwari, the Goddess, plays a central role in African divine kingship, Modjadji, the Rain Queen of the Lobedu, holds a special place as heir to the sacred monarchy of Zimbabwe. In his presentations on African kingship, Motshekga often singles out the Rain Queen for special attention. With respect to the crucial role of African royalty as mediators between heaven and earth, he observes: "African Divine Kings or Queens (e.g. the Mudjadji Rain-Queens) are intermediaries between the Nation on the One Side and the royal ancestors and God on the other."[38] With respect to the transcendent role of African royalty as gods on earth, he observes: "The African divine rulers, for instance the Rain-Queens (Mudjadji) of Balozwi (popularly known as Balobedu) were described as transformers of the clouds because they were believed to control, like the Solar God, the four quarters of the universe, time, and climate."[39] According to Motshekga, the Rain Queen has a special relationship with Mwari of the Karanga Empire, as the "incarnation of the Goddess" or as the center of a traditional institution that is "directly linked to the African cosmology and the goddess Mwari."[40] In theocratic terms, therefore, if all Africans in southern Africa worship the same God, the Goddess Mwari, then Modjadji, the Rain Queen of the Lobedu, should be at the center of African worship.

As documented in *The Realm of the Rain Queen*, the classic ethnographic monograph by Eileen Krige and J.D. Krige, the Lobedu ruler Modjadji embodied divine kingship, exercising rule over her people to ensure order and rule over nature to bring life-giving rain.[41] With a lineage going back to the nineteenth century, the fifth Rain Queen, Modjadji V, ruled for many years, preserving tradition from 1981 until her death in 2001. Because her daughter and designated successor died shortly after, the matrilineal succession fell upon her granddaughter, Mokobo, who was elevated to the divine station of Rain Queen in 2003. As documented in a media broadcast, the Venda King Mphephu presided over the coronation of Modjadji VI, declaring, "I now present to you our royal highness, Queen Modjadji of the Balobedu. May you enjoy many years of good life, and good relationship with your people, and that of South Africa at large." During the coronation it was raining, which made logistics difficult, but the rain was seen as a good sign, as "Royal family spokesman Mathole Motshekga says the key to her authority is her legendary ability to make it rain in a region prone to long periods of drought." Accordingly, since rain should not dampen but enliven the occasion, the event should be seen, Motshekga explained, as the renewal of the Rain Queen "as the intercessor or intermediary between the people, the royal ancestors, and the gods and God. So, she is the agent of the royal ancestors for bringing the rain. So she is responsible for the rituals to be conducted to make sure it rains." As Motshekga observed, even the original Zulu King Shaka came to the Modjadji for the secrets of making rain. Therefore, as spokesperson for the Lobedu, Motshekga explained how the continuation of this sacred dynasty was crucial for all of South Africa.[42]

In this ritual of crowning a Rain Queen, Motshekga, as "royal family spokesman," might have thought he was helping to maintain the lineage of divine kingship that he had traced from the pharaohs of ancient Egypt, through the emperors of the Karanga Empire of Zimbabwe, to the royal dynasty of his own kingdom, the Lobedu. However, the relations between theosophy and theocracy do not always run so smoothly in practice. During 1998, the weekly newspaper *Mail and Guardian* reported that Motshekga had made common cause with a former operative in the apartheid-era department of military intelligence to exploit the potential for developing the realm of the Rain Queen for cultural tourism, a hotel, and perhaps a casino. Reportedly, the community had approached Motshekga, in his capacity as a Lobedu and as a lawyer, to protect them from the predatory capitalist advances of a company, Ethnic Development and Productions, that was negotiating with the Royal Council of Queen Modjadji to carry out these development plans. According to press reports, Motshekga did intervene, ostensibly on behalf of the community, but Ethnic Development and Productions continued to pursue its projects among the Lobedu, merely changing its name to Kara Cultural Development, with further spinoffs, including Kara Interactive Solutions in the field of information technology.

It also began supporting Motshekga's political ambitions by financing events during his campaign for the premiership of Gauteng Province.[43] Not all of these allegations in the popular media may be true; certainly Motshekga denied them. But Motshekga has continued to be involved in controversies over land sales and tourism development.[44] Without pretending to be able to adjudicate any of these charges, as a historian of religions I can only observe in this case that the transmission of divine kingship, however it might be regarded as an ideal pattern of theocracy, does not always proceed without contestation. In the case of the Rain Queen, if an authentic inheritance of royal authority can be traced from ancient Egypt, through the Karanga Empire, to the Modjadji of the Lobedu Kingdom, it is clear that this theocratic tradition has culminated in different interests fighting over her sacred assets in a capitalist economy.

What the anthropologists Jean and John Comaroff have called "Ethnicity, Inc.," the emergence, within the pushes and pulls of global capitalism, of ethnic entrepreneurs, or "ethnopreneurs," has definitely been operating in the recent conflicts over theocracy among the Lobedu.[45] As ethnic entrepreneurs seek to capitalize on opportunities for marketing ethnicity through cultural tourism or casinos, new relations are emerging between local communities, traditionally based on reciprocity, and capitalist entrepreneurs, who are driven by maximizing profit. The Comaroffs have pointed to ethnic entrepreneurs, such as the CEO of the Royal Bafokeng Nation, as a problem, a sign that local communities are being exploited in a globalizing economy, but Motshekga has celebrated them as providing a solution to the economic challenges facing South Africans, a "model" that "could be emulated throughout the country."[46] According to Motshekga, exploiting ethnicity is crucial for economic development, especially if ethnicity can be linked with divinity.

Tragically, the Lobedu Rain Queen Modjadji VI died two years after her coronation in 2005. This young queen, who was educated, enjoyed popular culture, and was in a relationship with a commoner, which produced a daughter, died from meningitis, according to official reports, or from poisoning, according to her partner.[47] Once again, without pretending to adjudicate this dispute, as a historian of religions I can only observe that the death of the Rain Queen in 2005 created a rupture in the transmission of divine royalty that Motshekga has identified as the consistent thread in African religion going back to ancient Egypt and as the common focus of indigenous worship among all Africans in southern Africa. Motshekga, as well, has noticed this rupture, objecting to the male regent, Prince Mpapatla Modjadji, who has claimed the authority of the Rain Queen in presiding over the theocracy of the Lobedu, even daring in 2008 to reconvene the annual rainmaking rituals.[48] This appropriation of the authority of the Rain Queen by a male prince is unacceptable, according to Motshekga, who has claimed that "the successive Mudjadji Rain Queens were regarded as the incarnation of [the] goddess. Thus the 'temporary' replacement of a female Monarch with a male regent is a serious disruption of the relationship between the Balobedu Kingdom and its spiritual and cultural roots."[49] This rupture in divine kingship, which has spiritual, cultural, and material implications, has persisted, even as a lavish tourist hotel in honor of the Rain Queen was finally built in 2009. The Queen Modjadji V Hotel, a multi-million-rand construction, had been started over seven years earlier "but was delayed following a dispute between the Modjadji royal house and a senior member of the Balobedu Community Trust, Mathole Motshekga, over allegations of financial mismanagement during the construction process."[50] This dispute over the financial management and control of a hotel develop-ment in honor of the Rain Queen may not undermine the indigenous authenticity or theocratic authority of African divine kingship. But it does suggest that African theocracy, as promoted by Motshekga, is being renegotiated in local relations with the market economy and a democratic polity.

DEMOCRACY

On November 11, 2009, Mathole Motshekga, as chief whip of the ANC, introduced the following motion:

That the House—
(1) notes with great appreciation the approval by the United Nations (UN) of naming 18 July Nelson Mandela International Day;
(2) further notes that Nelson Mandela Day has already been declared an annual community work day for the cultivation of ubuntu values and principles that the nation's icon, Nelson Mandela, worked for and lived by;
(3) believes that Mandela's dedication to progressive values of human and social solidarity without regard to race, class and gender will continue to guide the nation in its efforts to create a non-racial, non-sexist, united, democratic and prosperous society in which the value of all citizens is measured by its common humanity;

(4) recognises that President Mandela's commitment to progressive values is encapsulated in the words of Lord Khem, an African sage, who says: ". . . the Light that is God resides in each and every one of us . . ." and further says: "Thou art the Light that shine [sic] upon others . . .";

(5) further recognises that the nation's icon, Nelson Mandela, has been the light that shines upon others; and

(6) supports and joins President Jacob Zuma in welcoming the recognition by the UN of Nelson Mandela Day and encourages the peoples and nations of the world to recognise the power within themselves to do something to improve the quality of life of others in celebration of Nelson Mandela International Day.[51]

This motion, which was subsequently adopted by the South African Parliament, did far more than comment approvingly on the United Nations' creation of an international Nelson Mandela Day; by invoking the wisdom of the African sage Lord Khem—in Hermetic tradition equated with the god Thoth of ancient Egypt, and with Thoth-Hermes of late Greco-Roman tradition, and considered the scribe of the gods and personification of divine wisdom—it also inserted the theosophy of the Kara Heritage Institute directly into the proceedings of the central democratic institution of South Africa.[52] Although the source of the quotation from Lord Khem is uncertain, his words recall the motto of Thoth—"Thou art the light, let that light shine"—appearing in Masonic and Theosophical texts.[53] But its deeper import is clear: Nelson Mandela, the "nation's icon," is associated with Kara, the Divine Light, as a being of divine light illuminating others and is portrayed as if he were also a member of the Kara Brotherhood, the Bonabakulu Abasekhemu, the Brotherhood of the Higher Ones of Egypt.

As we have seen, Motshekga's theosophy holds political implications by requiring the recovery of African theocracy. African monarchs and kings, representing God on earth, are intermediaries between humans and the heavens. Observing the Hermetic maxim "As above, so below," Motshekga sometimes calls for a restoration of an ancient Egyptian model of theocracy in which the "earthly order in both church and state reflected the heavenly order." The centralized, hierarchical authority of divine kingship, as Motshekga observes, represents a "governance structure [that] applied in heaven and in both church and state."[54] Although he is not a secessionist like the Thembu King Dalindyebo, Motshekga has insisted on restoring the "territorial integrity" of divine kingship. Looking back to the ancient model of divine kingship, he has argued that royal councils, on behalf of a king, must exercise administrative, judicial, and political powers over their kingdoms. He has criticized government efforts to accommodate traditional leaders, such as the formation of traditional councils and a government commission to resolve traditional leadership disputes, as measures undermining the authority of royal councils. Resources should rather be devoted to "building the infrastructures of royal courts," which could not only exercise political functions but also contribute to service delivery. As custodians of Africa's spiritual heritage, African royalty were essential for local government and economic development.[55]

On other occasions, however, Motshekga defers to democratic pluralism to identify African divine kingship as a "faith community" among other communities of faith in South Africa. "African kings, queens, chiefs, and other traditional authorities," he observes, "like faith communities, are custodians of spiritual and cultural values." Dedicated to preserving these African values, divine kingship can operate within a democratic division of labor between religion and politics in a modern democratic state, with African royalty performing "spiritual and cultural functions while political parties [assume] social and political functions."[56] Despite asserting an integrated authority over church and state within African theocracy, Motshekga has also positioned African divine kingship, religion, and spiritual heritage in the context of the constitutional separation of religion and state in a democratic order. Accordingly, he plays a leading role in the National Interfaith Leaders Council, representing the interests of African religion as one faith community among many in South Africa. However, he has also been able to extend the influence of his theosophic and theocratic understanding of African religion as chair of the ANC's Commission on Religious and Traditional Affairs and as chair of the selectors for the new commissioners appointed to the constitutionally mandated Commission for the Promotion and Protection of the Rights of Cultural, Religious, and Linguistic Communities.[57]

Asserting his religious values in a democratic society, Motshekga has angered Christians by proposing to "de-Christianize" Christmas on the grounds that Christians allegedly subverted the ancient Egyptian theosophy by appropriating the birthday of the God of Light, December 25.[58] He has angered neopagans, such as the witches of Wicca, by attacking witchcraft, and he has angered animal rights activists by defending the annual Zulu royal ritual Ukweshwama, which requires Zulu warriors to kill a bull with their bare hands.[59]

Christians, Muslims, and Jews in South Africa might all be offended if they learned that according to Motshekga their religions were degraded versions of an original African theosophy.[60] Motshekga's religious policy, however, departs from earlier efforts during the Mandela and Mbeki administrations to advance mutual understanding, civil toleration, and informed respect for religious diversity. Dedicated to those outcomes, the National Policy on Religion and Education of 2003, for example, began not with promoting religious values but with affirming constitutional values and human rights in a democratic South Africa. Motshekga's wife, Angie Motshekga, who has been involved in her husband's enterprises, became minister of basic education in the Zuma administration with responsibility for implementing this policy in South African schools.[61] Mathole Motshekga has argued, however, that human rights in South Africa must be interpreted within an African context. "We are therefore required as South Africans to contextualize our Bill of Rights," he has stated, "lest we negate our African humanity in the name of human rights."[62] African humanity, as Motshekga has insisted, is directly related to divinity, both collectively, since "all Africans in South Africa and the SADC region worship One and the same God," and individually, since each African is a bearer of divine light as a child of the one God.[63]

Maneuvering between faith communities and the state, Motshekga appears to be advocating a kind of civil religion for South Africa. Traced back to time immemorial and imagined as the shared spiritual heritage of all Africans, this religion aspires to fulfilling Robert Bellah's classic definition of civil religion as "a collection of beliefs, symbols, and rituals with respect to sacred things and institutionalized in a collectivity."[64] Bellah's original essay in 1967 on civil religion in America describes different renderings of civil religion—as a shared religious culture, as a religious nationalism, and as a shared history interpreted in the light of religious transcendence—all of which also appear in Mathole Motshekga's writings.

First, in celebrating a shared religious culture, Motshekga calls upon all South Africans to observe the African sacred calendar, derived from ancient Egypt, which divides the year into three seasons devoted to different ritual practices. In his speech to Parliament during a debate about Heritage Day in September 2009, Motshekga asserted that the "African Calendar embodies the intangible heritage of African people." All African people, according to this sacred calendar, observe the summer season (September to December), which is marked by the appearance of the Pleiades, with rainmaking ceremonies in October, fertility rituals in November, and first-fruits celebrations in December that culminate on December 25, the birthday of the God of Light, which "is not only a Christian holiday, . . . [but] a universal holiday which was celebrated in the solar temples of Great Zimbabwe, Maphungubwe, Mutokolwe (Lwandali), Meroe and various Egyptian temples." Entering the autumn season (January to April), which begins with the sacrifice of a black bull to God and the royal ancestors, this season is marked by harvest rituals, especially the celebrations of March 21–22 as "the sun enters the zodiacal sign of Amun [the lamb of God that is sacrificed to nourish humanity]." During the winter season (May to August), May 1 is a spiritual holiday, the birthday of the Queen of Heaven and Earth, not merely Workers' Day as it appears in the South African calendar of public holidays, and is followed by a May 25 holiday when the star Canopus signals the beginning of traditional ceremonies of initiation into adulthood. "The African Calendar," Motshekga maintains, "is an instrument for inculcating moral, social and economic values" that are essential for social cohesion and nation building in South Africa. As the basis for a shared cultural religion, it should be adopted by Parliament because it "would realign our spiritual and material existence and make us a truly value-centred society."[65]

Of course, in urging Parliament to adopt the African Calendar, Motshekga begs the question of whether the theosophy, astrology, and agricultural cycles of this calendar do in fact represent a shared cultural orientation in South Africa. Motshekga's theosophy can be contrasted with the neoshamanism of Credo Mutwa, custodian of African tradition, celebrated in 2009 at Freedom Park as "doyen of African culture," who has also related his encounters with aliens from outer space, or the traditionalism of Nokuzola Mndende, who focuses on the recovery of Xhosa oral tradition and ancestral rituals, to indicate that his version of African theosophy is not shared by all contemporary adherents of African religion.[66] Nevertheless, by persistently asserting his theosophy on public occasions and now in Parliament, Motshekga has established the possibility that his collection of Hermetic beliefs will be institutionalized in a collectivity. In the United States, by contrast, an African Hermeticist such as Muata Ashby, author of many Afrocentric books on Egyptian wisdom, translator of the Egyptian Book of the Dead, teacher of ancient Egyptian yoga, and director of the Sema Institute in Florida, must be content with developing a client relationship with his following. Occupying a different social location in South Africa, Motshekga aspires to integrate citizens into a communal relationship with ancient Egyptian theosophy.[67]

Second, in the service of South African nationalism, Motshekga calls for channeling all religious resources, but especially the spirituality of African religious heritage, into the Moral Regeneration Movement, social cohesion, and nation building in South Africa. Here Motshekga's civil religion appears not as a shared culture but as the religious legitimation of the nation and as a religious nationalism that sacralizes the nation. In the national interest, this form of civil religion calls for interreligious cooperation in nation building. Under the administration of Jacob Zuma, the new National Interfaith Leaders Council, which replaced the National Religious Leaders Forum of the previous administration, was enlisted to support the administration in achieving national goals. As President Zuma told the Presidential Religious Summit on November 27, 2008, his political movement, the ANC, "has always valued the interaction with faith communities because its history and moral vision are rooted in the religious sector."[68] In exchange for being valued by the ANC, communities of faith could add value by supporting government policies on poverty, crime, and service delivery, exercising oversight and assisting in implementation. The South African Council of Churches (SACC), which had played a crucial role in mobilizing religious opposition to apartheid, was excluded from the National Interfaith Leaders Council. In 1995 the SACC had adopted a policy of "critical engagement" with the ANC government, taking the view, as SACC secretary general Eddie Makue explained, "that governments come and go, but the church will always remain."[69] The new National Interfaith Leaders Council, however, was clearly constituted to provide religious support for the ANC government and according to Motshekga to become "a true engine of service delivery."[70]

However, religious nationalism, as a kind of idolatry, according to Bellah, does not require support from religious communities if the nation itself assumes a sacred aura. Certainly, the apartheid regime drew support from the Dutch Reformed Church, but the state established a Christian nationalism, an Afrikaner civil religion, or a political mythology that rendered the nation sacred in its own right.[71] Potentially, Motshekga's civil religion might become a religious nationalism in which African religion, culture, and tradition could be invoked to support anything done by the government. As we recall, in response to media reports of President Zuma's sexual impropriety in January 2010, a spokesperson for the Kara Heritage Institute, Moses Twala, insisted that the president's conduct was entirely consistent with African tradition. "It is normal for a man in our culture to be married but have children outside of his marriage," he explained. In keeping with African tradition, media should not have been reporting on the president's sex life because, according to Twala, "It is un-African to discuss private matters publicly."[72] Therefore, by underwriting a religious nationalism, the Kara version of African religion might serve to sacralize the prevailing government as it has sacralized divine kingship.

Finally, as Bellah argued, civil religion requires a sense of sacred history, "a genuine apprehension of universal and transcendent religious reality as seen in or, one could almost say, as revealed through the experience of . . . [a] people."[73] In this respect, Motshekga has reinterpreted African history in the light of religious transcendence, beginning in ancient Egypt and proceeding through the Karanga Empire to South Africa. But he has also traced the history of the ANC, in the light of his theosophy, back to an origin in Freemasonry and Pan-Africanism.[74] Referring to the early twentieth-century ANC presidents John Dube, Pixley Seme, and Z.R. Mahabane during the parliamentary debate on heritage in September 2009, Motshekga observed that "the founders of our democracy were both religious and political leaders."[75] In contrast to the Mandela and Mbeki administrations' emphasis on the ANC's secular human rights tradition, Motshekga's history of the ANC clearly seeks to merge religion and politics.[76] It is not merely a patriotic history but a sacred history.

Like any civil religion, Motshekga's cultural, nationalist, and transcendental civil religion is amorphous, allowing for multiple points of entry and multiple intersections of interests. Christians might enter, for example, where this civil religion recognizes the role of church leaders in the formation of the ANC or gives a political role to Christian churches, especially conservative Christian churches interested in challenging constitutional protections of abortion and sexual orientation, although their religious interests might not intersect with its revival of ancient Egyptian theosophy or its representation of Christianity as a degraded form of indigenous African religion. Nevertheless, as Jacob Olupona observed in Osogbo, Nigeria, such mixtures of religious and civic interests can produce a hybrid civil religion that draws together a legacy of ancestral heritage, the reality of religious diversity, and the changing conditions of urban modernity. If Motshekga is negotiating such a hybrid civil religion, it is a work in progress that has gained force but not a widespread following through his political position. As we have seen, this civil religion is founded on theosophy and theocracy: the theosophy of the Bonabakulu Abasekhemu, the mysterious and probably fictitious Higher Ones of Egypt, and the theocracy of Modjadji, the divine and now absent Rain Queen of the Lobedu. However it may have been constructed, this blend of theosophy and theocracy faces a profound challenge: a civil religion, in any form, requires an aura of authenticity for its collection of symbols, beliefs, and rituals to be incorporated in a social collectivity.

CHAPTER NINE

World Cup

Football, the world's game, the beautiful game, the sacred game, has often been characterized as a religion. In the advent of the 2010 Fédération Internationale de Football Association (FIFA) World Cup in South Africa, many commentators observed that football is a religion because it looks like religion and acts like religion.

Adopting a morphological analysis of religion by attending to characteristically religious forms, CNN national editor Dave Schechter declared his devotion to the "religion of football." Schechter identified forms of religion operating in football: prayers, curses, hymns, vestments, transcendent gods, and sacrificial rituals. "Deities will be implored," he noted. "Sacrifices will be pledged, some even offered." All of this religious activity, according to Schechter, must revolve around a sacred center, "a shrine that must be visited at least once in a lifetime."[1] For the "football worshipper," this sacred center, the holy of holies, is the FIFA World Cup, moving to a different location every four years but retaining its structural role as the central shrine of the religion of football. In these terms, football is a religion because it looks like religion.

Adopting a functional analysis of religion, the *Guardian* commentator Theo Hobson argued that football was a religion that was better than any institutionalized religion because it provided the world with a genuine ritual of social solidarity. In his article "The World Cup: A Ritual That Works," Hobson implicitly drew on Durkheim's definition of religion as beliefs and practices in relation to the sacred that draw people into a unified community.[2] In this respect, football is a religion because it acts like a religion, making us "feel that we are participating in something huge and communal." In British society, Christmas or royal events might achieve that religiously ritualized social solidarity, according to Hobson, but conventional religions, which form communities around churches, mosques, or temples, do not generate "a sense of solidarity with society in general." Accordingly, in functional terms, Hobson can conclude that recognized religions are less "religious" than the religion of football in forming social solidarity. Given the diversity of organized religions, "religion divides rather than unites," as religious festivities disguise the demands of authoritarian religious leaders, although Hobson acknowledges that conventional religious institutions can sometimes approach the pure religion of football, noting that he is "impressed by Catholic cultures in which holy days resemble big football events." Nevertheless, if we recognize the essential function of religion as creating a sacred sense of social solidarity, then football religion is more religious than any conventional religion. "The desire for society to be united in common ritual expression, or worship, is basic to religion, and perhaps politics too, but all actual realisations of this ideal should be viewed with suspicion." Hobson concluded, "We should be grateful for a harmless version of this deep-rooted instinct."[3] In these terms, football is a religion, better than most, because it acts like religion.

None of the commentaries on football religion that were framed outside South Africa, the sacred site of the 2010 FIFA World Cup, tried to relate religion to economics. Within South Africa, where hosting the World Cup required enormous capital investment in stadiums and infrastructure, neglecting pressing needs for addressing poverty, crime, housing, health care, and education, while ensuring record-breaking profits for FIFA, the intersection between religion and economics, between rituals of solidarity and financial calculations, could not be avoided. Accordingly, when one of South Africa's leading social anthropologists, Steven Robins, defended the religion of football, his article in the popular press was entitled "World Cup Ritual Worth Every Cent."[4]

How should we understand this intersection between football religion and economics? As I will propose, the World Cup was an instance of what Georges Bataille called *expenditure,* nonproductive expenditure evident in sacrifice, destruction of resources, and the "construction of sumptuary monuments, games, [and] spectacles," certifying "a *loss* that must be as great as possible in order for that activity to take on its true meaning."[5] As ritualized expenditure, the World Cup demonstrated the power of what Bataille identified as the general economy of excess, ostentatious loss, and exuberant destruction of resources that can never be contained within capitalist calculations of profit, wealth, and accumulation in the restricted economy. The 2010 FIFA World Cup in South Africa ritualized the relations between religion and economics in ways that cannot be contained by either morphological or functional analysis. Here Bataille might help us understand religion and economics in terms of the dynamics of sacrifice, festival, and sovereignty. Religion, including the religion of football, is not merely forms and functions but also the dynamics, energetics, and political economy of the sacred.

Bataille (1897–1962), as we will learn, is a good companion to bring along to the World Cup. As a student of the sociology of religion initiated by Emile Durkheim, Bataille began his own Collège de Sociologie in the 1930s to analyze the sacred dynamics of society but also to revitalize the sacred in France. Taking seriously the energizing potential of ritual sacrifice, he proposed performing a human sacrifice in Paris, even finding a volunteer, but he was unable to secure municipal permission for the ritual. Over a long career as a theorist of religion, sociologist, novelist, poet, and pornographer, he developed important insights into the dynamics of the sacred.[6] By taking Bataille to the World Cup, I do not intend to simply apply his theory to football, as if he would help us to answer the question: Is football a religion? The historian of religions Kocku von Stuckrad has argued that the answer to this question depends upon whether participants invoke religious discourses and enact religious practices. "As long as the cultural communication about football does not involve references to what the actors regard as religious, football does not belong to the religious field of discourse; however, when people start using religious semantics in their communication about football—which can also be non-verbal, such as the building of a prayer room in a football stadium—football definitely belongs to the religious field of discourse and is worthy the attention of scholars of religion."[7]

As we will see, the cultural officials of the 2010 FIFA World Cup in South Africa did more than build a prayer room. They officiated over blood sacrifices in keeping with the religious practices of African religion. Georges Bataille will have something to say about this sacrificial performance in the larger context of the sacrificial economy of the World Cup.

SACRIFICE

In December 2009, Zolani Mkiva, speaking on behalf of the Makhonya Royal Trust, which was coordinating cultural events for the 2010 FIFA World Cup, announced the plan to perform ritual sacrifices of cattle at each of the ten stadiums that had been prepared for the tournament. "We must have a cultural ceremony of some sort, where we are going to slaughter a beast," Mkiva explained. "We sacrifice the cow for this great achievement and we call on our ancestors to bless, to grace, to ensure that all goes well." In support of this proposal to perform ten sacrificial rituals, the South African minister of cooperative governance and traditional affairs, Sicelo Shiceka, argued that these ceremonies would not only sanctify but also Africanize the international event. "The World Cup will be on the African continent," Minister Shiceka observed, "and we will make sure that African values and cultures are felt by the visitors."[8] Although the term *sacrifice* is often used metaphorically in the religion of football, here was a proposal to perform actual blood sacrifices, rituals that required the killing of an animal, as an integral part of the cultural, spiritual, and religious significance of the World Cup. An international outcry erupted in the media, and animal rights organizations mobilized petition campaigns against the ritual. FIFA remained silent about its policy regarding the sacrifice of animals. As *Guardian* correspondent Matt Scott reported, "The plan, which apparently involves slicing the throat of a cow with a knife or an assegai, reportedly has the support of South Africa's traditional affairs minister, Sicelo Shiceka." Despite attempts to get a response, Scott found that FIFA was not prepared to say "whether it will allow the slaughter rituals to go ahead."[9]

During the previous month, ritual sacrifice had become the focus of controversy in South Africa as Animal Rights Africa went to court to stop the killing of a bull that forms part of the annual observance of Ukweshwama, the first fruits ceremony presided over by the Zulu king. Besides Zulu king Goodwill Zwelithini, respondents included Minister Shiceka, the minister of police Nathi Mthethwa, KwaZulu-Natal premier Zweli Mkhize, and the provincial minister for local government, housing and traditional affairs, Nomusa Dube. By naming these respondents, Animal Rights Africa was challenging both hereditary traditional leadership and elected democratic leadership in South Africa to prevent the ritual sacrifice of a bull at an annual celebration of Zulu royalty. In this ceremony, young men catch and kill a bull with their bare hands. Characterizations of this ritual differed dramatically. "During the Ukweshwama ritual," according to Animal Rights Africa, "men pulled out the bull's tongue, stuffed sand in its mouth and also attempted to tie its penis in a knot." By stark contrast to this visceral account, defenders of the ritual consistently rendered it as religious symbolism, observing that "Ukweshwama is a symbolic way of thanking God for the first crops of the season."[10] Accepting the argument that the ritual killing was religious symbolism, the judge in this case observed that "the activity was as important to the Zulu tradition as the Holy Communion was to Catholics."[11] Furthermore, acknowledging the royal symbolism of the ceremony, the judge found that the bull was killed by Zulu warriors in order to transfer "symbolic powers" to the Zulu king. "If this is stopped, the symbolic powers would be stopped," he said. "In effect, you are killing the king."[12] Accordingly, religious freedom, guaranteed by the South African Constitution, allowed for the ritual killing of a bull that symbolized thanksgiving to God and the sovereignty of the Zulu king.

On the eve of the 2010 FIFA World Cup, a sacrificial ritual was performed at one stadium, Soccer City, where the opening and closing ceremonies of the World Cup were scheduled. Organized by Zolani Mkiva, the ceremony was officiated by three hundred traditional diviners and healers, *sangomas* and *inyangas,* with about two thousand people in attendance. The ceremony began at 6:00 a.m. with the ritual killing of an ox by a seventy-year-old "Xhosa warrior" who speared the animal at the back of its neck, between its horns, according to tradition. Burning the traditional herb *impepho,* the ritual specialists, by Mkiva's account, called on "the spirits of our African ancestors to usher in their wisdom and energy in setting the scene of what was to follow in the day."[13] Phepsile Maseko, national coordinator for the Traditional Healers' Organisation, described the ceremony as having three effects—unifying people, welcoming visitors, and appeasing ancestors. "We burnt incense and other medicines and we slaughtered a cow near the stadium," Maseko recounted. "The cow symbolizes strength. . . . It is a unifying cow." Dealing with foreign fans and indigenous ancestors, the ritual was both the way "we bless the stadium as a symbol of welcome to the nations that are coming" and a way to alert the ancestors to the arrival of football fans from all over the world, because "we don't want our spirits to be scared of all the different languages."[14] Spiritually, the energy of this ritual was transmitted to all of the other stadiums throughout the country. As a result, despite abandoning the plan to perform sacrificial rituals at ten stadiums, Zolani Mkiva could conclude, "Our stadiums are now officially blessed according to our culture, for the tournament."[15]

Here we find different understandings of sacrifice, not merely in the rift between defenders of cultural traditions and defenders of animal rights, but in the contrasting interpretations of sacrifice by participants in the Zulu royal sacrifice and the World Cup sacrifice. On the one hand, the Zulu royal sacrifice during the annual observance of Ukweshwama was interpreted as a ritual of transcendence, invoking a transcendent deity, empowering the sovereign king, which reinforced the legitimacy of a traditional polity. As a ritual symbolizing the supreme power of God and king, this royal sacrifice was interpreted as reestablishing hierarchical relations of domination and subordination in Zulu society. Sacrifice, in this case, was understood as a religious ritual of political sovereignty. On the other hand, the World Cup sacrifice was understood by its officiants as a sacred event, generating a shared spiritual energy that effectively mediated relations among participants, strangers, and ancestors. Not a symbolic invocation of vertical transcendence, this sacrifice was understood to operate on a horizontal plane, extending spiritual energy to the ancestors in the earth, the stadiums throughout the country, and football fans all over the world. By contrast to the Zulu royal offering to the centralized, hierarchical power of God and king, the World Cup sacrifice radiated centrifugal force by transmitting spiritual energy everywhere and centripetal force by drawing everyone into the sacrificial space. Accordingly, this sacrifice was rendered as an act of ritual inclusion in a blessed community.

This distinction between transcendence and the sacred can be illuminated by Bataille's theory of sacrifice. According to Bataille, the sacred is the opposite of transcendence. While transcendence introduces hierarchy and alienation, a "religious" profanation of the sacred, the sacred transforms the profane world of utility into the sacred world of animality, intimacy, immediacy, and imminence. As the primary way of effecting this transformation, sacrifice removes both the victim and the sacrificer from the profane world of useful things, practical projects, economic calculations, and transcendental legitimations. As Bataille argued, "The first fruits of the harvest or a head of livestock are sacrificed in order to remove the plant and the animal, along with the farmer and the stock raiser, from the world of things."[16] In the religious symbolism of Christian Holy Communion and Zulu royal ritual, sacrifice is profaned by being turned back into a useful thing to the extent that it is deployed to legitimate the centralized authority of an ecclesiastical or political hierarchy. In the case of the World Cup ritual, we seem to have an instance of what Bataille regarded as sacrificial immediacy. "In sacrifice," he observed, "it is in the act itself that value is concentrated. Nothing in sacrifice is put off until later—it has the power to contest everything at the instant that it takes place, to summon everything, to render everything present."[17] Certainly, as understood by its organizers, the World Cup sacrifice was an act that brought everyone—foreigners, South Africans, and ancestral spirits—together in the moment of its enactment.

"In his strange myths, in his cruel rites," Bataille observed, "man is in search of a lost intimacy."[18] That intimacy, immediacy, and imminence of the sacred is achieved in the moment of sacrificial destruction and loss, in the sacrificial act of unconditional giving that relinquishes any expectation of return. In that moment of intimacy between sacrificer and victim, which removes both from the profane world of useful things, Bataille hears the sacrificer declare, "*Intimately,* I belong to the sovereign world of gods and myths, to the world of violent and uncalculated generosity."[19] By surrendering to the imminent presence of gods and myths, the sacrificer recovers what Bataille, in his specific definition of the term, identifies as "sovereignty," a momentary redemption of a sovereign self from its *thingification* in the profane world. Rupturing the world of useful things, sacrifice signifies sovereignty because in sacrifice both offering and offerer are "rescued from all utility."[20] Clearly, Bataille's notion of sovereignty is not the political sovereignty advanced in the renderings of Zulu royal ritual as a celebration of a transcendent God and king. Rather, this sovereignty, the recovery of free subjectivity from the world of things, is a breakthrough of the sacred, an interruption, disruption, or transgression of the profane world, in which a society may be transformed into a community. Although he often seemed to regard sovereignty as individual, as sovereign subjectivity, Bataille also focused on the dynamics of community, noting that "the sacred is only a privileged moment of communal unity, a moment of convulsive communication of what is ordinarily stifled."[21] Festival, carnival, and the display, giving, and destruction of wealth in rituals of potlatch, for Bataille, were instances of such convulsive communication of the sacred that transgressed the stifling order of economic rationality.

They rescued human beings from the world of things, the organization of projects, and the calculations of utility. Festivals, as free spaces and times of the sacred, can make anyone and everyone gods or kings. In festivals, sovereignty is not the political authority of royalty, state, or government but the ecstasy of being lost in the sacred.

FESTIVAL

On June 11, 2010, Zolani Mkiva, who has been named the Poet of Africa, began the opening ceremony of the 2010 FIFA World Cup at Soccer City with a performance of traditional African praise singing. Anticipating his appearance on the global stage, Mkiva said, "I am thrilled. It's a dream come true. I will be watched by more than three billion people from across world." Dedicating his performance to his late father, to the deceased monarch King Xolilizwe Sigcawu, and to the ninety-two-year-old former president Nelson Mandela, Mkiva called upon all South Africans to come together, in prayer, in support of their national team. "We must keep on praying for our boys, Bafana Bafana," Mkiva urged. "We must see them going to the finals. We must create a vibrant team spirit. They are patriots who have the entire world on their shoulders."[22] Like the sacrificial ritual he officiated at Soccer City before the World Cup, Mkiva's performance in the opening ceremony was intended to radiate sacred energy in larger and larger concentric circles of ancestral spirits, traditional royalty, national leadership, patriotic citizens, and a vast global community. Sixteen years earlier, Mkiva had been on a comparable stage, acting as the *imbongi*, the praise singer, at the inauguration of Nelson Mandela, the first democratically elected president of a new South Africa. His performance on that occasion had also mediated between local tradition, tracing Mandela back through heroic founders of the African National Congress, and a global audience, with special attention to singing the praises of Fidel Castro, Yasser Arafat, and Muammar Gaddafi.[23] Now he was opening the festival of the 2010 FIFA World Cup in South Africa.

According to Bataille, festival is "the place and the time of a spectacular letting loose."[24] In his defense of the World Cup, the anthropologist Steven Robins emphasized the spectacularization of sports as festival, as carnival, as an "ecstatic experience of solidarity and belonging." Individuals, in ecstasy, found themselves "losing one's self in the collective spirit of the carnival." As in Bataille's notion of sovereignty, which has nothing to do with normal politics, economics, or social order, the

World Cup provided an occasion for individuals to find their ecstatic sovereignty by abandoning the world of things, utility, projects, and economic calculations. During the World Cup, as the everyday, ordinary, and mundane world was "temporarily cordoned off," South African society was transformed into a community. As Robins concluded, we should appreciate the World Cup for the "benign social solidarity that occurred during this hyper-transient, yet wondrous, collective ritual."[25] Ecstasy and solidarity, as other analysts have observed, were the essence of the religion of football presented at the 2010 FIFA World Cup. For example, according to the political philosopher Achille Mbembe, football at the World Cup was "an act of communion that offers its members the opportunity to share, with countless pilgrims from around the world, the moments of a unique intensity."[26] Durkheim's notions of ecstasy and solidarity—collective effervescence, unified moral community—provided the template for these analyses of the World Cup festival.

However, as Bataille argued, the "spectacular letting loose" of the festival takes place in tension with the profane world of utility, economic calculation, and political authority that it can only temporarily disrupt. The festival's scope for personal ecstasy and social solidarity is "limited by a countervailing prudence that regulates and limits it." Although festival, with all of its sacrificial and celebratory giving, loss, waste, and destruction, may break through the limits of profane regularity into sacred immediacy, it is inevitably limited by the demands of the profane. Given the ongoing struggles between social taboos and their transgressions, "the festival is tolerated to the extent that it reserves the necessities of the profane world."[27] Although festivals are occasions for entering the sacred, for transgressing and disrupting the profane ordering of society, they are negotiated in the face of countervailing demands for restoring profane law and order. As a result, Bataille concluded, "The festival is not a true return to immanence but rather an amicable reconciliation, full of anguish, between the incompatible necessities."[28] Incompatible, yet entangled, with the profane world, the sacred excess of festival will inevitably be held to account by that world's standards.

Take the vuvuzela, the central aural icon of the 2010 FIFA World Cup in South Africa, a plastic horn that produced a noise compared to the buzzing of swarming bees, the moaning of distressed elephants, and the droning of airplanes, all at deafening volume. Certainly, this festive horn, celebrating football, transgressed conventional standards of the profane world by breaking the rules of music and producing senseless noise. Although it was frequently defended as a necessary part of African football culture, even by Sepp Blatter on behalf of FIFA, the vuvuzela was entangled in the profane world of property when its manufacturer was sued by the Nazareth Baptist Church. Founded in 1910 by the Zulu prophet Isaiah Shembe, the church had used such a horn in its worship services to invoke the Holy Spirit. As one follower of Shembe complained, the appropriation of their sacred horn by football meant that their Holy Spirit, rather than the spirit of the game, was being showered over the stadiums. As this dispute was settled out of court, the Nazareth Baptist Church secured a percentage of profits from the sale of vuvuzelas.[29] But profane claims on the sacred horn extended further. Moving from the local to the global, the president of the South African Council of Churches, Tinyiko Maluleke, described the vuvuzela as a "missile-shaped weapon" that was loud enough to awaken the rest of the world to Africa. Against the background of European colonization of Africa, Maluleke argued, the vuvuzela was an African rejoinder to imperial oppression, dispossession, and neglect. "Now," he asserted, "we have created the vuvuzela, which is one of the most obnoxious instruments: very noisy, very annoying. It will dominate the FIFA World Cup. I see the vuvuzela as a symbol, as a symbol of Africa's cry for acknowledgement."[30] Even the festive noise of the vuvuzela, therefore, could become property in legal disputes and a weapon in global politics during the World Cup.

The reconciliation of sacred and profane at the World Cup, the negotiation between festival and cost accounting, was difficult to adjudicate. Acknowledging the ecstatic enthusiasm and social solidarity generated by football, the South African political philosopher and social activist Richard Pithouse ultimately found that the World Cup festival was an indictment of the ANC government, which had abandoned the needs of the poor to offer "a mix of empty spectacle, participation in empty rituals like 'Football Friday,' and the fantasy of belonging in a society that is increasingly predicated on active and at times violent exclusion."[31] By any rational cost accounting, the festival of the World Cup represented a substantial financial loss to South Africa. Although the precise numbers remain in dispute, South Africa's investment of R24bn ($3bn) for six new and four upgraded stadiums and untold costs for new infrastructure, such as R8bn ($1bn) for the arguably unnecessary Shaka International Airport and R25bn ($3.1bn) for an elite train service between Johannesburg and Pretoria, suggest that enormous local resources were directed into expenditure for the World Cup. Although the anticipated financial benefits to South Africa in the form of tourism and job creation turned out to be negligible, the profit to FIFA, estimated at R24bn ($3bn), was substantial.[32] Clearly, FIFA was the winner of the 2010 FIFA World Cup in South Africa.

In his analysis of sacrificial expenditure, Bataille briefly considered competitive games. Like sacrificial rituals, games can be occasions for loss, waste, and destruction of resources that unleash the sacred. "In various competitive games," he observed, "loss in general is produced," confounding the presumption that games are all about winning. Instead, like sacrificial rituals of expenditure, competitive games waste money and energy. In these sports, such as the World Cup, "as much energy as possible is squandered in order to produce a feeling of stupefaction—in any case with an intensity infinitely greater than in productive enterprises." While South African citizens might have been stupefied by this exorbitant expenditure of resources and energy, their political leaders seemed to be engaging in a ritualized expenditure of resources similar to a potlatch, the sacrificial giving and sometimes destroying of wealth, which Bataille focused upon as the model of a general economy. Necessarily connected to festival, according to Bataille, the ritual of potlatch entailed giving, receiving, and returning under obligation, but in its purest form it was pure giving, without any expectation of return, especially when it was enacted "to defy rivals through the spectacular destruction of wealth." In South Africa, the festival of football seemed to inspire rivalry among politicians in the destruction of wealth as long as it could be linked to the spectacle of the World Cup. The entire proceedings, from this perspective, were devoted to sacrificial expenditure. The sacrificial ritual preceding the World Cup signaled this dedication to expenditure, a destruction of wealth like the potlatch, in which "what is destroyed is theoretically offered to the mythical ancestors."[33] The World Cup festival was a ritualized occasion for destroying resources and making myths.

SOVEREIGNTY

On November 5, 2009, Zolani Mkiva, president and director general of the Institute of African Royalty, convened a gathering of dignitaries at South Africa's Freedom Park, the central shrine of the nation, to bestow the first African Royal Award upon Nelson Mandela, who was praised as the Lion, the "king of the jungle," the icon of the nation. On the eve of the 2010 FIFA World Cup in South Africa, Mkiva presided over the second ceremony of the Institute of African Royalty, held in a Johannesburg hotel, at which the African Royal Award was presented to FIFA president Sepp Blatter.[34] Ironically, South African critics and cartoonists were fond of representing Blatter as a king, as in Jabulani Sikhakhane's indictment of the World Cup, "The Shame of Being Colonised by King Sepp," or as a pope, the head of "an organization that seems a bizarre cross between the Vatican and the IMF."[35] During the World Cup, FIFA enjoyed sovereignty over all the stadiums and their precincts, tax-exempt status, freedom from exchange controls, police escorts and security, enforcement of brands and trademarks, restrictions on media reports bringing FIFA into disrepute, and indemnity from any legal proceedings. As the criminologist Sophie Nakueira observed, "The traditional notion of national sovereignty is irrelevant when bodies like Fifa . . . use governments to advance their own objects, which in Fifa's case is to further its profits."[36] During the World Cup, FIFA was sovereign and Blatter a king, honoured with the African Royal Award by the Institute of African royalty.

While celebrating the global sovereignty of FIFA, African traditionalists took the opportunity of the World Cup to revitalize their own royal claims on political sovereignty. Since 1994, South Africa has been a unified, nonracial democracy under the sovereignty of one of the most progressive constitutions in the world, but governance has been shared with over 2,400 kings, queens, chiefs, and headmen, presiding over 774 chiefdoms that have maintained the same boundaries as were established under apartheid. Approximately 30 percent of the population lives under the authority of a chief. Responsible for security, dispute resolution, and allocation of land, these traditional leaders are also custodians of ancestral rituals, especially sacrifices, which link traditional sovereignty with the spiritual realm of myths, gods, and ancestors.[37] During the World Cup, the AmaGcaleka Xhosa king Zwelonke Sigcawu, whose predecessor had died in 2005, was installed in a traditional ceremony. Anticipating the coronation, Prince Xhanti Sigcawu asserted, "The build-up towards the coronation of the next Xhosa King will be an exciting activity that presents an opportunity to educate the general public about customs, rituals, norms, values, traditions and protocols of the cultural dynamics of our African Royalty." Besides educating the South African public, the organizers of the coronation hoped to attract foreign dignitaries, journalists, and tourists who would be in the country for the World Cup. In a statement issued by the chief executive officer of the Xhosa Royal Trust, Zolani Mkiva, the link between royal ritual and World Cup was important. "This event will take place at a time when the eyes of the entire world will be focused in South Africa given the 2010 Fifa World Cup," Mkiva declared. "Surely the coronation of His Majesty, King Zwelonke, will not only attract the local viewership and listenership but the whole world."[38] Asked about the costs of the coronation, which journalists estimated at around R10 million, Mkiva refused to answer any questions about money because "heritage is priceless."[39]

Although traditional heritage might be priceless, it nevertheless operates in a market economy. Accordingly, Makhonya Investments, on behalf of the Congress of Traditional Leaders of South Africa (Contralesa), was formed as a broad-based black empowerment company designed to advance the financial interests of traditional leaders. Under the leadership of its chairman, Zolani Mkiva, national executive director of Contralesa, Makhonya Investments was committed to providing financial support for South African royalty. In its mission statement, Makhonya Investments declared, "We take pride in having ensured that Kings and Queens together with senior Royals of our country are also direct beneficiaries of this investment initiative."[40] This initiative secured lucrative tenders from government, such as a five-year R3bn contract to manage the vehicle fleet of the Eastern Cape Province, which caused critics to wonder how a poet such as Zolani Mkiva could have the necessary experience to run such an operation.[41] However, as we have seen, Mkiva has had extraordinary experience in the sacred as Poet of Africa and praise singer to Nelson Mandela, as officiator of the World Cup sacrifice and performer in the World Cup opening ceremony, and as chairman of the Makhonya Royal Trust, president of the Institute of African Royalty, chief executive of the Xhosa Royal Trust, executive director of Contralesa, and chairman of Makhonya Investments, which presents him on its website as "HRH Zolani Mkiva," His Royal Highness, royalty in his own right.

In the ongoing transactions between sacred and profane, Georges Bataille observed, "sacred things are constituted by an operation of loss."[42] During the 2010 FIFA World Cup, the sacred was generated by sacrifices, festivals, and royal ceremonials, by stadium construction, infrastructural projects, and contractual obligations, all operating at a considerable financial loss to the people of South Africa. In all of these ways, the dynamics of the sacred was driven by sacrifice. The World Cup created a sacred time of sacrificial loss and waste, of destruction of resources and squandering of wealth, which transformed South Africa into a sacred space. As the traditionalist sacrificers of the cow at Soccer City on the eve of the World Cup observed, sacred space has centrifugal force, radiating everywhere, and centripetal force, drawing everyone inside, recalling Bataille's insight into the power of sacrificial ritual to "summon everything, to render everything present."[43] Harnessing the sacrificial dynamics of the sacred, the World Cup rendered everything and everyone present for the most important festival in the world. The spirit of the World Cup, which was explicitly identified as "spiritual" not only by praise singers and traditional healers but also by FIFA officials, the Local Organising Committee, advertising, and public relations, revealed an energetics of the sacred. Adapting insights from Bataille, we can say that the energetics of the sacred enables individuals to be sovereign and societies to be communities. For individuals, the event was spiritual. In promotions for the World Cup, the Afrikaans word for "spirit"—*gees*—was used for the spirit of the games. Individuals were urged to feel the *gees,* to catch the *gees,* to capture the *gees,* recapturing, in Bataille's peculiar sense, a personal sovereignty by being lost in the sacred. At the same time, the spirit of the games was communal, a Durkheimian "collective effervescence" that promised to transform society—local, national, and international—into community, a sacred solidarity into which personal subjectivity would be absorbed. The World Cup, therefore, mobilized the dynamics and energetics of the sacred.

The sacred, however, is also constituted by the operations of political economy. As I have proposed, it is produced through interpretive and ritual labor that generates surplus, immediately available for contested appropriations, in a political economy of the sacred. Even in a market economy, with its economic rationality, calculations of profit, and practices of accumulation, the sacred persists because, as Bataille observed, "ostentatious loss remains universally linked to wealth, as its ultimate function." Social rank, honor, glory, and even royalty in a capitalist economy are linked to an accumulation of wealth, but "only on the condition," as Bataille insisted, "that the fortune be partially sacrificed in unproductive expenditures such as festivals, spectacles, and games."[44] In the dialectic of sacred and profane, the extraordinary festival of the World Cup, during which individuals momentarily recovered personal sovereignty by losing themselves in the sacred, ultimately reinforced the sovereignty of capital in the political economy of the sacred in South Africa.

Beyond formal resemblance or functional equivalence, therefore, the religion of football at the World Cup in South Africa was religion because it demonstrated the dynamics, energetics, and political economy of the sacred. In the aftermath of the 2010 FIFA World Cup, South Africans struggled to figure out what to do with the stadiums, the "white elephants" that entailed massive maintenance costs in perpetuity with no hope of recovering losses or gaining profit. What would Bataille do? Although stadiums built for the 2002 World Cup in Japan and Korea were destroyed for sound fiscal reasons, Bataille might have advanced a different rationale, based on sacrificial loss, waste, and destruction of resources, for blowing them up. There could be ritual sacrifices, ecstatic festivals, and celebrations of solidarity. Tickets could be sold to behold these events of sacrificial expenditure. Blowing up the stadiums might provide new occasions not only for revitalizing the sacred but also for asserting competing claims on sovereignty in South Africa.

CHAPTER TEN

Staying Wild

Religion has always been wild. From a South African perspective, the term *religion* did not come from ancient Greco-Roman antiquity, medieval Christianity, or the European Enlightenment. It came from the sea, in ships, carried by European navigators, missionaries, and colonial agents who wielded the word as a weapon against indigenous people by declaring that they lacked any trace of religion and were instead subject to wild superstitions.[1] Religion, therefore, was a mark of difference separating the civilized from the wild.

Historian Paul Landau has argued that there actually was no religion in precolonial southern Africa. Indigenous African religion took shape out of the contacts, relations, and exchanges of the colonial encounter; it was a product of colonial crisis and intercultural translation. While Christian missionaries were busy finding local names for God by appropriating indigenous terms for an ancestor, such as *modimo* or *unkulunkulu,* Africans under colonial conditions found new ways to make their ancestors "spiritualized and sacralized."[2] In the wild and indeterminate terms of the colonial encounter, both Christian religion in Africa and African indigenous religion were made. Besides marking difference, therefore, religion was a wild arena in which new forms of the sacred were being produced.

For many years, the historical deployment of the word *religion* and the historical production of religion in South Africa have been obscured by the tendency to regard indigenous religion as if it were a stable religious system. For example, the notion of a Zulu religious system, which was inscribed in the classic text by Henry Callaway, *The Religious System of the Amazulu* (1868–70), was embedded in the boundaries imposed by the colonial location system or reserve system.[3] In academic research, a Zulu religious system has been constructed through an inventory of key features—belief in God, reverence for ancestors, rituals of sacrifice, practices of divination, and loyalty to political authority, asserted in collective rituals of fertility and warfare, but also claims to sacred kingship in the lineage of the thoroughly mythologized King Shaka, who was most frequently and consistently celebrated by British colonizers and imperialists.[4] In the colonial context, none of these features of indigenous Zulu religion could possibly be regarded as elements of a stable system. As religious resources, simultaneously symbolic and material, all of these elements were being deployed during the nineteenth century in complex and contested negotiations under colonial conditions.

Abstracted from colonial situations, indigenous African religion has been rendered as a distinctive spiritual mentality that pervades every aspect of African life, as in John S. Mbiti's understandable but untenable counterattack to the European denigration of African religion: "Wherever the African is, there is his religion: he carries it to the fields where he is sowing seeds or harvesting a new crop; he takes it with him to the beer party or to attend a funeral ceremony; and if he is educated, he takes religion with him to the examination room at school or in the university; if he is a politician he takes it to the house of parliament." In every sphere of economic, social, and political activity, Africans, according to Mbiti, are essentially religious. "Although many African languages do not have a word for religion as such," Mbiti admitted, "it nevertheless accompanies the individual from long before his birth to long after his physical death."[5] But such a "utopian" religion, which can be taken anywhere as a mobile mentality, is actually a consequence of colonial disruptions that detached the sacred from "locative" relations of ancestral exchange and orientation.[6]

Given these disruptions, we should not be surprised to find indigenous religion staying wild. Neither a stable and enduring system nor a perennial mentality that has persisted unchanged from time immemorial, African religion is an open set of resources and strategies for sacralizing. Nevertheless, indigenous African religion has been subjected to a variety of constructions, not only by anthropologists and historians, but also by adherents and advocates in postapartheid South Africa. As we have seen, these constructions can be very different. Credo Mutwa's neoshamanism can be contrasted with Mathole Motshekga's ancient Egyptian theosophy, and both differ dramatically from Nokuzola Mndende's profile of African traditional religion as comprising belief in the Creator, reverence for ancestors, ritual performances, and communal life.[7]

Going back to the colonial era, we find evidence of the relational production of indigenous religion. Shamans, for example, first emerged in the reports of European travelers, missionaries, and colonial agents as wild men. From a colonial perspective, shamanic practices often registered as incomprehensible noise, something like the vuvuzela during the 2010 FIFA World Cup. Songs, chants, and ritual performances were often described in colonial accounts not as music but as dissonant noise. As Giuseppe Acerbi reported, the song of the Siberian shaman, performed in secret in the mountains, was "the most hideous kind of yelling that can be conceived."[8] Likewise, in early reports from the Americas, shamans were said to produce the "most hideous Yellings and Shrieks."[9] The earliest colonial accounts from southern Africa claimed that indigenous ritual experts "sang only ha, ho, HO, HO, until one almost lost hearing and sight because of the terrible noise."[10] For colonial regimes relying upon visual surveillance, verbal command, and embodied discipline, the practices of shamans represented a kind of sensory disorganization. Inherently threatening to colonial rule, this alternative ordering of the senses was sometimes intentionally deployed by indigenous ritual specialists in opposition to colonial domination. In the Eastern Cape of southern Africa during the late 1830s and early 1840s, a Xhosa diviner by the name of Mngqatsi conducted regular rituals outside the British colonial settlement of Grahamstown, frightening the settlers with loud drumming and chanting. Often performed on Sundays, these rituals sought to disrupt the religious order of colonialism.[11] During the 1920s in central and southern Africa, anticolonial noise was transposed into a Christian idiom, under the influence of Pentecostal missions, in the practice of *chongo,* all-night sessions of loud drumming, singing, shouting, and speaking in strange tongues. *Chongo* was nothing more than "gibbering, shivering, and generally mad fits," according to the colonial administrator Charles Draper. His attempt to suppress this religious activity suggests that the sounds of shamanic ecstasy could be perceived as threatening colonial authority and control.[12] Although shamans were occasionally involved in explicitly anticolonial movements and revolts, their mere existence represented a wild noise beyond colonial control.

Under colonial conditions, indigenous forms of wild religion emerged to terrify both colonized and colonizer. In *The Wretched of the Earth,* the anticolonial theorist and strategist Frantz Fanon largely ignored religion, but he did reflect on recurring revivals in Africa of a wild religion, in which "terrifying myths" of maleficent spirits, the "leopardmen, serpent-men, six-legged dogs, zombies," generated an imaginary world of spiritual powers and prohibitions "far more terrifying than the world of the settler."[13] Such frightening forces, which further subdued the colonized, could also be deployed against the colonizer. In Mozambique, Eduardo Mondlane observed that traditional religious resources—indigenous religious forms of poetry, songs, dances, and art—were being revived and mobilized in resistance to colonialism. But they were also being recast under colonial conditions of interreligious contact in entirely new modes of engagement. Traditional woodcarvers, the Makonde, were performing their indigenous art by appropriating and transposing Christian symbols. As Mondlane recounted, these traditional artists were representing Christ as a demon, priests as animals, and the suffering of the crucifixion as a call for revenge. In these wood carvings, "a Madonna is given a demon to hold instead of the Christ Child; a priest is represented with the feet of a wild animal, a pieta becomes a study not of sorrow but of revenge, with the mother raising a spear over the body of her dead son."[14] Here was a kind of wild religion, employing indigenous art, but intervening in the colonial contest over religious meanings by appropriating, distorting, and reconfiguring a colonizing religion. This kind of hybridity, mixing and merging religious resources, appropriating and subverting religious signs, was a recurring feature of colonial situations.

WILD TRANSACTIONS

During the mid–twentieth century, the most celebrated African religious specialist in South Africa was Khotso Sethuntsa, a medicine man from the Eastern Cape town of Lusikisiki who drew his extraordinary healing powers and dangerous secrets for gaining wealth from the spirits of the river, the *abantu bomlambo,* of Xhosa tradition. Khotso was renowned for communing with two kinds of snakes: the *inkanyamba,* which gave luck, health, and prosperity, and the *mamlambo,* appearing as a beautiful woman in the depths of a river, who gave extraordinary wealth and power. With his many houses, luxury cars, and suitcases of cash, Khotso was famous for his mastery of the sacred secrets of money. According to one of his wives, "Money just had to flow in, one way or another. He loved the smell and touch of it, coins and notes. No getting out of it. There were pillows of money."[15] In exchange for this extraordinary wealth, blood was required. The spirits of the river required blood sacrifices, usually an animal sacrifice, but seekers after extraordinary wealth had to put their own lives and the lives of their families at stake. In Khotso's world, blood and money were unified in a sacrificial economy of exchange with the powerful spirits of the water that created wealth and power. As Khotso's fame extended throughout South Africa, Christians were also drawn to seek his services, including prominent Afrikaner politicians of the National Party. According to documentary and eyewitness accounts, the most powerful leaders of the emerging apartheid regime, D.F. Malan, H.F. Verwoerd, and J.G. Strijdom all visited Khotso. On the eve of the 1948 elections that brought the National Party to power, Verwoerd left a meeting with Khotso carrying a bottle of *muti*, powerful medicine, an event that gave rise to the popular tradition that the National Party achieved electoral victory only because they had the medicine man's *muti*.[16] Although he had mastered the secrets of the indigenous water spirits, Khotso also communed with a powerful spirit guide, who featured prominently as a tutelary deity in the shrine of his home: Paul Kruger, president of the Transvaal, who had led Afrikaners against the British during the South African War (1899–1902) and according to legend had hidden a vast fortune that was never discovered. Certainly, in the case of Khotso Sethuntsa, indigenous African religion was transaction.

In postapartheid South Africa, as we have seen, indigenous African religion has continued to transact. In 1996, Nicholas Gcaleka, who claimed to be a diviner, healer, and visionary in the Eastern Cape, was inspired by a dream to recover the skull of the nineteenth-century Xhosa king Hintsa. The death of Hintsa in 1835 in battle against British troops, who took the king's head as a trophy, was a critical moment in a long history of colonial warfare and Xhosa oral tradition. Although Gcaleka was denounced by Xhosa royalty as a fake, fraud, and charlatan, with the Xhosa king Xolilizwe Sigcawu calling him a "true con artist," he followed his dream to Scotland, where he was certain that he would find Hintsa's skull. In the indigenous idiom, as we have seen, dreams could be authorizing texts, certifying an ancestral intervention, demanding a response. Gcaleka responded to the demands of his dream. Securing a skull from a Scottish farm, he returned to South Africa hoping that the return of the Xhosa king would usher in a spiritual recovery from colonialism. However, when subjected to scientific testing, the skull was found to belong not to Hintsa but most likely to a middle-aged European woman.[17]

In 2001, Scotland Yard was baffled by an apparent murder of an African child, a child they called "Adam," whose mutilated body had been found in the Thames. Turning to African experts, Inspector Will O'Reilly enlisted the help of two experts from South Africa. First, he consulted with Colonel Kobus Jonker, an expert on Satanism, ritual murder, and other wild crimes who had founded the Occult-Related Crimes Unit of the South African Police during the apartheid era. Colonel Jonker showed the British policeman a "range of gruesome photographs," which had no doubt been drawn from his ongoing campaigns to protect Christians from the occult. Second, O'Reilly hired the indigenous Zulu religious specialist Credo Mutwa, "a well-known and powerful sangoma who abhorred the use of dark practices by some of his peers." Applying his expertise, Mutwa found that the child had been the victim not of a *muti* murder but of a sacrificial offering to a deity, a "human sacrifice committed by the worst black magicians in West Africa." On the basis of the spiritual insights of an apartheid-era Christian crusader against Satanism and a world-renowned Zulu shaman, O'Reilly reportedly returned to Scotland Yard "having established that Adam's murder bore all the hallmarks of a West African ritual killing."[18]

All of these wild transactions are instances of what the anthropologist Véronique Faure has called the "commodification and political manipulation of the notion of the occult."[19] Mysterious snakes produced wealth and power; dreamers, visionaries, and religious experts solved crimes. These manipulations of the occult were enacted through transactions with the capitalist economy, traditional authority, and the modern state. As a result, these cases defy any construction of African traditional religion as a stable system or a distinctive mentality. They demonstrate the relational character of indigenous religion. The transactions suggest the variety of ways in which indigenous religion is not preserved in splendid isolation from time immemorial but always entangled in a changing world. Drawing on indigenous religious understandings of sacrifice, snakes, and the liminal potential and danger associated with the river, Khotso created an extraordinary realm of spiritual power, attracting a following but also transacting with the colonial state. The diviners Gcaleka and Mutwa, who had both been accused of being fakes, one being a "true con artist," according to the Xhosa king, the other described in the popular press as a charlatan, asserted their indigenous religious authenticity by transacting with the United Kingdom, the former center of an empire that had once encompassed South Africa. According to the anthropologist Robin Horton, indigenous religion in Africa is supposed to be "microcosmic," focused on the small-scale relations of home, kinship, local chiefs, and ancestral spirits, by contrast to the "macrocosmic" worldviews ushered into Africa by the transcendent deities and transnational scope of Christianity and Islam.[20] However, these African diviners asserted their indigenous authenticity, not at home, but through international transactions with Scotland or Scotland Yard.

Reviewing their cases, we might easily conclude that they failed. Much as DNA testing disproved Gcaleka's claim that he had brought back Hintsa's skull, anthropological expertise refuted Mutwa's notions about human sacrifice in West Africa. The South African Adam Kuper, a professor of anthropology at Brunel University, dismissed the Zulu shaman's findings in the Adam case as nonsense. By following Mutwa, Kuper observed, "the police claimed, quite wrongly, that a [West African] Yoruba river god, Oshun, is associated with the colour orange, and that human sacrifices are made to him." Although he found that the Zulu shaman was wrong about West African religion, Kuper was more concerned that Scotland Yard had "reinforced dangerous delusions" by subscribing to "a farrago of contemporary myths" about African witchcraft, ritual murder, and human sacrifice. As a result, Scotland Yard was not only perpetuating stereotypes about occult Africa but also entangling itself in the projects of African occultists.[21]

Jonker was no doubt delighted with all this attention, since he had been campaigning since 1984, when he became a born-again Christian, to advance a Christian crusade against Satanism. According to Jonker, Satanism came in many forms, including witchcraft, mysticism, magic, and esotericism. Under the auspices of the Occult-Related Crimes Unit, he investigated crimes associated with medicine murders, witch purging, witchcraft-related violence, and the practices of religious sects or cults. Ultimately, from his Christian perspective, all of these crimes bore traces of the work of Satan. More than any Satanist, Jonker kept attention to Satanism alive in South Africa through his lectures, publications, and public profile in the South African Police as an expert on ritual murder.

As evangelical Christians had the most use for Satanism, Pentecostal churches made the most of indigenous notions of witches and witchcraft. The Reverend V.W. Khula, pastor of the True Faith of Apostolic Faith

Ministry in the Eastern Cape, distinguished his Pentecostal mission as a campaign against ancestral religion. "In my ministry," Khula explained, "the Holy Spirit has given me a gift to release those who are involved in Satanism, witchcraft, sangomas, and false prophets."[22] A recurring feature of his services was confessions by former witches. Usually young women, these members of Rev. Khula's congregation gave extraordinary accounts of their previous lives as witches, testifying to acts of harm they had caused against persons and property not only in South Africa but also in distant places all over the world. If anyone doubted the reality of witchcraft, these Christian testimonials provided "evidence" that witches were actually at work causing violence in the world.

Beliefs in witchcraft, as the anthropologist Adam Ashforth has argued, are symptomatic of a general "spiritual insecurity" in African life.[23] Christian campaigns against Satanism and witchcraft have only amplified that insecurity. When a postapartheid government commission was charged with investigating witchcraft in the mid-1990s, the findings did not provide any sense of security. According to the report of the Ralushai Commission, a witch is a person who, "through sheer malice, either consciously or subconsciously, employs magical means to inflict all manner of evil on their fellow human beings. They destroy property, bring disease or misfortune and cause death, often entirely without provocation to satisfy their inherent craving for evil doing."[24] Thus, instead of finding that witchcraft is a delusion, witches do not exist, and witch hunts are senseless acts of violence, the commission reinforced the general belief that witchcraft is real and witches cause violence. In this context, the South African Pagan Rights Alliance, including among its membership Wiccans and other neopagans who regard "witches" positively as persecuted bearers of ancient wisdom in Europe, provided the most vigorous defense of Africans accused of witchcraft. Criticizing government for perpetuating stereotypes, Pagans launched campaigns to call attention to the injustice of identifying, stigmatizing, and killing people as witches.[25]

Mixed up in all these transactions, indigenous religion in South Africa is a wild religion, not because it is practiced by wild savages, but because it is engaged with modernity. Given the Pew Forum finding that 56 percent of South Africans, predominantly Christian, adhere to beliefs in the protective power of sacrifices to spirits or ancestors, and that 52 percent participate in ancestral rituals, we have to recognize that Christianity and indigenous religion have been interwoven in South Africa.[26] Although the mixing and merging of religious practices is a fact of South African life, we find African traditionalists rejecting Christianity and Christians rejecting African indigenous tradition, displaying what we might regard as religious fundamentalisms in a world of ongoing religious transactions.

BLOCKING TRANSACTIONS

Some people do not want to transact. Some people want to maintain or restore the purity of their religion by protecting it from transactions. For example, Christian opponents of South Africa's new educational policy have objected to the inclusion of indigenous African religion. Irmhild H. Horn, professor of primary school education at the University of South Africa, argued in a South African academic journal, the *Journal for Christian Scholarship*, that African Traditional Religion (ATR), like contemporary postmodernism, is a threat to Bible-based Christianity. "Contemporary Africa," she noted, "is seeking to revive and reinstate its traditional primal worldview." Drawing on recent Christian polemics against indigenous African religion, Professor Horn provided a profile of ATR as a worldview based on animism, fetishism, and collectivism. "Both ATR and postmodernism," she asserted, "regard humans as primarily social beings." Horn accused this collectivist worldview of cultivating a "spiritual openness," whether based on primal religion or the postmodern "denial of truth," that runs contrary to the biblically informed spiritual discernment that is required of Christians. Objecting to the revival of indigenous religion among Africans, Horn also complained that "many Westerners, like many black Africans, are seeking to revitalize primal beliefs. The internet, television, films, books and games are primary vehicles for promoting primal beliefs and practices."[27] The inclusion of ATR in religion education, she insisted, was symptomatic of both African religious revival and New Age spirituality.

Professor Horn supplemented her religious objections with reflections on pedagogical method. In South African educational reforms of the 1990s, the entire curriculum had adopted the theory and methods of "Outcomes Based Education" (OBE). In principle, OBE promised a student-centered, lively, engaging, and participatory approach to teaching and learning.[28] But Horn worried that such an approach, with its emphasis on participation, would expose students to dangerous contact with spirits. "The OBE-approach favours experience and active participation," she noted. "It is therefore quite conceivable that children will, for example, participate in dances that induce spirit possession." Not only learning about an indigenous African worldview, students ran the risk, she warned, of participating in spiritual practices based on magic and ultimately on Satanism, because magic, she observed, "always has Satan as its source."[29]

Clearly, this professor of education had strong religious objections to the new policy for teaching and learning about religion, religions, and religious diversity in South African schools. As a trainer of teachers, she could not be expected to help teachers prepare for the challenges of the new curriculum. Although she objected to the inclusion of indigenous African religion, Professor Horn also attacked other religions, having achieved some notoriety in the popular press during 2001 by claiming that Hindu meditation practices "encourage psychological escapism and ultimately schizophrenia."[30] In her article in the *Journal of Christian Scholarship*, however, Professor Horn was most concerned with the consideration of ATR in religion education. She sought to counter its "animistic" worldview by advocating the teaching of intelligent design by a supreme God (although "Satan is prince of this world") and to counter its "collectivism" by advocating the theocratic Christian Reconstructionism of Rousas John Rushdoony as the best formula for religion and society. All of these religious concerns, however, were orchestrated against the use of education—and especially religion education—in the nation-building projects of a new South Africa. "In the name of unity and nation-building," Horn concluded, "our young are being influenced to accept unbiblical ideas and practices, even those that are expressly forbidden in the Bible"[31]

On the other side of this divide we find African *sangomas*, adhering to what they regard as fundamentals of indigenous tradition, who do not want to transact with the increasing number of white *sangomas* in South Africa and abroad. Dr. Nokuzola Mndende, a Xhosa *sangoma* with a PhD in religious studies, has been a prominent opponent of the initiation of white *sangomas*. She founded the Icamagu Institute in 1998 to advance the interests but also to defend the integrity of African religious heritage. In 2001 Dr. Mndende organized a gathering of *sangomas* at the University of Cape Town. "Sangomas take UCT by Storm," the popular press reported. Held in the university's Centre for African Studies, the daylong seminar featured *sangomas* and their initiates drumming, dancing, and singing in the thick smoke from burning traditional herbs. According to Mndende, the event signaled transformation in South Africa. As *sangomas* claimed space in the university, she said, "Now black people have the power to speak on their own."

A few white *sangomas,* however, were also in attendance. Chris Reid, who had adopted the name Ntombemhlope at his initiation in the mid-1990s, came in for special attention. He was challenged for wearing traditional Xhosa attire, was tested on the procedures of his initiation, and was mocked when he performed his dance. A former model, Reid had responded to "a calling from the spirits" to become a shaman. Reportedly he was sponsored by the Coca-Cola Company and South African Breweries to go to "*sangoma* school," where he learned the secrets of trance dancing, herbal healing, and divination. Eventually he entered the tourism industry, establishing Pure Pondo Adventures to lead township tours to herbalist shops and encounters with *sangomas.* At the seminar in 2001, according to the press account, Chris Reid had to flee from the grilling of *sangomas* who challenged his authenticity. "The important thing is that all of us belong to the ancestors," he argued. But the *sangomas* gathered at UCT insisted that he did not belong to their ancestors and that their ancestors could not belong to a white *sangoma.*[32]

In opposing the initiation of white *sangomas,* Mndende has stressed the importance of kinship in African religion. Religious practices, including the initiation of diviners, are deeply embedded in the sacred space of the home, the life of the family, and the extended kinship relations of the clan. Diviners, in Xhosa tradition, are called by the paternal or maternal ancestors of their family. If white aspirants to this calling are intent on taking Xhosa initiation, then they are claiming to be called not by their own ancestors but by African ancestors. Besides questioning the authenticity of this ancestral calling, Mndende has insisted that it is impossible for whites to fulfill the ritual requirements of initiation. She explains:

> You must perform certain rituals to show you have accepted the call; your family plays a major role in this. When you perform the acceptance of the call there are people responsible for certain duties. In the case of the Xhosa, the firstborn male at home slaughters the sacrificial goat and uses the sacred assegai; the paternal aunt makes the sacred necklace—the hair from the sacred cow is woven together with *usinga,* the ligament found in the vertebral column. When that goat is slaughtered there is a portion of meat taken first and roasted inside the kraal. It can *only* be clan members who perform this; all those things should be done by your own people in your own home.

In performing rituals of accepting the call, initiation, and graduation, one's own family is necessarily involved. Authenticity depends upon maintaining these sacralized kinship relations. "If a *sangoma* doesn't take you to your own family," Mndende warns, "it's a fake." According to her, *sangomas* who take on white initiates for a fee are corrupting the purity of indigenous African religion by promoting this fake practice for profit.[33]

Joanne Thobeka Wreford, anthropologist and *sangoma,* has argued against this necessary link between biological kinship and spiritual initiation in African religious tradition. Present at the UCT seminar in 2001, she was dismayed by the rejection of white *sangomas*. In arguing against Mndende's strictures, Wreford has accepted the centrality of kinship but has tried to broaden its definition in keeping with recent changes in African urban life. Not restricted to biology, kinship has expanded into larger networks of relationships of mutual recognition and support. According to ethnographic research in an African township of Cape Town, "People utilize the norms of kin-based relationships for reinforcing relationships between people acknowledged to have no *a priori* genealogical (kinship) link."[34] When Xhosa *sangomas* adopt white initiates into their households, therefore, they are applying this principle of expanding kinship. As a result, white *sangomas* do not have to return to their own homes, let alone their ancestral homeland somewhere in Europe, because they have a new home, family, clan, and ancestral lineage of spiritual kinship.

As Irmhild Horn rejected any transaction with African traditional religion, which she regarded as Satanic, Nokuzola Mndende rejected this "spiritual kinship" with neoshamans as violating the fundamental integrity of African traditional religion in South Africa. Both, in different ways, were trying to protect the purity of their respective religions. In the ongoing history of what Jean and John Comaroff have called the "long conversation" between Africans and the West, between indigenous religion and European Christianity, mixtures rather than purity have been the rule.[35] But not all mixtures have been mixed in the same way. For example, the poet, novelist, and antiapartheid activist Mongane Wally Serote, who is also a *sangoma,* has found his own way to transact with Christianity. In his novel *Revelations,* Serote formulates a specific relation with the religion of the West, as his main character declares: "This young religion on the African continent, Christianity, had cost us dearly indeed, but we had made friends with Christ and asked him daily since then to liberate us from the West."[36] Making friends with Christ for the liberation of Africa from the West, Serote captured a religious strategy, deployed throughout colonial Africa, in which Africans might be in Christianity but not of it. Something of this strategy, perhaps, filtered into his role as director of the national heritage shrine of Freedom Park.

PURITY, POWER, AND FESTIVAL

We have seen African religious resources deployed in recent South African politics, from the national shrine of Freedom Park to the neotraditionalism of the Zuma era, raising questions about the relation between African indigenous religion and the state. A modern state, as Max Weber proposed, is the organized exercise of legitimated violence over a territory.[37] All of these features of the state—coercive power, compelling legitimacy, and territorial sovereignty—have recently been called into question. In recent social and cultural analysis of the state, power has been disaggregated into multisited processes of governmentality, institutionalized functions, and everyday practices.[38] Legitimacy has been recast as fluid and unstable circulations of imagination and even magic.[39] Sovereignty has been rendered a social construction, critiqued as "organized hypocrisy," reconstructed as spatial, and deconstructed as "spectral."[40] In theory and practice, these challenges to the modern state have carried specific force in South Africa. During the antiapartheid struggle, the legitimacy of the apartheid state was vigorously challenged by liberation movements, international organizations, and religious bodies. After the democratic elections of 1994, with legitimacy ostensibly underwritten by popular mandate, the postapartheid state was faced with the challenge of sovereignty. Becoming a nation just when nations were supposedly going out of style, as national sovereignty was allegedly being swept away by global market forces, the new South Africa was faced with crucial dilemmas of nation building and social cohesion.[41]

The new democratic government was also confronted with the risk of being captured by the state. In education, for example, the new government Ministry of Education inherited all of the bureaucratic structures and racist inequities established by the apartheid state. Faced with the monumental task of creating a unified educational system out of this fractured legacy, even the most radical, revolutionary educationalists from the liberation movements soon found themselves "seeing like a state."[42] As Mongane Wally Serote observed in his novel *Revelations,* Africans in the democratic dispensation suddenly found themselves responsible for healing the damage that had been done to them by apartheid.[43]

Although indigenous religion is transactional, we have seen how its guardians have opposed certain transactions in the name of purity. During the annual festival of the Royal Reed Dance in 2010, the Zulu king Goodwill Zwelithini gave a speech to twenty thousand bare-breasted Zulu maidens about the dangers of pornography. The king complained, "Some people are doing this dirty thing of inviting photographers during the virginity testing of maidens." As we recall, the festival had long been a tourist attraction. Perhaps the recent introduction of the ritual of virginity testing, which was a response to the AIDS epidemic under the auspices of revitalizing indigenous tradition, raised the king's concern about tourist photography. In any case, the Zulu king railed against enemies of the kingdom who were defiling the sanctity of the Reed Dance by exploiting the Zulu maidens on display during the ceremony as a "source of material for international pornography websites." As the king exclaimed, "I was shocked when I received these pictures on my website!" Here was a transaction between traditional authority and modern communication technology. The Zulu king had a website. But he did not like what he was seeing. The Zulu kingdom had to be mobilized, King Zwelithini concluded, to fight the pornographic enemies of "this solemn culture of ours."[44]

Addressing the sexual politics of South Africa, Nokuzola Mndende has commented on polygamy, gender, and sexual orientation. In response to the scandal in early 2010 when it was revealed that President Jacob Zuma had fathered a child outside of wedlock, Mndende was adamant that the president's conduct was not consistent with African tradition. "Polygamous marriage is like any other marriage," she explained, "it doesn't allow extra-marital affairs." In African tradition, prescribed procedures had to be followed for a man to take another wife. But African tradition did not permit conceiving a child outside the sanctity of marriage. Moving from African tradition to a more general observation about gender, Mndende concluded that the real problem was that Zuma was a man. "An extra-marital affair is beyond race, religion or culture," she observed. "It's a weakness of men."[45] By contrast to Zuma's supporters in the Kara Heritage Institute, who announced that the president's behavior was consistent with African tradition, Mndende insisted that the president had violated both indigenous tradition and gender justice. For her, the issue of gender was important, since she argued that African traditional religion was a "genderless faith," in which God and ancestors were spiritual, without gender, and that male and female human beings both had prominent roles in the tradition.[46] Turning to sexual orientation, however, she noted a problem in traditional accommodation of same-sex marriages that were recognized under the constitution. The traditional exchange of *lobola,* the bridewealth paid before marriage, posed a problem. "Normally the man pays it," she noted. "In this case who's going to pay?"[47]

As the anthropologist Graeme Reid has shown, the freedom of sexual orientation, enshrined in the South African Constitution, which entails the right to same-sex marriage, became a flashpoint for revealing the gap between progressive constitutionalism and religious tradition in South Africa. In a series of public hearings on same-sex marriage conducted by the National House of Traditional Leaders in 2005, the African public overwhelming opposed homosexuality as un-African and un-Christian, a violation of both domains of religious purity. Citations of the Christian Bible mixed with concerns about traditional practices of *lobola,* procreation, and inheritance in African religious tradition. As we have seen, traditional leadership can make strong claims on indigenous African religion and can invoke African religion in claims on political power and authority. During one of the hearings on sexuality, after many people had spoken, the master of ceremonies introduced the local chief by saying, "As a chief who is anointed, not a voted chief, he must tell us what he thinks. A voted chief would say same-sex marriages are okay." Contrasting this God-given chief with democratically elected representatives, who in principle should represent the will of the people, the master of ceremonies proposed that the anointed traditional leader was a better representative of their popular will than any elected politician. The chief took up his role in this ritual drama by sanctifying the voices of the people. "The nation has spoken," he proclaimed. "As a creation of God and your leader I am not going to go against the word of God and come up with my own things." While the audience applauded, the chief concluded: "I agree with the nation because there would never be a leader without a nation that supports him. So I am not going to go against what the people of God had to say. What we are hearing shocks me as well."[48] In keeping with conservative public sentiment that homosexuality was un-African and un-Christian, traditional leadership could render popular prejudice as the sacred mandate of indigenous tradition and the Christian God.

In the strained relations between a progressive constitution and conservative tradition in South Africa, homosexuality became a benchmark for reinforcing tradition against the incursions of modernity. However, as Graeme Reid found during his ethnographic research on the public hearings on sexuality, everyone in these communities, even the most religiously conservative, admired the most modern hairstyling, which was associated with the artistry that could be provided only by gay hairdressers. Accordingly, even conservative Christians and African traditionalists, who were opposed to homosexuality and same-sex rights, sought out gay hairstylists to do their hair in a modern style. Hair, as demonstrated in Chris Rock's documentary, *Good Hair,* can be sacred in the difficult transactions between religious tradition and modernity.

However, moving from purity to power, the sacralized claims to anointed authority by traditional leaders remained in tension with constitutional democracy in South Africa. Although various initiatives in education and public pedagogy have tried to cultivate a democratic ethos, the Pew Forum study in 2010 found that only 54 percent of South Africans supported democracy. Rejecting any democratic form of government, 40 percent wanted a strong leader with a strong hand to solve the country's problems.[49] Although South Africa's constitution affirms freedom of religion, many Christians want a religious state. According to the Pew Forum study, 66 percent of Christians in South Africa wanted the constitution to be replaced by the Bible as the official law of the land.[50] We might question the statistical validity of these findings, but they suggest profound contradictions in the South African polity. Fortunately, everything was resolved during the 2010 FIFA World Cup.

The World Cup was the ultimate festival in South Africa. Although I have focused on indigenous rituals, with special attention to sacrifice, the event was blessed by other religious ceremonies. As the newly built Cape Town Stadium was getting ready for the festival, it was tested by a series of events—a football match for twenty thousand, a rugby match for forty thousand, and then the final test, a Christian evangelical prayer rally for sixty thousand people. On May 29, 2010, a prayer rally was held at Super Stadium, Atteridgeville, to mark a national day of prayer for the World Cup and South Africa's national team, known as Bafana Bafana, "the boys, the boys." Reverend Mcebisi Xundu, president of the National Interfaith Leaders Council, prayed for strength, wisdom, and victory for the national team. "We are here to ask God to give our team Bafana Bafana strength and wisdom during this World Cup," he explained, "and only through prayer can they really go far in the tournament." Dr. Mathole Motshekga, chief whip of the ruling African National Congress in Parliament, prayed for national unity. "We are of the view that through sports our nation can prosper," Motshekga declared, "and as we pray for Bafana we must appreciate how we have worked all of us black and white to bury apartheid so let's use this event to unite us behind the team." Spiritually, the National Interfaith Leaders Council was mobilized for the World Cup.[51]

The Anglican archbishop in Cape Town, Thabo Makgoba, announced a simple prayer that he hoped would be embraced not only by Christians but also by people of other faiths. "It is a short and simple prayer which is easy to learn," Archbishop Makgoba explained. "I hope many people, of many backgrounds, will join me in praying it daily in the coming weeks."

> God bless the 2010 World Cup:
> Bless those who compete, and those who watch,
> Bless those who host, and those who visit,
> And help all who love "the beautiful game"
> Grow in the love you have given us to share. Amen.[52]

The Catholic Church of South Africa, with a following of about 10 percent of the South African population, also prayed for the World Cup. Designing a "Soccer World Cup Prayer" in the shape of a soccer ball, the South African Catholic Bishops' Conference prayed that South Africans would be good hosts, especially by refraining from crime, and that God's spirit would infuse the games:

> Almighty God, creator of all
> as people from every nation gather with
> excitement and enthusiasm for the 2010 World
> Soccer Cup may South Africans be good hosts, our visitors
> welcomed guests and the players from every team be blessed
> with good sportsmanship and health. May your Spirit of fairness,
> justice and peace prevail amongst players and all involved.
> May each contribute in his own positive ways to prevent, control
> and fight crime and corruption, hooliganism of any kind and
> exploitation and abuse, especially of those most vulnerable.
> May those far away from home and those in their families
> find much joy in this occasion to celebrate the beautiful
> game of soccer and the beautiful game of life
> according to Your plan for the common
> good of all. Amen.[53]

Tragically, one of the first religion stories to hit the media during the World Cup was an account of a family dispute between devotees of the Christian gospel and a devotee of the religion of football. According to an article entitled "Man Killed by Family for Watching World Cup Instead of Gospel Show," "David Makoeya, a 61-year-old man from the small village of Makweya, Limpopo Province, fought with his wife and two children for the remote control on Sunday because he wanted to watch Germany play Australia in the World Cup. The others, however, wanted to watch a gospel show." In the ensuing religious battle between football and Gospel in the Makoeya home, members of David Makoeya's family beat his head against the wall. He was dead by the time the police arrived.[54]

In its Soccer World Cup Prayer, the Catholic bishops asked not God but ordinary South Africans to prevent, control, and fight crime and corruption. As South Africans prepared for the World Cup, crime seemed to touch every household; corruption seemed to pervade the entire polity; and an undercurrent of violence had become normalized. Reflecting on the accumulative practices of current leaders in South Africa, Simphiwe Sesanti, a journalism lecturer at the University of Stellenbosch, urged a return to tradition. His son had recently gone through the month-long traditional initiation into manhood, learning that to be a man means "never to take away what does not belong to you." But he also carried with him into the bush a gift from his father, *The Wisdom of Ptah-Hotep,* discovering in the sacred teachings of ancient Egypt that greed is the root of all evil. Arguing that corruption is an insult to the ancestors, from the seers of ancient Egypt to the martyrs in the struggle against apartheid, Sesanti called for a revitalization of "cultural rituals to mould men and women that are going to be caring leaders."[55] Moving between domestic and political spheres, this hope for the future is also a feature of wild religion.

Wild religion, as we have seen, lives in the home, the polity, and the practices of sacred specialists who move between domestic and public space, operating within the most intimate relations of the home and the most contested politics of the state. In all of these domains, wild religion can configure spiritual insecurity, fear, and terror. But it can also generate surprising creativity, energizing a variety of personal, social, and political projects. This wild religion, in all its aspects, has permeated South Africa's recent history from the advent of democracy to the euphoria of the World Cup. We can only expect that the sacred in South Africa, having always been wild, will be staying wild.

Notes

PREFACE

1. Afrika Msimang, "Going Back to Our Past with Praise," *Cape Times,* March 1, 1999, 17.

2. David Chidester, *Religions of South Africa* (London: Routledge, 1992), 6.

3. Ibid., 9–10.

4. David Chidester, *Savage Systems: Colonialism and Comparative Religion in Southern Africa* (Charlottesville: University Press of Virginia, 1996), and "Dreaming in the Contact Zone: Zulu Dreams, Visions, and Religion in Nineteenth-Century South Africa," *Journal of the American Academy of Religion* 76, no. 1 (2008): 27–53.

5. Nokuzola Mndende, "African Traditional Religion: A Brief Overview," in *Tears of Distress: Voices of a Denied Spirituality in a Democratic Society* (Dutywa, South Africa: Icamagu Institute, 2009), 111–28.

6. David Chidester, *Authentic Fakes: Religion and American Popular Culture* (Berkeley: University of California Press, 2005), 104–6, 113.

7. William Sims Bainbridge and Rodney Stark, "Client and Audience Cults in America," *Sociological Analysis* 41, no. 3 (1980): 199–214.

8. Vuya Africa, "Spirit of Religion—South Africa," 2005, www.vuyaafrica .co.za/spirit-of-religion.php.

9. BBC, "US Chat Show Host Could Be Zulu," *BBC News,* June 15, 2005, http://news.bbc.co.uk/2/hi/africa/4096706.stm.

10. Kathryn Lofton, *Oprah: The Gospel of an Icon* (Berkeley: University of California Press, 2011).

11. Kader Asmal, David Chidester, and Wilmot James, eds., *Nelson Mandela: From Freedom to the Future* (Johannesburg: Jonathan Ball, 2003), elsewhere published as *Nelson Mandela, In His Own Words: From Freedom to the Future*

(London: Little, Brown, 2003) and as *Nelson Mandela, In His Own Words* (New York: Little, Brown, 2003).

12. David Chidester, Adrian Hadland, and Sandra Prosalendis, "Globalisation, Identity, and National Policy in South Africa," in *What Holds Us Together: Social Cohesion in South Africa,* ed. David Chidester, Phillip Dexter, and Wilmot James (Cape Town: HSRC Press, 2003), 295–321.

13. Kader Asmal, David Chidester, and Cassius Lubisi, eds., *Legacy of Freedom: The ANC's Human Rights Tradition* (Johannesburg: Jonathan Ball, 2005).

14. David Chidester, "Studying Religion in South Africa," in *The Next Step in Studying Religion: A Graduate's Guide,* ed. Mathieu E. Courville (London: Continuum, 2007), 101–15.

1. GOING WILD

1. Peter Harris, *Birth: The Conspiracy to Stop the '94 Election* (Cape Town: Umuzi, 2010), 209, 219.

2. Richard Calland, Lawson Naidoo, and Andrew Whaley, *The Vuvuzela Revolution: Anatomy of South Africa's World Cup* (Johannesburg: Jacana, 2010), 138.

3. Luis Lugo et al., *Tolerance and Tension: Islam and Christianity in Sub-Saharan Africa* (Washington, DC: Pew Forum on Religion and Public Life, 2010), 5, 160.

4. H. Jurgen Hendriks and Johannes C. Erasmus, "Religion in South Africa: The 2001 Population Census Data," *Journal for Theology in Southern Africa* 121 (2005): 88–111.

5. F. W. J. Schelling, *Historical-Critical Introduction to the Philosophy of Mythology,* trans. Mason Richey and Markus Zisselsberger (Albany: SUNY Press, 2007), 171.

6. Bradford Keeney, "What Is Shaking Medicine?" 2009, www .shakingmedicine.com/shaking-medicine/shaking-medicine.php, and *Bushman Shaman: Awakening the Spirit through Ecstatic Dance* (Rochester, VT: Destiny Books, 2005).

7. David Chidester, *Authentic Fakes: Religion and American Popular Culture* (Berkeley: University of California Press, 2005), 119–20.

8. David Chidester and Edward Tabor Linenthal, introduction to *American Sacred Space,* ed. David Chidester and Edward Tabor Linenthal (Bloomington: Indiana University Press, 1995), 1–42.

9. Anthony Synnott, "Shame and Glory: A Sociology of Hair," *British Journal of Sociology* 38, no. 3 (1987): 284. See also Edmund R. Leach, "Magical Hair," *Journal of the Royal Anthropological Institute* 88, no. 2 (1958): 147–64; C. R. Hallpike, "Social Hair," *Man,* n.s., 2 (1969): 256–64; Raymond Firth, "Hair as Private Asset and Public Symbol," in *Symbols: Public and Private* (London: Allen and Unwin, 1973), 262–98; Paul Hershman, "Hair, Sex and Dirt," *Man,* n.s., 9, no. 2 (1974): 274–98; Gananath Obeyesekere, *Medusa's Hair: An Essay on Personal Symbols and Religious Experience* (Chicago: University of Chicago Press, 1981), 13–46.

10. Dir. Jeff Stilson, prod. Chris Rock Entertainment, 2009.

11. Synnott, "Shame and Glory," 390.

12. Britta Sandberg, "Hindu Locks Keep Human Hair Trade Humming," *Spiegel Online International,* February 10, 2008, www.spiegel.de/international/business/0,1518,536349-2,00.html.

13. Saritha Rai, "A Religious Tangle over the Hair of Pious Hindus," *New York Times,* July 14, 2004, www.nytimes.com/2004/07/14/world/a-religious-tangle-over-the-hair-of-pious-hindus.html?pagewanted=all.

14. Jonathan Z. Smith, "The Bare Facts of Ritual," in *Imagining Religion: From Babylon to Jonestown* (Chicago: University of Chicago Press, 1978), 53–65.

15. Leach, "Magical Hair," 154.

16. Jean Comaroff and John L. Comaroff, "Millennial Capitalism: First Thoughts on a Second Coming," *Public Culture* 12, no. 2 (2000): 291–343.

17. Georges Bataille, "The Notion of Expenditure," in *Visions of Excess: Selected Writings, 1927–1939,* ed. Allan Stoekl, trans. Allan Stoekl, Carl R. Lovitt, and Donald M. Leslie Jr. (Minneapolis: University of Minnesota Press, 1985), 118.

18. Access Hollywood, "Bad Day: Chris Rock Is Sued over 'Good Hair,'" *MSNBC: Entertainment,* October 6, 2009, www.msnbc.msn.com/id/33200833/ns/entertainment-access_hollywood/.

19. Leach, "Magical Hair," 162–63.

2. MAPPING THE SACRED

1. On Plinian people, see J.B. Friedman, *The Monstrous Races in Medieval Art and Thought* (Cambridge, MA: Harvard University Press, 1981).

2. Aristotle, *Politics,* trans. Benjamin Jowett (Oxford: Oxford University Press, 1905), 29.

3. Jean-Pierre Vernant, *Myth and Society in Ancient Greece,* trans. Janet Lloyd (Brighton: Harvester Press, 1979).

4. Thabo Mbeki, *Africa, the Time Has Come: Selected Speeches* (Tafelberg, South Africa: Mafube, 1998), 239.

5. Ibid., 241.

6. Vsevolod Slessarev, *Prester John, the Letter and the Legend* (Minneapolis: University of Minnesota Press, 1959).

7. Mbeki, *Africa,* 241.

8. Keith B. Richburg, *Out of America: A Black Man Confronts Africa* (New York: Basic Books, 1997), xxiv.

9. Mbeki, *Africa,* 240.

10. Paul Wheatley, *The Pivot of the Four Quarters* (Chicago: Aldine, 1971), 225–26.

11. Richard W. Bulliet, ed., *The Columbia History of the Twentieth Century* (New York: Columbia University Press, 1998).

12. Camoens, *The Lusiads* (Harmondsworth: Penguin, 1952), 130–31.

13. Pauline Podbrey, *White Girl in Search of a Party* (Pietermaritzburg: Hadeda Books, 1993), 97, and *Cape Times,* April 9, 1996, both cited in Vivian

Bickford-Smith, Elizabeth van Heyningen, and Nigel Worden, *Cape Town in the Twentieth Century: An Illustrated Social History* (Cape Town: David Philip, 1999), 7.

14. David Chidester and Edward T. Linenthal, introduction to *American Sacred Space,* ed. David Chidester and Edward T. Linenthal (Bloomington: Indiana University Press, 1996), 9–16.

15. Albert Grundlingh and Hilary Sapire, "From Feverish Festival to Repetitive Ritual? The Changing Fortunes of Great Trek Mythology in an Industrializing South Africa, 1938–1988," *South African Historical Journal* 21 (1989): 19–37.

16. Ciraj Rassool and Leslie Witz, "The 1952 Jan van Riebeeck Tercentenary Festival: Constructing and Contesting Public National History in South Africa," *Journal of African History* 34 (1993): 447–67. See also Leslie Witz, *Apartheid's Festival: Contesting South Africa's National Pasts* (Bloomington: Indiana University Press, 2003).

17. Adam Smith, *An Inquiry into the Nature and Causes of the Wealth of Nations,* ed. R.H. Campbell, A.S. Skinner, and W.B. Todd, 2 vols. (Oxford: Clarendon Press, 1976), 2:626.

18. H.B. Thom, ed., *Journal of Jan van Riebeeck,* 3 vols. (Cape Town: Balkema, 1952–58), 3:185–86, 23–25; Gerrit Schutte, "Company and Colonists at the Cape, 1652–1795," in *The Shaping of South African Society, 1652–1840,* ed. Richard Elphick and Hermann Giliomee (Cape Town: Maskew Miller Longman, 1989), 292.

19. Patricia Seed, *Ceremonies of Possession in Europe's Conquest of the New World, 1492–1650* (Cambridge: Cambridge University Press, 1995).

20. A. Böeseken, ed., *Dagregister en Briewe van Zacharias Wagenaer, 1662–1666* (Pretoria: Staatsdrukker, 1973), 238; Martin Hall, "Small Things and Mobile, Conflictual Fusion of Power, Fear, and Desire," in *The Art and Mystery of Historical Archaeology,* ed. Anne Elizabeth Yentsch and Mary C. Beaudry (Boca Raton, FL: CRC Press, 1992), 381; Martin Hall, David Halkett, Pieta Huigen van Beek, and Jane Klose, "'A Stone Wall Out of the Earth That Thundering Cannon Cannot Destroy'? Bastion and Moat at the Castle, Cape Town," *Social Dynamics* 16, no. 1 (1990): 22–37.

21. Thabo Mbeki, "Statement of the President of the ANC Thabo Mbeki, on the Report of the TRC: Joint Sitting of the Houses of Parliament," February 1999, www.anc.org.za/ancdocs/speeches/1999/sp0225.html.

22. Michael Keath, *Herbert Baker: Architecture and Idealism, 1892–1913* (Gibraltar: Ashanti, 1992), 130.

23. Hermann Wittenberg, "Rhodes Memorial: Imperial Aesthetics and the Politics of Prospect," unpublished paper, University of Cape Town, Africa seminar. See also Paul Maylam, *The Cult of Rhodes: Remembering an Imperialist in Africa* (Cape Town: David Philip, 2005).

24. Keath, *Herbert Baker,* 130.

25. David Chidester, *Savage Systems: Colonialism and Comparative Religion in Southern Africa* (Charlottesville: University Press of Virginia, 1996).

26. See Edward W. Soja, *Postmodern Geographies: The Reassertion of Space in Critical Social Theory* (London: Verso, 1989), 149, 151; Slavoj Žižek, *The Sublime Object of Ideology* (London: Verso, 1989), 87.

27. Frantz Fanon, *The Wretched of the Earth* (Harmondsworth: Penguin, 1990), 40.

28. Mahmood Mamdani, *Citizen and Subject: Contemporary Africa and the Legacy of Late Colonialism* (Princeton: Princeton University Press, 1996).

29. David Bunn, "Whited Sepulchres: On the Reluctance of Monuments," in *Blank____: Architecture, Apartheid, and After,* ed. Hilton Judin and Ivan Vladislavić (Cape Town: David Philip, 1999).

30. Fanon, *Wretched of the Earth,* 40.

31. J. A. Loubser, *The Apartheid Bible: A Critical Review of Racial Theology in South Africa* (Cape Town: Maskew Miller Longman, 1987).

32. André Du Toit, "No Chosen People: The Myth of the Calvinist Origins of Afrikaner Nationalism and Racial Ideology," *American Historical Review* 88 (1983): 920–52; Leonard Thompson, *The Political Mythology of Apartheid* (New Haven: Yale University Press, 1985).

33. S. W. Pienaar, *Believe in Your People: D. F. Malan as Orator, 1908–1954* (Cape Town: Tafelberg, 1964), 128–29; David Chidester, *Shots in the Streets: Violence and Religion in South Africa* (Cape Town: Oxford University Press, 1992), 7.

34. "Draft Memorandum on the Group Areas Bill, Act 111/2, 12 April 1950," Central Archives, ARG 9; Alan Mabin, "Comprehensive Segregation: The Origins of the Group Areas Act and its Planning Apparatuses," *Journal of Southern African Studies* 18 (1992): 405–29, and "Dispossession, Exploitation, and Struggle: An Historical Overview of South African Urbanization," in *The Apartheid City and Beyond,* ed. David M. Smith (London: Routledge, 1992), 13–24; Uma Mesthrie, "Tinkering and Tampering: A Decade of the Group Areas Act (1950–1960)," *South African Historical Journal* 28 (1993): 177–202, and "'No Place in the World to Go'—Control by Permit: The First Phase of the Group Areas Act in Cape Town in the 1950s," *Studies in the History of Cape Town* 7 (1994): 184–207.

35. Vivian Bickford-Smith, "A 'Special Tradition of Multi-Racialism'? Segregation in Cape Town in the Late Nineteenth and Early Twentieth Centuries," in *The Angry Divide: Social and Economic History of the Western Cape,* ed. Wilmot G. James and Mary Simons (Cape Town: David Philip, 1991), 48, and *Ethnic Pride and Racial Prejudice in Victorian Cape Town* (Cambridge: Cambridge University Press, 1995); Paul Maylam, "Explaining the Apartheid City: 20 Years of South African Urban Historiography," *Journal of Southern African Studies* 21 (1995): 19–38.

36. Christopher C. Saunders, "Segregation in Cape Town: The Creation of Ndabeni," *Africa Seminar: Collected Papers* (Cape Town: University of Cape Town, 1978), 1:47; M. W. Swanson, "The Sanitation Syndrome: Bubonic Plague and Urban Native Policy in the Cape Colony, 1900–1909," *Journal of African History* 18 (1977): 387–410.

37. Christopher C. Saunders, "From Ndabeni to Langa," *Studies in the History of Cape Town* 1 (1984): 194–230.

38. Marco Bezzoli, Rafael Marks, and Martin Kruger, eds., *Texture and Memory: The Urbanism of District Six* (Cape Town: Urban Housing Research Unit, 1998); Shamil Jeppie and Crain Soudien, eds., *The Struggle for District Six: Past and Present* (Cape Town: Buchu Books, 1990).

39. Harriet Deacon, ed., *The Island: A History of Robben Island, 1488–1990* (Cape Town: David Philip, 1996).

40. Nelson Mandela, "Nelson Mandela's Address to the People of Cape Town on the Occasion of His Inauguration as State President, Grand Parade, Cape Town, 9 May 1994," www.polity.org.za/polity/govdocs/speeches/1994/spo509a.html.

41. White House, Office of the Press Secretary, "Remarks by Mr. Kathrada, President Bill Clinton, and President Mandela during Visit to Robben Island, 27 March 1998," http://clinton2.nara.gov/Africa/19980327–10850.html.

42. Sapa, "Sangomas Cleanse Robben Island," *Cape Times*, October 3, 1997.

43. W.D. Hammond-Tooke, "The Symbolic Structure of Cape Nguni Cosmology," in *Religion and Social Change in Southern Africa*, ed. M.G. Whisson and M. West (Cape Town: David Philip, 1975), 15–33; David Chidester, *Religions of South Africa* (London: Routledge, 1992), 9–13.

44. Jean Comaroff, "Healing and Cultural Transformation: The Case of the Tswana of Southern Africa," *Social Science and Medicine* 15, no. 2 (1981): 367–78.

45. Philip Mayer and Iona Mayer, *Townsmen or Tribesmen: Conservatism and the Process of Urbanization in a South African City* (1961; repr., Cape Town: Oxford University Press, 1971); Philip Mayer, "The Origin and Decline of Two Rural Resistance Ideologies," in *Black Villagers in an Industrial Society*, ed. Philip Mayer (Cape Town: Oxford University Press, 1980), 1–80.

46. Archie Mafeje, "Who Are the Makers and Objects of Anthropology? A Critical Comment on Sally Falk Moore's 'Anthropology and Africa,'" *African Sociological Review* 1, no. 1 (1997): 9–10; see also Bernard Magubane, "The 'Xhosa' in Town Revisited: Urban Social Anthropology—A Failure in Method and Theory," *American Anthropologist* 75 (1973): 1701–14.

47. P.A. McAllister, "Work, Homestead, and the Shades: The Ritual Interpretation of Labour Migration among the Gcaleka," in Mayer, *Black Villagers*, 210.

48. Ibid., 238.

49. Victor Turner, *The Ritual Process: Structure and Anti-Structure* (London: Routledge and Kegan Paul, 1969), 112.

50. Janet J. Mills, "Diviners as Social Healers within an Urban Township Context," *South African Journal of Sociology* 18, no. 1 (1987): 7–13; see Teboho Victor Soul, "A Comparative Study of Rural and Urban Africans on their Attitudes towards Amagqira" (MA thesis, University of Fort Hare, 1974).

51. Homi Bhabha, *The Location of Culture* (London: Routledge, 1994), 112.

52. Saunders, "From Ndabeni to Langa," 219.

53. Maylam, "Explaining the Apartheid City," 35.

54. Archie Mafeje, "Religion, Class, and Ideology in South Africa," in Whisson and West, *Religion and Social Change in Southern Africa*, 164–84.

55. James P. Kiernan, "Poor and Puritan: An Attempt to View Zionism as a Collective Response to Urban Poverty," *African Studies* 36 (1977): 31–41, and "The Healing Community and the Future of the Urban Working Class," *Journal for the Study of Religion* 7, no. 1 (1994): 49–64.

56. David Chidester, Gordon Mitchell, Isabel Apawo Phiri, and A. Rashied Omar, *Religion in Public Education: Options for a New South Africa,* 2nd ed. (Cape Town: UCT Press, 1994), 150.

57. John Murray Cuddihy, *No Offense: Civil Religion and Protestant Taste* (New York: Seabury, 1978).

58. Dennis Radford, "South African Christian Architecture," in *Christianity in South Africa: A Political, Social, and Cultural History,* ed. Richard Elphick and Rodney Davenport (Oxford: James Currey, 1997), 327–36.

59. Hilton Judin and Ivan Vladislavić, "Positions A to Z: ZCC," in Judin and Vladislavić, *Blank____.*

60. James P. Kiernan, "Where Zionists Draw the Line: A Study of Religious Exclusiveness in an African Township," *African Studies* 33 (1974): 79–90, and "A Cesspool of Sorcery: How Zionists Visualize and Respond to the City," *Urban Anthropology* 13 (1984): 219–36.

61. Chidester, *Shots in the Streets,* 104.

62. Quoted in ibid., 110.

63. Yusuf Da Costa and Achmat Davids, *Pages from Cape Muslim History* (Pietermaritzburg: Shuter and Shooter, 1994), 130–32; M.K. Jeffreys, "The Malay Tombs of the Holy Circle," *Cape Naturalist* 1–6 (1934–39).

64. I.D. du Plessis, *The Cape Malays,* 2nd ed. (Cape Town: A.A. Balkema, 1972), 33.

65. Achmat Davids, "The Revolt of the Malays: A Study of the Reactions of the Cape Muslims to the Smallpox Epidemics of Nineteenth Century Cape Town," *Studies in the History of Cape Town* 5 (1984): 59.

66. Ibid., 73.

67. Shamil Jeppie, "I.D. du Plessis and the 'Re-Invention of the Malay'" (BA Honors thesis, University of Cape Town, 1988).

68. Nelson Mandela, "Speech by President Nelson Mandela at an Intercultural Eid Celebration, Johannesburg, 30 January 1998," www.info.gov.za/speeches/1998/98202_0x8009810647.htm.

69. "Full-Scale Gang War Threatens Flats," *Mail and Guardian,* August 8, 1996, www.mg.co.za/article/1996-08-08-full-scale-gang-war-threatens-flats.

70. Abdulkader I. Tayob, "Jihad against Drugs in Cape Town: A Discourse-Centred Analysis," *Social Dynamics* 22, no. 2 (1996): 23–29; Sindre Bangstad, "Hydra's Heads: PAGAD and Responses to the PAGAD Phenomenon in a Cape Muslim Community," *Journal of Southern African Studies* 31, no. 1 (2005): 187–208; Heinrich Matthee, *Muslim Identities and Political Strategies: A Case Study of Muslims in the Greater Cape Town Area of South Africa, 1994–2000* (Marburg: Kassel University Press, 2008).

71. Nelson Mandela, "Address by President Nelson Mandela to Parliament, 5 February 1999," www.info.gov.za/speeches/1999/99205_opening99_10091.htm.

72. PAGAD, "People against Gangsterism and Drugs," n.d., www.pagad.co.za/, accessed April 14, 1999.

73. Chidester and Linenthal, introduction to *American Sacred Space,* 5–6.

74. Claude Lévi-Strauss, "Introduction à l'oeuvre de Marcel Mauss," in *Sociologie et anthropologie,* by Marcel Mauss (Paris: Presses universitaires de France, 1950), xlix; Jonathan Z. Smith, *To Take Place: Toward Theory in Ritual* (Chicago: University of Chicago Press, 1978), 107.

75. John Urry, "Social Relations, Space and Time," in *Social Relations and Spatial Structures,* ed. Derek Gregory and John Urry (New York: St. Martin's Press, 1985), 30.

76. David Chidester, "Stealing the Sacred Symbols: Biblical Interpretation in the Peoples Temple and the Unification Church," *Religion* 18 (1988): 137–62.

77. John P. Sullivan, "Gangs, Hooligans, and Anarchists: The Vanguard of Netwar in the Streets," in *Networks and Netwars: The Future of Terror, Crime, and Militancy,* ed. John Arquilla and David Ronfeldt (Santa Monica, CA: RAND, 2001), 116.

78. Harvie Ferguson, *The Science of Pleasure: Cosmos and Psyche in the Bourgeois World View* (London: Routledge, 1990), 61.

79. Chiara Carter and Marianne Merten, "Rites and Wrongs of Cape Gangs," *Mail and Guardian,* January 11, 1999.

80. Don Pinnock, *Gangs, Rituals, and Rites of Passage* (Cape Town: African Sun Press, 1997), 27–41; see also Don Pinnock, *The Brotherhoods: Street Gangs and State Control in Cape Town* (Cape Town: David Philip, 1984).

81. Jeffrey Henderson and Manuel Castells, introduction to *Global Restructuring and Territorial Development,* ed. Jeffrey Henderson and Manuel Castells (Beverly Hills, CA: Sage Publications, 1987), 7.

82. David Harvey, *The Condition of Postmodernity* (Oxford: Basil Blackwell, 1989); Anthony Giddens, *The Constitution of Society* (Berkeley: University of California Press, 1984), 110–44; Arjun Appadurai, "Disjuncture and Difference in the Global Cultural Economy," *Theory, Culture, and Society* 7 (1990): 295–310.

83. Wilfried Scharf and Clare Vale, "The Firm: Organised Crime Comes of Age during the Transition to Democracy," *Social Dynamics* 22, no. 2 (1996): 30–36.

84. Gustav Thiel, "Cape Drug War Heads for Polls," *Mail and Guardian,* April 4, 1997.

85. Marianne Merten, "God and the Gangster," *Mail and Guardian,* July 2, 1999.

86. Eric Ntabazalila, "Gangsters' Paradise 'Reborn' as Church," *Cape Times,* July 2, 1999.

87. Marianne Merten, "In the Name of the Lord," *Mail and Guardian,* April 30, 1999.

88. Ibid.

89. Marianne Merten, "Married to the Mob," *Mail and Guardian,* July 9, 1999.

90. Thabo Mbeki, "Prologue," in *African Renaissance: The New Struggle,* ed. Malegapuru William Makgoba (Tafelberg, South Africa: Mafube, 1999), xviii, xv.

91. Mbeki, *Africa,* 31.

3. VIOLENCE

1. Desmond Tutu, "Archbishop Desmond Tutu's Address to the First Gathering of the Truth and Reconciliation Commission, 16 December 1995," www.justice.gov.za/trc/media/pr/1995/p951216a.htm.

2. Truth and Reconciliation Commission, "Faith Communities Hearing— 17–19 November 1997," www.justice.gov.za/trc/special/faith/faith_a.htm and www.justice.gov.za/trc/special/faith/faith_b.htm; RICSA, "Faith Communities and Apartheid: A Report Prepared for the Truth and Reconciliation Commission by the Research Institute on Christianity in South Africa," in *Facing the Truth: South African Faith Communities and the Truth and Reconciliation Commission*, ed. James Cochrane, John de Gruchy, and Stephen Martin (Cape Town: David Phillip, 1999), 13–77.

3. Kairos Theologians, *Challenge to the Church: The Kairos Document* (Johannesburg: Skotaville, 1985).

4. Nelson Mandela, "Nelson Mandela's Address to Rally in Cape Town on His Release from Prison, 11 February 1990," www.sahistory.org.za/pages/people/special%20projects/mandela/speeches/1990s/1990/1990_address_on_his_release.htm.

5. John Lamola, "Does the Church Lead the Struggle? A Caution," *Sechaba*, July 1988, 7–11; David Chidester, *Shots in the Streets: Violence and Religion in South Africa* (Cape Town: Oxford University Press, 1992), 130–32.

6. Robert B. Miller, "Violence, Force, and Coercion," in *Violence*, ed. Jerome A. Schaffer (New York: David McKay, 1971), 25–26.

7. Kaare Svalastoga, *On Deadly Violence* (New York: Columbia University Press, 1982), 7. The most widely used quantitative instrument for measuring violence is the Conflict Tactic Scales originally introduced in Murray A. Straus, "Measuring Intrafamily Conflict and Violence: The Conflict Tactics (CT) Scales," *Journal of Marriage and Family* 41, no. 1 (1979): 75–88.

8. Paul Heelas, "Anthropology, Violence, and Catharsis," in *Aggression and Violence*, ed. Peter Marsh and Anne Campbell (New York: St. Martin's Press, 1982), 47–61.

9. Newton Garver, "What Violence Is," in *Philosophy for a New Generation*, ed. A.K. Berman and James A. Gould (London: Macmillan, 1970), 353–64.

10. Ninian Smart, "René Girard: Violence and the Sacred," *Religious Studies Review* 6 (1980): 175.

11. John Dewey, *Intelligence in the Modern World,* ed. Joseph Ratner (New York: Modern Library, 1939), 488. See also Joseph Betz, "Violence: Garver's Definition and a Deweyan Correction," *Ethics* 87 (1976–77): 339–51.

12. Gerald Runkle, "Is Violence Always Wrong?" *Journal of Politics* 38 (1976): 367–89.

13. H.L. Nieburg, *Political Violence: The Behavioral Process* (New York: St. Martin's Press, 1969), 13.

14. Edward N. Muller, "A Test of a Partial Theory of Potential for Political Violence," *American Political Science Review* 66 (1979): 928–59, and *Aggressive Political Participation* (Princeton: Princeton University Press, 1979).

15. Paul R. Brass, *Theft of an Idol: Text and Context in the Representation of Collective Violence* (Princeton: Princeton University Press, 1997).

16. C. Wright Mills, *The Power Elite* (New York: Oxford University Press, 1956), 71.

17. Max Weber, *From Max Weber: Essays in Sociology,* ed. H.H. Gerth and C. Wright Mills (London: Routledge and Kegan Paul, 1970), 78; V.I. Lenin, *The State and Revolution* (London: Allen and Unwin, 1917), 154.

18. Johan Galtung, "Violence, Peace, and Peace Research," *Journal of Peace Research* 6 (1969): 167–91.

19. Johan Galtung, *The True Worlds: A Transnational Perspective* (New York: Free Press, 1980), 67.

20. Ted Gurr, *Why Men Rebel* (Princeton: Princeton University Press, 1970).

21. Henry Bienen, *Violence and Social Change* (Chicago: University of Chicago Press, 1968), 21–22; Lewis Coser, *The Functioning of Social Conflict* (Glencoe, IL: Free Press, 1956).

22. Charles Tilly, *From Mobilization to Revolution* (New York: McGraw-Hill, 1978).

23. Hannah Arendt, *On Violence* (London: Allen Lane, 1970), 46, 51–52.

24. Georges Sorel, *Reflections on Violence* (New York: Macmillan, 1961).

25. Frantz Fanon, *The Wretched of the Earth,* trans. Constance Farrington (New York: Grove Press, 1968), 29–32, 48.

26. David E. Apter, ed., *The Legitimation of Violence* (New York: New York University Press, 1997); Maurice Bloch, *From Blessing to Violence: History and Ideology in the Circumcision Ritual of the Merina of Madagascar* (Cambridge: Cambridge University Press, 1986); *Prey into Hunter: The Politics of Religious Experience* (Cambridge: Cambridge University Press, 1992); Paul Brown and Ilsa Schuster, eds., "Culture and Aggression," special issue, *Anthropological Quarterly* 59, no. 4 (1986); Randall Collins, "Three Faces of Cruelty: Toward a Comparative Sociology of Violence," *Sociology since Midcentury* (New York: Academic Press, 1981), 133–60; Natalie Zemon Davis, "Rites of Violence," in *Society and Culture in Early Modern France: Eight Essays* (Stanford: Stanford University Press, 1976), 152–87; Kenneth M. George, *Showing Signs of Violence: The Cultural Politics of a Twentieth-Century Headhunting Ritual* (Berkeley: University of California Press, 1996); Sudhir Kakar, *Colors of Violence: Cultural Identities, Religion, and Conflict* (Chicago: University of Chicago Press, 1996); David Riches, ed., *The Anthropology of Violence* (Oxford: Basil Blackwell, 1986); Stanley Jeyaraja Tambiah, *Leveling Crowds: Ethno-Nationalist Conflicts and Collective Violence in South Asia* (Berkeley: University of California Press, 1997); Daniel E. Valentine, *Charred Lullabies: Chapters in an Anthropology of Violence* (Princeton: Princeton University Press, 1996).

27. Réne Girard, *Violence and the Sacred,* trans. Patrick Gregory (Baltimore: Johns Hopkins University Press, 1977); *The Scapegoat,* trans. Yvonne Freccero (Baltimore: Johns Hopkins University Press, 1986). See Robert Hamerton-Kelly, ed., *Violent Origins: Walter Burkert, René Girard, and Jonathan Z. Smith on Ritual Killing and Cultural Formation* (Palo Alto: Stanford University Press, 1987).

28. Mary Douglas, *Purity and Danger: An Analysis of the Concepts of Pollution and Taboo* (London: Routledge and Kegan Paul, 1966).

29. Chidester, *Shots in the Streets*, 1–20.

30. Mircea Eliade, *The Myth of the Eternal Return*, trans. Willard R. Trask (Princeton: Princeton University Press, 1954), ix.

31. Regina M. Schwartz, *The Curse of Cain: The Violent Legacy of Monotheism* (Chicago: University of Chicago Press, 1997).

32. Allen Feldman, *Formations of Violence: The Narrative of the Body and Political Terror in Northern Ireland* (Chicago: University of Chicago Press, 1991).

33. Chidester, *Shots in the Streets*, 1–2.

34. Orlando Patterson, *Slavery and Social Death: A Comparative Study* (Cambridge, MA: Harvard University Press, 1982).

35. Chidester, *Shots in the Streets*, 76.

36. Martha Himmelfarb, *Tours of Hell: An Apocalyptic Form in Jewish and Christian Literature* (Philadelphia: Fortress Press, 1985).

37. Talal Asad, "Notes on Body Pain and Truth in Medieval Christian Ritual," *Economy and Society* 12 (1983): 287–327; Steven Gregory and Daniel Timerman, "Rituals of the Modern State: The Case of Torture in Argentina," *Dialectical Anthropology* 11 (1986): 63–71; Michael Taussig, "Culture of Terror—Space of Death: Roger Casement's Putumayo Report and the Explanation of Torture," *Comparative Studies in Society and History* 26 (1984): 467–97.

38. Elaine Scarry, *The Body in Pain: The Making and Unmaking of the World* (New York: Oxford University Press, 1985).

39. Arnold van Gennep, *The Rites of Passage*, trans. Monika B. Vizedom and Gabrielle L. Caffee (Chicago: University of Chicago Press, 1960). See also David Chidester, "Rituals of Exclusion and the Jonestown Dead," *Journal of the American Academy of Religion* 56 (1988): 681–702.

40. Chidester, *Shots in the Streets*, 75–76.

41. Régis Debray, *A Critique of Political Reason* (London: Verso, 1983).

42. Republic of South Africa, *White Paper on Defence, 1977* (Pretoria: Government Printers, 1977).

43. Nico Steytler, "Policing Political Opponents: Death Squads and Cop Culture," in *Towards Justice: Crime and State Control in South Africa*, ed. Desirée Hansson and Dirk van Zyl Smith (Cape Town: Oxford University Press, 1980), 121; M.D. Dippenaar, *Die Geskiedenis van die Suid Afrikaanse Polisie* (Silverton: Promedia, 1988), 246; Chidester, *Shots in the Streets*, 212–14.

44. Chidester, *Shots in the Streets*, 17.

45. Peter Harris, *Birth: The Conspiracy to Stop the '94 Election* (Cape Town: Umuzi, 2010), 219.

46. Charles Villa-Vicencio, *A Theology of Reconstruction: Nation-Building and Human Rights* (Cape Town: David Philip, 1992).

47. Jonny Steinberg, *The Number: One Man's Search for Identity in the Cape Underworld and Prison Gangs* (Johannesburg: Jonathan Ball, 2004), 18, 8, 7. See also Jonny Steinberg, *Nongoloza's Children: Western Cape Prison*

Gangs during and after Apartheid (Johannesburg: Centre for the Study of Violence and Reconciliation, 2004), www.csvr.org.za/docs/correctional/nongolozaschildren.pdf.

48. Steinberg, *Number,* 47.

49. Charles van Onselen, *The Small Matter of a Horse: The Life of "Nongoloza" Mathebula, 1867–1948* (Johannesburg: Ravan, 1984); Van Onselen, *New Babylon and New Nineveh: Everyday Life on the Witwatersrand, 1886–1914* (Johannesburg: Jonathan Ball, 2001), 368–97.

50. Steinberg, *Number,* 54–55.

51. Ibid., 154.

52. Ibid., 4.

53. Ibid., 74.

54. Ibid., 28–29.

55. Kenelm Burridge, *Mambu: A Melanesian Millennium* (London: Methuen, 1960); Peter Lawrence, *Road Belong Cargo: A Study of the Cargo Movement in the Southern Madang District, New Guinea* (Manchester: Manchester University Press, 1964); Peter Worsley, *The Trumpet Shall Sound: A Study of "Cargo" Cults in Melanesia,* 2nd ed. (London: MacGibbon and Kee, 1968; orig. ed. 1957).

56. Nils Bubandt, "Violence and Millenarian Modernity in Eastern Indonesia," in *Cargo, Cult, and Culture Critique,* ed. Holger Jebens (Honolulu: University of Hawaii Press, 2004), 115.

57. Karl-Heinz Kohl, "Mutual Hopes: German Money and the Tree of Wealth in East Flores," in Jebens, *Cargo, Cult,* 87.

58. Centre for Development and Enterprise, *Under the Radar: Pentecostalism in South Africa and Its Potential Social and Economic Role* (Johannesburg: Centre for Development and Enterprise, 2008); Jean Comaroff and John L. Comaroff, eds., "Millennial Capitalism and the Culture of Neo-Liberalism," special issue, *Public Culture* 12, no. 2 (2000); Birgit Meyer, "Pentecostalism and Neo-Liberal Capitalism: Faith, Prosperity and Vision in African Pentecostal-Charismatic Churches," *Journal for the Study of Religion* 20, no. 2 (2007): 5–28.

59. Steinberg, *Number,* 54–55.

4. FUNDAMENTALISMS

1. Jacob Sherman, "Summary for the September 4 to 9, 2005 Islamic Fundamentalism Conference Hosted by Esalen's Center for Theory and Research (CTR)," n.d., www.esalenctr.org/display/fundamentalism/shermano5.cfm, accessed February 26, 2007. See R. Scott Appleby, *The Ambivalence of the Sacred: Religion, Violence, and Reconciliation* (Lanham, MD: Rowman and Littlefield, 2000); Gabriel A. Almond, R. Scott Appleby, and Emmanuel Sivan, *Strong Religion: The Rise of Fundamentalisms around the World* (Chicago: University of Chicago Press, 2003).

2. Christopher R. Stones, "The Jesus People: Changes in Security and Life-Style as a Function of Non-Conformist Religious Influence," *Journal of Social Psychology* 97 (1977): 127–33, "The Jesus People: Fundamentalism and Changes

in Factors Associated with Conservatism," *Journal for the Scientific Study of Religion* 17, no. 2 (1978): 155–58, and "Fundamentalism and Conservatism among Jesus People in South Africa," *Journal of Psychology* 98 (1978): 225–29.

3. Stones, "Jesus People: Fundamentalism," 157.

4. Paul Gifford, *The New Crusaders: Christianity and the New Right in Southern Africa* (London: Pluto Press, 1991), 35.

5. David Chidester, *Christianity: A Global History* (San Francisco: Harper Collins, 2000), 531.

6. Concerned Evangelicals, *Evangelical Witness in South Africa: A Critique of Evangelical Theology and Practice by Evangelicals Themselves* (Dobsonville, South Africa: Concerned Evangelicals, 1986), 4.

7. Roger A. Arendse, "The Gospel Defence League: A Critical Analysis of a Right Wing Group in South Africa," *Journal of Theology for Southern Africa* 69 (1989): 95–105; Paul Gifford, *The Religious Right in Southern Africa* (Harare: University of Zimbabwe, 1988); Pippa Green, "Apartheid and the Religious Right," *Christianity and Crisis* 47, no. 14 (1987): 326–28.

8. Uta Lehmann, "The Impact of the Iranian Revolution on Muslim Organizations in South Africa during the Struggle against Apartheid," *Journal for the Study of Religion* 19, no. 1 (2006): 23–39.

9. C.J.B. Le Roux and H.W. Nel, "Radical Islamic Fundamentalism in South Africa: An Exploratory Study," *Journal for Contemporary History* 23, no. 2 (1998): 1–24.

10. But see Farid Esack, "Three Islamic Strands in the South African Struggle for Justice," *Third World Quarterly* 10, no. 2 (1988): 473–98; Desmond C. Rice, "Islamic Fundamentalism as a Major Religiopolitical Movement and Its Impact on South Africa" (MA thesis, University of Cape Town, 1987).

11. Christian Centre, *Views on the Draft Curriculum 2005 Statements,* October 9, 2001, www.cellchurchonline.com/downloads/views_on_the_new_curriculum.doc.

12. R.J. Rushdoony, *The Institutes of Biblical Law* (Nutley, NJ: Craig Press, 1973), 294.

13. Gary North, "The Intellectual Schizophrenia of the New Christian Right," *Christianity and Civilization* 1 (1982): 25.

14. Bruce Lincoln, *Holy Terrors: Thinking about Religion after September 11* (Chicago: University of Chicago Press, 2003), 100, 103.

15. "The Sociology of Public Discourse in a Democratic South Africa, Part I," *ANC Today,* January 14–20, 2005, www.anc.org.za/ancdocs/anctoday/2005/ato2.htm.

16. "The Sociology of Public Discourse in a Democratic South Africa, Part II," *ANC Today,* January 21–27, 2005, www.anc.org.za/ancdocs/anctoday/2005/ato3.htm.

17. U.S. State Department, *International Religious Freedom Report 2006: South Africa,* September 2006, www.state.gov/g/drl/rls/irf/2006/71325.htm.

18. Bruno Latour, *We Have Never Been Modern,* trans. Catherine Porter (Cambridge, MA: Harvard University Press, 1993); Jean Comaroff and John L. Comaroff, "Occult Economies and the Violence of Abstraction: Notes from the

South African Postcolony," *American Ethnologist* 26 (1999): 279–303; David R. Loy, "Religion of the Market," *Journal of the American Academy of Religion* 65 (1997): 275–90.

19. Mike Davis, *Buda's Wagon: A Brief History of the Car Bomb* (London: Verso, 2007). See also Ivan Strenski, "Sacrifice, Gift, and the Social Logic of Muslim 'Suicide Bombers,'" *Terrorism and Political Violence* 15, no. 3 (2003): 1–34, and responses: Richard D. Hecht, "Deadly History, Deadly Actions, and Deadly Bodies: A Response to Ivan Strenski's 'Sacrifice, Gift, and the Social Logic of Muslim "Suicide Bombers,"'" *Terrorism and Political Violence* 15, no. 3 (2003): 35–47; Richard C. Martin, "Ivan Strenski's Analysis of Human Bombers: A Response," *Terrorism and Political Violence* 15, no. 3 (2003): 48–56.

20. Homa Hoodfar, "Bargaining with Fundamentalism: Women and the Politics of Population Control in Iran," *Reproductive Health Matters* 8 (1996): 30–40, www.hsph.harvard.edu/Organizations/healthnet/gender/docs/hoodfar.html. See also John Stratton Hawley, *Fundamentalism and Gender* (Oxford: Oxford University Press, 1994); Courtney W. Howland, ed., *Religious Fundamentalisms and the Human Rights of Women* (London: Palgrave Macmillan, 2001).

21. Jonathan Xavier Inda, ed., *Anthropologies of Modernity: Foucault, Governmentality, and Life Politics* (London: Blackwell, 2005).

22. Roger Friedland, "Money, Sex and God: The Erotic Logic of Religious Nationalism," *Sociological Theory* 20, no. 3 (2002): 381–425.

23. Almond, Appleby, and Sivan, *Strong Religion*, 1.

24. A. Rashied Omar, "Religion, Violence, and the State: A Dialogical Encounter between Scholars and Activists" (PhD diss., University of Cape Town, 2005).

25. Tariq Ali, *The Clash of Fundamentalisms: Crusades, Jihads, and Modernity* (London: Verso, 2003), xiii.

26. Lisa Marie Laegreid Sunday, "Struggling against Fundamentalism and Intolerance," *South Africa Independent Media Centre,* January 26, 2003, http://southafrica.indymedia.org/news/2003/01/2931.php.

27. Kader Asmal, David Chidester, and Wilmot James, introduction to *Nelson Mandela: In His Own Words,* ed. Kader Asmal, David Chidester, and Wilmot James (New York: Little, Brown, 2003), xxvi.

28. "Eish, 2005!," editorial, *Mail and Guardian,* December 9, 2005, www.mg.co.za/article/2005-12-09-eish-2005.

29. Kader Asmal, David Chidester, and Cassius Lubisi, eds., *Legacy of Freedom: The ANC's Human Rights Tradition* (Johannesburg: Jonathan Ball, 2005), 11.

30. Nelson Mandela, "Full Democratic Rights," in Asmal, Chidester, and James, *Nelson Mandela,* 11–12.

31. Nelson Mandela, *The Struggle Is My Life* (New York: Pathfinder Press, 1986), 76.

32. Nelson Mandela, "Courageous Leadership for Global Transformation," International Women's Forum, Sandton, South Africa, January 30, 2003, Nowar-Paix, www.nowar-paix.ca/documents/2003-03-08iwd/nelsonmadela.htm.

33. John Metzler, "Karen Hughes' Mission: Explaining America Abroad," *World Tribune.com,* May 19, 2006, www.worldtribune.com/worldtribune/WTARC/2006/mz5_19.html.

5. HERITAGE

1. South Africa, Department of Education, *National Policy on Religion and Education* (Pretoria: Department of Education, 2003), www.info.gov.za/otherdocs/2003/religion.pdf.

2. National Education Coordinating Committee, *Curriculum: Report of the National Education Policy Investigation Curriculum Research Group* (Cape Town: Oxford University Press, 1992), 74–75.

3. South Africa, Department of Education, *Religion in Curriculum 2005: Report of the Ministerial Committee on Religious Education* (Pretoria: Department of Education, 1999); Janet Stonier, "A New Direction for Religious Education in South Africa? The Proposed New Religious Education Policy," *Journal for the Study of Religion* 11, no. 1 (1998): 93–115.

4. South Africa, Department of Education, *Revised National Curriculum Statement Grades R-9 (Schools)* (Pretoria: Department of Education of South Africa, 2002), www.education.gov.za/LinkClick.aspx?fileticket=WJoXaOgvys4%3D&tabid=266&mid=720, and *National Curriculum Statement Grades 10–12: Life Orientation* (Pretoria: Department of Education of South Africa, 2002), www.polity.org.za/article/national-curriculum-statement-grades-10-12-october-2002–2002-10-27.

5. Daleen Joan Christiaans, "Empowering Teachers to Implement the Life Orientation Learning Area in the Senior Phase of the General Education and Training Band" (MEd thesis, University of Stellenbosch, 2006).

6. Chrissie Steyn, *Religion in Life Orientation* (Pretoria: Unisa Press, 2004).

7. Michel Clasquin, "Religious Studies in South(ern) Africa: An Overview," *Journal for the Study of Religion* 18, no. 2 (2005): 5–22.

8. David Chidester, Gordon Mitchell, Isabel Apawo Phiri, and A. Rashied Omar, *Religion in Public Education: Options for a New South Africa,* 2nd ed. (Cape Town: UCT Press, 1994); David Chidester, "Religion Education in South Africa: Teaching and Learning about Religion, Religions, and Religious Diversity," *British Journal of Religious Education* 25, no. 4 (2003): 261–78, and "Religion Education in South Africa," in *International Handbook of the Religious, Spiritual and Moral Dimensions of Education,* ed. Marian de Souza, Kathleen Engebretson, Gloria Durka, Robert Jackson, and Andrew McGrady (New York: Springer, 2007), 433–48.

9. René Ferguson and Cornelia Roux, "Teachers' Participation in Facilitating Beliefs and Values in Life Orientation Programmes," *South African Journal of Education* 23, no. 4 (2003): 273–75, and "Possibilities for Mediation in the Context of Teaching and Learning about Religions," *South African Journal of Education* 23, no. 4 (2003): 292–96; Cornelia Roux, "Religion in Education: Perceptions and Practices," *Scriptura* 89 (2005): 293–306; Cornelia Roux and Petro du Preez, "Clarifying Students' Perceptions of Different Belief Systems and

Values: Prerequisite for Effective Educational Praxis," *South African Journal of Higher Education* 30, no. 2 (2006): 293–306.

10. David Chidester, "Religion Education and the Transformational State in South Africa," *Social Analysis: The International Journal of Cultural and Social Practice* 50, no. 3 (2006): 61–83.

11. Bruce Lincoln, "Ritual, Rebellion, Resistance: Once More the Swazi Ncwala," *Man* 22, no. 1 (1987): 132–56.

12. Nelson Mandela, "Speech by President Nelson Mandela at a State Banquet in His Honour, Jakarta, Indonesia, 14 July 1997," www.anc.org.za/ancdocs/history/mandela/1997/sp970714.html.

13. South Africa, *National Policy on Religion*, art. 10.

14. Ibid., art. 70.

15. South Africa, Department of Education, "Introducing Religion Education into Schools," in *Manifesto on Values, Education, and Democracy* (Pretoria: Department of Education, 2001), 43–45; Kader Asmal and Wilmot James, eds., *Spirit of the Nation: Reflections on South Africa's Educational Ethos* (Pretoria: Human Sciences Research Council, 2002).

16. South Africa, *National Policy on Religion*, art. 14, art. 7; Malegapuru William Makgoba, ed., *African Renaissance: The New Struggle* (Tafelberg, South Africa: Mafube, 1999); Janine Rauch, "Linking Crime and Morality: Reviewing the Moral Regeneration Movement," *SA Crime Quarterly* 11 (2005), www .iss.org.za/pubs/CrimeQ/No.11/Rauch.htm; *Crime Prevention and Morality: The Campaign for Moral Regeneration in South Africa* (Pretoria: Institute for Security Studies, 2005), www.iss.org.za/pubs/Monographs/No114/Mono114 .pdf.

17. South Africa, *National Policy on Religion*, art. 7.

18. Alan Barnard, "Coat of Arms and the Body Politic: Khoisan Imagery and South African National Identity," *Ethnos* 69, no. 1 (2004): 19; see also Alan Barnard, "!Ke e: /xarra //ke: Multiple Origins and Multiple Meanings of the Motto," *African Studies* 62 (2003): 243–50.

19. Thabo Mbeki, "Address by President Thabo Mbeki at the Unveiling of the Coat of Arms, Kwaggafontein, 27 April 2000," www.info.gov.za/speeches/2000/000502438p1001.htm.

20. Annie E. Coombes, *History after Apartheid: Visual Culture and Public Memory in a Democratic South Africa* (Durham: Duke University Press, 2003); Martin Hall, "The Reappearance of the Authentic," in *Museum Frictions: Public Cultures/Global Transformations,* ed. Ivan Karp et al. (Durham: Duke University Press, 2006), 70–101; Sabine Marschall, *Landscape of Memory: Commemorative Monuments, Memorials and Public Statuary in Post-Apartheid South Africa* (Leiden: Brill, 2010); Ciraj Rassool, "The Rise of Heritage and the Reconstruction of History in South Africa," *Kronos* 26 (2000): 1–21; Nick Shepherd, "Roots and Wings: Heritage Studies in the Humanities," in *Shifting Boundaries of Knowledge: A View of Social Sciences, Law, and Humanities in South Africa,* ed. A. Hofmaenner and T. Marcus (Durban: University of KwaZulu-Natal Press, 2006), 125–40; "Heritage," in *New South African Keywords,* ed. Nick Shepherd and Steven Robins (Johannesburg: Jacana, 2008), 116–28.

21. Leslie Witz, Ciraj Rassool, and Gary Minkley, "Repackaging the Past for South African Tourism," *Daedalus* 130, no. 1 (2001): 277–96.

22. Régis Debray, "Marxism and the National Question," *New Left Review* 105 (1977): 26–27.

23. Andrew Crampton, "The Voortrekker Monument, the Birth of Apartheid, and Beyond," *Political Geography* 20 (2001): 221–46; Elizabeth Delmont, "The Voortrekker Monument: Monolith to Myth," *South African Historical Journal* 29 (1993): 70–102; Albert Grundlingh, "A Cultural Conundrum? Old Monuments and New Regimes: The Voortrekker Monument as Symbol of Afrikaner Power in a Post-Apartheid South Africa," *Radical History Review* 81 (2001): 94–112.

24. Janet Hodgson, "*Ntaba kaNdoda:* Orchestrating Symbols for National Unity in Ciskei," *Journal of Theology for Southern Africa* 58 (1987): 18–31; see David Chidester, *Religions of South Africa* (London: Routledge, 1992), 204–12.

25. Gerard Corsane, "Using Ecomuseum Indicators to Evaluate the Robben Island Museum and World Heritage Site," *Landscape Research* 31, no. 4 (2006): 399–418; Harriet Deacon, "Intangible Heritage in Conservation Management Planning: The Case of Robben Island," *International Journal of Heritage Studies* 10, no. 3 (2004): 309–19; Myra Shackley, "Potential Futures for Robben Island: Shrine, Museum, or Theme Park?" *International Journal of Heritage Studies* 7, no. 4 (2001): 355–63; John E. Tunbridge, "Penal Colonies and Tourism with Reference to Robben Island, South Africa: Commodifying the Heritage of Atrocity?" in *Horror and Human Tragedy Revisited: The Management of Sites of Atrocities for Tourism,* ed. Gregory Ashworth and Rudi Hartmann (New York: Cognizant, 2005), 19–40.

26. Constitution Hill Foundation, *Number 4: The Making of Constitution Hill* (London: Penguin, 2006); Mark Gevisser, "From the Ruins: The Constitution Hill Project," *Public Culture* 16, no. 3 (2004): 507–19.

27. Charmaine McEachern, "Mapping the Memories: Politics, Place and Identity in the District Six Museum, Cape Town," in *Social Identities in the New South Africa: After Apartheid,* vol. 1, ed. Abebe Zegeye (Cape Town: Kwela, 2001), 223–47; Ciraj Rassool, "Making the District Six Museum in Cape Town," *Museum International* 58, nos. 1–2 (2006): 9–18; "Community Museums, Memory Politics and Social Transformation: Histories, Possibilities and Limits," in Karp et al., *Museum Frictions,* 286–321; Ciraj Rassool and Sandra Prosalendis, eds., *Recalling Community in Cape Town: Creating and Curating the District Six Museum* (Cape Town: District Six Museum, 2001).

28. Sabine Marschall, "Visualizing Memories: The Hector Pieterson Memorial in Soweto," *Visual Anthropology* 19, no. 2 (2006): 145–69; Ruth Kerkham Simbao, "The Thirtieth Anniversary of the Soweto Uprisings: Reading the Shadow in Sam Nzima's Iconic Photograph of Hector Pieterson," *African Arts* 40, no. 2 (2007): 52–69.

29. Freedom Park Trust, "Freedom Park," n.d., www.freedompark.org.za/, accessed September 10, 2007.

30. David Chidester, *Savage Systems: Colonial and Comparative Religion in Southern Africa* (Charlottesville: University Press of Virginia, 1996), 261–62.

31. Freedom Park Trust, *The Freedom Park: Interpreting the Past, Informing the Present, Imagining the Future,* brochure, November 2008, www.docstoc .com/docs/71611551/Freedom-Park-brochure---Freedom-Parkindd.

32. Gerhard Schutte, "Tourists and Tribes in the 'New' South Africa," *Ethnohistory* 50, 3 (2003): 473–87.

33. Anne Mager, "'One Nation, One Soul, One Beer, One Goal': Nationalism, Heritage and the South African Breweries," *Past and Present* 188 (2005): 163–94; "Trafficking in Liquor, Trafficking in Heritage: Beer Branding as Heritage in Post-Apartheid South Africa," *International Journal of Heritage Studies* 12, no. 2 (2006): 159–75.

34. Martin Hall, "The Legend of the Lost City: Or the Man with the Golden Balls," *Journal of Southern African Studies* 21, no. 2 (1995): 179–99; Martin Hall and Pia Bombardella, "Las Vegas in Africa," *Journal of Social Archaeology* 5, no. 1 (2005): 5–24.

35. Philip Bonner, "History Teaching and the Apartheid Museum," in *Toward New Histories for South Africa: On the Place of the Past in Our Present,* ed. Shamil Jeppie (Cape Town: Juta, 2004), 140–47; Lindsay Bremner, "Memory, Nation Building and the Post-Apartheid City: The Apartheid Museum in Johannesburg," in *Desire Lines: Space, Memory and Identity in the Post-Apartheid City,* ed. Noëleen Murray, Nick Shepherd, and Martin Hall (London: Routledge, 2007), 85–103; Chana Teeger and Vered Vinitzky-Seroussi, "Controlling for Consensus: Commemorating Apartheid in South Africa," *Symbolic Interaction* 30, no. 1 (2007): 57–78.

36. Sunday Times, "Sunday Times Heritage Project," www.sundaytimes .co.za/Heritage/Index.asp, accessed September 10, 2007. See also Charlotte Bauer, "Sunday Times Heritage Project: New Street Memorials: Goodbye to Big Men on Bronze Horses," Iziko Museum Summer School, 2007, www .iziko.org.za/education/pastprogs/pdfs/2007Charlotte_Bauer.pdf; Cynthia Kros, "Prompting Reflections: An Account of the *Sunday Times* Heritage Project from the Perspective of an Insider Historian," *Kronos* 34 (2009): 159–80; Sabine Marschall, "Private Sector Involvement in Public History Production in South Africa: The *Sunday Times* Heritage Project," *African Studies Review* 53, no. 3 (2010): 34–59.

37. Henry A. Giroux, "Public Pedagogy and the Politics of Neo-Liberalism: Making the Political More Pedagogical," *Policy Futures in Education* 2, nos. 3–4 (2004): 498.

38. Petra Engelbrecht and Lena Green, eds., *Responding to the Challenges of Inclusive Education in Southern Africa* (Pretoria: Van Schaik, 2007).

39. Penny Enslin, "Citizenship Education in Post-Apartheid South Africa," *Cambridge Journal of Education* 33, no. 1 (2003): 73–83.

40. Serena Nanda, "South African Museums and the Creation of a New National Identity," *American Anthropologist* 106, no. 2 (2004): 379–85; Rooksana Omar, "Meeting the Challenges of Diversity in South African Museums," *Museum International* 57, no. 3 (2005): 52–59.

41. Herbert Prins, Bernard Scholtz, and Ed February, *Future Directions for Heritage Conservation in South Africa* (Cape Town: National Monuments Council, 1994), 8.

42. Shane Graham, "Memory, Memorialization, and the Transformation of Johannesburg: Ivan Vladislavić's *The Restless Supermarket and Propaganda by Monuments,*" *MFS Modern Fiction Studies* 53, no. 1 (2007): 70–97.

43. Jonathan Z. Smith, "Narratives into Problems: The College Introductory Course and the Study of Religion," *Journal of the American Academy of Religion* 56, no. 4 (1988): 727–39.

44. Vicki Crowley and Julie Matthews, "Museum, Memorial, and Mall: Postcolonialism, Pedagogies, Racism, and Reconciliation," *Pedagogy, Culture, and Society* 14, no. 3 (2006): 263–77; Nigel Worden, "Signs of the Times: Tourism and Public History at Cape Town's Victoria and Alfred Waterfront," *Cahiers d'études africaines* 141/142 (1996): 215–36.

45. Tomoko Masuzawa, *The Invention of World Religions: Or, How European Universalism Was Preserved in the Language of Pluralism* (Chicago: University of Chicago Press, 2005); David Chidester, "Global Citizenship, Cultural Citizenship, and World Religions in Religion Education," in *International Perspectives on Citizenship, Education, and Religious Diversity,* ed. Robert Jackson (London: Routledge, 2003), 31–50.

46. Cheryllyn Dudley, "Freedom Park Affront to Christianity," African Christian Democratic Party, www.acdp.org.za/oldpress/PRESS10.htm, accessed September 5, 2007 (no longer available).

47. I.H. Horn, "African Traditional Religion, Western Religious Shifts and Contemporary Education," *Journal for Christian Scholarship/Tydskrif vir Christelike Wetenskap* 39, nos. 3–4 (2003): 51–66.

48. Lourens du Plessis, "Freedom *of* or Freedom *from* Religion? An Overview of Issues Pertinent to the Constitutional Protection of Religious Rights and Freedom in 'the New South Africa,'" *Brigham Young University Law Review* 4 (2001): 439–66; Johan D. van der Vyver, "Constitutional Perspective of Church-State Relations in South Africa," *Brigham Young University Law Review* 4 (2001): 635–73.

6. DREAMSCAPES

1. C.G. Jung, *Collected Works,* 20 vols., trans. R.F.C. Hull (London: Routledge and Kegan Paul, 1964), 10:63–64.

2. Frank McLynn, *Carl Gustav Jung: A Biography* (New York: St. Martin's Press, 1997), 282; see also Blake Burleson, *Jung in Africa* (New York: Continuum, 2005).

3. Henry Callaway, *The Religious System of the Amazulu* (1868–70; repr., Cape Town: Struik, 1970), 228, 260, and "On Divination and Analogous Phenomena among the Natives of Natal," *Proceedings of the Anthropological Institute* 1 (1872): 163–83. See also Norman Etherington, "Missionary Doctors and African Healers in Mid-Victorian South Africa," *South African Historical Journal* 19 (1987): 77–91; David Chidester, *Savage Systems: Colonialism and Comparative Religion in Southern Africa* (Charlottesville: University Press of Virginia, 1996).

4. Callaway, *Religious System,* 6, 142.

5. David Chidester, "Dreaming in the Contact Zone: Zulu Dreams, Visions, and Religion in Nineteenth-Century South Africa," *Journal of the American Academy of Religion* 76, no. 1 (2008): 27–53.

6. David Chidester, *Authentic Fakes: Religion and American Popular Culture* (Berkeley: University of California Press, 2005), 230–31.

7. Credo Mutwa, *Zulu Shaman: Dreams, Prophecies, and Mysteries,* ed. Stephen Larsen (Rochester, VT: Destiny Books, 2003); David Chidester, "Credo Mutwa, Zulu Shaman: The Invention and Appropriation of Indigenous Authenticity in African Folk Religion," *Journal for the Study of Religion* 15, no. 2 (2002): 65–85, and *Authentic Fakes,* 172–89. See also Joan B. Townsend, "Core Shamanism and Neo-Shamanism," in *Shamanism: An Encyclopedia of World Beliefs, Practices and Culture,* 2 vols., ed. Mariko Namba Walter and Eva Jane Neumann Fridman (Santa Barbara, CA: ABC-Clio, 2004), 1:49–57.

8. Arjun Appadurai, "Disjuncture and Difference in the Global Cultural Economy," in *Modernity at Large: Cultural Dimensions of Globalization* (Minneapolis: University of Minnesota Press, 1996), 27–47; Jean Comaroff and John L. Comaroff, "Occult Economies and the Violence of Abstraction: Notes from the South African Postcolony," *American Ethnologist* 26, no. 2 (1999): 279–303.

9. James Hall, *Sangoma: My Odyssey into the Spirit World of Africa* (New York: G.P. Putnam's Sons, 1994), 202.

10. David M. Cumes, *Africa in My Bones: A Surgeon's Odyssey into the Spirit World of African Healing* (Claremont, South Africa: Spearhead, 2004), 84.

11. Jeremy Stolow, "Religion and/as Media," *Theory, Culture and Society* 22, no. 4 (2005): 129.

12. Hazel Friedman, "Of Culture and Visions," *Mail and Guardian,* March 27, 1997; Angela Johnson, "The Angela Johnson Interview," *Mail and Guardian,* July 18, 1997.

13. Bradford Keeney, ed., *Vusamazulu Credo Mutwa: Zulu High Sanusi* (Stony Creek, CT: Leete's Island Books, 2001); Credo Mutwa, *Song of the Stars: The Lore of a Zulu Shaman,* ed. Stephen Larsen (Barrytown, NY: Station Hill Openings, 1996).

14. David Icke, *The Reptilian Agenda* (Venice, CA: UFO TV, 2005).

15. David Icke, "The Reptilian Brain," May 25, 2011, www.davidicke.com/headlines/48911-david-icke-the-reptilian-brain.

16. Nicky Molloy, "David Icke's Lecture: The Biggest Secret," *Ufonet,* December 2, 1999, http://tech.groups.yahoo.com/group/ufonet/message/3019. See David Icke, *The Biggest Secret* (London: Bridge of Love Publications, 1999).

17. Icke, *Reptilian Agenda.*

18. Cumes, *Africa in My Bones,* ix, 7, 18.

19. Susan Schuster Campbell, *Called to Heal: African Shamanic Healers* (Twin Lakes, WI: Lotus Press, 2000), and *Spirit of the Ancestors* (Twin Lakes, WI: Lotus Press, 2002).

20. David M. Cumes, "Holistic Urology and Surgery, Psycho-Spiritual Healing," n.d., www.davidcumes.com/, accessed January 20, 2006 (no longer available).

21. Malidoma Patrice Somé, *Ritual: Power, Healing, and Community* (Portland: Swan Raven, 1993).

22. Kenton Johnson, "Indigenous Healers Day, January 31, 2001," *Wellness eJournal,* January 31, 2001, www.compwellness.com/eJournal/2001/0131.htm.

23. "Whites Embrace Traditional Healing in Swaziland." *Panafrican News Agency,* August 9, 2000, www.ancestralwisdom.com/whitethwasas.html; Jeanne Viall, "Claudia Uses Old Ways to Help with the New," *Cape Argus,* November 22, 2004, 13; P.H. Mtshali, *The Power of the Ancestors: The Life of a Zulu Traditional Healer* (Mbabane, Swaziland: Kamhlaba Publications, 2004).

24. Kenneth Cohen, "About Kenneth 'Bear Hawk' Cohen," n.d., www.kennethcohen.com/sacred_earth/about.html, accessed January 13, 2011.

25. Tom "Blue Wolf" Goodman, "Rekindling the Ancient Fires: Sacred Journey to South Africa," *Aquarius: A Sign of the Times,* August 2004, www.aquarius-atlanta.com/aug04/balance.shtml.

26. Lisa Aldred, "Plastic Shamans and Astroturf Sundances: New Age Commercialization of Native American Spirituality," *American Indian Quarterly* 24, no. 3 (2000): 329–52; Alice Kehoe, "Primal Gaia: Primitivists and Plastic Medicine Men," in *The Invented Indian: Cultural Fictions and Government Policies,* ed, James Clifton (New Brunswick, NJ: Transaction, 1990), 193–209.

27. Sibongile Nene, "Sibongile Nene, Sangoma: African Traditional Healer," www.sangoma.ca/, accessed April 14, 2006 (no longer available).

28. Rex Weyler, "Singer Interrupted by Life: Journeys with Ann Mortifee," *Shared Vision,* 2005, www.shared-vision.com/2005/sv1807/viewpoint1807.html, accessed December 24, 2005 (no longer available).

29. Ann Mortifee, *Into the Heart of the Sangoma* (Vancouver: Jabula Music, 2005).

30. Ange Frymire, "What's Sacred Got to Do with It?" *Common Ground,* November 2003, http://commonground.ca/iss/0311148/music_festival.shtml.

31. Rudolf Otto, *The Idea of the Holy,* trans. John W. Harvey (Oxford: Oxford University Press, 1923), 49, 68.

32. Mutwa, *Song of the Stars,* 30.

33. Hall, *Sangoma,* 61.

34. Mutwa, *Song of the Stars,* 29.

35. Hall, *Sangoma,* 12, 196.

36. Mtshali, *Power of the Ancestors,* 22.

37. David Chidester, *Word and Light: Seeing, Hearing, and Religious Discourse* (Urbana: University of Illinois Press, 1992); Lawrence Sullivan, "Sound and Sense: Towards a Hermeneutics of Performance," *History of Religions* 26 (1986): 1–33.

38. Hall, *Sangoma,* 54.

39. Cumes, *Africa in My Bones,* 6.

40. Ibid., 105.

41. Ibid., 44.

42. John E. Mack, *Passport to the Cosmos: Human Transformation and Alien Encounters* (New York: Three Rivers Press, 1999).

43. Louise Meintjes, *Sound of Africa! Making Music Zulu in a South African Studio* (Durham: Duke University Press, 2003).

44. Mutwa, *Song of the Stars,* 173.
45. Cumes, *Africa in My Bones,* 92, 30.
46. Ibid., 30.

7. PURITY

1. Accommodation Direct, "Attend the Royal Reed Dance Festival in Zululand," n.d., www.durban-direct.com/activity/attend-the-royal-reed-dance-festival-in-zululand, accessed February 9, 2010.

2. C. de B. Webb and J.B. Wright, eds., *The James Stuart Archive,* vol. 5 (Pietermaritzburg: University of Natal Press, 2001), 186, n. 103.

3. Axel-Ivar Berglund, *Zulu Thought-Patterns and Symbolism* (London: C. Hurst, 1976), 159. See Harriet Ngubane, "Some Notions of 'Purity' and 'Impurity' among the Zulu," *Africa* 46 (1976): 274–84.

4. Carol Ann Muller, *Rituals of Fertility and the Sacrifice of Desire: Nazarite Women's Performance in South Africa* (Chicago: University of Chicago Press, 1999), 21.

5. Adam Ashforth, "An Epidemic of Witchcraft? The Implications of AIDS for the Post-Apartheid State," *African Studies* 61, no. 1 (2002): 121–43; Benedict Carton, "The Forgotten Compass of Death: Apocalypse Then and Now in the Social History of South Africa," *Journal of Social History* 37, no. 1 (2003): 199–218.

6. Suzanne Leclerc-Madlala, "Virginity Testing: Managing Sexuality in a Maturing HIV/AIDS Epidemic," *Medical Anthropology Quarterly,* n.s., 15, no. 4 (2001): 533–52.

7. Katherine Kendall, "The Role of Izangoma in Bringing the Zulu Goddess Back to Her People," *Drama Review* 43, no. 1 (1999): 94–117; Michael Lambert, "Nomkhubulwane: Reinventing a Zulu Goddess," in *Zulu Identities: Being Zulu, Past and Present,* ed. Benedict Carton, John Laband, and Jabulani Sithole (Scottsville: University of KwaZulu-Natal Press, 2008), 545–53. See also Max Gluckman, "Rituals of Rebellion in South-East Africa," in *Order and Rebellion in Tribal Africa* (London: Cohen and West, 1963), 110–36.

8. Preben Kaarsholm, "Moral Panic and Cultural Mobilization: Responses to Transition, Crime and HIV/AIDS in KwaZulu-Natal," *Development and Change* 36, no. 1 (2005): 133–156; Suzanne Leclerc-Madlala, "Popular Responses to HIV/AIDS and Policy," *Journal of Southern African Studies* 31, no. 4 (2005): 845–56; Fiona Scorgie, "Virginity Testing and the Politics of Sexual Responsibility: Implications for AIDS Intervention," *African Studies* 61, no. 1 (2002): 55–75; Louise Vincent, "Virginity Testing in South Africa: Re-Traditioning the Postcolony," *Culture, Health and Sexuality* 8, no. 1 (2006): 17–30.

9. "Castro Hlongwane, Caravans, Cats, Geese, Foot & Mouth and Statistics: HIV/AIDS and the Struggle for the Humanisation of the African," March 2002, www.virusmyth.com/aids/hiv/ancdoc.htm. See also Robert J. Thornton, *Unimagined Community: Sex, Networks, and AIDS in Uganda and South Africa* (Berkeley: University of California Press, 2008).

10. "Davos 2010: South Africa's Zuma Defends Polygamy," *BBC News*, January 28, 2010, http://news.bbc.co.uk/2/hi/8485730.stm.

11. Mahmood Mamdani, ed., *Beyond Rights Talk and Culture Talk: Comparative Essays on the Politics of Rights and Culture* (New York: St. Martin's Press, 2000).

12. Jacob Zuma, "Statement by President Jacob Zuma on Media Reports about His Child," *Mail and Guardian Online*, February 3, 2010, www.mg.co .za/article/2010–02–03-zuma-confirms-love-child.

13. Jacob Zuma, "Love Wisely and Responsibly: Message from Deputy President Jacob Zuma, Chairperson of the South African National Aids Council, 14 February 2002," www.thepresidency.gov.za/show.asp?type= sp&include=former_deputy/pr/2002/pro214.htm.

14. Jacob Zuma, "Opening Address by Deputy President Jacob Zuma, at the Launch of the Moral Regeneration Movement, Summit Held at the Waterkloof Air Force Base, Pretoria, 18 April 2002," http://74.125.95.132/ search?q=cache:eHy64JrJY7MJ:mrm.org.za/index2.php%3Foption%3Dcom_ docman%26task%3Ddoc_view%26gid%3D50%26Itemid%3D72+moral+reg eneration+movement+south+africa+%22Jacob+Zuma%22&cd=4&hl=en&ct =clnk&gl=za. See also "Moral Regeneration Movement," www.mrm.org.za/, n.d., accessed February 9, 2010; Louise Vincent, "Moral Panic and the Politics of Populism," *Representation* 45, no. 2 (2009): 213–21.

15. Peter Mason, *Deconstructing America: Representations of the Other* (London: Routledge, 1990), 63. See also Norman Cohn, *Europe's Inner Demons: An Enquiry Inspired by the Great Witch-Hunt* (New York: New American Library, 1975).

16. Robert Moffat, *Missionary Labours and Scenes in Southern Africa* (London: John Snow, 1846), 64. See David Chidester, *Savage Systems: Colonialism and Comparative Religion in Southern Africa* (Charlottesville: University Press of Virginia, 1996), 189.

17. Samuel Broadbent, *A Narrative of the First Introduction of Christianity amongst the Barolong Tribe of Bechuanas, South Africa* (London: Wesleyan Mission House, 1865), 204.

18. Robert Young, *African Wastes Reclaimed: The Story of the Lovedale Mission* (London: J.M. Dent, 1902), 127.

19. Donovan Williams, "The Missionaries on the Eastern Frontier of the Cape Colony, 1799–1853" (PhD diss., University of the Witwatersrand, 1959), 311.

20. Jacklyn Cock, "Domestic Service and Education for Domesticity: The Incorporation of Xhosa Women into Colonial Society," in *Women and Gender in Southern Africa to 1945,* ed. Cherryl Walker (London: James Currey; Cape Town: David Philip, 1990), 76–96.

21. Deborah Gaitskell, "Christian Compounds for Girls: Church Hostels for African Women in Johannesburg, 1907–1970," *Journal for Southern African Studies* 6 (1979): 44–69.

22. Heather Hughes, "A Lighthouse for African Womanhood: Inanda Seminary 1869–1945," in Walker, *Women and Gender,* 218.

23. Deborah Gaitskell, "Housewives, Maids or Mothers? Some Contradictions of Domesticity for Christian Women in Johannesburg, 1903–1939," *Journal of African History* 24 (1983): 241–56.

24. Deborah Gaitskell, "Devout Domesticity? A Century of African Women's Christianity in South Africa," in Walker, *Women and Gender,* 251–72.

25. David Chidester, *Religions of South Africa* (London: Routledge, 1992), 100–106.

26. Sheila Meintjes, "Family and Gender in the Christian Community at Edendale, Natal, in Colonial Times," in Walker, *Women and Gender,* 125–45.

27. Webb and Wright, *James Stuart Archive,* 5:332; Benedict Carton, "Awaken *Nkulunkulu,* Zulu God of the Old Testament: Pioneering Missionaries During the Early Age of Racial Spectacle," in Carton, Laband, and Sithole, *Zulu Identities,* 140.

28. Webb and Wright, *James Stuart Archive,* 5:229–30.

29. Deborah Gaitskell, "Wailing for Purity: Prayer Unions, African Mothers and Adolescent Daughters, 1912–1940," in *Industrialisation and Social Change in South Africa,* ed. Shula Marks and Richard Rathbone (London: Longman, 1982), 341.

30. See, for example, Eileen J. Krige, *The Social System of the Zulus* (London: Longmans, Green, 1936), 34 n. 4; H.O. Mönnig, *The Pedi* (Pretoria: Van Schaik, 1967), 331; Monica Wilson, *Keiskammahoek Rural Survey,* vol. 3, *Social Structure* (Pietermaritzburg: Shuter and Shooter, 1952), 97, and *Reaction to Conquest: Effects of Contact with Europeans on the Pondo of South Africa* (London: Oxford University Press, 1961), 208.

31. Paul B. Rich, *White Power and the Liberal Conscience: Racial Segregation and South African Liberalism, 1921–60* (Johannesburg: Ravan Press, 1984), 54–76.

32. Max Gluckman, "Kinship and Marriage amongst the Lozi of Northern Rhodesia and the Zulu of Natal," in *African Systems of Kinship and Marriage,* ed. A.R. Radcliffe-Brown and Daryll Forde (London: Oxford University Press, 1940), 203.

33. Isaac Schapera, "Premarital Pregnancy and Native Opinion: A Note on Social Change," *Africa* 6 (1933): 61.

34. Eileen J. Krige, "Changing Conditions in Marital Relations and Parental Duties among Urbanized Natives," *Africa* 9 (1936): 1.

35. Bronislaw Malinowski, "Parenthood, the Basis of Social Structure," in *The New Generation: The Intimate Problems of Parents and Children,* ed. V.F. Calverton and Samuel D. Schmalhausen (London: Allen and Unwin, 1930), 113–68; Schapera, "Premarital Pregnancy," 59.

36. Schapera, "Premarital Pregnancy," 73.

37. Ibid., 85, 89.

38. Krige, "Changing Conditions," 14.

39. Ibid., 4–5.

40. Ibid., 11.

41. Ibid., 6, 22.

42. H.P. Junod, *Bantu Heritage* (Johannesburg: Hortors, 1938), 92.

43. Wilmot G. James, "From Segregation to Apartheid: Miners and Peasants in the Making of a Racial Order, South Africa, 1930–1952" (PhD diss., University of Wisconsin-Madison, 1982), 144; Alan Jeeves, *Migrant Labour in South Africa's Mining Economy: The Struggle for the Gold Mine's Labour Supply, 1890–1920* (Livingston: McGill Queen's University Press; Johannesburg: Witwatersrand University Press, 1985), 115; David Chidester, *Shots in the Streets: Violence and Religion in South Africa* (Boston: Beacon Press; Cape Town: Oxford University Press, 1991), 69–76.

44. J.M. Coetzee, "The Mind of Apartheid: Geoffrey Cronjé," *Social Dynamics* 17 (1991): 1–35; Geoffrey Cronjé, *'n Tuiste vir die Nageslag* (Johannesburg: Publicite, 1945). See also Robert Gordon, "Apartheid's Anthropologists: The Genealogy of Afrikaner Anthropology," *American Ethnologist* 15 (1988): 535–53.

45. Pumza Fihlani, "Is Zuma's Sex Life a Private Matter?" *BBC News*, February 3, 2010, http://news.bbc.co.uk/2/hi/africa/8495446.stm.

46. Krige, "Changing Conditions," 4.

47. Jeff Guy, "Analysing Pre-Capitalist Societies in Southern Africa," *Journal of Southern African Studies* 14, no. 1 (1987): 32. See also Peter Delius and Clive Glaser, "Sexual Socialization in South Africa: A Historical Perspective," *African Studies* 61, no. 1 (2002): 27–54, and "The Myths of Polygamy: A History of Extra-Marital and Multi-Partnership Sex in South Africa," *South African Historical Journal* 50, no. 1 (2004): 84–114.

48. Henry Callaway, *The Religious System of the Amazulu* (1868–70; repr., Cape Town: Struik, 1970), 250.

49. Webb and Wright, *James Stuart Archive*, 5:332.

50. Mathole Motshekga, "Kingship and Religion," 2008, www.kara.co.za/Profs%20public/KINGSHIP%20AND%20RELIGION.pdf. See also Melissa Littlefield Applegate, *The Egyptian Book of Life: Symbolism of Ancient Egyptian Temple and Tomb Art* (Deerfield Beach, FL: Health Communications, 2001); Timothy Freke and Peter Gandy, *The Hermetica: The Lost Wisdom of the Pharaohs* (New York: Tarcher, 1999).

51. Wisani wa ka Ngobeni, "Motshekga Scandal Widens," *Mail and Guardian Online*, September 24, 2004, www.mg.co.za/article/2004-09-24-motshekga-scandal-widens.

52. Myolisi Gophe, "Bull Sacrificed in Bid to Reduce Train Death Toll," *Cape Argus*, January 28, 2007, www.capeargus.co.za/index.php?fArticleId=3650209.

53. R.W. Johnson, "All Eyes on the Man from Inkandla," *Business Day*, October 10, 2006.

54. Siyabonga Mkhwanazi, "ANC to Rule until Jesus Comes Back," *Cape Times*, May 5, 2008.

55. "Challenge Unchristian Laws, Urges Zuma," *City Press* (Johannesburg), April 8, 2007.

56. Mhlaba Memela, "JZ Slams Same-Sex Marriage," *Sowetan*, September 26, 2006.

57. Mandy Rossouw, "Zuma's New God Squad Wants Liberal Laws to Go," *Mail and Guardian Online*, September 11, 2009, www.mg.co.za/article/2009-09-11-zumas-new-god-squad-wants-liberal-laws-to-go.

58. D.L. Mosoma, "National Interfaith Leaders Council (NILC) Responds to President Jacob Zuma's Apology," February 6, 2010, www.anc.org.za/caucus/docs/pr/2010/pro206.html.

59. BBC, "SA's Zuma Showered to Avoid HIV," *BBC News,* April 5, 2006, http://news.bbc.co.uk/2/hi/africa/4879822.stm. See Deborah Posel, "Sex, Death and the Fate of the Nation: Reflections on the Politicization of Sexuality in Post-Apartheid South Africa," *Africa* 75, no. 2 (2005): 125–53.

8. POWER

The epigraphs to the sections "Theosophy" and "Theocracy" are both from Mathole Motshekga's "The Intermediary Role of the African Monarchy," a paper presented at the South African Heritage Resources Agency's Annual Heritage Indaba, September 4, 2007, 3 and 16 respectively.

1. Donna Bryson, "African Kings, Queens to Honour Madiba," *Times Live,* November 3, 2009, www.timeslive.co.za/news/local/article178629.ece.

2. Sapa, "Tribe Suspends Secession Plans," *News 24,* January 6, 2010, www.news24.com/Content/SouthAfrica/News/1059/d73b673c21fd43a8a35f7fbcd88b487c/06-01-2010-06-02/Tribe_suspends_secession_plans.

3. Gerald James Larson, *India's Agony over Religion* (Albany: SUNY Press, 1995), 286.

4. Jacob K. Olupona, "Orisa Osun: Yoruba Sacred Kingship and Civil Religion in Osogbo, Nigeria," in *Osun across the Waters: A Yoruba Goddess in Africa and the Americas,* ed. Joseph M. Murphy and Mei-Mei Sanford (Bloomington: Indiana University Press, 2001), 46–67. See also Olupona's "Religious Pluralism and Civil Religion in Africa," *Dialogue and Alliance* 2, no. 4 (1988): 41–48, and *Kingship, Religion, and Rituals in a Nigerian Community: A Phenomenological Study of Ondo-Yoruba Festivals* (Stockholm: Almqvist and Wiksell International, 1991); Jacob K. Olupona and Rosalind I.J. Hackett, "Civil Religion in Nigeria," in *Religion and Society in Nigeria: Historical and Sociological Perspectives,* ed. Jacob K. Olupona and Toyin Falola (Ibadan: Spectrum Books, 1991); Simeon O. Ilesanmi, "The Civil Religion Thesis in Nigeria: A Critical Examination of Jacob Olupona's Theory of Religion and the State," *Bulletin of the Council of Societies for the Study of Religion* 24, nos. 3–4 (1995): 59–63.

5. Mahmood Mamdani, *Citizen and Subject: Contemporary Africa and the Legacy of Late Colonialism* (Princeton: Princeton University Press, 1996); J.C. Myers, *Indirect Rule in South Africa: Tradition, Modernity, and the Costuming of Political Power* (Rochester: University of Rochester Press, 2008).

6. Cheikh Anta Diop, *The African Origin of Civilization: Myth or Reality?* (Chicago: Lawrence Hill Books, 1974) and *Precolonial Black Africa* (Chicago: Lawrence Hill Books, 1987); Molefi Kete Asante, *Kemet, Afrocentricity, and Knowledge* (Trenton, NJ: Africa World Press, 1990) and *Afrocentricity* (Trenton, NJ: Africa World Press, 1992).

7. Mathole Motshekga, *Self-Knowledge and the Art of Being* (Pretoria: Kara Heritage Institute, n.d.).

8. Mathole Motshekga, "Restoration and Advancement of Cultural and Traditional Governance in a Democratic South Africa," paper presented for the Local Government Sector Education Training Authority at the launch of "Traditional Leadership Training: Local Economic Development and Community Development," August 30, 2007, 10, and "Kingship and Religion," paper presented at the Kara Roundtable, Richards Bay, Kwazulu Natal, April 18–19, 2008, 3, 5.

9. Robert N. Bellah, "Civil Religion in America," *Daedalus* 96 (1967): 1–21. See David Chidester, *Patterns of Power: Religion and Politics in American Culture* (Englewood Cliffs, NJ: Prentice Hall, 1988), 81–109.

10. Mathole Motshekga, *African Unity in Diversity from Antiquity to the Dawn of the African Century* (Pretoria: Kara Heritage Institute, 2001), 8; Albert Churchward, *The Origin and Evolution of Freemasonry Connected with the Origin and Evolution of the Human Race* (London: G. Allen and Unwin, 1920), 114; Charles H. Vail, *Ancient Mysteries and Modern Masonry* (New York: Macoy Publishing and Masonic Supply Co., 1909), 178–79.

11. Kara Heritage Institute, *Kara News: Introducing the Kara Heritage Institute* (Pretoria: Kara Heritage Institute, 2002). See also Brian P. Copenhauer, *Hermetica: The Greek "Corpus Hermeticum" and the Latin "Asclepius"* (Cambridge: Cambridge University Press, 1992); Antoine Fauvre, *The Eternal Hermes: From Greek God to Alchemical Magus* (Grand Rapids, MI: Phanes Press, 1995); Garth Fowden, *The Egyptian Hermes: A Historical Approach to the Late Pagan Mind* (Princeton: Princeton University Press, 1993); Timothy Freke and Peter Gandy, *The Hermetica: The Lost Wisdom of the Pharaohs* (New York: Tarcher, 1999).

12. Mathole Motshekga, "Building the Character of the African Youth for Moral and Social Regeneration," paper presented for the Department of Education at the 2006 2nd Provincial Representative Council of Learners' Lekgotla, September 29, 2006, 6, and "Indigenous Knowledge's Systems in the African Century," paper presented at the Black Management Forum's 30th Anniversary Annual Conference, October 12–13, 2006, 1. See Corey D.B. Walker, *A Noble Fight: African American Freemasonry and the Struggle for Democracy* (Urbana: University of Illinois Press, 2008).

13. Stephen Howe, *Afrocentricism: Mythical Pasts and Imagined Homes* (London: Verso, 1998), 66–67.

14. David Stevenson, *The Origins of Freemasonry: Scotland's Century, 1590–1710* (Cambridge: Cambridge University Press, 1988), 77–96; Vail, *Ancient Mysteries*, 192–93.

15. Kara Heritage Institute, *Education and Training Programmes* (Pretoria: Kara Heritage Institute, n.d).

16. Mathole Motshekga, "The Influence of Africa in the Development of Western Civilisation," paper presented to Cultural Reclamation Forum, Johannesburg, March 17, 2001, 14.

17. Motshekga, "Restoration and Advancement," 6.

18. Motshekga, "Influence of Africa," 17.

19. Mathole Motshekga, *Dawn of the African Century: The African Origins of Philosophy and Sciences: An Insight by Necherofho Motshekga*

(Johannesburg: Kara Publishers, 1999), 86, n. 52, quoted in Joseph Head and S.L. Cranston's *Reincarnation: The Phoenix Fire Mystery* (New York: Julian Press, 1977), 191.

20. Patrick G. Bowen, "The Ancient Wisdom in Africa," from *Theosophist Magazine, July 1927-September 1927*, ed. Annie Wood Besant (Whitefish, MT: Kessinger, 2003), 558–59.

21. Patrick G. Bowen, "Africa's White Race," in *Theosophical Path Magazine, July to October 1932*, ed. G. De Purucker (Whitefish, MT: Kessinger, 2003), 179–90, and "The Sayings of the Ancient One," in *Theosophical Path Magazine, January to December 1934*, ed. G. De Purucker (Whitefish, MT: Kessinger, 2003), 328–36.

22. Bowen, "Ancient Wisdom in Africa," 560.

23. Motshekga, *African Unity in Diversity*, 11.

24. David Lan, *Guns and Rain: Guerillas and Spirit Mediums in Zimbabwe* (Berkeley: University of California Press, 1985).

25. Mathole Motshekga, "The African Renaissance and Theosophical Movement," paper presented at the Theosophical Society, Johannesburg, 1998, 4.

26. Mathole Motshekga, "The Philosophy and Art of Human Regeneration," paper presented at the Kara Roundtable, Richards Bay, Kwazulu Natal, April 18–19, 2008, 12–16; "Sun Exercise," Actualize Yoga Asanas, n.d., http://asana .yoga-at-sense.com/Actualize-Yoga-Asanas/soorya-namaskar, and "Soorya Namaskar (Sun Exercise)," Yoga2Learn, n.d., www.yoga2learn.com/learn/ suryan.htm, both accessed March 14, 2010.

27. Jacques Berlinerblau, *Heresy in the University: The "Black Athena" Controversy and the Responsibilities of American Intellectuals* (New Brunswick: Rutgers University Press, 1999).

28. J. Olumide Lucas, *The Religion of the Yorubas* (Lagos, Nigeria: CMS Bookshop, 1948); Jacob K. Olupona, "The Study of Yoruba Religious Tradition in Historical Perspective," *Numen* 40, no. 3 (1993): 240–73.

29. O. Kwame Osei, *The Ancient Egyptians Are Here* (Accra, Ghana: Vytall, 2001); Kojo Duffu Yankson, *Africa's Roots in God: The Knowledge of the True God Embedded in the African Culture* (Accra, Ghana: Sankofa Heritage Books, 2007), 87. See T.C. McCaskie, "Asante Origins, Egypt, and the Near East: An Idea and Its History," in *Recasting the Past: History Writing and Political Work in Modern Africa*, ed. Derek R. Peterson and Giacomo Macola (Athens: Ohio University Press, 2009), 125–48.

30. Ntuma Mase, "Le mystere de Sirius," *Bundu Dia Kongo*, January 11, 2008, http://mbutamassee.afrikblog.com/archives/2008/01/11/7524739.html.

31. Aeneas S. Chigwedere, *The Karanga Empire* (Harare: Books for Africa, 1985) and *Roots of the Bantu* (Harare: Mutapa Publishing House, 1998). See also Terence Ranger, "Nationalist Historiography, Patriotic History and the History of the Nation: The Struggle over the Past in Zimbabwe," *Journal of Southern African Studies* 30, no. 2 (2004): 215–34.

32. Byron E. Shafer, ed., *Religion in Ancient Egypt: Gods, Myths, and Personal Practice* (London: Routledge, 1991).

33. Motshekga, "Restoration and Advancement," 6–8.

34. Ibid., 10.

35. Motshekga, "Intermediary Role," 4.

36. Chirevo V. Kwenda, "Religious Myth and the Construction of Shona Identity," in *Religion and the Creation of Race and Ethnicity: An Introduction* ed. Craig R. Prentiss (New York: New York University Press, 2003), 204 n. 13.

37. Motshekga, "Restoration and Advancement," 6–7, and "Building the Character," 5.

38. Motshekga, "Intermediary Role," 11.

39. Mathole Motshekga, "Traditional and Local Governance in a Democratic South Africa: A Non-Governmental Perspective," paper presented at the 4th National Annual Local Government Conference: Traditional Leadership and Local Governance in a Democratic South Africa, Quo Vadis?, July 30–31, 2007, 6–7.

40. Quoted in Meiki Nzewi, "The *Avu* of Alafrika: A Narrative on an Encounter with Musical Arts Knowledge," *Journal of the Musical Arts in Africa* 1 (2004): 80; University of Pretoria, "Book of the Month, July 2009," June 2009, http://bookmonth.blogspot.com/2009/06/book-of-month-july-2009 .html.

41. Eileen Jensen Krige and J.D. Krige, *The Realm of the Rain Queen* (Oxford: Oxford University Press, 1943).

42. Challiss McDonough, "Rain Queen," April 11, 2003, www.globalsecurity .org/military/library/news/2003/04/mil-030411-3e19179f.htm.

43. Stefaans Brummer, "Mathole's Business Links with MI Agent," *Mail and Guardian,* May 8, 1998, www.mg.co.za/article/1998–05–08-matholes-business-links-with-mi-agent, and "Premier Denies Personal Links with MI Agent," *Mail and Guardian,* May 22, 1998, www.mg.co.za/ article/1998–05–22-premier-denies-personal-links-with-mi-agent.

44. Ngwako waga Modjadji, "Outrage over Royal Land Sale," *News 24,* October 9, 2006, www.news24.com/Content/SouthAfrica/News/1059/3367174caacf468 4a51cd4ae2cccbbff/09–10–2006–12–50/Outrage_over_royal_land_sale#.

45. John L. Comaroff and Jean Comaroff, *Ethnicity, Inc.* (Chicago: University of Chicago Press, 2009).

46. Motshekga, "Traditional and Local Governance," 13; see Comaroff and Comaroff, *Ethnicity, Inc.,* 98–114.

47. Liz McGregor, "Rain Queen's Heir Is Pawn in a Battle Royal," *Observer,* October 14, 2007, www.guardian.co.uk/world/2007/oct/14/southafrica .theobserver, and "Who Killed the Rain Queen?" in *At Risk: Writing on and over the Edge of South Africa,* ed. Liz McGregor and Sarah Nuttall (Johannesburg: Jonathan Ball, 2007), 15–47.

48. Alex Matlala, "Rain-Making Rituals Start," *Sowetan,* October 10, 2008, www.sowetan.co.za/News/Article.aspx?id=860069.

49. Motshekga, "Restoration and Advancement," 15.

50. Michael Sakuneka, "Hotel Opens to Honour Rain Queen Modjadji," *Sowetan,* April 20, 2009, www.sowetan.co.za/News/Article.aspx?id=983822.

51. Republic of South Africa, *Minutes of Proceedings: National Assembly, No. 39–2009* (Pretoria: Government Printers, 2009), 1590–91.

52. Mathole Motshekga, "The African Past, Identity, and Human Civilization," paper presented at the Bokamoso Social Club, Mohlaletsi, Limpopo, September 1, 2006, 7, and "Philosophy and Art," 2, 6.

53. C.W. Leadbeater, *Ancient Mystic Rites* (Wheaton, IL: Theosophical Publishing House, 1986), originally published as *Glimpses of Masonic History* (1926), 425; Eleanor Stakesby-Lewis, "The Mystery Tradition of Africa," in *Theosophy Magazine, February 1951 to October 1951*, ed. C. Jinarajadasa (Whitefish, MT: Kessinger, 2003), 324, 425.

54. Motshekga, "Kingship and Religion," 4–5.

55. Motshekga, "Traditional and Local Governance," 8, 11.

56. Motshekga, "Kingship and Religion," 5.

57. Sicelo Shiceka, "Address by the Minister for Provincial and Local Government, Mr Sicelo Shiceka (MP) on the Inauguration of the Commission for the Promotion and Protection of the Rights of Cultural, Religious and Linguistic Communities (CRL Rights Commission), 23 February 2009," South African Government Information, www.search.gov.za/info/previewDocument.jsp?dk =%2Fdata%2Fstatic%2Finfo%2Fspeeches%2F2009%2F09022710451001 .htm%40Gov&q=(+((shiceka)%3CIN%3ETitle)+)+%3CAND%3E(+Category %3Cmatches%3Es+)&t=S+Shiceka%3A+Inauguration+of+Commission+for+ Promotion+and+Protection+of+Cultural%2C+Religious+and+Linguistic+Com munities.

58. Leané du Plessis, "Christelike afdae se name moet verander," *Beeld,* April 19, 2007, http://jv.news24.com//Beeld/Suid-Afrika/0,,3–975_2101630,00.html.

59. South African Pagan Rights Alliance, "Kara Heritage Institute Defames Witches," November 2, 2007, www.paganrightsalliance.org/ karaheritagedefameswitchcraft.pdf; Dominic Mahlangu, "ANC Joins Row over Bull-Killing Ritual," *Times Live,* December 2, 2009, www.timeslive.co.za/news/ article218055.ece.

60. Motshekga, "Intermediary Role," 16, and "Culture, Religion, and Traditions in a Democratic South Africa," paper presented at the Seminar of the Gender Commission on Widowhood, April 10, 2008, 4.

61. Wisani wa ka Ngobeni, "Motshekga Scandal Widens," *Mail and Guardian Online,* September 24, 2004, www.mg.co.za/article/2004–09–24- motshekga-scandal-widens.

62. Motshekga, "Culture, Religion, and Traditions," 8.

63. Motshekga, "Restoration and Advancement," 6.

64. Robert N. Bellah, *The Broken Covenant: American Civil Religion in a Time of Trial* (New York: Seabury Press, 1975), 175.

65. Mathole Motshekga, "'Celebrating Our Tangible and Intangible Cultural Heritage for Nation Building and Social Cohesion,' speech by the ANC Chief Whip, Dr. Mathole Motshekga, during the National Assembly Debate on Heritage Day, 17 September 2009," www.anc.org.za/caucus/index .php?include=docs/sp/2009/sp0917.html.

66. Freedom Park, "Doyen of African Culture, Credo Mutwa's Historic Visit to the Freedom Park," July 31, 2009, www.freedompark.co.za/cms/index .php?option=com_docman&task=doc_details&gid=169&Itemid=47; Nokuzola

Mndende, *Tears of Distress: Voices of a Denied Spirituality in a Democratic South Africa* (Dutywa, South Africa: Icamagu Institute, 2009).

67. Muata Ashby, *The Egyptian Book of the Dead* (Miami: Sema Institute, C.M. Book Publishing, 1998); *Egyptian Yoga: The Philosophy of Enlightenment* (Miami: Cruzian Mystic Books, 2005).

68. Motshekga, "Celebrating."

69. Mandy Roussow, "Zuma's New God Squad Wants Liberal Laws to Go," *Mail and Guardian Online,* September 11, 2009, www.mg.co.za/article/2009-09-11-zumas-new-god-squad-wants-liberal-laws-to-go.

70. Mathole Motshekga, "Partnership for Reconstruction, Development, and Progress," *ANC Today,* August 22, 2009, 3–4, www.polity.org.za/article/anc-statement-by-mathole-motshekga-african-national-congress-chief-whip-on-a-partnership-for-reconstruction-development-and-progress-in-the-anc-today-newsletter-22082009-2009-08-22.

71. T. Dunbar Moodie, *The Rise of Afrikanerdom: Power, Apartheid, and the Afrikaner Civil Religion* (Berkeley: University of California Press, 1975); Leonard Thompson, *The Political Mythology of Apartheid* (New Haven: Yale University Press, 1985).

72. Pumza Fihlani, "Is Zuma's Sex Life a Private Matter?" *BBC News,* February 3, 2010, http://news.bbc.co.uk/2/hi/africa/8495446.stm.

73. Robert N. Bellah, *Beyond Belief: Essays on Religion in a Post-Traditional World* (New York: Harper and Row, 1970), 179.

74. Motshekga, "Building the Character," 6, and "Indigenous Knowledge's Systems," 1.

75. Motshekga, "Celebrating."

76. See Kader Asmal, David Chidester, and Cassius Lubisi, eds., *Legacy of Freedom: The ANC's Human Rights Tradition* (Johannesburg: Jonathan Ball, 2005).

9. WORLD CUP

1. Dave Schechter, "The Religion of Football," *CNN Belief Blog,* June 4, 2010, http://religion.blogs.cnn.com/2010/06/04/the-church-of-football.

2. Emile Durkheim, *The Elementary Forms of the Religious Life,* trans. Joseph Ward Swain (New York: Free Press, 1965), 62.

3. Theo Hobson, "The World Cup: A Ritual That Works," *Guardian,* June 12, 2010, www.guardian.co.uk/commentisfree/belief/2010/jun/12/world-cup-ritual-religion.

4. Steven Robins, "World Cup Ritual Worth Every Cent," *Cape Times,* October 25, 2010, 13.

5. Georges Bataille, "The Notion of Expenditure," in *Visions of Excess: Selected Writings, 1927–1939,* ed. Allan Stoekl, trans. Allan Stoekl, Carl R. Lovitt, and Donald M. Leslie Jr. (Minneapolis: University of Minnesota Press, 1985), 118.

6. Paul Hegarty, *Georges Bataille: Core Cultural Theorist* (Newbury Park, CA: Sage Publications, 2000); Michael Surya, *Georges Bataille: An Intellectual*

Biography, trans. Krzysztof Fijalkowski and Michael Richardson (London: Verso, 2002).

7. Kocku von Stuckrad, "Reflections on the Limits of Reflection: An Invitation to the Discursive Study of Religion," *Method and Theory in the Study of Religion* 22, no. 2 (2010): 166.

8. BBC, "World Cup Stadium 'Cow Sacrifice' Plan Sparks Row," *BBC News*, December 1, 2009, http://news.bbc.co.uk/2/hi/africa/8388001.stm.

9. Matt Scott, "Fifa in a Stew over Ritual Slaughter of Cows in World Cup Stadiums," *Guardian*, December 23, 2009, www.guardian.co.uk/sport/2009/dec/23/fifa-world-cup-stadium-cow-slaughter.

10. Bongani Mthembu, "Bull-Killing Ritual to Be Debated in Durban," *Mail and Guardian*, November 24, 2009, www.mg.co.za/article/2009–11–24-bullkilling-ritual-to-be-debated-in-durban; Sapa, "Mkhize: Bull-Killing Ruling Promotes Cultural Tolerance," *Mail and Guardian*, December 4, 2009, www.mg.co.za/article/2009–12–04-mkhize-bullkilling-ruling-promotes-cultural-tolerance.

11. BBC, "World Cup Stadium."

12. Sharika Regchand, "Bull-Killing Ritual Compared to Communion," *Star*, December 2, 2009, www.thestar.co.za/?fSectionId=&fArticleId=vn20091202042612982C697058.

13. Sapa, "Sangomas Sacrifice Ox to Bless the World Cup Stadiums," *Cape Times*, May 26, 2010, www.capetimes.co.za/index.php?fArticleId=5486198.

14. Reuters, "Cow Slaughtered at World Cup Stadium to Appease Spirits," *National Post*, May 26, 2010, http://sports.nationalpost.com/2010/05/26/cow-slaughtered-at-world-cup-stadium-to-appease-spirits/#ixzzopAGwG3dK.

15. Sapa, "Sangomas Sacrifice Ox."

16. Georges Bataille, *Theory of Religion*, trans. Robert Hurley (New York: Zone Books, 1989), 43.

17. Georges Bataille, *Inner Experience*, trans. Leslie Anne Boldt (New York: SUNY Press, 1988), 137.

18. Georges Bataille, *The Accursed Share: An Essay on General Economy*, vol. 1, *Consumption*, trans. Robert Hurley (New York: Zone Books, 1988), 57.

19. Bataille, *Theory of Religion*, 44.

20. Ibid., 49.

21. Georges Bataille, "The Sacred," in *Visions of Excess*, 242.

22. Lulamile Feni, "King's Voice Fulfils Dying Father's Wish," *Herald*, June 14, 2010, www.epherald.co.za/article.aspx?id=573036. See also Zolani Mkiva, "Zolani Mkiva: His Royal Heritage," The Poet of Africa, http://poetofafrica.com/new1, accessed August 29, 2011.

23. Russell H. Kaschula, "Praise Poetry: Xhosa Praise Poetry for President Mandela," in *African Folklore: An Encyclopedia*, ed. Phillip M. Peek and Kwesi Yankah (London: Routledge, 2004), 362–64.

24. Bataille, *Theory of Religion*, 54.

25. Robins, "World Cup Ritual," 13.

26. Tom Devriendt, "Vuvuzelas All Around," *Africa is a Country*, July 11, 2010, http://africasacountry.com/2010/07/11/the-vuvuzela/.

27. Bataille, *Theory of Religion*, 54.

28. Ibid., 55.

29. Jonah Fisher, "Unholy Row over World Cup Trumpet," *BBC News*, January 16, 2010, http://news.bbc.co.uk/2/hi/8458829.stm; Mpume Madlala, Kanina Foss, and Sapa-AFP, "Vuvuzela Deal for Shembe Church," *IOL News*, June 22, 2010, www.iol.co.za/news/south-africa/vuvuzela-deal-for-shembe-church-1.487721.

30. Tinyiko Sam Maluleke, "South Africa, Christianity, and the World Cup," *Ekklesia: A New Way of Thinking*, June 5, 2010, www.ekklesia.co.uk/node/12326.

31. Richard Pithouse, "On the Path to Crony Capitalism," *Daily Dispatch*, September 25, 2010, www.dispatch.co.za/article.aspx?id=436143.

32. Patrick Bond, *A Political Economy of the 2010 World Cup in South Africa, Six Red Cards for FIFA* (Durban: Centre for Civil Society, University of KwaZulu Natal, 2010), http://ccs.ukzn.ac.za/files/Bond%20%20A%20Political%20Economy%20of%20the%20Soccer%20World%20Cup%20 2010%20over2.pdf.

33. Bataille, "Notion of Expenditure," 119, 121.

34. Makhonya.com, "Our Team Visited the Royal African Awards," www.makhonya.com/?page_id=134, accessed November 20, 2010.

35. Jabulani Sikhakhane, "The Shame of Being Colonised by King Sepp," *Sunday Tribune*, May 2, 2010, www.highbeam.com/doc/1G1–225354713.html; Nikhil Pal Singh, "World Cup 2010," *Social Text: Periscope*, July 20, 2010, www.socialtextjournal.org/periscope/2010/07/introduction-south-africas-world-cup.php.

36. Niren Tolsi, "Fifa Called the Shots—and We Have Said 'Yes,'" *Mail and Guardian*, June 4, 2010, http://2010.mg.co.za/article/2010–06–04-fifa-called-the-shots-and-we-said-yes.

37. J. Michael Williams, *Chieftancy, the State, and Democracy: Political Legitimacy in Post-Apartheid South Africa* (Bloomington: Indiana University Press, 2010), 5–9.

38. Mayibongwe Maqhina, "Government to 'Assist' with King's Coronation," *Daily Dispatch*, May 10, 2010, www.dispatch.co.za/article.aspx?id=400264.

39. "King Xolilizwe *[sic]* Sigcawu Coronation," *MyPE.co.za*, May 7, 2010, www.mype.co.za/modules.php?name=News&file=print&sid=4805.

40. Makhonya Investments, "Welcome: Creating Wealth and Sustainable Growth for Rural Communities," www.makhonyainvestments.co.za/, accessed November 20, 2010.

41. Thanduxolo Jika, "BEE Shock in R3bn Bisho Fleet Contract," *Daily Dispatch*, October 3, 2009, www.dispatch.co.za/article.aspx?id=349332.

42. Bataille, "Notion of Expenditure," 119.

43. Bataille, *Inner Experience*, 137.

44. Bataille, "Notion of Expenditure," 123.

10. STAYING WILD

1. David Chidester, *Savage Systems: Colonialism and Comparative Religion in Southern Africa* (Charlottesville: University Press of Virginia, 1996).

2. Paul S. Landau, *Popular Politics in the History of South Africa, 1400–1948* (Cambridge: Cambridge University Press, 2010), 235. See also Paul S. Landau, "'Religion' and Christian Conversion in African History: A New Model," *Journal of Religious History* 23, no. 1 (1999): 8–30.

3. Henry Callaway, *The Religious System of the Amazulu* (1868–70; repr., Cape Town: Struik, 1970); Chidester, *Savage Systems,* 116–72. See also Axel-Ivar Berglund, *Zulu Thought-Patterns and Symbolism* (London: C. Hurst, 1976); David Chidester, Chirevo Kwenda, Robert Petty, Judy Tobler, and Darrel Wratten, *African Traditional Religion in South Africa: An Annotated Bibliography* (Westport, CT: Greenwood Press, 1997), 212–75; Eileen Jensen Krige, *The Social System of the Zulus* (London: Longmans Green, 1936); E.M. Preston-Whyte, "Zulu Religion," in *Encyclopedia of Religion,* ed. Mircea Eliade (New York: Macmillan, 1987), 15:591–95.

4. W. Wanger, "The Zulu Nation of God according to the Traditional Zulu God-Names," *Anthropos* 18/19 (1923–24): 656–87; 20 (1925): 558–78; and 21 (1926): 351–85; Jennifer Weir, "Whose Unkulunkulu?" *Africa* 75, no. 2 (2005): 203–19; Irving Hexham, ed., *Texts on Zulu Religion: Traditional Zulu Ideas about God* (New York: Edwin Mellen Press, 1987); Luc de Heusch, *Sacrifice in Africa: A Structuralist Approach,* trans. Linda O'Brien and Alice Morton (Manchester: Manchester University Press, 1985), 38–64; Michael Lambert, "Ancient Greek and Zulu Sacrificial Ritual: A Comparative Analysis," *Numen* 40, no. 3 (1993): 293–318; Brian M. Du Toit, "The Isangoma: An Adaptive Agent among Urban Zulu," *Anthropological Quarterly* 44, no. 2 (1971): 51–65; Harriet Ngubane, *Body and Mind in Zulu Medicine: An Ethnography of Health and Disease in Nyuswa-Zulu Thought and Practice* (London: Academic Press, 1977); Max Gluckman, "Social Aspects of First Fruits Ceremonies among the South-Eastern Bantu," *Africa* 11 (1938): 25–41; Jeff Guy, *The Maphumulo Uprising: War, Law, and Ritual in the Zulu Rebellion* (Scotsville: University of KwaZulu-Natal Press, 2005); Carolyn Hamilton, *Terrific Majesty: The Powers of Shaka Zulu and the Limits of Historical Invention* (Cape Town: David Philip, 1998); Dan Wylie, *Savage Delight: White Myths of Shaka* (Pietermaritzburg: University of Natal Press, 2000).

5. John S. Mbiti, *African Religions and Philosophy* (London: Heinemann, 1969), 1–2; see also John S. Mbiti, *Introduction to African Religion* (London: Heinemann, 1975). For critique, see Jan Platvoet and Henk J. van Rinsum, "Is Africa Incurably Religious? Confessing and Contesting an Invention," *Exchange: Journal of Missiological and Ecumenical Research* 32, no. 2 (2003): 123–53.

6. On the distinction between "locative" orientations, fixed in place, and "utopian" orientations toward anyplace (or no place), see Jonathan Z. Smith, *Map Is Not Territory: Studies in the History of Religions* (Leiden: E.J. Brill, 1978), 100–101, 293, 309.

7. Nokuzola Mndende, "African Traditional Religion: A Brief Overview," in *Tears of Distress: Voices of a Denied Spirituality in a Democratic Society* (Dutywa, South Africa: Icamagu Institute, 2009), 111–28. See also Nokuzola Mndende, "From Underground Praxis to Recognized Religion: Challenges Facing African Religions," *Journal for the Study of Religion* 11, no. 2 (1998):

115–24, and "From Racial Oppression to Religious Oppression: African Religion in the New South Africa," in *Religion and Social Transformation in Southern Africa*, ed. Thomas G. Walsh and Frank Kaufmann (St. Paul, MN: Paragon House, 1999), 143–56.

8. Giuseppe Acerbi, *Travels through Sweden, Finland, and Lapland, to the North Cape in the Years 1798 and 1799*, 2 vols. (London, 1802), 2:311.

9. Gloria Flaherty, *Shamanism and the Eighteenth Century* (Princeton: Princeton University Press, 1992), 26.

10. Chidester, *Savage Systems*, 40–41.

11. David Chidester, *Religions of South Africa* (London: Routledge, 1992), 43.

12. Karen E. Fields, *Revival and Rebellion in Colonial Central* Africa (Princeton: Princeton University Press, 1985), 156.

13. Frantz Fanon, *The Wretched of the Earth*, trans. Constance Farrington (London: Penguin, 1967), 43.

14. Eduardo Mondlane, *The Struggle for Mozambique* (Harmondsworth: Penguin, 1969), 104.

15. Felicity Wood, "Blood Money: An Analysis of the Socio-Economic Implications of Oral Narratives Concerning Wealth-Giving Snakes in the Career of Khotso Sethuntsa," *Journal of South African Literary Studies* 21, nos. 1–2 (2005): 84.

16. Felicity Wood, "The Shape-Shifter on the Borderlands: The Trickster Figure and the Relationship between Twentieth Century Oral Narrative in Xhosa Speaking Communities in South Africa and their Socio-Political and Spiritual Context," *International Journal of the Humanities* 4, no. 7 (2007): 23. See also Felicity Wood and Michael Lewis, *The Extraordinary Khotso, Millionaire Medicine Man from Lusikisiki* (Auckland Park, South Africa: Jacana, 2007).

17. Nomalanga Mkhize, "Nicholas Gcaleka and the Search for Hintsa's Skull," *Journal of Southern African Studies* 35, no. 1 (2009): 211–21.

18. Evy Barry, "The Witchcraft Murder," *National Geographic.com*, February 5, 2005, http://ngccommunity.nationalgeographic.com/ngcblogs/explorer/2005/02/the-witchcraft-murder.html; Terence Ranger, "Scotland Yard in the Bush: Medicine Murders, Child Witches, and the Construction of the Occult," *Africa* 77, no. 2 (2007): 272–83.

19. Véronique Faure, "In Pursuit of the Occult: The Investigation of Satanism and Witchcraft in South Africa," in *The Power of the Occult in Modern Africa: Continuity and Innovation in the Renewal of African Cosmologies*, ed. James Kiernan (Berlin: Lit Verlag, 2006), 153.

20. Robin Horton, "African Conversion," *Africa* 41 (1971): 85–108.

21. Jimmy Lee Shreeve, "Thames Torso Killing: Sacrifice or Extremist Christian Scam?" *Libertarian Enterprise*, September 28, 2008, www.ncc-1776.org/tle2008/tle486–20080928–02.html.

22. Jennifer Badstuebner, "'Drinking the Hot Blood of Humans': Witchcraft Confessions in a South African Pentecostal Church," *Anthropology and Humanism* 28, no. 1 (2003): 11.

23. Adam Ashforth, *Madumo: A Man Bewitched* (Chicago: University of Chicago Press, 2000), and *Witchcraft, Violence and Democracy in South Africa* (Chicago: University of Chicago Press, 2005).

24. Ralushai Commission, *Report of the Commission of Inquiry into Witchcraft Violence and Ritual Murders in the Northern Province of the Republic of South Africa* (Northern Province: Ministry of Safety and Security, 1996). See Peter Geschiere, "Witchcraft and the Limits of the Law: Cameroon and South Africa," in *Law and Disorder in the Postcolony*, ed. Jean Comaroff and John L. Comaroff (Chicago: University of Chicago Press, 2006), 219–46; Isak Niehaus, "Witchcraft in the New South Africa: From Colonial Superstition to Postcolonial Reality," in *Magical Interpretations, Material Realities: Modernity, Witchcraft, and the Occult in Postcolonial Africa,* ed. Henrietta L. Moore and Todd Sanders (London: Routledge, 2001), 184–205.

25. Damon Leff, Morgause Fontleve, and Luke Martin, "A Pagan Witches Touch Stone: Witchcraft and Witch-Hunts in South Africa," n.d., www .paganrightsalliance.org/A_Pagan_Witches_Touchstone.pdf, accessed January 24, 2011.

26. Luis Lugo et al., *Tolerance and Tension: Islam and Christianity in Sub-Saharan Africa* (Washington, DC: Pew Forum on Religion and Public Life, 2010), 180, 223, http://features.pewforum.org/africa/.

27. I.H. Horn, "African Traditional Religion, Western Religious Shifts and Contemporary Education," *Journal for Christian Scholarship/Tydskrif vir Christelike Wetenskap* 39, nos. 3–4 (2003): 52, 64, 60. Professor Horn refers to two Christian accounts of indigenous African religion: Richard J. Gehman's *African Traditional Religion in Biblical Perspective* (Kijabe, Kenya: Kesho, 1990) and Yusuf Turaki's *Christianity and African Gods: A Method in Theology* (Potchefstroom, South Africa: Potchefstroom University, 1999).

28. I.A. Coetzer, "A Survey and Appraisal of Outcomes-Based Education (OBE) in South Africa," *Educare* 30, nos. 1–2 (2001): 73–93.

29. Horn, "African Traditional Religion," 62–63.

30. Buddy Naidu, "Hindus Labeled Heathens: University of SA Lecturer Claims Yoga Could Cause Mental Derangement," *Sunday Times,* July 1, 2001, www.suntimes.co.za/2001/07/01/news/durban/ndbn02.htm.

31. Horn, "African Traditional Religion," 65.

32. Sabata Ngcai, "Sangomas take UCT by Storm: But Where Does the White Sangoma Fit In," *City Press,* April 22, 2001, http://152.111.1.87/argief/berigte/ citypress/2001/04/22/18/2.html; Emma Dowson, "Umtata: 'Trust Me, I'm a Witch Doctor,'" *Independent,* May 5, 2001, www.independent.co.uk/travel/ africa/umtata-trust-me-im-a-witch-doctor-615533.html; Simon Richmond and Helen Ranger, *Lonely Planet Cape Town City Guide* (Victoria, Australia: Lonely Planet Publications, 2009), 237.

33. Brendon Bosworth, "Testing Time for White Sangomas," *Street News Service,* July 26, 2010, www.streetnewsservice.org/news/2010/july/feed-242/ testing-time-for-white-sangomas-.aspx.

34. A.D. Spiegel and A.M. Mehlwana, *Family as Social Network: Kinship and Sporadic Migrancy in the Western Cape's Khayelitsha,* Co-operative Research Programme on Family Life (Pretoria: Human Sciences Research Council, 1997),

2; Jo Thobeka Wreford, *Working with Spirit: Experiencing Izangoma Healing in Contemporary South Africa* (Oxford: Berghan, 2008), 188. See also Jo Thobeka Wreford, "'Long-Nosed' Hybrids? Sharing the Experiences of White Izangoma in Contemporary South Africa," *Journal of Southern African Studies* 33, no. 4 (2007): 829–43.

35. Jean Comaroff and John L. Comaroff, *Of Revelation and Revolution: Christianity, Colonialism, and Consciousness in South Africa,* vol. 1 (Chicago: University of Chicago Press, 1991), 428 n.73.

36. Mongane Wally Serote, *Revelations* (Auckland Park, South Africa: Jacana, 2010), 115.

37. Max Weber, *From Max Weber: Essays in Sociology,* ed. and trans. H.H. Gerth and C. Wright Mills (New York: Basic Books, 1958), 78.

38. Michel Foucault, "Governmentality," in *The Foucault Effect: Studies in Governmentality,* ed. Graham Burchell, Colin Gordon, and Peter Miller (Chicago: University of Chicago Press, 1991), 87–104; Timothy Mitchell, *Rule of Experts: Egypt, Techno-Politics, Modernity* (Berkeley: University of California Press, 2002); Michael Herzfeld, *The Social Production of Indifference: Exploring the Roots of Western Bureaucracy* (Oxford: Berg, 1992).

39. Benedict Anderson, *Imagined Communities: Reflections on the Origins and Spread of Nationalism* (London: Verso, 1991); Thomas Hanson and Finn Stepputat, eds., *States of Imagination: Ethnographic Explorations of the Postcolonial State* (Durham: Duke University Press, 2001); Michael Taussig, *The Magic of the State* (London: Routledge, 1997).

40. Thomas J. Bierstecker and Cynthia Weber, eds., *State Sovereignty as Social Construct* (Cambridge: Cambridge University Press, 1996); Stephen Krasner, *Sovereignty: Organized Hypocrisy* (Princeton: Princeton University Press, 1999); James Ferguson and Akhil Gupta, "Spatializing States: Toward an Ethnography of Neoliberal Governmentality," *American Ethnologist* 29 (2002): 981–1002; Judith Butler, *Precarious Life: The Powers of Mourning and Violence* (London: Verso, 2004), 61.

41. Tristan Anne Borer, *Challenging the State: Churches as Political Actors in South Africa, 1980–1994* (Notre Dame: University of Notre Dame Press, 1998); Peter Vale, *Security and Politics in South Africa: The Regional Dimension* (Boulder, CO: Lynne Rienner, 2003); David Chidester, Phillip Dexter, and Wilmot James, eds., *What Holds Us Together: Social Cohesion in South Africa* (Cape Town: HSRC Press, 2003).

42. James Scott, *Seeing Like a State: How Certain Schemes to Improve the Human Condition Have Failed* (New Haven: Yale University Press, 1998).

43. Serote, *Revelations,* 119.

44. Sipho Khumalo, "Photos of Reed Dance Virgins Anger Zulu King," *Cape Times,* September 13, 2010, 4.

45. Tabelo Timse, "Zuma's Lovechild Provokes Debate on Polygamy in South Africa," *Telegraph,* February 2, 2010, www.telegraph.co.uk/expat/expatnews/7155266/Zumas-lovechild-provokes-debate-on-polygamy-in-South-Africa.html.

46. Nokuzola Mndende, "A Genderless Faith," *Mail and Guardian,* April 13, 2006.

47. Michael Fleshman, "African Gays and Lesbians Combat Bias: An 'Invisible' Minority Seeks Legal Safeguards, Acceptance," *Africa Renewal,* April 2007, www.un.org/ecosocdev/geninfo/afrec/vol21no1/211-gays-lesbians-combat-bias.html.

48. Graeme Reid, "The Canary of the Constitution: Same-Sex Equality in the Public Sphere," *Social Dynamics* 36, no. 1 (2010): 43.

49. Lugo, *Tolerance and Tension,* 90.

50. Ibid., 11, 285.

51. BuaNews, "A Prayer for Bafana Bafana," *2010 FIFA World Cup South Africa,* May 31, 2010, www.sa2010.gov.za/node/3130.

52. Delaine Zendran, "2010 FIFA World Cup: Unity in Diversity," *Interfaithing,* May 26, 2010, www.interfaithing.com/2010-fifa-world-cup-unity-diversity-317/.

53. Catholic Church of South Africa, "2010 World Cup: Church on the Ball!," South African Catholic Bishops' Conference, www.sacbc.org.za/Site/index.php?option=com_content&task=view&id=292&Itemid=29, accessed January 22, 2011.

54. Associated Press, "Man Killed by Family for Watching World Cup Instead of Gospel Show," *News One,* June 18, 2010, http://newsone.com/world/associatedpress3/man-killed-by-family-for-watching-world-cup-instead-of-gospel-show/.

55. Simphiwe Sesanti, "Corruption Is an Insult to Ancestors," *Cape Times,* January 25, 2011, 9.

Index

abantu baselokishini, 29, 31
abantu bekhaya, 27
abantu bomlambo, 27–28, 194
abortion, 42, 77, 86, 149
Acerbi, Giuseppe, 193
Adamastor, 17
Afghanistan, 82, 86
African American: ancestors, 16;
   hairstyling, 5–9; hip-hop, 113
African Calendar, 171–72
African Christian Democratic Party, 79–80,
   109–10
African indigenous religion: and African
   Renaissance, 35; and ancient Egypt,
   12, 148, 154–75, 208; and Cape Town,
   10, 18, 22, 27–35; and Christianity,
   viii, 13, 34, 147, 198–200, 202; and
   colonialism, viii, 13, 22, 191–94; and
   education, 34; and Freedom Park, 11,
   103–105, 172, 186, 203; as hybrid,
   30–35; inventory of, viii, 192; and
   Jacob Zuma, ix, 4, 8, 11, 134–35,
   146–51; and kinship, 201–2; as
   mentality, 192; as microcosmic,
   197; and migrant labor, 29–30; and
   national prayer, 34; and neoshamanism,
   112–131; and Robben Island, 26–27;
   and sex, 11–12, 132–36, 146–51,
   204–5; and social class, 32; and
   space, 3, 27–28; as system, viii, 192;
   and traditional leadership, 4, 12; and

transactions, 196–97; and wild
   space, 3; and World Cup, ix, 4, 13,
   178–83
African-initiated churches, 18, 32–33,
   37
African Muslim Party, 79
African National Congress: and
   antiapartheid struggle, 38, 66–67;
   election advertising of, 79; as
   government, 2, 12, 67, 153, 185; and
   human rights, xiii; and Islam, 40–41;
   sacred history of, 173–74; and theology,
   54
African Renaissance, 14–16, 35–36, 49–50,
   98, 108, 162
Africans' Claims in South Africa, 88
Afrikaner: anthropology, 31; Broederbond,
   40; civil religion, 173; nationalism, 19,
   24, 62–63, 102
Afrocentricism, 154, 158–59, 162–63,
   172
AIDS, 134–35, 150
Algeria, 86
Ali, Tariq, 87
Almond, Gabriel, 86
amagoduka, 28–29
American Board for Foreign Missions,
   138–39
Americans gang, 45–46, 67
Amissah, Nana Ama, 152
ANC Today, 82–83

ancestors: African American, 16; and
   calling, 119; and Christianity, 33; and
   coat of arms, 100; and dreams, 113,
   123–24; emergence of, vii; and Freedom
   Park, 11, 103–4; and healing, viii; and
   home, 18, 26–28, 114; and migrant
   labor, 29–30; and *sangomas,* 201–2;
   sacralized, 191; and white *sangomas,*
   130, 200–202; and World Cup, 180–81
Ancient Egypt, ix, 12, 16, 21, 116, 148,
   154–75
Ancient Ones of Khem, 12, 159–61, 169,
   175
Anglican Church: and Cape Town, 32,
   37–38; and confession; and sexual purity,
   138; and World Cup, 207
Animal Rights Africa, 179–80
Antichrist, 78
apartheid: and alienation, 119; and
   Cape Town, 18–19, 23–27; and Dutch
   Reformed Church, x, 78; and Kairos
   theologians, 53–55; and National Party,
   69, 76, 102; and religious diversity,
   24–25; and sexual purity, 146–147;
   as separate development, 102; as
   separateness, 23; struggle against, 35,
   37–40, 53–55, 66–67; theology of, 24
Apartheid Museum, 105
apocalypse, 88–90
Appleby, Scott, 73, 86, 88, 90
Arafat, Yasser, 183
Arendt, Hannah, 59
Aristotle, 15
Armageddon, 88
Armed Islamic Group, 86
Aromaa-Wolf scale, 56, 58
Asante, Molefi Kete, 154, 158, 162
Ashby, Muata, 172
Ashforth, Adam, 198
Asmal, Kader, 94, 96–97
Atlanta, 104
Atlantic Charter, 88
Augustine of Hippo, 124
authenticity, 73–74, 83, 113, 115–16, 121,
   123–24, 175
Axum, 16

Bafana Bafana, 183, 206
Baker, Herbert, 21–22
Bambaataa, Afrika, 113
Bantustans, 102, 114, 116, 154
Barnard, Alan, 99
Bataille, Georges: and expenditure, 13,
   177–78, 186, 188–90; and festival,
   183–86; and general economy, 178,

   186; and sacred, 181–82, 188–90;
   and sacrifice, 178–79; and sovereignty,
   182–84
beer, 29, 33
Bellah, Robert, 157, 171
Ben-Jochannan, Yosef, 158
Bhabha, Homi, 30–31
bhayiskhobbo, 126
Bible: and fundamentalism, 75, 81; and
   God, 164; as law, 206; and Ninevites,
   68; and religion education, 109, 199–
   200; and sex, 205
Bickford-Smith, Vivian, 25
Black Management Forum, 155
Blair, Tony, 128
Blatter, Sepp, 185, 187
Blavatsky, Helena Petrovna, 159
blood: and money, 45–46, 50, 195; and
   reptilians, 117
Blood River, 24, 51
Board of Directors, xii
Bonabakulu Abasekhemu, 12, 159–61, 169,
   175
Bonteheuwel, 38
Bophutatswana, 114, 116
Bosnia, 87
botho, 162
Botswana, vii–viii
Bowen, Patrick, 159–61
Brass, Paul R., 58
Brazil, 88
British: and Cape Town, 17; colonialism,
   112–13; imperialism, 21–22; royalty, 116
Broadbent, Samuel, 136–37, 148
Broederbond, 40
Bronner Bros. International Hair Show, 5–6
Brown and Lowe Inventory of Religious
   Belief, 74–75
Brutus, Dennis, 87–88
Bubandt, Nils, 70
Buddhism, 1, 4
Bulhoek massacre, 106
Bundu Dia Kongo, 163
Bush, George W., 82, 88–89, 128
Bushmen: and national symbols, 96–100;
   and neoshamanism, 4
butongo, 129

California, 114
Callaway, Henry, 112–13, 192
Camoens, 17
Campbell, Susan Schuster, 119
Canada, 121
Cape Flats, 25, 48
Cape of Good Hope, 17, 19–20

Cape Peace Initiative, 48–49
Cape Town: and African indigenous
religion, 22, 27–35; and apartheid,
18–19, 23–27; and bull sacrifice,
148; cannon, 3; castle, 3, 20; and
Christianity, 10, 18, 22, 26, 32, 35–39;
and colonialism, 10, 18–23; and
contradictions, 10; and Dutch, 19–21;
and festival, vii; and gangs, 41, 43–49;
and Hinduism, 22; and imperialism,
21–22; and Islam, 10 18, 22, 25–26,
39–42; and Judaism, 22; and liberating
the city, 38–39; and sanitation, 25; and
segregation, 25; and Van Riebeeck's
hedge, 3
cargo cults, 9, 70–71
casinos, 104–5, 166–67
Cassiem, Achmad, 78
Castro, Fidel, 183
cemeteries, 37–38, 40
ceremony: of first-fruits, 179–82; of
possession, 20, 45; and World Cup,
179–81, 183
Charismatic churches, 47–49
Chechnya, 86
Cheops, 117, 159
chi-rho monogram, 158
Chitauri, 117–18, 127–29
chongo, 193
Christian Centre, 80
Christian National Education, 34, 91
Christian Reconstructionism, 11, 80–81,
200
Christianity: and African American, 6;
and African indigenous religion, viii,
13, 34, 198–200, 202; and architecture,
18, 36–37; and Bulhoek, 106; and
Cape Town, 10, 18, 22, 26, 32, 35–39;
and cargo, 71; Charismatic, 47–49;
and cult of domesticity, 137–40,
150; Dutch, 20–21; and election of
1994, 79; evangelical, 6, 8, 78; and
fundamentalism, 10–11, 74–81, 83,
85–90; and gangs, 47–49, 68; as
indigenous religion, 33; and Jacob
Zuma, 4, 8, 11, 149–50; legitimating
apartheid, 24; as macrocosmic, 197;
and missionaries, 12, 32–33, 37, 89–90,
136–40; and national prayer, 34; and
opposition to heritage projects, 110; and
opposition to religion education, 79–81,
109–10, 199–200; and police, 66; and
Reconstructionism, 11, 80–81, 200; and
sanitation, 39–40; and sex, 12, 136–40,
143–44; and social class, 32; and

struggle against apartheid, 53–55; and
Truth and Reconciliation Commission
(TRC), 51–55; and wild, 4; and World
Cup, 4, 12–13, 124, 206–7; and Xhosa,
28–29.
Churchill, Winston, 88
Churchward, Albert, 158–59
circumcision, x, 137
citizenship, 95, 107
civil religion: Afrikaner, 173; in Nigeria,
153–54, 157, 174; theosophical, 12, 157,
171–75
civilization, 14
class, 32
Clinton, Bill, 26
coat of arms, 97–100
Coetzee, J.M., 146
Cohen, Kenneth "Bear Hawk," 120
colonialism: and African indigenous
religion, viii, 13, 22, 191–94; British,
112–13; and Cape Town, 10, 18–23;
Dutch, 3; and hybridity, 30–31, 194
Coloureds, 31, 45
Comaroff, Jean, 9, 167, 202
Comaroff, John, 9, 167, 202
Commission for the Promotion and
Protection of the Rights of Cultural,
Religious, and Linguistic Communities,
111, 170
Commission on Religious and Traditional
Affairs, 2, 170
communion, 180, 184
Community Outreach Forum (CORE), 47
Concerned Evangelicals, 78
confession, 51–53
Congo, 163
Congregational Church, 138–39
Congress of Traditional Leaders of South
Africa (Contralesa), 152, 188
conspiracy, 116–17
constitution, 4, 92, 98; and religion,
109–11, 180; and sexual orientation, 205
Constitution Hill, xiii, 102
Constitutional Court, 102
constitutionalism, 4, 11–12, 135, 150
conversion, 47–49
Cradle of Humankind, 4, 100, 103
Credo Mutwa village, 114
crime: and gangs, 44–49; as religious
problem, 71–72, 207–8
Cronjé, Geoffrey, 145
Cuba, 105
Cuddihy, John Murray, 35
Cumes, David M., 114–15, 119–21,
126–27, 129–30

Dalindyebo, Buyelekhaya, 152–53, 169
dancing, 4
darkness, 123
Day of Reconciliation, 51
Day of the Covenant, 51
De Klerk, F.W., 63
Debray, Régis, 65–66, 101
democracy: and fundamentalism, 10–11,
    81; and pluralism, 156–57, 170–71;
    and traditional leadership, 12, 187,
    205–6
Department of Arts and Culture, 101
Department of Education, 92, 94–95, 97,
    155
desecration, 22, 38, 153
Dewey, John, 3, 56–57, 59–61
Dikeni, Sandile, 17
Dionysians, 15
Diop, Cheikh Anta, 154, 162
District Six, 19, 25–26, 102–3
District Six Museum, 102–3
Diverse people unite, 2, 96
diversity, ix, 1–2, 35, 91–93, 96, 107
divination, x, viii, 119
diviners: and sex, 133; as social healers, 30.
dog, 15
Doggy Dog, 70
Douglas, Mary, 62
Draper, Charles, 193
dreams: and ancestors, 113, 123–24;
    blocking, 130; and dream-loss, 112; and
    media, 114–15; and neoshamanism, 11,
    115, 119–23, 129–31; and power, 112;
    and sacrifice, 113; and senses, 113–15;
    Zulu, 112–13, 129–31
Du Plessis, I.D., 40
Dube, John, 174
Dube, Nomusa, 179
Durkheim, Emile, xii, xiii, 5, 43, 101,
    176–78, 184, 189
Dutch: and Cape Town, 19–21;
    colonialism, 3
Dutch East India Company, 17
Dutch Reformed Church: and apartheid,
    52–53, 78; and Cape Town, 17,
    19–21, 36; and civil religion, 173; and
    National Party, 24, 66; and Truth and
    Reconciliation Commission (TRC),
    52–53

Eastern Cape, 27–28, 31, 33, 152–53, 188,
    194–95, 197–98
economy: and ethnicity, 167–68; general, 9,
    13, 178, 186; global, 8–9, 20, 85, 114;
    market, 188–89; occult, 71, 84, 114

Eid, 41
Eiselen, W.M., 31
election: of 1948, 19, 24, 69; of 1994, 1,
    40, 78–79, 98
Eliade, Mircea, 5, 43, 63, 101
energetics, 113–15, 129, 178, 189
ET: The Extraterrestrial, 128
ethnopreneurs, 167
European Renaissance, 15
exclusion, 2, 10–11, 18, 20–21, 31–32
expenditure, 9, 13, 177–78, 186,
    188–90
extraterrestrials, 11, 114–19, 127–29

Falwell, Jerry, 77–78, 85
Family Protection Scoreboard, 77
Fanon, Frantz, 23, 60–61, 194
Fassie, Brenda, 105
Faure, Véronique, 196
Fédération Internationale de Football
    Association (FIFA), 1, 4, 12, 176–90
Feldman, Allen, 63
Ferguson, Harvie, 45–46
festival: and Georges Bataille, 183–86; of
    One City, Many Cultures, vii, 35–36; of
    Van Riebeeck, 19; of World Cup, 1, 13,
    183–86, 206
fetishism, 84
Firm, 47
football, 4, 12, 176–78
Foucault, Michel, 23, 85
Freedom Day, 98
Freedom Front, 79
Freedom Park, ix, 11, 103–5, 172, 186,
    203
Freemasonry, 154, 157–59, 163, 169,
    174
Friedland, Roger, 85
Frontline Fellowship, 78, 80
fundamentalism: American, 11, 82, 86–90;
    as blocking transactions, 199–202;
    Christian, 10–11, 74–81, 83, 85–90;
    and crisis, 74; and gender, 85; and
    globalization, 87; of Jesus People, 10,
    74–77; and media, 84; Muslim, 11,
    78–83, 87, 90; of New Christian Right,
    77–78; opposing democracy, 78–82; and
    polarization, 82–87; as political problem,
    86–87; and state, 86–87; supporting
    apartheid, 77–78; as wild religion, 3
funerals, 35, 37–39

Gaddafi, Muammar, 183
Galtung, Johan, 58–59
game parks, 4, 114

gangs: of Cape Town, ix, 10, 41,
43–49; Number, ix, 47, 49, 67–71;
and urbanization, 45; and violence,
67–72
Garver, Newton, 56
Gauteng Province, 148, 154, 167
Gcaleka, Nicholas, 195–97
gees, 189
Gemmill, James, 145
Gemmill, William, 144–45
gender: and African indigenous religion,
204; and fundamentalism, 85; and God,
164; and sexual purity, 132–51
genocide, 49–50, 99
Gervais, Tchiffi Zie Jean, 152
Ghana, 152, 162
Giroux, Henry A., 106
globalization: and ancestral orientation,
114; and economy, 85; and
fundamentalism, 87; and nations,
85–86; and neoshamanism, 113–15; and
polarization, 82; and sacrificial exchange,
114
Gluckman, Max, 140
God: and African indigenous religion, viii,
156, 164–66, 169–71, 180–82, 187,
191–92, 197, 204–5; and Afrikaners, 24,
51, 62; and American fundamentalism,
82; ancient Egyptian, 148, 154, 157–59,
161–63, 165, 169–72; and beasts,
15; child of, 155, 171; and Christian
fundamentalism, 75, 77, 81; and
Desmond Tutu, 38, 83; and dreams, 112;
and election advertising, 79; and football,
176, 206–8; and gangs, 46, 68; as
Great Separator, 24; and hair, 6, 9; and
intelligent design, 200; and Jacob Zuma,
149; and Jesus People, 75; as market,
49; and missionaries, 164, 191; and
money, 46; and Muslim fundamentalism,
82; and People Against Gangsterism
and Drugs (PAGAD), 41–42; and royal
ritual, 180–82; and sacrifice, 62–63; and
traditional leadership, 205; unknown,
136; and World Cup, 206–8; Yoruba,
197
Goddess, 134, 164–65, 168
Gogo, viii-viii
Gold Reef City, 105
Good Hair, 5–9, 206
Goodman, Tom "Blue Wolf," 120
Gospel Defence League, 78
Grahamstown, 193
Greco-Roman antiquity, 14–15, 154,
169

Greys, 118, 127
Groote Kerk, 36
Group Areas Act (1951), 24–25, 31
Gugulethu, 30
Gujarat, 87
Guy, Jeff, 147

Haffajee, Ferial, 88
hair, 5–9, 206
Hall, James, 114–15, 120, 124–27, 129
Hall, Prince, 158
Hamas, 86
Hard Livings, 45–47
Harris, Peter, 1, 67
Havana, 105
healing: and Freedom Park, 104; and
money, 194–95; national, 51–52, 102;
ritual, vii, 11, 18, 32; social, 30; village,
119
Hector Pieterson Memorial, 103
hell, 64–65
Heritage Day, 155, 171–72
heritage: and Christian opposition, 110;
and coat of arms, 99–100; market-
driven, 104–6; and nation building,
11, 99–104; as priceless, 188; and
public pedagogy, 107–11; and religion
education, 91–100; state-driven, 102–4;
and tourism, 104–5
hermeneutics, 113, 115, 129
Hermes Trismegistus, 154, 169
Hermeticism, 12, 148, 154–55, 157–59,
161–63, 169, 172
Heroes Day, 51
Himmelfarb, Martha, 64
Hinduism: and Cape Town, 22; and
hair, 6–9; and national prayer, 34; and
schizophrenia, 200; and yoga, 162
Hintsa, 195–97
His People, 48
Hitler, Adolf, 88
hlobonga, 147
Hobson, Theo, 176–77
Hollywood, 128–29
Holomisa, Patekile, 152
home: and ancestors, 114; and dreams,
113; as sacred space, 10, 18, 27–30; in
townships, 32
homosexuality: and Jacob Zuma, 149; and
rights, 42, 79; and traditionalists, 149,
205–6
Hood, C.J., 120
Hoodfar, Homa, 85
Horn, Irmhild H., 199–200, 202
Horus, 163

house of dreams, 113–14
Hughes, Karen, 89–90
human rights, 42, 79, 77, 89, 91–92, 102, 171
hybridity, vii, 10, 14, 18, 30–31, 46–47, 194

Icamagu Institute, 200
Icke, David, 116–18, 127, 129
idliso, 134
illegitimacy: and anthropologists, 140–46; and apartheid, 146–47; and Christian missions, 136–40; and Jacob Zuma, 11–12, 135, 146–51
Illuminati, 116, 128
imbongi, 183
impepho, 180
imperialism: American, 87, 89; British, 19, 21–22
incorporation, 2, 10–11, 18, 22, 31–32
Independent Electoral Commission, 1
India, 6–9, 86
Indonesia, 96
inhlawulo, 135, 146
initiation: into adulthood, x, 137; of sangomas, 114, 119, 133, 201–2
inkanyamba, 194
Inkatha Freedom Party, 79
inquisition, 51
Institute for Comparative Religion in Southern Africa (ICRSA), xii
Institute for Contextual Theology, 53
Institute of African Royalty, 152, 186–88
International Religious Freedom Report, 83
Into the Heart of the Sangoma, 121–23
intonjane, 137
intsonyama, viii
inyangas, 180
ipupo, 129
Iran, 86, 89
Ireland, 63
Isivivane, 104
Islam: and Cape Town, 10, 18, 22, 25–26, 39–42; and election of 1994, 79; and fundamentalism, 78–83, 87, 90; and gangs, 47–49, 68; and karamats, 26, 39, 41; as macrocosmic, 197; and Malays, 25; and national prayer, 34; in Nigeria, 154; and People Against Gangsterism and Drugs (PAGAD), 41–42, 47–49; and Qibla, 11, 78–79, 83
Israel, 88
Itongo, 160
Ivory Coast, 152

Jack, Buyiswa, 26–27, 34
Jakarta, 96
Jerusalem, 88
Jesus People, 10, 74–77
JFKs, 46
Jit, 121
Johannesburg, 10, 102, 104–5, 116; and Jesus People, 74–77; and mining, 68–69
Johnson, Glen, 49
Jonker, Kobus, 196–197
Judaism: and Cape Town, 22; and hair, 7; and Jewish underground, 86; and national prayer, 34; as wild, 4
Jung, C.G., 112
Junod, H.P., 144–45
Junod, Henri-Alexandre, 144

Kairos Document, 53–55
Kara Cultural Development, 166
Kara Heritage Institute, 146–48, 150–51, 154–55, 159, 162, 173–74, 204
Kara Interactive Solutions, 166
karamats, 26, 39, 41
Karanga Empire, 163–67, 174
Karnak, 21
Kathrada, Ahmed, 26
!Ke e: /xarra //ke, 96–98
Keeney, Bradford, 4, 116
Kgatla, 140–42
Khan, Glen, 49
Khem, 169
Khoisan National Consultative Council, 99
Khoisan: genocide of, 49–50; and national symbols, 96–100; resistance, xiii; shamans, 193; as wild, 20
Khoza, Irvin, 134–35
Khula, V.W., 197–98
Kiernan, James, 37
Kilikijan, 69–70
kings: divine, 156, 162, 169–70; dog, 15; Xhosa, 187, 195; Zulu, 179–82
kinship, 64, 82–83, 201–2
Kipling, Rudyard, 21
Kirk, Kevin, 6
Kirstenbosch Botanical Gardens, 21
Kohl, Karl-Heinz, 70
kraal, 27, 33
Kriel, Ashley, 38
Krige, Eileen, 140–45, 165
Krige, J.D., 165
Kruger, Paul, 195
Kuper, Adam, 197
Kwenda, Chirevo V., 164

Laden, Osama bin, 82, 90
Lamb, Debbie, 48
Lamola, John, 54
Landau, Paul S., 191
Langa, 31–32
Langa Baptist Choir, x
Larsen, Stephen, 116
Larson, Gerald, 153
Latour, Bruno, 84
Leach, Edmund, 8–9
Lekganyane, Barnabas, 54
Lennon, John, 105
Leo Africanus, 15
Lesotho, 118
Lévi-Strauss, Claude, 44
liberation, x, xii-xiii, 19, 37–39, 59–60, 66–67
lidloti, 124–25
Life Orientation, 91–92
Lighthouse, 48
liminality, 27–30, 124
Limpopo Province, 120, 208
Lincoln, Bruce, 82, 95
Lobedu, 154, 164–68, 175
lobola, 135, 143, 205
Locke, John, 3
Lofton, Kathryn, xi
London, 15
Long, Charles H., xii
Lost City, 104–5
Lucas, J. Olumide, 162
Lusiads, 17
Lusikisiki, 194–95
Luther, Martin, 8
Lutheran Church, 36

madrasahs, 39
Mafeje, Archie, 28, 31–33
magic, 84
Magubane, Bernard, 28
Mahabane, Z.R., 174
Majola, Votani, 153
Makeba, Miriam, 120
Makgoba, Thabo, 207
Makhonya Investments, 188
Makhonya Royal Trust, 179, 188
Makoeya, David, 207–8
Makue, Eddie, 173
Malan, D.F., 24, 195
Malays, 25, 40
Mali, 15
Malinowski, Bronislaw, 141
Maluleke, Tinyiko, 13, 185
Mamdani, Mahmood, 23
mamlambo, 194

Mandela, Nelson: and African royalty, 186; birthday, xii-xiii; inauguration of, 34, 183; and Islam, 41; and People Against Gangsterism and Drugs (PAGAD), 41–42; and Robben Island, 26, 102; as servant of the people, 54; and theosophy, 168–69; and traditional leadership, 152–53; and United States, 89; and unity in diversity, 2, 96; and World Cup, 183
Mandhlalanga, 160
Manenberg, 45
Manetho, 159
Manifesto on Values in Education, 98
Mankanyezi, 159–60
Mannenberg Memorial, 105
manyano, 138–39
market: and ancient city, 16; as god, 49; in hair, 6, 8–9; as religion, 84
marriage: as absent, 136–37; polygamous, 11, 134–37, 141–42, 204; same-sex, 149, 205–6
Martins, Albern, 47
Marx, Karl, 58
Maseko, Phepsile, 180
Masey, Francis Edward, 21–22
Mashinini, Tsietsi, 106
Masons, 154, 157–59, 163, 169, 174
Mathebula, Mzuzephi, 68–69
Maul, Darth, 128
Mayer, Philip, 28, 34
Maylam, Paul, 31
Mbande, Mpengula, 147
Mbeki, Thabo: and African Renaissance, 14–16, 49–50, 98; and AIDS, 134–135; and coat of arms, 98–100; and Desmond Tutu, 82–83; and Freedom Park, ix, 11, 104; inauguration of, 34; and policy, xiii; and unity in diversity, 2; and Van Riebeeck's hedge, 21
Mbembe, Achille, 184
Mbiti, John S., 192
McAllister, P.A., 29–30
McBride, Robert, 63
McCauley, Ray, 149
McKay, Gretchen, 120
McLynn, Frank, 112
media: and dreams, 114–15; and fundamentalism, 84; as limits, 125; and neoshamanism, 113; as potential, 126–27; as validation, 127–29
medicine, 134, 195
Meintjes Louise, 129
Melanesia, 70–71

memorials: colonial, 18; and Freedom Park, 103–5; imperial, 21–22; postapartheid, 107; and Sunday Times Heritage Project, 105–6
memory, 19
Men in Black, 128
Merovingian dynasty, 116
Methodist Church, 32, 138–39
mhondoro, 161
migration, 10, 18, 27–30
Mills, C. Wright, 58
Mills, Janet, 30
mines: and gangs, 68–69; and sex, 144–45; and torture, 65; and tourism, 105
Mkhatshwa, Smangaliso, 64
Mkhize, Zweli, 179
Mkiva, Zolani: and African royalty, 186–88; and investments, 188; as Poet of Africa, 183; and Word Cup opening, 183; and World Cup sacrifice, 179–81
Mndende, Nokuzola: and African religion, viii-x, 172, 193; and sexual politics, 204–5; and white *sangomas,* 200–202
Mngqatsi, 193
Mobaba, 128
mockery, 12, 150
modernity, 84
modimo, 191
Modjadji, 154, 156, 163, 165–68, 175
Modjadji V, 165
Modjadji VI, 166–68
Modjadji, Mpapatla, 168
Moffat, Robert, 136
Mogale-Lefakane, Joyce, 152
Mohamed, Nazeem, 39
Mondlane, Eduardo, 194
money: and blood, 45–46, 50, 195; cult, 70; and healing, 194–95; and sex, 85; as sacred, 46
Mongrels, 45
monuments: colonial, 18; postapartheid, 107; propaganda by, 108–9
Moral Majority, 77
Moral Regeneration Movement, 71, 98, 135, 173
Mortifee, Ann, 115, 121–23, 129
motse, 28
Motshekga, Angie, 171
Motshekga, Mathole: and civil religion, 157, 171–75; and theocracy, 12, 154–57, 162–70; and theosophy, 12, 148–49, 154–62, 193; and World Cup, 206–7

Mozambique, 194
Mpondo, 69
Mthethwa, Nati, 179
Mtshali, P.H., 115, 119, 126–27
mujahideen, 87
Muller, Carol Ann, 133
Muller, Edward N., 58
museums, 102–03, 105, 107
music, 121–23, 129
Muslim Judicial Council, 39
muti, 195–96
Mutwa, Vusamazulu Credo: and dreams, 129; and extraterrestrials, 114–19, 126, 128–29; and globalization, 113–14, 129; and media, 125–29; and medicine, 119; and Native American shamans, 120; and neoshamanism, 119, 121–23, 160, 193; and Scotland Yard, 196–97; and senses, 117–18, 124–27; at Freedom Park, 172
Mwari, 164–65
My Nappy Roots, 9
myth: ancient Egyptian, 157–58; of apartheid, 24–25, 63; of cargo, 70–71; and Freedom Park, 103; of gangs, 45–46, 69; and nationalism, 101; of origin, vii-viii, 63; terrifying, 194

naga, 28
Nakueira, Sophie, 187
National Education and Training Forum, 92
National Education Policy Investigation, 91–92
National Heritage Council, 101
National Interfaith Leaders Council, 2, 71, 149–50, 170, 173, 206–7
National Monuments Council, 107
National Party: and Afrikaner nationalism, 19, 24; and apartheid, 31, 69, 76, 102; and Christian National Education, 34; election advertising of, 79; and *muti,* 195
National Policy on Religion and Education (2003), ix, 11, 91–99, 103, 171
National Religious Leaders Forum, 2, 111, 149
nationalism: African, 51; Afrikaner, 19, 24, 51, 62–63, 102; failed, 102; and globalization, 85–86; and heritage, 99–104; religious, 101–2, 173–74; Xhosa, 102; and wild, 3–4
Native American religion, 120
nature, 3

Nazareth Baptist Church, 12–13, 133, 185
Ndabeni, 25
Nene, Sibongile, 121
Neoplatonism, 11, 154
neoshamanism: and dreams, 115, 119–23, 129–31; and globalization, 113–15; and media, 114–15, 123–29; and senses, 114–15, 123–27; and wild, 4
New Age, 4, 11, 80, 114, 116, 199
New Christian Right, 77–78, 149
New Partnership for Africa's Development (NEPAD), 98
Nigeria, 153–54, 162, 174
Ninevites, 68–69
Nobel Peace Prize, 88–89
Nomkhubulwane, 134
Nongoloza, 68–71
North, Gary, 80
Northern Cape, 28
Ntaba kaNdoda, 102
Ntombemhlope, 201
Number gangs, 49, 67–72
numinous, 123

O'Reilly, Will, 196
Occult-Related Crimes Unit, 196–97
Olupona, Jacob, 153–54, 162, 174
Omar, A. Rashied, 87
One City, Many Cultures, vii, 35–36
Ohaah, xiii
Osei, O. Kwame, 162
Oshun, 197
Osiris, 163
Otto, Rudolph, 5, 43, 123

Paris, 15
Parliament, ix, xiii, 12, 155, 168–69, 171–72
Parliament for the World's Religions, vii
Patterson, Orlando, 64
Pentecostal churches: and economy, 71; as wild, 193; and witchcraft, 197–98
People Against Gangsterism and Drugs (PAGAD), 41–42, 47–49
Pestalozzi Trust, 80–81
Pew Forum, 1, 198, 206
pharaohs, 116
Phenethi, Macfarlane, 79
Physical Energy, 21
Pietermaritzburg, 69
pilgrimage, 26, 104
Pinnock, Don, 46

Pithouse, Richard, 185
Pliny the Elder, 14–16
Podbrey, Pauline, 17
police, 66
pornography, 77, 204
potlatch, 182
Powell, M. Norman (Ingwe), 120
prayer: as antisocial, 139, 147; and hairstyling, 6; interfaith, 34; unions, 138–39; and World Cup, 4, 12, 206–7
premodern, 84–85
Presbyterian Church, 32
Prester John, 15
Pretoria, 62–63
primitive, 14, 21
prisons: and gangs, 67–71; Old Fort Prison, 102; and torture, 64–65
propaganda, 108–9
prophets: and hip-hop, 113; Isaiah Shembe, 12, 133, 185; and neoshamanism, 125; and Truth and Reconciliation Commission (TRC), 53–54
prostitution, 42
Protestant: cult of domesticity, 137–40; ethic, 33, 71; sensibility, 7–8, 123
Ptah, 157–58, 208
Public Health Act (1883), 40
public pedagogy, 106–9
Purity League, 138
purity: and order, 62; and sacrifice, 62; and sanitation, 25; racial, 20; ritual, 4, 11, 26–27, 32, 132–134; sexual, 11–12, 20, 132–51, 204–6
pyramids, 16, 117
Pythagoreans, 15

al-Qaeda, 86–87
Qibla, 11, 78–79, 83
Qur'an, 78

race: and purity, 20; and segregation, 25
Rain Queen, 154, 156, 163, 165–68, 175
Rainbow Culture Village, 104
Ralushai Commission, 198
rape, xiii
Rauber, Claudia, 120
Red People, 28, 34
Reed Dance, 132–33, 146, 204
Reid, Chris, 201
Reid, Graeme, 205–6
Reiki, 120

religion: as absent, 136, 191; and ancient
cities, 15; armed, 10, 49, 65–67; as
being human 17; civil, 12, 153–54,
157, 171–75; of civility, 35; and class,
32; and colonialism, 22, 191–94; and
constitution, 109–11, 180; and crime,
71–72; and diversity, 1–2, 35; and
economics, 177–78; and education,
79–81; of football, 4, 12, 176–78;
and fundamentalism, 73–90; of gangs,
68–70; of market, 84; and nationalism,
101–2; of Oprah, xi; as oppositional
term, 83; as private, 35; as resources and
strategies, ix, 17, 44, 95–96; revealed, 3;
of secular humanism, 80–81; as stealing
sacred symbols, 44; and state, 83; strong,
73; and struggle against apartheid,
37–39; and tourism, ix–x; and violence,
10, 51–72; and wild, 2–4; and world
religions, 109
religion education: and Christian
opposition, 79–81, 95, 109–10, 199–200;
and citizenship, 95; curriculum, 92–94;
and heritage, 91–100; and nation
building, 94–100; policy, ix, 94–98; and
public pedagogy, 106–9; and state, 95; as
teaching subject, 91–95
religion studies, 94
Religions of South Africa, vi–viii
Religious System of the Amazulu, 112, 192
Reptilian Agenda, 116–19, 128
reptilians, 116–19, 128–29, 131
Republic of the Ciskei, 102
Revelations, 202–3
Rhema Church, 48, 149
Rhodes Memorial, 21–23
Rhodes, Cecil John, 19, 21–23, 45
Richburg, Keith, 16
rites of passage: and gangs, 46; and
migrant labor, 29–30; and mines, 65
ritual: of acclimatization, 65; as attention,
8; communion, 180, 184; confession,
51–53; divination, x, 119; as empty, 185;
and Freedom Park, 103–4; funerals, 35,
37–39; and gangs, 46, 69–70; and hair,
5–9; healing, viii, 11, 18, 32, 51–52, 104,
195; homecoming, 113; initiation, x, 114,
119; killing, 61–63; murder, 196–197;
and nationalism, 10, 101; pilgrimage,
26, 104; political, 37–39, 153; power,
69–70; and production of truth, 51–52;
of protection, 39; purity, 4, 7, 11, 26–27,
32, 69, 132–34; of rainmaking, 168; rites
of passage, 29–30, 46, 65; royal, 132–33,
170, 179–82, 204; sacrifice, 4, 12, 15,

18, 113, 117, 170, 178–83, 195; space,
33; specialists, 12, 28, 112, 180; speech,
33; and synesthesia, 126; of tonsure,
6–9; of torture, 64–65; and Truth and
Reconciliation Commission (TRC), 10,
51–53; of World Cup, ix, 4, 12–13,
178–83
rivers, 27–28, 194–96
Rix, Vivian, 48
Robben Island, ix, 19, 26, 34, 39, 41, 102
Robins, Steven, 177, 183–84
Rock, Chris, 5–9, 206
Roman Catholic Church: and Cape Town,
32; and confession, 52; and hair, 7; and
World Cup, 207
Rome, 14–15
Roosevelt, Franklin D., 88
Rosicrucianism, 154, 157
Rousseau, Jean-Jacques, 3
Royal Bafokeng Nation, 167
royalty, ix, 12, 18, 132–33, 152–53, 170,
179–82, 186–88, 204
Rushdoony, Rousas John, 80, 200

S'khumbuto, 103
sacred: calendar, 51, 155, 171–72; and city,
14–50; definition of, 5; and desecration,
22; as empty, 44; and Georges Bataille,
181–82, 188–90; and hair, 5–9; as
hybrid, ix, 18, 30–35, 46–47; kingship,
153–57, 162–170; logic of, 65–66;
mapping of, 10; memory, 19; as
migrating, ix, 18, 27–30, 46–47; money,
46; music, 123; and nationalism, 101–2;
as numinous, 123; ownership of, 9, 43;
pivoting of, 43; political economy of,
4, 13, 18–19, 22–23, 43–50, 62, 178,
189; production of, ix; and ritualization,
8; and sacrifice, 8–9; as set apart, 2, 5,
43–44, 101; space, ix, 2, 10, 19, 26–27,
37–38, 42–43, 101–4; specialists, vii–viii,
ix; surplus, 9, 43, 48; time, ix–x, 1–2,
101–3; and transcendence, 5, 181–82;
and wild, 2
sacrifice: ancient Greek, 15; and dreams,
113; as exchange, 113–14; and Georges
Bataille, 178–79; and hairstyling, 6; for
healing, viii; human, 69–70, 117, 178,
196–97; and initiation of *sangomas*, 201;
as offering, 61–62; for power, 62–63;
for protection, 148; for purification,
ix, 26–27, 62; royal, 170, 179–82; and
sacred, 8–9; and tonsure, 6–9; for wealth,
195; and World Cup, ix, 4, 13, 178–83
Salaam, Abdullah Kadi Abdus, 39

sangomas: and kinship, 201–2; and Robben
Island, 26–27, 34; theosophical, 160–61;
and tourism, x; white, 114–15, 119–23,
130, 200–2; and World Cup, 180; Xhosa,
200–202; Zulu, 113–15, 119–27
sanitation, 25, 39–40
Sankofa, 163
Santa Barbara, 119
sanusi, 113, 115, 120, 160
Satan, 196–98, 200, 202
scarcity, 18–19, 43–44
Scarry, Elaine, 65
Schapera, Isaac, 12, 140–45
Schechter, Dave, 176
Schelling, F.W.J., 3
School People, 28, 34
Schwartz, Regina M., 63
Scotland Yard, 196–97
Scott, Matt, 179
secular humanism, 77, 80–81, 95
segregation, 15, 40
Seme, Pixley, 174
senses: and dreams, 113–15; extraordinary,
118; and extraterrestrials, 117–19; as
limits, 124–25; as potential, 126–27; and
synesthesia, 126; as validation, 127
Serote, Mongane Wally, 202–3
Sesanti, Simphiwe, 208
Sethuntsa, Khotso, 194–96
sex: and African indigenous religion,
11–12, 204–5; and anthropologists,
140–46; and Christian missionaries,
12, 136–40; with extraterrestrials, 118;
and hair, 5; and heat, 133; and Jacob
Zuma, 4, 11–12, 146–51, 173–74; and
mines, 144–45; and mockery, 141–42;
and money, 85; and purity, 11–12, 20,
132–51, 204–6; and Zulu tradition, 12,
132–36, 146–51
Sexy Boys, 45
Shaka, 166, 192
shaman: Khoisan, 193; and media, 113;
musical, 121, 129; Native American, 120,
193; plastic, 120–21; Siberian, 193; as wild,
2, 4, 11, 193; Zulu, 113, 115–16, 121
Shamwari, 114, 122
Shapiro, Jonathan (Zapiro), 150
shebeen, 48
Shekinah Tabernacle Church, 48
Shembe, Isaiah, 12, 133, 185
Shiceka, Sicelo, 179
Shona, 164
Sigcawu, Xhanti, 152, 187
Sigcawu, Xolilizwe, 183, 195
Sigcawu, Zwelonke, 187

Sightings, 117
Sikhakhane, Jabulani, 187
Sikhism, 86
Sikhowe, 122
silence, 123
Sivan, Emmanuel, 86
smallpox, 40
Smart, Ninian, 56
Smith, Adam, 20
Smith, Jonathan Z., xii, 8, 108
snakes, 194
social death, 64, 68
"Sociology of Public Discourse in a
Democratic South Africa," 82–83
Somé, Malidoma Patrice, 120
Sorel, Georges, 60
South African Breweries, 104, 201
South African Broadcasting Corporation,
xiii, 155
South African Catholic Bishops'
Conference, 207–8
South African Council of Churches (SACC),
13, 53, 173, 185
South African Heritage Agency, 101, 155
South African Human Rights Commission,
155
South African Pagan Rights Alliance, 198
South African Schools Act (1996), 92
sovereignty: and Georges Bataille, 182–84;
and state, 203; and theocracy, 4, 12,
154–57, 162–70; and traditional
leadership, 4, 153; and World Cup,
186–90
Soweto, 78, 106, 114, 116, 125
space: and coat of arms, 99; of flows, 47;
home, 10, 18, 27–28; liminal, 27–28;
locative, 192; and money, 45–46; outer,
117–119; ritual, ix, 33; sacred, 2, 10,
19, 26–27, 37–38, 42–43, 103–4, 189;
urban, ix, 14–50; utopian, 192; wild, 10,
18, 27–28
sphinxes, 21
Sri Venkateswara Temple, 6–9
St. George's Cathedral, 37–38
St. Stephen's Church, 36
Staggie, Rashaad, 41, 47, 49
Staggie, Rashied, 47–49
Star Wars, 128
Stargate II, 128
state: bifurcated, 23; Christian, 78; and
fundamentalism, 86–87; and heritage,
102–4; and legitimacy, 203; Muslim, 78;
and pastoral power, 23; and religion, 83;
and religion education, 95; and sex and
money, 85; and violence, 58, 64–67, 203

statues, 18–21, 23
stealing: and cargo cults, 70–71; and gangs, 44–45; sacred symbols, 44
Steinberg, Jonny, 67–69
Stones, Christopher R., 74–77
Strijdom, J.G., 63, 195
Strijdom Square, 63
Strydom, Barend, 62–63
Sudan, 86
Sunday Times Heritage Project, 105–6
surplus, 10, 18–19, 43–44, 48
Swaggert, Jimmy, 77–78
Swaziland, 119
syncretism, 31, 33
synesthesia, 126
Synnott, Anthony, 5

Table Mountain, 39
Tambo, Oliver, 66
terrorism, 41, 84
Thembu, 152–53, 169
theocracy, 4, 12, 154–57, 162–70
theology: apartheid, 24; and African National Congress, 54; Kairos, 53–55; of reconstruction, 67
Theosophical Society, 154, 157, 159–61
theosophy, ix, 4, 12, 148, 154–62
Thoth, 169
thwasa, 114
Timbuktu, 15–16
time: and coat of arms, 99; sacred, ix, 1–2, 188–89
Tirupati, 6–9
Tokyo, 14–16
toleration, 35–36
torture: and alien abduction, 118–19; and prison, 64–65
tourism, ix–x, 104–5, 132–33, 166–67, 201, 204
Traditional Healers' Association, 180
traditional leadership, 4, 12, 187, 205–6.
transcendence, 5, 181–82
True Faith of Apostolic Faith Ministry, 197–98
Truth and Reconciliation Commission (TRC), 10, 51–53
Tshisimane, 120
Tswana: emergence myth, vii–viii; and home, 28; and illegitimacy, 140–42
Tuan Guru, 39
Turkey, 86
Turner, Victor, 30

Tutu, Desmond: and Jerry Falwell, 77; and liberating Cape Town, 38–39; and Nelson Mandela, xiii; and Thabo Mbeki, 82–83; and Truth and Reconciliation Commission (TRC), 10, 51–53
Twala, Moses, 146–48, 173–74

ubuntu, 155, 162
Ukweshwama, 170, 179–82
Umkhonto we Sizwe, 51, 63
ungqingili, 149
United States: and Americans gang, 45–46; and E pluribus unum, 96; and fundamentalism, 11, 77–78, 82, 86–90; and New Christian Right, 149; and reptilians, 116
Unity in diversity, ix, 2, 96–98, 107, 156
Universal Declaration of Human Rights, 89
University of Cape Town, viii, 200–202
unkulunkulu, 191
urbanization, 16–18; and gangs, 45; and social class, 32; and Xhosa, 28–34
Urry, John, 44

values: constitutional, 92, 98, 171; and education, 95, 97–98
Van der Leeuw, Gerardus, 5, 43
Van Gennep, Arnold, 29, 43
Van Riebeeck, Jan, 19–20, 45
Van Riebeeck, Maria, 19–20
Van Riebeeck's hedge, 3, 20–21, 23, 27
Verwoerd, H.F., 195
Victoria and Alfred Waterfront, 17
violence: as armed religion, 10, 65–67; and ethical justification, 57, 59–61; and gangs, 41, 45–49, 67–72; as illegitimate force, 3, 55–56, 59; as institutionalized dehumanization, 10, 64–65; as liberating, 60–61; and People Against Gangsterism and Drugs (PAGAD), 41–42, 47–49; as physical harm, 55–56, 57–58; political, 51–52, 57–61; as ritual killing, 10, 61–63; and state, 86–87, 203; and Truth and Reconciliation Commission (TRC), 51–53; as violation, 56, 58–59; as wild, 3
virginity, 132–34, 146, 204
Vladislavić, Ivan, 108
Vlok, Adriaan, 66
Von Stuckrad, Kocku, 178
Voortrekker Monument, 11, 62, 102

vuvuzela, 12, 184–85, 193
Vuya Africa, x

Wagenaer, Zacharias, 20–21, 45
Wealth of Nations, 20
Weber, Max, 58, 84, 203
Wentzel, Magadien, 68, 70
Westminster Confession, 52
Wheatley, Paul, 16, 49
Wicca, 170, 198
wild: as bad, ix, 3. 10–11; as energy, 3; as good, ix, 3–4, 11; as mixed, ix, 4, 11–12; as obstacle, 3; as situational, 2–4; space, 3, 10, 18, 27–28; transactions, 194–99
wilderness, 2
Williams, Donovan, 137
Wilson and Patterson Conservative Scale, 74–75
Winfrey, Oprah, xi–xi
Wisdom of Ptah-Hotep, 208
Wise Man, 69
witchcraft: and inquisition, 51–52; and medicine, 133; and neopagans, 170; and Pentecostals, 197–98; and spiritual insecurity, 198; and wild space, 27–28
Women's Help Society, 138
World Cup: and ancestors, 180–81; as festival, 183–86; prayers, 4, 12–13, 206–7; and religion of football, 176–78; and sacrifice, ix, 13, 178–83; and sovereignty, 186–190; and vuvuzela, 184–85, 193; as wild, 4, 12–13
World of Beer, 104
World of Coca-Cola, 104
world religions, 109
World Social Forum, 88
Wreford, Joanne Thobeka, 202
Wretched of the Earth, 194

Xam, 96–98
Xhosa: and Christianity, 28–29; diviners, 193; healing ritual, viii; and Hintsa, 195–97; and home, 27–30; initiation, x; nationalism, 102; Red and School, 28, 34; and rivers, 27–28, 194; *sangomas,* 200–202; and urbanization, 28–34
Xhosa Royal Trust, 188
Xundu, Mcebisi, 206

Yankson, Koju Duffu, 162–63
yoga, 120, 155, 162
Yoruba, 197
Yusuf, Shaykh, 39

Zimbabwe, 16, 118, 161, 163–67, 174
Zion Christian Church, 32, 37, 52, 54
zodiac, 155, 159, 162
Zulu: and Blood River, 24; dreams, 112–13, 129–31; and illegitimacy, 140; and Number gangs, 69; Oprah Winfrey as, x–xi; popular music, 129; religious system, 192; royal ritual, 132–33, 170, 179–82, 204; *sangomas,* 113–15, 119–27; and sex, 12, 132–36, 146–151; shaman, 113, 115–16, 121; Shembes, 12–13, 133, 185; tradition, ix, 4, 8, 11, 134–35, 146–51; white, 120
Zulu Nation, 113
Zuma, Jacob: and Christianity, 4, 8, 11, 149–50; and crime, 71–72; and human rights, xiii; and interfaith council, 173; and sex, 4, 8, 11–12, 134–36, 146–51, 173–74, 204–5; and unity in diversity, 2; and Zulu tradition, ix, 4, 8, 11, 134–35, 146–51
Zwelithini, Goodwill, 179, 204

COVER DESIGNED BY
Claudia Smelser

TEXT
10/13 Sabon

DISPLAY
Sabon

COMPOSITOR
Toppan Best-set Premedia Limited

PRINTER AND BINDER
Maple-Vail